The German Army and the Nazi Party, 1933-1939

ROBERT J. O'NEILL

The German Army and the Nazi Party, 1933-1939

Foreword by Captain Sir Basil Liddell Hart

H James H. Heineman, Inc., New York

© Robert J. O'Neill 1966   First published 1966

Published in the United States of America by
James H. Heineman, Inc.
60 East 42nd Street
New York, New York 10017

Library of Congress Catalogue Card No. 67-11678
British publishers: Cassell and Company Ltd.
Printed in Great Britain and bound in the United States of America

Foreword

by CAPTAIN SIR BASIL LIDDELL HART

THIS is a very revealing book and a highly interesting one to read—two qualities that are rarely combined in a work of history. Indeed, it is the most illuminating study that has appeared of the way in which Hitler, gaining office, by degrees gained an ascendancy over the German Army and its professional heads, who in previous generations had been the most secure as well as the strongest factor in the state. Earlier studies have tended to be an indictment of the General Staff for succumbing to Hitler, or even conniving at his ascent, while some more recent ones have tended to whitewash it, as a natural reaction.

Thus the time was ripe for a more objective study—which Captain (and Doctor) Robert O'Neill is well fitted to supply. The first serving officer from the Australian Army to come to Oxford as a Rhodes scholar, he spent four years there, two of which were occupied by work for his D.Phil. on the subject of which his book is a distillation. In the course of that task he has not only explored the documents, and unearthed some that were not available or not known to exist earlier, but has had extensive discussions with many of the generals. (The Weichs memoranda show that Hitler was planning, as early as 1934, for a European war to be fought on both the Western and Eastern fronts.) The generals interviewed included a number whom I interrogated in or soon after the war, and I know from them how much they were impressed by Robert O'Neill's high intelligence and acute grasp of the matters he was investigating or on which he was cross-examining them. He benefits by a knowledge of military technique, and a close acquaintance with military habits of mind, that are blended with the approach and basic attitude of the scholar.

This blend, and his investigation, does not lead him to exculpate the generals but does help him to understand them, and thereby to provide a convincing explanation of how they became subservient to Hitler, were turned from being his most formidable obstacle into unwitting assistance of his purpose, and eventually launched into the kind of war that all their strategic teaching had warned them to avoid. Their very qualities, and particularly their desire to become non-political, were turned to their disadvantage and Hitler's advantage. From being an obstacle they became a tool—a fact, and a change into reverse, that they realized too late.

In the process Hitler was consciously aided, yet unwittingly, by a few of the leading generals who *were* politically interested, particularly Blomberg and Reichenau. The effect is ably traced and brought out in Dr O'Neill's book.

B.H.L H.

Contents

Illustrations

The Reichs Cabinet at the proclamation of the new Defence Law, 16 March 1935*

The Army parading under the banners of the Nazi Party*

Blomberg greeting 88-year-old General Karl Litzmann*

Blomberg, Göring, Fritsch and Hitler at the Party Rally, Nuremberg, 1935*

Motorized heavy artillery parading before Hitler at the Party Rally*

The Team of Two—Fritsch and Beck at Army exercises, 1935*

The Ceremonial Re-opening of the Kriegsakademie in Berlin*

following page 120

The Opening of the Officer Training School, Potsdam†

The Army training members of the National-Socialist Motor Corps*

The Army training members of the Hitler Youth in marksmanship*

Two members of the Hitler Youth being taught field craft by an Army instructor*

Schoolboys being taught marksmanship as part of their normal education under the Third Reich*

The tanks of the German Army:
  (1) before Hitler came to power
  (2) after Hitler's abrogation of the Versailles Treaty‡

Soldiers parading in Potsdam before the Garnisonkirche with the new National War Flag*

The old colours of the Imperial Army being borne in procession through Nuremberg*

The new colours being paraded before Hitler and Göring in Berlin*

Newly dedicated colours being paraded before Fritsch and Blomberg*

Motorized units of the Army parade past Hitler at the Party Rally, Nuremberg 1936*

Blomberg publicly honours the Hitler-Putsch of 1923 by participating in the repetition of the march to the Feldherrnhalle*

Party military propaganda at the exhibition staged in 1937 entitled 'Give me four years time!'*

Hitler nominating Blomberg to be Colonel-in-Chief of Infantry Regiment 73*

Hitler presenting Blomberg to Mussolini*

following page 160

Firtsch handing over the Seeckt memorial to members of the Seeckt family*

* Bundesarchiv, Koblenz   † General Hermann Flörke
‡ Bibliothek für Zeitgeschichte, Stuttgart

Acknowledgement and Note on Translations

THIS book which began life as an academic thesis owes an enormous amount to the information, wisdom, and guidance which I have been fortunate to receive from many kind people. Professor Norman Gibbs, Chichele Professor of the History of War at Oxford, supervised the preparation of my thesis throughout two intense years. Both his critical comments and his architectural suggestions have been of the greatest assistance to the development of the work into its present form. E. T. Williams, Warden of Rhodes House, read the manuscript while in the midst of many other demanding activities and was a bountiful source of helpful criticism. Captain Sir Basil Liddell Hart most generously gave access to his voluminous collection of private papers and library relating to the German Army and provided me with the benefit of many valuable discussions and his wide personal experience of the German High Command. James Joll of St Antony's College, Oxford, Professor Michael Howard, Professor of War Studies at King's College, London, and Brian Melland gave me much valuable advice and comment.

Naturally, I owe a great debt of gratitude to those who helped me in Germany for Germany is a country which defies comprehension without personal acquaintance. First and foremost I am grateful to General Hermann Flörke for the enormous amount of time and trouble which he took to help my work in many ways, and to his family for the warmth of their hospitality. General Gotthard Heinrici also gave me much assistance, both in discussion and correspondence. All those who granted me interviews (listed at the end of the bibliography on p. 257) gave me indispensable and often unique information which has been vital for filling the inevitable gaps which occur in a picture built up entirely from documentary evidence. These and many others did much to alleviate by their personal kindness and hospitality the difficulties of my travels in the winter of 1963–64.

However, the chief fundament of material on which this book is based was the documentary evidence supplied by the relevant archives within Germany. I am very grateful to the following in this respect:

the Director and staff of the Bundesarchiv/Militärarchiv, Koblenz, particularly Dr Schmalz,
the Director and staff of the Militärgeschichtliches Forschungsamt, Freiburg im Br., particularly Dr Arenz,

the Director and staff of the Institut für Zeitgeschichte, Munich, particularly Dr Hoch,

Dr Rohwer, Director of the Bibliothek für Zeitgeschichte, Stuttgart, and his staff.

There are many others to whom I owe thanks—they know who they are and I know that they will understand that space prohibits me from adding to this list, apart from thanking the following for their assistance in administrative matters: the Committee for Advanced Studies, Oxford University, the Principal and Fellows of Brasenose College, Oxford, and Dr G. Feith, who produced an immaculate final draft of the thesis.

For performing the unenviable task of correcting the proofs and for other assistance, I am grateful to Captain J. E. Bullen, to my parents and to my wife Sally.

Finally, I am most grateful to the Australian Army for giving me both the time and the support necessary for the preparation of the thesis on which this book is based.

In the course of my preparation I have been allowed access to unpublished documents in official custody, and in accordance with official practice, I am not allowed to give their reference numbers; but sources referring indirectly to statements based on these documents are quoted.

The general principle which I have used in handling German words has been to translate them into English in all cases in which there were clear English equivalents, except for those few words such as *Wehrmacht*, and abbreviations such as *OKH* (the Army High Command) and *OKW* (the Armed Forces High Command) which were thought to be sufficiently well-known for their translation in all cases to be unnecessary. In the many cases in which exact English equivalents do not exist, I have used the German forms in the interests of accuracy and clarity.

This applies particularly to military ranks, because I feel that there is very little direct correspondence between British ranks as in present use and the German ranks of the pre-war period. A *Hauptmann* was much senior both in authority and in age to a Captain. An *Oberst* could command a division, so the equivalent of Colonel applies only to some particular appointments. I have attempted to give an approximate scale of comparison for the military ranks of Germany and Britain in Appendix E. Admittedly, this is inconvenient, because it means much more memory work, but it is hoped that a truer picture of the scope of the authority of the various German officers will result. In particular, this method enables the avoidance of the relatively useless and misleading term 'Colonel-General'—useless because the term has no direct meaning in British terminology and misleading through the automatic translation of *Oberst* by Colonel. Because a Major General is junior to a Lieutenant General, a Colonel General is sometimes thought to be junior to both. In this particular case, *Generaloberst* is more accurately thought of as '*ein oberster General*', i.e. in adhering to the literal meaning of '*oberst*' rather than to its idiomatic equivalent in one special case.

Other German appointments, organizations, ranks and offices raise similar difficulties, so there are a number of other German terms besides military ranks throughout the text. In difficult cases, an approximate English equivalent has been added in brackets. Departments and offices of the German High Command are given in both languages in Appendix D.

The camouflaged titles, such as *Chef des Truppenamts*, have not been translated literally. Instead their functional equivalent, such as Chief of the General Staff, has been used, so that confusion regarding continuity of functions before and after the removal of the camouflaged titles in 1935 might be avoided.

Documents, speeches, etc., have been translated with moderate freedom in order to convey as much of the sense as possible into readable English. In some cases the attainment of flowing English would have demanded so great a reformation of the German structure that emphasis, atmosphere or clarity would have been lost, so there are several pieces of very clumsy English amongst the translations of documents and speeches. In a few cases, namely some of the documents cited by British authors, I have not been able to see the German originals in order to make more fluent translations, so I have adhered to the English versions given by the authors in question, rather than attempt any revision by guesswork.

Introduction

|F this book can be said to be dedicated to anything, then it is to illustrating that the conduct of political-military relations is neither a simple, nor a one-sided process. In general, neither the praise for victories and wise policies, nor the blame for disasters belongs exclusively to the politicians or to the soldiers who are involved, for the two groups are linked inextricably by their functions within a process of balance. This balance is composed of forces pulling in opposite directions. The process is seldom static because the determinants of these forces are as changeable as human thoughts. As one force weakens, the others take up the slack until a new equilibrium is reached. Either the politicians or the soldiers, or both, will have had to take up a new position.

A government normally has a policy to which it would like to adhere. Yet, in order to carry out the business of governing, it is sometimes necessary to alter the policy to suit the means of implementation. In the matter of military policy, it may be necessary to make modifications for such reasons as dependence on the Army for the maintenance of internal order, the relative weakness of the national military power, fear of a coup, or a desire to keep the military under control without their realizing it.

Similarly, soldiers have their particular goals. They may be Machiavellian in character, or they may be idealistic or somewhere in between. Often they can be trapped by the nature of the military ethic*[1] which governs their life into a desire to extend this ethic into civilian society. A system which works so well in ruling the complex affairs of military life may easily delude an oversimplifying mind into applying it where it does not belong. Civilian society in the Western World places the emphasis on the obligations of the state to care for its members. Military society emphasizes the duty of its members to devote themselves to the well-being of the State. Failure to perceive this difference may cause soldiers to concern themselves in every aspect of politics, down to the smallest details.

But even the least politically minded of soldiers have to take into account a modicum of political factors. Their goals are affected by the budget or the state of international tension, and thus their policies must be adjusted to harmonize. Political-military relations, the interaction of the

---

* Throughout the book, superior figures refer to source notes, which are at the back of the book, commencing on page 259.

I

policies of each group, are determined fundamentally by the individual goals of the two.

But this is not enough. Different cases may be imagined in which the aims of both politicians and soldiers do not vary from one instance to another, yet the outcome of one case may bear very little relation to others. If, in one instance, the political and military organizations are linked only at the very highest level, through the person of the Head of State, it is to be expected that the soldiers will have more influence than when the senior military officer is subordinate to a Cabinet Minister. The nature of the connection between the politicians and the soldiers is also an important factor in their interrelation. The nature of this connection is influenced by many other factors besides structure, such as the relative wisdom or obstinacy of the contending parties or the mood of public opinion.

During the early years of the Nazi régime, political-military relations in Germany went through a far-reaching process of change. Before 1933 the German Army had enjoyed a considerable degree of autonomy within the state. It was kept small and without modern equipment by political circumstances, it was unpopular with the people, and its High Command was averse to Nazism. By 1939, to a large extent each of these factors had been reversed. How did this happen? Was it due to the personalities involved, to the nature of the German command structure, to the international situation, or to the internal environment within Germany at the time? What was the role of the Army—did it actively assist the Nazi Party in carrying out this reversal, did it offer resistance, did it feel content to let sleeping dogs lie, or did it remain passive because of a sense of duty to its political master? This book is aimed at investigating these questions.

In carrying out this investigation, it seemed better to split the subject up into individual topics as far as possible, such as:

The Army and the S.A.,
The Army and the S.S.,
Organizational Disputes within the High Command,
The Army and Hitler's War Plans, etc.

However, since there were several events which had a broad influence on many factors comprising Army-Party relations such as Hitler's accession to power and the Fritsch crisis, it has been necessary to make a compromise in the arrangement of material by including some chronological chapters. This compromise has been eased by the way in which several subjects were of importance for periods of a few years only, e.g. the S.A. ceased to complicate Army-Party relations after mid-1934, the important stages of the ideological penetration of the Army occurred between 1934 and 1938, etc.

In making the final arrangement of chapters, note was taken of the influence of events on the subsequent course of Army-Party relations. With the positions of the chronological chapters dictated by the order of events, the other chapters were fitted into the arrangement to illustrate cause and effect as clearly as possible.

Thus Chapters 1–4 precede Chapters 5–7 because the former set the atmosphere in which the events of the latter chapters occurred. Similarly Chapters 4–9 describe the background against which the larger issues of war and peace were fought out as related in Chapters 10–12. In brief, this story describes a three-stage process:

(a) how Hitler made a favourable impression on the Army,
(b) how this was exploited by the Party to make the bulk of the Army obedient to Hitler,
(c) how the resistance of the High Command was overcome and the Army launched into aggressive war.

1

The Army and the Accession of Hitler to Power

HITLER and the Nazi Party had been objects of great interest to the Reichswehr during the later years of the Weimar Republic. This interest expressed itself in many different attitudes, ranging from unbridled enthusiasm to deep despondency. At this time, the greater part of the officer corps had been in the service of the Kaiser, and might thus have been expected to have preserved an atmosphere of conservatism, if not outright monarchism, through the years following 1918. But this was far from being so.

During the intervening years many difficulties had arisen for the Reichswehr, such as restrictions on its size and equipment, low rates of pay, internal civil disorders of many kinds, and strained, if not openly hostile, relations with some of the political parties and the press. Some officers were not content to confine their reactions to these circumstances to passive acceptance, and threw their energies behind one or other of the parties which seemed to offer a solution to their problems and a return to the more pleasant way of life which they had enjoyed before 1914. The cases of the young Leutnants Scheringer, Ludin and Wendt serve as prime examples of this type of outlook.[2] From frustration with the conditions of service in 1929–30, they attempted to spread National-Socialism throughout the officer corps, and were tried for this offence at Leipzig, on 23 September 1930. During his imprisonment, Scheringer wrote an article for the *Völkischer Beobachter*, which included the following:

> The actual purpose of the Reichswehr as a citadel of the military idea and the basic nucleus for the future war of liberation pales. The need of earning bread becomes all important. Soldiers turn into officials, officers become candidates for pensions. What remains is a police troop. People know nothing of the tragedy of the four words: 'Twelve years as subalterns.'[3]

How concisely this expressed the low morale, the monotony and the seeming hopelessness of the predicament of the German Army at that time!

Thus there was fertile soil awaiting the policies and ideas of Adolf Hitler. National-Socialist nationalism, its fight against the conditions of the Treaty of Versailles, its rearmament policies, and its professed respect for the Army attracted the sympathies of many officers. The anxieties of the Army High Command concerning a possible Polish incursion into East Prussia were partly relieved by the co-operation of the S.A.* in East Prussia, and along the Pomeranian and Silesian frontiers in forming a large part of the Grenzschutz.[4]

When Groener banned the S.A. in 1932, widespread dissatisfaction was reported throughout the Officer Corps, not only in the Eastern regions.[5] Hitler had been making specific appeals to the Reichswehr for several years, and although the putsch of 1923 had brought about an appreciable drop in his popularity with the Reichswehr, he had had plenty of time to make reparation. In his speech at the trial of Scheringer, Ludin and Wendt in 1930, he said:

> We will see to it that, when we have come to power, out of the present Reichswehr shall rise the great Army of the German people.[6]

His promises also included a restoration of the Monarchy.[7] But the real strength of Hitler's appeal to the Reichswehr lay in its breadth. There were some officers who were only indirectly affected by the strategic problems of Germany, but there were very few indeed who were not affected by the atmosphere of the times. Soldiering during the 'twenties had been a difficult profession, because of the isolation of the Army (and not only of the German Army) from civilian life. The atmosphere of disillusionment and pacifism had given rise to a feeling of rejection in the minds of the soldiers.[8] They felt that they were regarded as something less than responsible members of a modern society and that they were accused of being one of the basic causes of the recent troubles and upheavals. Thus, Hitler only had to voice his respect and admiration for the Reichswehr and the 'Old Army' in order to extend his appeal to the greater part of the German Army.

Hitler was also in the fortunate position of being able to point to his own experience to give the picture of complete sincerity. His own war record was, in its way, exemplary. He had been a volunteer from the outset, he had fought for four years in the trenches, and had been awarded the rare distinction for his rank of the Iron Cross, First Class. The peculiar fact that, despite this decoration, he had never risen above the rank of Corporal would not have been beyond the rationalizing powers of men who were familiar with the ways of armies.

However, not all of what the Reichswehr saw of Nazism made a favourable impression. The violent methods which the Nazis used to obtain their objectives, such as the battles in the streets and the use of force to coerce individuals to render them obedient, the mania of the Party for uniforms of every sort, and the clearly recognizable military ambitions of Röhm and his Brown Shirts, all had a chastening effect on those members of the Army who saw them, and who could see where the cause of these symptoms lay.[9] The unsavoury nature of the characters of Röhm and Heydrich

---

* The S.A. (Sturmabteilung) was the private army of the Nazi Party.

was known to some who had been able at first or second hand to observe their former service careers. There were those who had to read the police reports of the many brutal acts committed by the Nazis during their 'Kampfzeit'. In 1932, 23·8% of the officer corps was of aristocratic lineage.[10] The socialist doctrine of Goebbels had little appeal for them. The candidature of Hitler for the Presidency in 1932, against Field-Marshal von Hindenburg was the cause of further disapproval of the Nazis, on the part of the Reichswehr.[11] Thus there were men such as Rundstedt, Fritsch, Hammerstein, Witzleben and Weichs, middle ranking and senior officers, who were more impressed by the evil qualities of Nazism.

These several factors produced within the Army a mixed set of reactions towards Nazism. In 1932, Groener felt sure enough of the loyalty of the Army to dismiss any suggestion that it might not obey orders.[12] However Groener expressed this opinion with reference to an armed Nazi uprising, which would have been clearly illegal. Whether or not the Reichswehr would have obeyed any orders from its own High Command to prevent the legal accession to power of Hitler as part of a coalition government, which had been approved by the President and Supreme Commander, is a very dubious matter.[13]

The military side of the story of the crisis which led to Hitler's accession to power began in late 1932. At this time, the internal political situation caused grave concern within the Reichswehr Ministry. In early November, the Ministry for the Interior informed the Reichswehr Minister, General Kurt von Schleicher, that a Communist uprising was imminent.[14] On 8 November, this was promulgated to the Wehrkreis* Commanders with an outline of the supposed tactics which the Communists would employ.[15] Shortly afterwards, the transport workers of Berlin went on strike, under the leadership of a Nazi-Communist coalition.[16] Communists by themselves were danger enough, but when combined with the forces which had been their counterweight, a situation had arisen which could have got out of control.

On 25 November, a detailed study of the matter was made at the Reichswehr Ministry, by means of a 'Planspiel', or war-game. This investigation was made under the direction of Oberstleutnant Eugen Ott,† head of the Wehrmachtabteilung (Armed Forces Branch) of the Ministeramt, the political department of the Reichswehr Ministry. The Reichswehr Minister, Schleicher, had hesitated long over giving his approval for this study,[17] as he did not want to start a process which would automatically cause the Reichswehr to become actively involved in the political struggle. The participants in the Planspiel included representatives of the Wehrkreise, of the Ministry of the Interior, and of the Police. The main difficulty encountered in attempting to use troops to restore order in Berlin,

* Germany was divided into a number of military districts called Wehrkreise. There were seven of these in 1933. See Appendix C for the organization of the German Army.
† Botschafter a.D. Eugen Ott. Chef Wehrmachtabteilung, Ministeramt, Reichswehr Ministerium, as a Major, 1.10.31. Promoted Oberstleutnant 1.4.32. Sent to Japan for attachment to the Imperial Japanese Army on 17.4.33. Appointed Military Attaché in Tokyo, 1.4.34, and Ambasssador to Japan on 1.4.38.

and in the other large cities, if severe trouble broke out, was transport. The Reichswehr possessed very few motor vehicles, and was dependent upon the railways for rapid movement. Garrisons were small and were scattered throughout Germany in the more remote parts. Attempts to move troops into the cities in the case of civil disorder could have been countered by the opposition of the transport workers. If it were decided to move in troops as a precautionary measure, this might precipitate the very trouble which it was designed to prevent.

Apart from the numerical inferiority of the Reichswehr to the Rotfront-kämpferbund and to the Sturmabteilung, there were acute fears of Polish intentions. It was known that Pilsudski had formulated plans for a preventive war against Germany, and that Polish troops had been concentrated in the Polish Corridor and on parts of the East Prussian border.[18] Consequently, all available soldiers were needed in the East.

When the conference broke up on 26 November 1932, the outlook of the participants was pessimistic. On 2 December 1932, Ott laid the conclusions of the conference before Schleicher.[19] The essence of these conclusions was that it was feared that, in the event of a combined blow from the forces of the Nazi and Communist Parties the joint efforts of the Reichswehr and the Police would be insufficient to maintain law and order. Ott emphasized that the Nothilfe (Emergency Service) was of inadequate numerical strength, and because of the presence of Nazis in its ranks, partly unreliable. Strengthening of the Army and of the Police was an urgent necessity, he continued. If a strike took the form of passive resistance, it would be very difficult to combat, since there were no resources for moving food. The psychological situation of the Army and of the Police was very difficult, Ott concluded, since agitators were spreading the belief that any use of force would not be for the maintenance of law and order, but for the interests of a ruling class against the population at large.

Thus the Reichswehr felt incapable of dealing with the worst of the possible cases of political strife. The Army did not, however, refuse to assist in the restoration of law and order in the event of trouble. On 13 December 1932, another conference between the Reichswehr, the Police, and the Ministry for the Interior took place in the Reichswehr Ministry.[20] They discussed the orders necessary for putting troops under command of the Police, and for the arming of the Police with heavier weapons.* On 15 December Wehrkreis representatives met at the Reichswehr Ministry to discuss 'exceptional military circumstances'.[21] Instructions to deal with these circumstances were issued under Schleicher's signature on 27 January 1933. The orders stressed close co-operation between the Wehrkreise and their local civil authorities, and introduced an optimistic note by requesting further suggestions, which were to reach the

---

* The police had already received some weapons from the Army. On 23 July 1931, the Berlin Police had 18 machine-guns and 1,965 carbines, while all other cities were armed on an approximate pro-rata basis. The heaviest concentration was in the Ruhr, where the police had 55 machine-guns and 620 carbines. The Prussian Minister of the Interior, Severing, signed a certificate to the effect that the Army was the only supplier of weapons to the police. OKH File H 24/74.

Ministry by 1 March 1933. In the event of a lack of co-operation on the part of the State (Land) Governments, command over their police might be removed from them, single recalcitrant officials might be replaced by the Wehrkreis Commanders and officials might be placed in protective custody.[22]

In the meantime, the wider political events of January 1933 were taking place. Schleicher had failed to split the Nazi Party. His favour with Hindenburg had sunk so low that the President would not grant him a dissolution of the Reichstag, so he and his Cabinet resigned on 28 January 1933. Schleicher's only ally was the Chef der Heeresleitung (Commander-in-Chief of the Army), General der Infanterie Kurt Freiherr von Hammer-stein-Equord.

Hammerstein was a man of great courage and initiative and thoroughly worthy of his post.[23] Perhaps the most eloquent praise of his ability would be that he was the only lazy man to get to the top of the German Army. Unfortunately, his penchant for hunting often took him away from his work when there were official matters requiring his attention.[24] His attitude towards the Nazis was one of frank and open contempt.[25] He had remarked earlier to Carl Severing, 'The Reichswehr will never allow them to come to power.'*[26] In later years, his opposition to Nazism led him into close friendship with General Ludwig Beck, with whom he formed many plans for ridding the world of Hitler, between 1939 and 1943, the year of his death.†

Hammerstein's opinion in January 1933 was the same as that of Schleicher, in that both thought that the appointment of a Papen-Hugenberg coalition would result in civil war, and provide a good pretext for the feared Nazi-Communist revolt.[27] He thus had to make the choice between a possible civil war and the coming to power, albeit by legal means, of a man and a system detested by him. Such a civil war might have allowed the Communists to gain control and might have afforded Poland an opportunity to strike at her old foe with impunity. Whether or not he perceived the possible consequences of a Nazi Government is not clear. We do know, by his actions, that he decided that Hitler would be the lesser of the two evils, and that he was not prepared to call out the Reichswehr, provided that Hitler confined himself to legal methods in attempting to come to power. On Thursday, 26 January 1933, he placed his views before Hindenburg. He said that if the situation developed into a general revolt as the result of a new Papen Government, the Reichswehr would be in difficulties, especially in the matter of firing on Nazis, as the troops could succumb to Nazi influence.[28]

---

* In view of what eventuated, this statement cannot be taken completely at face value, unless it was used in the context of an *illegal* seizure of power by the Nazis. However, it does indicate that Hammerstein was a public foe of the Nazi Party. Perhaps, had he been freer of other worries, such as the Eastern Frontier and the internal threats to law and order, he might have caused the literal fulfilment of this declaration.

† Hammerstein died on 24 April 1943, Wheeler-Bennett, *Nemesis of Power*, p. 567. Hammerstein was a frequent visitor to Beck's house, Goethestrasse 9, Lichterfelde, during the war years, where they discussed their plans for removing Hitler from power. Conversation with Frau Gertrud Neubaur-Beck, the daughter of General Beck, 16 March 1964.

Hindenburg received several military visitors during that week. Amongst them were the openly pro-Nazi Generalleutnant von Blomberg, Commander of Wehrkreis I (East Prussia), his Chief of Staff, Oberst von Reichenau, and the Chaplain of Wehrkreis I, Chaplain Müller.[29] Blomberg at that time was also a member of the German Delegation to the Disarmament Conference at Geneva. How it came about that he was received by Hindenburg at such a critical moment is not known. Blomberg, a former Chief of the General Staff (then called Chef des Truppenamts), was well known to the old Field-Marshal,[30] and either one may have taken the initiative in arranging this conversation.[31] Blomberg recommended a National Front Government under Hitler as the best solution from the point of view of the Reichswehr. If it came to an armed conflict with the S.A. and S.S., he said, both officers and men would be defeated, and the Army would be smashed to pieces.[32]

Hindenburg was having great trouble in deciding on the next Chancellor. He was resolved that Schleicher had to be replaced by someone more dependable, in both of his capacities. He discussed the question of a new Reichswehr Minister with Papen on the evening of 28 January.[33] Papen suggested Generalleutnant von Fritsch, Commander of Wehrkreis III (Berlin), with whom Papen had spent his early military career, and whom Papen greatly admired.[34] Hindenburg said nothing against Fritsch, but stated a preference for Blomberg, because he was better known to him. Hindenburg's judgement of Blomberg was that he was a gifted professional soldier, completely apolitical, with a pleasant personality, and one who had, by his conduct of affairs at Geneva, shown that he possessed all the necessary qualities of a minister.[35] This misjudgement of Blomberg, especially the underestimation of his political inclinations, was to have tragic consequences. After the decision for Blomberg had been made, Hindenburg sent him a telegram, recalling him from the Geneva Conference, on the morning of 29 January.[36]

At 10 a.m. on 29 January, Schleicher and Hammerstein met with Generalmajor von dem Bussche-Ippenburg, head of the Army Personnel Office, and with another officer, probably Oberst von Bredow, head of the Ministeramt and Schleicher's right-hand man.[37] They were resolved not to attempt any military action against Hindenburg, but to use whatever influence was available to them short of force, to prevent the calamity of the return of Papen. They discussed the old problem of the Chancellorship once again, but apart from agreeing that there were strong objections to both Papen and Hitler, no progress towards a solution of the dilemma was made. Schleicher showed himself to be disappointed and was resigned to accept whatever should come. He reiterated the need for the Reichswehr to remain loyal to the President, irrespective of the outcome of the struggle for the Chancellorship.[38] As they left Hammerstein's office, they met Oberst von Reichenau, who was standing in Hammerstein's reception room. He remarked to them, 'Now is the time to arrest the Field-Marshal'. Bussche retorted, 'Nonsense!' In view of what Hindenburg had already decided with respect to Blomberg this was surely an odd remark for Reichenau to let fall, unless he was still uninformed, and thought that the outcome would be a Papen Government, with someone other than Blomberg as Reichswehr Minister.

Around midday,[39] by pure chance, Schleicher learned from an industrialist friend, Otto Wolff,[40] that Blomberg had been recalled from Geneva. Schleicher informed Hammerstein, who went to see Hitler, at the house of Carl Bechstein, between 3 and 4 p.m. to try to obtain some information on what was really happening.[41] Hammerstein and Schleicher were afraid that Hindenburg would decide in favour of a Papen-Hugenberg Cabinet. They felt that this would be disastrous, and they had already sent a messenger to the President, with their views.[42] This attempt to make contact was fruitless, and Hammerstein was now afraid of a *fait accompli* in favour of Papen and Hugenberg. Hitler was able to tell Hammerstein little, apart from his willingness to retain Schleicher as Reichswehr Minister. Hammerstein offered to use what influence he had left with Hindenburg on Hitler's behalf, and returned to the Ministry.[43]

Werner von Alvensleben, Schleicher's liaison man with the Nazis, then came to Schleicher and Hammerstein and offered to go to Hitler again. He arrived at Goebbels's house around 7 p.m., to find that an agreement had been reached between the Nazis and Papen, whereby Hitler was to have the Chancellorship. However, Hitler was still insisting upon a dissolution of the Reichstag, and it was by no means certain that Hindenburg would agree to this. Alvensleben expressed the opinion that the men advising Hindenburg—Papen, Oskar von Hindenburg, and Secretary Meissner—should be arrested. This immediately alarmed the Nazis, who thought that they might be exploited for the purposes of setting up a military dictatorship. They therefore informed the Hindenburg group that they were in danger of becoming the victims of a Reichswehr putsch. These rumours produced great alarm within the Presidential Palace. Whether Hindenburg himself believed that the Reichswehr were preparing a putsch is open to doubt.[44] However the possibility that Schleicher would attempt some further means of delaying the formation of a new Cabinet may well have been enough to force Hindenburg to an immediate decision. On the evening of 29 January 1933, Hindenburg chose Hitler to succeed Schleicher as Chancellor; the swearing in of the new Cabinet was arranged for 11 a.m. on the following day, and Oskar von Hindenburg was detailed to meet Blomberg at the Anhalter Bahnhof on the latter's arrival from Geneva at 8.30 a.m. on the 30th, so that Schleicher would be denied any further possibility for intervention.

Thus was the die cast. The old President was forced to make a rapid decision about a problem which had been troubling him for some time, and to which he had previously been unable to find an answer. The force which triggered him was probably, although not certainly, the fear that Schleicher was about to do something which would inhibit Hindenburg's already narrow range of possible solutions. Schleicher, for his part, had lost the initiative of his December machinations so completely that even his information system had failed to keep him abreast of events. He was in no position to plan a putsch and was doing nothing more than attempt to use his personal influence with Hindenburg to prevent the formation of a

Papen-Hugenberg Government. The fact that Hindenburg had lost patience completely with Schleicher made contact between them impossible, and so facilitated the growth of suspicion in Hindenburg's mind that Schleicher was working actively against him. The blame for this must, of course, rest almost entirely with Schleicher, whose record of intrigue and inconsistency gave Hindenburg very little reason for trusting him. With Schleicher, on the fringes of the momentous events, lay the Reichswehr. Its commander, Hammerstein, was in no better a position than Schleicher to influence events, as Hindenburg had sharply rejected Hammerstein's efforts to give advice.[45] The Reichswehr itself was not strong enough to support the structure of the Republic, come what might, even had its heart been in its task. As it was its sympathies were such that if called upon to do battle with the forces of the Right, the internal tensions generated thereby would have rendered it completely ineffective.

In the midst of these crises of confidence and threats of civil disorder stood one man, who, despite the initial disapproval of those in power, contrived to play off these internal disharmonies, one against the other, until he had become a lesser evil than the other choices open to the President, and his nomination to the Chancellorship followed automatically. The part which Hitler played in securing office for himself by causing severe anxiety within the Presidential Palace, at a time when Hindenburg needed all the peace that he could get, must also be given considerable weight.

The conduct of the Reichswehr during the critical period prior to the Machtübernahme has been the subject of much controversy. The Reichswehr has been condemned, notably by Wheeler-Bennett[46] and Craig,[47] for tolerating the coming to power of a man and of a system of the greatest evil, and for seeking to exploit these circumstances for its own military ends, at the expense of the welfare of Germany as a whole. It has been defended by Ritter,[48] on the grounds that the coming to power of Hitler and the Nazi Party was not due to the support of the German Army, but to the popular enthusiasm and general support which Nazism enjoyed amongst the German people.

This bald defence by Ritter does not exactly meet the criticisms of Wheeler-Bennett and Craig. It simply assigns a role of insignificance to the Reichswehr throughout the period of crisis, and possibly by default of further comment, implies that the charges of tolerance and exploitation of evil are groundless. This, however, leaves the explanation too loose.

The concept of the word 'tolerance' implies a choice between interference and non-interference in a particular situation, between active participation on behalf of one's beliefs, and remaining, by conscious choice, passive. In this case, then, it is necessary that there should have been at least a feasible possibility that the Reichswehr could by force have prevented Hitler's accession to power, and could also have dealt with any consequent disorders until Germany was once again fully under the control of a civil government.

This alternative course has two bases, one theoretical, the other practical. The theoretical basis is the assumption that any army has the right to interfere in the internal workings of the political system of the country which has raised it, even though none of the contending political parties has resorted to illegal means, though law and order is being maintained by the civil police, and though the Head of State or Commander-in-Chief does not desire any military assistance. Needless to say, the law of no civilized nation, including the Weimar Republic, has recognized the validity of any such principle.

The practical basis for the employment of the Reichswehr to stop Hitler was that there should have been some clear gain out of the operation. The possibility that the use of the Army could have worsened the course of events even further must be considered. A deleterious effect could have resulted in either of two major ways. First, if the Army had been defeated in internal civil war, a total collapse of law and order could have resulted. Secondly, if the Army had won, but had proved unable to find any means of returning to civil government better than that which existed before the conflict had broken out, in January 1933, the additional bitterness and other passions aroused by the actual physical fighting would scarcely have made the situation any easier to solve than it had been originally.

Whether Hammerstein, the Chef der Heeresleitung, was deterred from acting against the Nazis because of the weakness of the Reichswehr in physical strength, or because he saw no ultimate benefit to the internal political situation within Germany as a result, or whether he and Schleicher, as Wheeler-Bennett states,[49]

... were still dreaming in their blindness of a martial State in which the masses, galvanized and inspired by modified National-Socialism, would be directed and disciplined by the Army,

is by no means certain. However, to a man of Hammerstein's character, training, background and position, it seems likely that some of the preceding difficulties presented themselves. In principle, there seemed to be at the most, only dubious justification for a putsch. In practice, the effects of a putsch could well have been negative. Doubtful of the reliability of the Reichswehr, troubled by the Polish threat, with no plans for the requisite conspiracy, organization of trusted sympathizers throughout the Army, and the disposition of troops, it seems small wonder that Hammerstein was prepared to leave the initiative to someone else, for the time being at least. The accusations that the Reichswehr tolerated the coming to power of Nazism and endeavoured to exploit it for the Reichswehr's private ends would seem to require further evidence than has been provided to date.

Conversely, there seems to be insufficient evidence to state with certainty that the conduct of the Reichswehr during the Machtübernahme was entirely determined by the military difficulties apparent at the time. The role played by Schleicher, characterized by intrigue, self interest, and deceit, may also have had an influence on his subordinate and friend, Hammerstein. Certainly the two men remained in the closest of contact throughout the whole affair, and Schleicher may have planted some other ideas into Hammerstein's policy, reinforcing his feelings against Papen, or, later, for Hitler. It is also possible that some officers of lower rank exerted an additional influence on Hammerstein, to ensure the neutrality of the Reichswehr.

But if the verdict is to remain open, it would seem that in view of the preceding consideration a much greater stretch of the imagination is required to find the Army, under a man of the character of Hammerstein, guilty of exploitation of the circumstances, than is required to conclude that it had been waiting on the outcome of events.

2

The Rearrangement of the High Command 1933-1934

THE operation of the High Command was immediately affected by the character and personality of the new Reichs Chancellor. Prior to the Machtübernahme, Chancellors had come and gone, some with moderate influence on the Reichswehr, others with almost no influence. While personalities such as the Reichswehr Ministers Gessler and Groener enjoyed a relatively stable position of authority, the scope for the transient Chancellors to acquire influence in military affairs was much more limited. But once the old team, and their successor, Schleicher, had been removed from office, Hitler, a man of many military interests, began to rule at the same time as his new Reichswehr Minister. Although he began rather tentatively to give his interests rein, and exerted himself far more in later years, his personality had its immediate effects, and was a factor in maintaining harmony between the Army and its new political masters from the very outset.

Enough has already been written concerning the details of Hitler's personality.[50] However, the richness of the available descriptions is so great that a small amount of recapitulation of those characteristics which had a large influence upon the senior officers of the Reichswehr might be of some assistance in gauging the attitude of these officers towards Hitler, and the nature of the atmosphere in which they worked together.

It should not be forgotten that Hitler could, when he liked, be thoroughly charming, interesting in conversation, and gay. He could meet difficult situations with a calmness which was very difficult for those who met it to reconcile with his excitable temperament.[51] His working hours were chaotic but he seemed to make a more genuine effort to adapt himself to the regular methods of the Wehrmacht than he did to those of other departments.[52] He went away at week-ends spending most Sundays of the pre-war period at the Berghof.[53] Thus he spent his most relaxed moments away from his official mentors, and in the company of his old Party comrades, who exercised a counteracting influence to that of the department heads in Berlin. The many surprises which greeted Hammerstein's successor, Fritsch, on Hitler's return from these week-ends caused Fritsch to express the desire that Hitler should always be accompanied on these journeys by his Wehrmacht Adjutant,[54] the then Major Friedrich Hossbach.*

Hitler was very bored by paper work. This had two advantages—first, it was easy to talk with him and to use thereby more techniques of persuasion than written communications allowed; and second, he usually signed orders without reading them when they concerned personnel changes or administrative detail.†[55] Correspondingly, it was easier for those who had the ear of the Führer most often, men such as Göring, Goebbels, Himmler, Ribbentrop and Ley, to gain a relative advantage over the Wehrmacht in obtaining support for their various projects and schemes. The habit of giving orders only a casual perusal sometimes resulted in administrative chaos, since Hitler did not approve of any appreciable interchange of information between departments which might weaken his own position. When he himself failed to fulfil the role of 'universal joint' conscientiously, the administration of Germany was coordinated only by coincidence.

He made a favourable impression on the Army leaders by refraining from interference in internal Army affairs. He left the basis of selection for the promotion of officers as professional efficiency, rather than political outlook.[56] He did not alter the judgements of courts martial,[57] nor did he take any part in the planning of operations, until January 1938.[58] He received briefings in silence while on exercises and did not make criticisms.[59] When asked a question which he did not want to discuss, he would gradually diverge from the topic of conversation, so that the person talking had to exert extreme persistence in order to get his difficulty dealt with.‡ This appearance of complete confidence in his subordinates, coupled with his strong interest in the rebuilding of Germany's armed strength, must have done much to create an atmosphere of trust. The Generals probably felt that while dealing with an Austrian Corporal might not be very gratifying, things could be a lot worse.

He managed to give some people the impression that he was a far-seeing genius, by such things as his plans for the reconstruction of Berlin, to make the city capable of sustaining another two centuries of development,

---

* Hossbach was Wehrmacht Adjutant to Hitler from 3 August 1934 to 28 January 1938. For details of his career see Appendix B.

† Hossbach, *Zwischen Wehrmacht und Hitler*, also relates an interesting example of Hitler's working methods. Hitler wanted to grant the Army some new battle colours. Hossbach persuaded him to re-institute the old Imperial Colours. However, when Blomberg suggested that a new form of colours be adopted, Hitler was just as ready to agree as he had been with Hossbach, and so the decision was reversed, and the Army received new colours. Grand Admiral Karl Dönitz also made frequent reference to these characteristics of Hitler in conversations with the writer in April 1964. He regarded the use of written material as one of Raeder's chief errors in dealing with the Führer.

‡ Hossbach, *op. cit.*, p. 37, and conversation with Generalleutnant Hermann Flörke, December 1964. General Flörke relates how Hitler treated officers who returned from the Front during the war, and who tried to bring unwelcome matters to the attention of the Führer. Flörke was once in this position, having returned from the Russian Front in 1944, to receive a decoration for his bravery. He had a great number of matters to question Hitler about, or to inform him of, but Hitler gave him no chance to speak, by indulging in one of his well known monologues, until an Adjutant appeared and informed Hitler that the time allocated for the conversation had expired.

and his ideas for a new capital at Neu Strelitz.[60] As late as 1935, it was felt by many men in the Bendlerstrasse* that Hitler found the early measures of totalitarianism repugnant, and that he would relax them shortly.[61] He had the ability to discern what people wanted to hear from him, and he was then able to tell them whatever it was in a convincing manner. In short, he was well equipped for exploiting the atmosphere of the time within the German Army, and the Army was largely unaware that the benefits which it was receiving were only to enable Hitler to expend its strength on his desperate schemes for spreading Nazism and German hegemony throughout the Eastern European lands.†

Hitler's chief military subordinate, General der Infanterie Werner von Blomberg,‡ had been appointed to the Cabinet as Reichswehr Minister one day before Hitler himself was chosen by Hindenburg to lead the next Government.[62] It is a strange coincidence that Blomberg would have been Hitler's most likely choice as well.[63] He was Hitler's leading protagonist among the Generals, and he had made a very favourable impression on Hitler for many reasons, including his classic physique and appearance, his modern military ideas, and his political inclinations. His Chief of Staff during his immediately previous appointment as Commander of Wehrkreis I (East Prussia) was Oberst von Reichenau, who was also known personally to Hitler as one of his most enthusiastic supporters within the Army.[64] Hindenburg may well have chosen Blomberg with the possibility of a Papen Government in mind, as well as for his seeming compatibility with Hindenburg's picture of the non-political soldier[65] who would be a restraining influence on the wild schemes of the Nazis. It is interesting that Papen made no objection to having the pro-Nazi Blomberg as his Reichswehr Minister when he discussed the matter with Hindenburg on 28 January 1933.[66]

Blomberg had shown great distinction in his military career. In the First World War, he had won the *Pour le Mérite*, the highest decoration of the German Army, for his brilliant planning work. His service in the General Staff was eventually rewarded by the attainment of the position of Chief of the General Staff (at that time Chef des Truppenamts). In this capacity, he visited the Soviet Union in 1928,[67] to inspect the various training establishments which were run by the Germans in Russia in defiance of the Treaty of Versailles. He was so impressed by the simplicities and advantages of the military life in Russia that he was verging on becoming Communist after his return.[68] This is an illustration of his impetuous, intense, and over-simplifying nature. His failure to perceive the drawbacks of being a Soviet soldier indicated a grave narrowness in political outlook. It would be interesting to know what he thought when his Russian friends and colleagues were purged four years later, some months before his own downfall.

---

* The Reichswehr Ministry and the Army High Command were situated in the block bounded by the Bendlerstrasse on the east and by the Tirpitz Ufer of the Landwehr Canal on the south. Thus these terms became synonyms similar to Whitehall and No. 10.

† See below, Chapter 10, for Hitler's ultimate military policy.

‡ For details of the career of Field-Marshal von Blomberg, see below, Appendix B.

As the responsible defender of the outpost of East Prussia, he had grave difficulties to face, because of the discrepancies between the threatening Polish forces and his own. The fact that Reichenau found the solution to this manpower problem through the co-operation of the S.A.[69] may have helped to transfer his absolutist tendencies to the side of Nazism. Another influence was Wehrkreis Chaplain Müller, a convinced Nazi who was to become the Reichsbischof of the Protestant Church. During these years in Königsberg his thought culminated in conceiving the execution of the process of bringing together the Wehrmacht and the Party as his 'great historical mission'.[70]

Blomberg's personality was an unusual, but by no means unique combination of many strong drives.[71] He was frank and open. He showed great energy, keenness, and intensity both in his conversation, and in his work. He was spontaneous to the point of impulsiveness. With his great energy and self-discipline he was all the easier for someone else to dominate. Hitler quickly exerted his will over Blomberg's to the extent that Blomberg's nick-name became 'Hitler-Junge Quex', after a character in a propaganda film, a member of the Hitler Youth, who idolized the Führer. He was also known as 'Gummi-Löwe', or 'Rubber Lion', for the same reasons.[72] His impulsiveness has been evidenced by Hossbach[73] who has described how Blomberg became carried away by the frequent use of the word 'Heil!' on a Navy exercise which he was attending. He ordered on the spot that the normal form of greeting throughout the Wehrmacht be changed to 'Heil!' He has been characterized by Fritsch, his direct subordinate of both the late 1920s and the 1930s,* as being very difficult to work under, for his nature was inclined too much in the direction of romantic fantasy, which made him vacillating, always seeking novelties, and, on occasions, too susceptible to outside influence.[74]

Thus it was far from difficult for Hitler to play on Blomberg's misplaced idealism, and so make him comply with his Führer's wishes. In one regard, the choice of Blomberg was fortunate for the Army. While he was at the head of the Wehrmacht, the evil influence of Himmler, Ley, and other leaders of that ilk, was minimized for the soldiers. The Party leaders lacked an excuse for interfering in the internal affairs of the Army, because Blomberg left no doubt about his loyalty to Hitler. Blomberg resisted the attempts of Göring to convert the Luftwaffe into a private force to such an extent that he incurred Göring's enduring enmity, which was to play a significant role in Blomberg's ultimate downfall.† Blomberg never permitted officers to join the Nazi Party, and while he remained at the Tirpitz Ufer, there was no incident in which Hitler interfered in the internal workings of the Wehrmacht against the advice of his Minister.[75] This advice may seldom have been forthcoming, but at least he was actuated by a set of ideals rather than by the naked power hunger of the

---

* When Blomberg was Chef des Truppenamts, Fritsch was head of his most important department, the Operations Abteilung, 1926–29.

Fritsch served under Blomberg as Commander-in-Chief of the Army from 1934–38, while Blomberg was Reichswehr and Reichskriegs Minister.

† For Göring's enmity and later role, see below, Chapter 11.

C

Party leaders. But as far as the Wehrmacht was concerned, this may have been worse than no ideals at all, for this made it easy for soldiers to mistake the shadow of correct and chivalrous conduct for the substance of a wise and responsible defence policy. There is no doubt that a significant part of the credit for the unprecedented military successes of 1939-40 belongs to him. There is equally little doubt that the total disaster which befell his country was partly due to his uncritical acceptance of the heavily over-simplified 'Führer Prinzip'.

Blomberg's nominee to succeed Schleicher's assistant, Generalmajor von Bredow, was his old Chief of Staff, von Reichenau, who was immediately promoted to Generalmajor on taking office on 1 February 1933.[76] This was also a fateful choice with far-reaching consequences for the conduct of military-political relations, for Reichenau's political views were akin to those of his chief, with the difference that Reichenau was a more forceful personality. While Blomberg could be moved by sudden impulses, Reichenau did not make decisions without pause for thought, insight and calculation.[77] His National-Socialism centred on Hitler, rather than on the Party as a whole, and his drive and determination brought him into conflict with several of the Party organizations, especially the S.A.* and the Reichsarbeitsdienst (National Labour Corps).† However initially his relations with the S.A. were very good by virtue of the assistance which the S.A. rendered to the defence of East Prussia.[78] The friction began to grow only when Reichenau saw that the S.A. was attempting to encroach on the Army's sphere of activity in a way which could have prejudiced its position as the one and only defence force of the Reich.

Reichenau's personality was that of an active sportsman.[79] He could not bear to be restricted and was continually seeking outlets for his ideas and energies. In military thought, he was one of the most progressive, and gave much assistance to Guderian in the development of the techniques of Blitzkrieg.[80] He appealed to Hitler's conception of a modern soldier, and was a frequent guest at the Reichs Chancellery and at the Berghof.[81] He participated in sport regularly and was fond of competing with his men.[82] He was appointed to the International Olympic Committee as the German representative.[83]

One of the many aspects of Reichenau's nature was a pronounced leaning towards England, both in personal matters and in military policy. He spoke English at home, wore English clothes, and attempted for some months to convince Hitler that he should attempt to form an alliance with England, rather than with Italy.‡[84] When Hitler finally rejected this advice, Reichenau's affection for him moderated,[85] and several observers have stated that by 1941, shortly before his death, Reichenau had swung around to extreme dissatisfaction with Hitler.[86]

* See below, Chapter 3.
† See below, Chapter 6.
‡ According to Blumentritt, Reichenau worked hard in 1936 to try to convince Hitler that he should direct his foreign policy towards an alliance with Britain. In 1941, Reichenau prepared a minute on the inadvisability of attacking Russia. After the rejection of this by Hitler, Reichenau swung round to general criticism of Hitler. Generals von Vietinghoff, Röhrricht, Foertsch and Speidel have given evidence that in 1941 Reichenau had changed his views appreciably.

The first personal contact between Hitler and Reichenau was arranged by Wehrkreis Chaplain Müller, in April 1932.[87] Correspondence began between the two concerning the conduct of S.A. men serving in the Grenzschutz, and German foreign policy.[88] Hitler's letter to Reichenau of 2 December 1932,[89] not only indicates the close degree of co-operation which existed between Hitler, Blomberg and Reichenau, but also gives an interesting outline of Hitler's foreign policy and of his appreciation of the dangers threatening the Eastern frontier. The relationship between Reichenau, Blomberg and Hitler appears to have been a smooth one, which endured two and a half years of intensive effort during the rebuilding and reforming of the German military forces.

As soon as Reichenau took up his new appointment he began to threaten the position of Hammerstein as Commander-in-Chief of the Army by displaying his own ambitions for becoming Hammerstein's successor.[90] Hammerstein was in a difficult position.* He was resolved to stay on in the hope of influencing Hindenburg to take action against the Nazis.[91] There was considerable friction between him and Blomberg, his former junior. Shortly after the Machtübernahme, Blomberg had invited Fritsch, the Commander of Wehrkreis III, Berlin, to dinner. At this dinner, Blomberg warned Fritsch that he would be appointed Commander-in-Chief of the Army should Hammerstein have to retire suddenly for any reason.† Blomberg gradually circumscribed Hammerstein, so that by June 1933, he had no direct access to the President, save on strictly military matters.[92]

A further complication for Hammerstein was the formation of the Reichs Defence Council. This was the last of Hitler's initial structural reforms. The Council was formed on 4 April 1933 with the task of planning and co-ordinating all State activities which could strengthen Germany's war position. It was composed of the Ministers for Foreign Affairs, Interior, Propaganda, Finance and Defence under the chairmanship of the Reichs Chancellor.[93] This body had the effect of tying the Wehrmacht more closely to the structure of the Nazi Party, for another voice, almost wholly Nazi, was added to those which could exercise control over defence policy and the Army. The Council had no direct power to alter the policies of the Commander-in-Chief of the Army, but its indirect

---

* Hammerstein's difficulties are illustrated by the order which he gave in February 1933 concerning the liaison of members of the Army with persons connected with politics. He forbade the officers to invite any people who might have political influence, especially Göring, to messes or to social gatherings. Weichs' memoirs. The relationship between Göring and Hammerstein was particularly bad. Hammerstein always referred to Göring by his true rank, i.e. Hauptmann a.D., or Captain retired, or by the nickname, 'Verrücktgewordener Flieger', or 'the crazy airman'. Weichs, *op. cit.*, and confirmed by conversation with Generaloberst Heinrici, March 1964.

† Fritsch's own reactions to this suggestion were:

1. The sudden dismissal of Hammerstein presumably for political reasons, would have had a bad effect on the Army.

2. He did not look forward to working with Blomberg in the light of his past experience as a subordinate of Blomberg.

The account of this dinner is given in Fritsch's memorandum of 1 February 1938.

This also indicates that Blomberg had not then begun to favour Reichenau as Hammerstein's successor.

effect was to give more power to Blomberg and Reichenau to control factors which affected the decisions of the Army Commander by virtue of their increased closeness to the various policy-making centres of the Reich.

Thus in a short time, effective control of the Reichswehr Ministry had passed to Hitler, while his opposition had become confined and, to a large extent, bypassed. All that Hammerstein was left with was the personal allegiance of the soldiers, together with command over the Army in the specific matters in which his policy agreed with the views of Blomberg and Reichenau.

Hammerstein, however, still had one loyal friend in close support—the Chef des Truppenamts, Generalleutnant Wilhelm Adam. Adam had been Chef des Truppenamts since the commencement of Hammerstein's period of office,[94] and was one of the most senior Generals of the Reichswehr. Consequently when there was a reshuffle of Generals, he was bound to be included, and Hammerstein would have the problem of selecting a successor. In September 1933, the Commander of Gruppenkommando 2 (Kassel), General von Seutter retired.[95] His successor was General der Artillerie Ritter von Leeb, who was moved from the important post of Commander of Wehrkreis VII (Munich). Adam was appointed to replace him, and the important station at the right hand of the Chef der Heeresleitung fell vacant.

Amongst the Divisional Commanders at that time was Generalmajor Ludwig Beck, Commander of the First Cavalry Division at Frankfurt an der Oder.[96] During his thirty-five years in the Army, Beck had achieved an outstanding military reputation. He had also experienced personal misfortune which had tempered the spirit that was to withstand so much in the following eleven years remaining to him.

Beck was born a Rhinelander, at Biebrich, near Wiesbaden, into a quiet, respectable, upper middle class family.[97] His father was a highly skilled metallurgical engineer, with a strong academic bent. This bent was present in the young Ludwig, and became one of his most outstanding characteristics. He entered the Prussian Field Artillery Regiment No. 15 in 1898, and spent most of the period before the First World War in Alsace-Lorraine. This beautiful country aroused in him a deep love of its characteristic villages, its woods, and its valleys, and to retire to a house in Alsace always remained one of his pipe-dreams. His service as a junior officer had been sufficiently outstanding to enable him to be selected for General Staff training, which he completed between October 1908 and July 1911.

During the First World War, he served as a Staff Officer in divisional and higher headquarters. For the last two years of the war, he served on the Staff of the Army Group *Deutscher Kronprinz* with the then Major Max von Viebahn, who relates how Beck carried enormous responsibilities which sometimes in effect embraced command of the entire Army Group. In this position, Beck acquired the habits of intense industry which were to mould the whole shape of his future life. He became accustomed to working fifteen hours a day, and to going for long periods without any free time. He even gave up one of his few relaxations—playing the violin. He particularly distinguished himself at the end of the war by his planning of the withdrawal of German forces totalling ninety divisions, under the most difficult and pressing circumstances.

The only romance of his life blossomed briefly in the mid-war period. He married Amalie Pagenstecher, the daughter of a Bremen merchant, on 12 May 1916. They had a brief war-time honeymoon, and he returned to the Front. Their daughter Gertrud was born in 1917. However, the health of Frau Beck deteriorated severely, and she died on 16 November 1917, leaving the upbringing of Gertrud to Ludwig. His reaction to this loss was, similar to that of Field-Marshal Montgomery, to immerse himself totally in his profession. He grew more and more apart from the social life that tended to surround rising young officers. He was shy and withdrawn. Few things revolted him more than the artificial bonhomie of the Officers' Messes. Life also became more difficult for him on account of his health. He developed a stomach complaint which robbed eating of pleasure for him. He ate two simple meals a day, with a warm drink as his only sustenance in the middle of the day. Whether this made for efficient work is doubtful. However, he used to continue his work to a late hour after dinner. Despite the few opportunities which he had for using it, he never lost his personal charm. This is an outstanding feature in the memories of those few of his intimate friends who still survive.

On 1 October 1929, he became Commander of Artillery Regiment No. 5, in Fulda. During this time, his political views began to incline towards the desirability of experimenting with Hitler and the Nazi Party as the government of Germany. His part in the trial of Scheringer, Ludin and Wendt, the young officers charged with spreading Nazism throughout the Army, is illustrative of his views at the time. He spoke in open court in defence of the character of Scheringer, which, as his Commanding Officer, he was obliged to do. However, he went beyond the bounds of military duty by showing his sympathy with Scheringer's ideas. As soon as Groener, the Reichswehr Minister, heard of this he wanted to have Beck dismissed. Hammerstein, who was Chef der Heeresleitung at that time, and very impressed with Beck's soldierly qualities, dissuaded Groener, and Beck went on to become a divisional commander.

In the years 1931 to 1933, he was busy with the writing of a manual of tactics which was to become one of the most renowned of German military publications—the *T.F.* or *Truppenführung*. This became his most famous work, and gained him a great reputation for the clarity of his ideas and expression. For a military publication, this work has one other outstanding feature—it is written in prose of great elegance. This, together with the large number of other studies which he wrote during his lifetime mark him as a thinker of the same rank as the great Moltke.

Thus, in October 1933, it was difficult to go beyond Beck in the quest for a successor to Adam, and despite their earlier political differences, he was the man whom Hammerstein chose to be his closest adviser and assistant. In view of the difficulties of that first year of the Nazi rule, Hammerstein must have been aware that his period of office was drawing to a close. Beck would have to serve as the only sort of bridge which he could build between his era and that of his successor.

Moving to Berlin was a mixed blessing for Beck, for he much preferred life in the open country to office work in a city. However, he had scope for his one form of recreation, horsemanship, in the Tiergarten and the Grunewald, and he settled down to a busy routine. He had ridden regularly since he was a youth, and was an expert judge of horses. An equestrian gift was the one sort which gave him great pleasure on birthdays and other anniversaries. He rose every morning at 5.30 and rode from 6 until 8 o'clock. Breakfast followed, and by 8.30 he was being driven towards the Bendlerstrasse. Work commenced at 9 o'clock, and continued without a break until nearly 7 p.m. Then he would return home, and dine. After dinner, he would usually go to his desk and do another three hours' work before midnight.

He resided in a simple double-fronted, grey stucco house, No. 9, Goethestrasse, Lichterfelde. He deliberately chose a simple house which he could afford entirely on his income without any special allowance. He shunned the more luxurious official residence which could have been his, since he realized the tentacles which favours of that sort could send out to bind a man's honour to his job, long after the two had become incompatible. Beck's honour was not to be bought. As he said to his daughter, he did not want to owe anything to anyone, especially Hitler. His friends were chiefly military colleagues, especially Manstein, Hammerstein, Hossbach, Heinrich von Stülpnagel, and above all, Fritsch. This group was to widen later as the difficult times of conspiring against Hitler approached, and included men of renown from all walks of life, such as Friedrich Meinecke, and the members of the 'Mittwochgesellschaft'[98] (the Wednesday Club).

The main criticism which has been made of Beck is that he was too conservative,[99] and incapable of making a decision in an unfamiliar environment. There is no doubt that his basic mould of character was conservative. He was also cautious, and adhered strictly to the dictum of Moltke: 'Erst wägen, dann wagen', or, 'First consider, then venture'. But both parts of this must be given weight—he was prepared to take risks, after due consideration. It may be that his idea of consideration was somewhat more thorough than the notions of others, but he carried the greater responsibility. His planning of exercises for the General Staff using armoured formations of the size of a division, or even of a corps, in 1935,[100] when Germany scarcely had any tanks at all, and no combat models, shows anything but excessive conservatism. His decision-making powers had been proved during the First World War under conditions in which he bore abnormally large responsibility, and where an inability to make up his mind would have resulted in his rapid dismissal, instead of his distinguished record of promotion.[101]

However, he was no match for the fast play of the Nazis. He attacked practical details of their plans in which they might have recognized an error, rather than moral aspects. His resistance was made ineffective by the simple expedient of shutting him out. Beck obtained a face to face interview with Hitler twice on official matters, during his five years of office as Chief of the General Staff. However, the quantity and scope of the studies which he wrote at this time show what a clear grasp he had of the international strategic issues of his day. He could see the best solutions, but was not able to put them into effect. It is indeed tragic that this insight was not wedded to the dashing, driving personality of Seeckt.

Throughout the course of 1933, relations between the Nazi Government and the Chef der Heeresleitung became steadily worse.[102] Hammerstein had stayed on in the hope of effecting a reconciliation with Hindenburg, so that the progress of the dictator might have been checked by some joint action.[103] Blomberg kept Hammerstein away from Hindenburg, and the old President for his part showed no desire to restore good relations. Hitler waited until he was sure that Blomberg also wanted a new Commander-in-Chief of the Army, and then suggested to Hindenburg, whose prerogative it was to appoint the Chef der Heeresleitung, that Reichenau should have Hammerstein's position.[104] This infuriated Hindenburg, since he could not tolerate this sort of interference in military affairs. He had not forgiven Hammerstein for his willing subordination to Schleicher in January 1933, and so he was ready to make a change, but he had the strongest objections to giving the command of the Army into the hands of Reichenau. Reichenau's reputation as a 'Partei General' was widespread, and he had never even held a divisional command.

Blomberg aggravated the situation by telling Papen that he would resign if Reichenau was not appointed.[105] When Papen told this to Hindenburg, Blomberg was summoned to the Presidential Palace, and told that his post was a political one, and that if he wished to do so, he could resign for political reasons. On the other hand, he was not free to challenge a Presidential decision in military matters, on political grounds. In Hindenburg's view, this was tantamount to insubordination.

While this may have provided, intentionally or unintentionally, an escape for Blomberg, the reasoning used deserves some comment. Hindenburg was the Supreme Commander of the German Armed Forces according to the Constitution (article 47), and Blomberg was a Cabinet Minister and, according to the Reichsminister Law of 27 March 1930, was a civilian. This law specifically stated that if an active officer was appointed to be Reichswehr Minister, then he was to be automatically retired from the day of his appointment. Blomberg's official duties then were essentially civilian and political in nature despite the illegal deferment of his retirement from military duty until 1938. But Hindenburg's argument assumed that a Defence Minister had no military responsibilities whatsoever.

Hindenburg's concept of mutually exclusive categories is far too simple for the general case. With respect to the situation in Germany at that time, it was patently false, because of the nature of the Weimar Constitution. This Constitution specifically gave the power of command in administrative matters to the Reichswehr Minister.[106] The Chef der Heeresleitung could only exercise command by representing the Minister.[107] While Blomberg's action in attempting to coerce Hindenburg to choose Reichenau showed poor judgement, he could not be denied some legitimate interest in the person who was to succeed Hammerstein. In addition, Hindenburg's conduct towards Blomberg was inconsistent. Having told Blomberg that his post was of a purely political nature, Hindenburg accused him of military insubordination.

Hindenburg discussed the matter in detail with Papen. They went through a list of alternatives, and Papen recommended Fritsch.[108] Whether Papen played the decisive role in the appointment of Fritsch which he has claimed is not independently verifiable. There were a number of other factors which Papen fails to mention which could have influenced the decision. Fritsch was the Commander of Wehrkreis III, with his head-quarters in Berlin. Thus he must have been noticed many times by Hindenburg at official occasions, exercises and inspections. His personal qualifications were at least as high as those of the other contenders, and he was relatively young at 53, active and with several years of work ahead of him. Furthermore, he was previously the first choice of Blomberg for the position, if what Blomberg said to Fritsch in February 1933* is to be believed; and so it is possible that Blomberg told Hindenburg that if he could not have Reichenau, then he would prefer Fritsch.

Real signs of trouble over the succession became noticeable to the press in December 1933. The Alsatian Press which was on many occasions the first to report new happenings within Nazi Germany, reported that a complete reorganization of the High Command was likely with Hammer-stein resigning, Blomberg taking over command of the Army, and Röhm becoming the Defence Minister.[109] While these newspapers were a long way from the truth in these instances, they did describe how Hitler had pressed for Reichenau to succeed Hammerstein, and how this had been rejected by Hindenburg. According to Hossbach,[110] Hitler had said that Hindenburg had threatened to resign if Fritsch's appointment was not confirmed by the Cabinet.

When the matter was made known to Fritsch in late 1933, he hesitated for some time before accepting the appointment.[111] He had imagined that his current posting was to have been his last before retirement, and had little desire to inherit the difficulties of Hammerstein.[112] He accepted only after consultation with Seeckt one evening.[113] On 3 January 1934, Fritsch began the process of taking over from Hammerstein,[114] and on 1 February he became the new Chef der Heeresleitung,[115] 'against the wishes of the Führer and of Blomberg', as he wrote four years later.[116]

The character of Werner Freiherr von Fritsch is perhaps the greatest enigma of the whole period of this study. There are almost as many different pictures of him as there are authors who have written about him, ranging from the exemplary to the despicable.[117] The least confusing way to treat his character might be to consider separately two main sections of his life—first Fritsch as a soldier, pure and simple, and secondly, as a man (taken in the sense of 'political animal') in a complicated society.

As far as his capability as a soldier can be estimated without the test of command in war, he appears to have reached heights touched by only a

* See above, Chapter 2, p. 19.

Fritsch, Blomberg and Hitler at Army Exercises,
Munsterlager, 1935

ARBEITER

WÄHLT DEN FRONTSOLDATEN
HITLER!

Nazi Election Poster, exploiting Hitler's record
in the First World War

The Chancellor and the President at the ceremonial opening of the
Reichstag in the Garnisonskirche, Potsdam, 21 March 1933.
Hitler for the Nazi Party bows to the traditions of Old Prussia as
embodied in Hindenburg.

The Reichswehr Ministry.

A German Chart of the early 'Thirties showing the organization of the Reichswehr.

The Seven Military Districts (Wehrkreise) of Germany in 1933.

Field-Marshal Freiherr von Weichs whose memoirs have left a vivid picture of German political-military relations in the pre-war years.

Field Marshal von Reichenau, who as Blomberg's political assistant fought to contain the growing ambitions of the S.A. under Röhm.

Generaloberst Heinrici as commander of the First Panzer Army, January 1945. From 1933 to 1937, Heinrici was a staff officer and departmental head within the Army Command. His memoranda written at the time of the S.A. crisis are of historical importance.

Generaloberst Dollmann, whose letters have provided new material for this story.

Himmler in humbler days, standing by Röhm's horse at the first rally of the S.S. at Döberitz, one year before Röhm was shot by Himmler's men.

S.A. banners at the Party Rally in 1936. Although politically decapitated, the S.A. remained a vast organization after 1934.

An indication of the growing strength of the S.A.—Hitler addressing a rally of the S.A. at Dortmund in 1933.

The induction of recruits which began the expansion of the German Army—1 April 1934. Note the presence of two S.A. men in uniform in this photograph taken by the commander of the Tenth Company of Infantry Regiment Halberstadt (I.R.12) looking into the courtyard of the Anger-Kaserne, Magdeburg.

Hitler and Röhm at a rally of the S.A. and S.S. in the Sportpalast,
Berlin on 8 April 1933

handful of generals in any country. He was one of those rare soldiers who could inspire through his personality, by its combination of stimulating zest and quiet confidence, not only those who came into close and regular contact with him, but the greater part of his subordinates from the Bendlerstrasse to the Grenzschutz. The obvious standard to measure him against is that of Seeckt. There seems no doubt that amongst the members of the German Army of the Fritsch era, his popularity and authority, two qualities which are not always linked, exceeded those of Seeckt by a marked degree.*

While the essence of Fritsch's ability was personality, it was based also on several other more assessable qualities. His performance at the Kriegsakademie in the years 1907–10,[118] where he topped his class with the extraordinary grades of nine in both Tactics and Military History, the two dominating subjects, gave him a status which in Oxford parlance could be equalled only by a double first.†[119] His first confidential report as a young officer comments: 'An excellent officer, a passionately keen horseman,‡ and an outstanding comrade.' Here again, the combination of outstanding ability in a technical sense and comradeship is worth noting.

During the First World War he served chiefly as a Staff Officer, although the head wound which he received from a grenade in 1917[120] testified that he was not one of those Staff Officers who never went near the Front. While he was serving with the German forces in the Baltic campaign in 1919, as Chief of Staff to the Commander, General Graf von der Goltz, a report was made on him by the French head of the Inter-Allied Commission, General Niessel. Niessel wrote:

Major von Fritsch is young, arrogant and extremely self confident. It seems he has no qualms about playing hide and seek with truth or evading uncomfortable issues. He has all the faults of character of the Prussian General Staff officer, who frequently considers himself superior—and rightly too—to the ordinary mortal.[121]

This description tells almost as much about the writer as about the subject. It was as if Niessel had expected to find such a man in the uniform of an officer of the Great General Staff. When he did find him, or was allowed

---

* This appraisal of Fritsch is based on discussion of the character and personality of Fritsch with over 100 men and women, who either knew him personally through direct contact, or who knew his image from their service under him as Staff Officers, junior commanders, N.C.O.s and privates in the various units which he commanded. Many of these served under Seeckt also. In making such a comparison, some weight must be allowed for a tendency to magnify Fritsch out of sentiment or sympathy. Seeckt had his personal triumph in the creation of the Reichswehr.

† It is interesting to note that two of Fritsch's classmates at the Kriegsakademie were Hammerstein and Papen.

‡ Horsemanship remained Fritsch's greatest joy in life, apart from his work. His journey books as Commander-in-Chief of the Army for 1936–37 (OKH file H 24/39) show that when he took a week-end off, six horses always accompanied his party to Achterburg. His well known love of horses made him a target for requests for favours of one sort of another by many equestrian associations. OKH file H 24/37 contains nothing but invitations to gymkhanas and frequent requests for Fritsch to donate trophies, which he appeared to do, to the tune of RM 70 each, regularly. He always wrote letters of congratulation to the winners of his trophies, irrespective of rank or class, and replied to letters of thanks.

to gain the impression that he had, his excitement was so great that he was prepared to commit his secret admiration for the Prussian General Staff officer to paper, and, furthermore to bare these feelings before the eyes of his seniors. It probably gave Fritsch and his colleagues a great deal of amusement to have such a chaperon.

During the years after the First World War, Fritsch served in several postings, alternating between the General Staff and the regimental. His papers show that he regarded the Freikorps as a danger threatening the new Reich, and that its members ought to be prevented from returning home in organized bands.[122] He saw the Kapp putsch as a calamity as it had led only 'to renewed splits amongst the people'.[123] The same memorandum showed that he regarded Bolshevism as the chief danger, not only for Germany, but for Europe, and that German assistance should have been given to Pilsudski, so that the Bolshevist forces might have been defeated as close to the Russian border as possible. His service in the Baltic campaign brought him into contact with Seeckt, and a friendship developed which was to last until Seeckt's death in 1936.[124] In 1924 he was appointed Chief of Staff to the Commander of Wehrkreis I.*[125] After two years, he became head of the Operations Abteilung of the General Staff[126] (1 Abteilung, Truppenamt), another key position, where he worked directly under Blomberg, who was at that time Chef des Truppenamts. When he was appointed to command Wehrkreis III in October 1932[127] he was in the front rank of the leaders of the Reichswehr, modern and progressive in his outlook on military problems[128] and capable of inspiring the devotion of those who served under him. He was an outstandingly good choice for handling the military problems of the German Army.

Unfortunately, the problems which faced the German Army in the years after the appointment of Fritsch were of many types. The difficulties of re-expanding the Army were small compared with the political complications which attended the functions of the Army under the Nazi régime. While Fritsch may have been well equipped to handle the former, it is to be greatly deplored that this military excellence was accompanied by a low order of political consciousness and dexterity. Fritsch's development was not broadly based, and this had its origins in his childhood.

Fritsch was born a Rhinelander,† and he served in a Hessian Regiment.‡ He was the only son of middle class parents,§ and he had a rather isolated childhood. His father exercised extremely strict control over him, which inhibited him to such a degree that very few people ever came to know him on personal terms.[129] In a letter of 4 September 1938[130] he writes:

---

* It is interesting that most of the leading men in the German Army had served for some time in Wehrkreis I, East Prussia. This was a nursery for talent.

† Fritsch was born on 4 August 1880 at Benrath, near Düsseldorf. See Kielmansegg, *Der Fritsch Prozess* 1938, p. 15.

‡ Field Artillery Regiment No. 125, Darmstadt. He entered on 21 September 1898. Kielmansegg, *op. cit.*, p. 18. For full details of his career, see below, Appendix B.

§ His brother did not survive infancy. He had three sisters. His father was a soldier, reaching the rank of Generalleutnant, and was the first of his line to break the tradition of being a civil servant. Kielmansegg, *op. cit.*, p. 16.

When you write further that I am often difficult to understand, you are doubtless correct. From my earliest days, I have never spoken with anyone about myself. I simply cannot do it, and if anyone tries to penetrate me in this direction, he only achieves the reverse.

This loneliness and isolation, strange though they may seem, are not incompatible with his success in an exclusively male profession, where personal relations would appear to be of great importance. In many ways this isolation may have suited him, and could have helped him to become such a devoted professional soldier. He was able to get along with people quite well, yet they never saw inside him. He automatically maintained a front of reserve over his personal life and so it was no difficulty for him to subscribe to the military code of ethics, which demanded a high degree of self abnegation. He did not like talking about himself, and so he abhorred social occasions, where his only activity would be to listen to someone else talking about himself. It is not that he was anti-social in principle. With company which he liked and respected, he could be the most charming companion, or interesting host.[131] When this company was lacking he was much more interested in riding. He enjoyed his work, so he could usually find much to interest himself, and as a result, he tended to become more proficient. This may have developed into a cyclical process, which assisted his progress, and increased his yield of satisfaction. As military leadership demands a large amount of self sufficiency on the part of the leader, he could have found himself well suited to command men, and the satisfaction of inspiring their confidence could have been an acceptable substitute for human companionship on the intimate level.

These considerations may also explain his life-long bachelorhood. In his youth, he was on occasions, a very gay subaltern, but it had to be an outstanding woman to attract his attention.[132] His internal nervous energy, his isolation and his ability may have combined to make him into a perfectionist, and raised a barrier between him and anything which might compromise what he had achieved already. Furthermore, at the age at which a rising young officer was most likely to marry, the mid-thirties, he was away fighting a war.*

If these were his attitudes towards normal social life, then it would have been difficult for him to avoid a lack of sympathy, or even a feeling of repulsion, towards politicians. Not only did their seemingly self-centred behaviour conflict with his military code of ethics, but they also contradicted his personal reserve, his principles of making as little fuss as possible,† and possibly even his strict Protestant Christianity.[133] Above

---

* A further indication of his attitude towards marriage occurs in the letter of 4 September 1938, cited by Kielmansegg, *op. cit.*, p. 18:

I openly confess that at that time—years ago—I would gladly have married—and certainly wished to have some children.

† When Fritsch later paid official visits to units as the Commander-in-Chief of the Army, he would often specifically order that there were to be no flags or decorations in his honour, work was not to be kept waiting until his arrival, nor was work to be interrupted while he was looking about. (However, the same sources usually mention that the unit which he was to visit was to provide a luggage van, rather than a light car for his impedimenta.) OKH file H 24/39.

all, he disapproved of political soldiers, of whom Schleicher seemed to be the perfect model. In 1932, when he was commanding the First Cavalry Division at Frankfurt an der Oder, his Chief of Staff, Oberst Freiherr von Weichs,* reported back to him after a conference which he had attended at the Reichswehr Ministry, conducted by Schleicher. Weichs was about to report what had happened, when Fritsch broke him off with 'No! It is all lies!'[134]

He did once turn his thoughts in a political direction when Seeckt was dismissed from office in 1926. As one of Seeckt's closest advisers, he advised Seeckt to resist his removal by force.[135] This wild counsel shows at least as much political ignorance as loyalty to Seeckt. However, he was not unaware of his limitations in this direction. In 1937, he wrote:[136]

I have made it my guiding rule to limit myself to the military field alone, and to keep myself apart from any political activity. I lack everything necessary for politics. Furthermore, I am convinced that the less I speak in public, the more speedily can I fulfil my military task.

With these views on politics and politicians in general, he was not likely to be a keen supporter of Hitler and his National-Socialists. He became known for making numbers of most unguarded critical comments about the Nazis to all and sundry when he felt annoyed by them. One morning, Oberst Gotthard Heinrici† entered his office for the usual morning discussion. There was much celebrating and revelry going on in the streets. Fritsch asked Heinrici why they were celebrating. Heinrici replied that it was the Führer's birthday. 'Why celebrate that!' was the loud ironic response.[137] At the parade at Saarbrücken on 1 March 1935, to mark the return of the Saar to Germany, Fritsch stood on the reviewing platform, where, according to a witness standing next to him[138] 'he poured out a running fire of sarcastic remarks about the S.S., the Party, and various Nazi leaders from Hitler on down. He did not disguise his contempt for them all.' He was thus an easy target for the secret microphones of the Gestapo in the telephones and offices which he used in the course of his work.[139]

So it was an odd set of relationships within the High Command, once Fritsch had overcome his doubts and had taken office. Hitler and Fritsch had very little to do with each other.[140] Fritsch had no right of direct access, and Blomberg transacted all the usual defence business. When Fritsch did see Hitler, it was usually in Blomberg's presence.[141] Their relations therefore were restricted to formal correctness, which was, until 1938, always observed on both sides.[142] Fritsch's presence had a strange effect on Hitler. While Hitler would talk quite freely with Blomberg, and even argue, he always felt inhibited when Fritsch was present, and never let anything slip—either in substance or in form.[143] Fritsch, for his part, never tried to argue things out with Hitler until 5 November 1937, preferring to thrash matters out with Blomberg, or simply to voice a protest

* For details of the career of Field-Marshal von Weichs see below, Appendix B.
† For details of the career of Generaloberst Heinrici, see below, Appendix B.

to Hitler. Hitler once described Fritsch as 'the incorruptible English-man'.[144] Fritsch's outlook on Hitler is summed up in his oft-repeated words:

Hitler is Germany's fate for good and for bad.[145]

Whether Hitler had studied the nature of his new Army Commander or not is not known, but the words which he chose to greet Fritsch on the latter's assumption of office would have confirmed Fritsch in his conception of his task.

Create an army of the greatest possible strength, inner resolution and unity, on the best imaginable foundation of training.[146]

He would have been wiser to have given more weight to the prophetic words with which Ludendorff advised him:

Hitler remains loyal to no one—he will betray even you inside a few years![147]

The relationship between Fritsch and Blomberg was always tense.[148] Although Fritsch often got along well enough with Blomberg,[149] he must have found great difficulty in feeling sympathetic towards a man who was playing a part which Fritsch felt ought not to exist. Moreover, his past experience of Blomberg* had made him aware of Blomberg's propensities for romanticism fantasy and novelties, and of his habit of acting from a sudden impulse.[150] However, they were able to co-operate sufficiently well for the discharge of their official duties, and a major crisis in their relations was avoided until January 1938, when a certain amount of strong feeling came to the surface.† Fritsch was usually able to persuade Blomberg to take to Hitler matters which Fritsch had complained about, but he was exasperated by the ease with which Blomberg allowed himself to be beaten down by the Führer.[151]

The strongest partnership within the High Command was that between Fritsch, and his Chief of Staff, Beck. They were old friends,[152] and Fritsch had worked with Beck on the committee which had directed the writing of *Die Truppenführung*.[153] However, their relations in early 1934 became clouded, due to Fritsch's mistrust that in the debates taking place about reorganization,‡ Beck was attempting to restore the General Staff to its former, pre-1918 position, and to render Fritsch superfluous.[154] It did not take very long for them both to realize that there was grave misunderstanding between them, and all doubts were speedily dissolved in what became a very strong personal friendship.[155]

This was the environment in which Fritsch had to attempt to carry out his task. He was quite clear what this was—on the one hand to give correct

---

* 1927–29, when Blomberg was Chef des Truppenamts, and Fritsch was in charge of the Operations Abteilung, and thus was Blomberg's first adviser.
† See below, Chapter 11.
‡ See below, Chapter 8.

strategic advice so that all hazardous wars, both single front and several front could be avoided, and on the other hand, to see that the re-establishment of German military parity was efficiently conducted.[156] He wished the Army to go through the process of growth gradually, so that its skill and efficiency would not be sacrificed for numbers of men. He wished to base this new Army on the old traditions, despite the efforts of the Nazis to stress the complete break with the past.[157] He took office at a critical point when the efforts of the S.A. to replace the Army were near their height, and he became involved in a struggle with Röhm from the outset. In view of all these complications, it is not to be wondered that he wrote the following words about the situation which confronted him on the assumption of his duties:

> I found before me a heap of ruins, and in particular there was a far-reaching lack of confidence in the highest authority.[158]

Thus, the four senior positions within the German High Command were occupied by two different types of men. Blomberg and Reichenau represented the spirit of the new political era, while Fritsch and Beck embodied the traditions of the old.

Initially, these differences do not appear to have been apparent. Relations between Fritsch and Blomberg had been close enough in 1933 to enable Blomberg to tell Fritsch that he wanted Fritsch to succeed Hammerstein,* and Beck took office in a spirit of confidence.[159] However, the differences between the functions of their positions swiftly accentuated their differences in personality. Blomberg and Reichenau were concerned with the adaptation of the Reichswehr to the Nazi Government, the Nazi Party, and Nazi ideology, so that political-military relations ran as smoothly as possible. The outstanding task before Fritsch and Beck was to increase greatly the size and standard of efficiency of the Army.

As soon as these two different activities began to conflict with each other, the forces of individual personality set these two pairs onto ever-diverging courses, splitting the potential unity of the Armed Forces which could have formed a restraint on Hitler. Out of this, Hitler was able to increase his personal power by allowing the two groups to fight each other, while he remained as an onlooker, or sometimes performed the functions of an adjudicator, until he finally broke both groups individually.

* See above, p. 19.

3

The Army and the S.A.

THE coming to power of the Nazi Party brought with it a new danger to the position of the Army. While the policies of Hitler might have given the Army more freedom from foreign influence, the private armed force of the Nazi Party, the Sturmabteilung, began to challenge the Army from within. In this situation, the German Army found itself in difficulties which seemed to defy a legal solution. The only forces which were capable of keeping the S.A. within the narrow limits of internal party-political duties were the Chancellor Adolf Hitler, using both his national and his party authority, and the Army itself, exploiting its physical strength in battle with the S.A. It did not seem likely that Hitler would strike down the loyal party troops who had fought the street battles of the Nazi Party through many years. The interests of both Hitler and the S.A. appear to have been far closer together than the interests of Hitler and the Reichswehr. Yet, if the dread prospect of internal civil war were to be avoided, the winning of Hitler to the side of the Army seemed to be the only alternative to an abdication by the Army of its principal functions.

Consequently, there was a special influence acting within the framework of German political-military relations during the period of rivalry between the Army and the S.A. This influence was the desire of the Army for Hitler to take the part of the Army against his own party troops. Initially, in the first months of the Third Reich, this force appears to have been existent in embryonic form, in the minds of very few soldiers. Gradually the course of events aroused the Reichswehr to the realization that it was being subjected to a serious threat. It is possible that the action of this influence on the Army was similar to that of a strong spin on a heavy flywheel. Certainly the loyalty of the Army to Hitler was exploited by the initiators of the purge of 30 June 1934.

Before an examination of the particular circumstances of the rivalry between the German Army and the S.A., the general question of what right, if any, an army has to act in domestic politics to ensure its own existence should be considered. In most western countries the relationship of the Army to the other component groups of the nation is a matter for politicians alone. From this can it be deduced that an army has no legitimate interest in its own existence within such a society? Clearly not, for there is a distinction to be made between an army's actually acting in an unconstitutional sense, by taking decisions of this nature into its own hands, and an army's remaining alert to the possibility of any internal threat to its own efficiency, and reporting this threat to the responsible politicians when and if it arises. An army is in a unique position to see such threats as they occur. If the government, legally appointed and supported by a clear majority of the people, refuses to take any action once warned by the Army, then the duty of the Army in this regard has been completed, and any soldier who subsequently takes matters into his own hands is guilty of a serious crime.

The nature of Hitler's government gave the Nazi Party and its leaders an enormous amount of influence. In the ranks of this party was a body of partly armed troops, which outnumbered the Army by three to one[160] on the day of the Machtübernahme. Amongst the leaders of the S.A. were the most extreme type of Nazi revolutionary, whose sense of statesmanship was open to doubt. It would seem then, that the Army had a definite responsibility to take note of the activities of the S.A., and to inform Hitler of any threat to the position of the Army which the S.A. presented by either explicit or implicit action.

The relationship between the Army and the S.A. began several years before Hitler came to power. There had been co-operation and there had been conflict. The S.A. had assisted the Army to form Grenzschutz units in the Eastern border regions.[161] S.A. units had established excellent relations with their local Reichswehr units, by turning out to give tired troops a cheer as they marched back on cold evenings from the manœuvre field, or to provide hot drinks.[162] On the other hand, there had been a number of clashes between the men of the S.A. and the Army ever since the putsch of 1923, especially the banning of the S.A. in 1932, in which the Reichswehr Minister, General Groener, and his adviser, General von Schleicher, played the leading roles in the attempted suppression of the S.A.

If these events are viewed on the surface, it would appear that the S.A. had some reason to be antagonistic towards the Army. When the Army needed assistance, the S.A. gave it, only to be stamped on by the Army for trying to spread a creed which included the abolition of the military restrictions which had been in force throughout the Weimar period.

Beneath this surface lay some more fundamental causes of antagonism. Within the S.A. were many veterans of the First World War who held the Reichswehr in high regard for its military efficiency but who thought that its political and social views were antiquated and reactionary. These men sincerely thought that a modern army ought to be organized on more radical lines with less emphasis on class distinction and social background and more on efficiency. They felt that this could be achieved only by the gradual replacement of the Reichswehr by the S.A. so that the former faded out of existence.

The first significant contact between the Army and the S.A. after the Machtübernahme concerned the administration of youth organizations.[163] These organizations had been run by a body called the 'Reichkuratrioum für Jugendertüchtigung', under the Ministry for the Interior.[164] Blomberg for reasons of efficiency[165] caused it to be placed under the Ministry of

Labour, which was headed by Seldte, who was also head of the Stahlhelm[*] and an obvious counterweight to Röhm.[166] Röhm wanted to place the Kuratorium under control of the S.A.,[167] the Stahlhelm was rapidly losing power,[168] and Blomberg was faced with the necessity for taking some action which would prevent the control of the Kuratorium from gradually passing into the hands of Röhm.

On 18 March 1933, Blomberg announced that he had prepared a study of the youth movements.[169] This study made the following points:

1. The Reichswehr had more to do with youth than any other authority.

2. The present situation of disorganization, shortages and restrictions needed to be dealt with.

3. A Reichs Youth Minister was needed, instead of the chaos which resulted from the current system, in which four government departments could influence the administration of the Kuratorium. Also, a special organization for girls should be established.

Nothing came of these thoughts, except, possibly the appointment of Baldur von Schirach as Reichsjugend Führer.[170]

It was left to Reichenau to come to a compromise agreement with the S.A., at a conference between the leaders of the S.A. and Reichenau at Bad Reichenhall between 1 July and 3 July 1933.[171] During the months prior to this conference, the Reichswehr had been active in preparing the ground for as favourable an agreement as possible. On 15 May, Blomberg ordered that all members of the Wehrmacht were to salute the members of the 'Nationale Verbände',[†] and that the flags and colours of these organizations were to be saluted when carried with formed bodies of men, and at national public rallies and parades.[172] Soldiers attending these rallies had to avoid giving any impression of indifference towards the 'National Movement'. Accordingly, when indoors, or without a hat, soldiers were to raise their right arm when other people were doing so. Finally, soldiers had to join in the singing of songs at these gatherings.

Two days later, an agreement was reached, sanctioned by Hitler, between the Reichswehr and the S.A., which placed the S.A., S.S., and Stahlhelm under Reichswehr control in military matters.[173] Hitler also gave his support to the Reichswehr against any possible rivals for the position of 'bearer of the arms of the nation', by making several speeches which specifically affirmed that this was the Army's right.[174]

The Bad Reichenhall conference resulted in an agreement which dissolved the Kuratorium, and replaced it by a new body, the Ausbildungswesen (AW), which was to be directed by Obergruppenführer Krüger of the S.A.[175] Thus the Army made the major concession. However, in view of the overriding control which the Army had over the S.A. in military matters by virtue of the agreement of 17 May, this might not have been

---

[*] The Stahlhelm was one of the major German War Veterans' Associations.
[†] 'Verbände' is a term with special connotation. Often it occurs prefixed by 'Wehr-' or National-'. In all of these cases, it was simply a way of referring to the armed or equipped forces of the Nazi Party, together with the Stahlhelm. The components of these forces included: The S.A.; the S.S.; the N.S.K.K. (Nationalsozialistisches Kraftfahrkorps—the N.S. Motor Corps); the H.J. (Hitler Jugend).

thought too great a price to pay for harmony and efficiency in youth matters. In point of fact, this agreement weakened the position of the Army considerably, as the Army had also agreed to assist with the provision of military training for the leaders of the Ausbildungswesen.* Eventually this provided 13,000 leaders who had been given military training,[176] and so made a significant increase in the military strength of the S.A.

The Army did not lose sight of its primary interest, that of building up a large reserve of trained men. The use of the S.A. enabled the letter of the Versailles Treaty to be observed, while the agreement provided for the preparation of 250,000 reserves for the use of the Reichswehr in an emergency.[177] The Army took a gamble, knowingly or unknowingly, on keeping the S.A. within its limits, for the sake of gaining a badly needed increase in German military strength. Until the challenges of the S.A. had been silenced, the Army was more dependent than ever before on the good will of Hitler, who did not hesitate to exploit this period of weakness on the part of the Army to spread Nazism as widely as possible throughout the Army, from the bottom upwards, thereby circumscribing any opposition to his régime within the upper echelons of the Army.†

The consequences of this agreement went further than national defence and the rivalry between Röhm and the Reichswehr. It implied to the men in the ranks of the Army that the S.A. was on the same footing as themselves, and therefore was a body with national, rather than just party status. Thus the grip of Nazism on the Army was strengthened. The increase of contact between the two also provided an avenue for Nazi ideas and propaganda to flow back into the Army at a low and uncritical level.

During August 1933 a further agreement was made between the Reichswehr and the S.A. concerning recruiting for the Army. This established the S.A. and the other Nationale Verbände as the main source of recruits.[178] The weakening effect of this on the Army with reference to the S.A. must have been obvious to Blomberg, as all recruits could thus have been preconditioned by the S.A. However he may have taken this risk in order to gain a steady supply of recruits without having to organize it.

The Army and the S.A. continued to have conferences, and in mid-August, at Bad Godesberg, the possibilities of giving military training to the S.A. in general were discussed.[179] The conference came to nought, however, because the representatives of the S.A. brought forward accusations against the Army that it was not National-Socialist in outlook.[180] Hitler attended on the 19th, and made a speech which emphasized the rights of the Army to remain the 'sole bearer of the arms of the nation',[181] but this was not sufficient to restore an atmosphere of co-operation.

The policy of Röhm was to replace the Army by the S.A., while using

---

* The Army had begun to train S.A. men in short week-end courses in April 1933. See Sauer, *die Nationalsozialistische Machtergreifung*, pp. 726, 797, 886, 892. On 5 July 1933, Blomberg and Krüger conferred about the control of the budget of the AW. Reichenau wanted it to be under the control of the Reichswehr. Blomberg agreed to it being controlled by the Minister for the Interior. Sauer, *op. cit.*, p. 894.
† See below, Chapter 5.

the professional soldiers as a means of training the S.A. in basic military skills.[182] The head of the Ausbildungswesen, Obergruppenführer Krüger, an old Army man, had been following a policy of close co-operation with the Reichswehr. This did not accord with the views of Röhm, and Krüger's influence began to go into a decline.[183] Hitler continued to support the Army against any suggestion that it was less suited to its tasks than any other military body, but he had to find some new role for Röhm and his masses, which had grown to over two and one half millions.[184] Since the coming to power, the S.A. had had very little to do, apart from administrative and propaganda duties, and Hitler was faced with deciding between expansion of the S.A. as a military force, and the reduction of the ambitions of its leaders to conformity with the then insignificant role of the S.A.

During this time, a number of incidents occurred which indicated the growth of friction between the Army and the S.A. On 21 September, Wehrkreis VII (Munich) began to express concern about the high proportion of those men who had been dishonourably discharged from the Reichswehr and who were occupying leading positions in the S.A.[185] On 19 September, Blomberg had ordered that when soldiers in plain clothes met members of the S.A., etc., they were to use the Nazi salute.[186] This was emphasized further in the *Militär-Wochenblatt* of 4 October.[187] Shortly afterwards, on 17 October, a young officer, Leutnant Lindwurm of Infanterie Regiment 15 was struck in the face by some S.A. men for not saluting an S.A. flag in Giessen. The seriousness of this incident was indicated by Blomberg's conduct. He had Lindwurm before him immediately, and then instructed the commander of Lindwurm's regiment to settle the matter with the local S.A. leader, and to confine Lindwurm to three days' room-arrest.[188]

Co-operation with the S.A. was extended widely by an order of the Reichswehr Minister of late October 1933.* This stated that units of the Reichswehr were to co-operate directly with local units of the S.A. in the following matters:

1. Military training, both within and outside the Army.
2. Systematic recruiting for the Army.
3. The obtaining of short term replacement personnel for the Army.
4. Preparations to meet emergencies by the co-ordination of personnel requirements and equipment.

In November, Reichenau revealed his anxiety about the whole situation when he remarked, 'Should things go wrong in the co-operation with the S.A., then we will be in severe trouble.'[189] He stressed to officers who were being sent to train the S.A. that they were to report any apparent danger,

---

* The details of this order are given in an instruction which was issued by Wehrkreis VII on 24 October 1933. WK VII file 741. I have not been able to discover the order which went out from the Reichswehr Ministry to Wehrkreis VII, but judging from many other instances, it is likely that this was issued on 23 October. From other examples of the handling of business within the Reichswehr Ministry, it is likely that the draft of this order would have taken approximately one week to circulate amongst the relevant heads of departments for comment and modification before being finally released. Therefore, it is likely that there was a conference between the Army and the S.A. prior to 15 October 1933.

and the appropriate measures would then be taken by the High Command.

Röhm received a huge addition to those under his command during late 1933 and early 1934.[190] On 6 November 1933, he published an order outlining how the Stahlhelm and Kyffhäuser Bund, another large veterans' organization, were to be incorporated into the S.A., as reserves.[191] On 1 December, Röhm's personal position was enhanced by the declaration of the S.A. as an official branch of the Government, and the award of a seat in the Cabinet and on the Reichs Defence Council.[192] These positions would have enabled him to see the struggles which were taking place for the post of Commander-in-Chief of the Army, and to note the internal divisions of the Army into radical and conservative groups.

The importance to Blomberg of making an effort to keep up with the S.A. in matters of Nazi doctrine was shown in an 'Important Political Instruction of the Reichswehr Minister', of 8 December, on the subject of patronizing Jewish shops.[193] In this instruction, Blomberg said:

S.A. members have been banned from so doing [purchasing in Jewish shops]. I cannot issue a general Wehrmacht ban, as it would conflict with the directives of the Ministry of Economics concerning the boycott of non-Aryan businesses. Nevertheless, there is a danger of friction if Wehrmacht members continue to make purchases in Jewish shops.

Local commanders must decide in each case whether this shopping disrupts local discipline.

Local commanders are to co-operate with S.A. leaders in this matter.

Where there is no danger to discipline, any local S.A. ban on Jewish shops is to be promulgated to the troops in local orders.

By this means, Blomberg resigned the direction of a cruel policy to those most fitted to be brutal, and left the Reichswehr without any other guidance, apart from what little personal authority local commanders were able to retain to influence the conduct of their men towards Jews.

In late 1933, Reichenau suggested to Röhm that a compromise solution for their mutual difficulties might be reached.[194] Reichenau proposed that the military activities of the S.A. might be expanded, but that the S.A. was to remain under the direction of the Reichswehr as a type of militia. Röhm would have none of this, as he felt that his strength was sufficient to enable him to press Hitler for higher status. Röhm may have received reports of attitudes within the Army which gave him reason to feel that the Army was not so sternly set on limiting the S.A. as Reichenau was. In January 1934, the Commander of Wehrkreis V, Stuttgart, General-leutnant Liebmann, addressed the following remarks to the officers of his staff:

I consider that the S.A. is an absolute necessity to the State, and the good elements who wish to work with us must be supported.[195]

While these thoughts were probably aroused by concern for the weakness of Germany, they illustrate the strength of nationalist movements in their influence on the Army.

During early 1934, plans were being made by the Reichswehr Ministry for the reintroduction of conscription.[196] It was realized that this would require delicate handling. A large increase in the strength of the Army would have ended Röhm's plans for a mass militia under the control of the S.A. Accordingly, negotiations with Röhm were begun by the Reichswehr Ministry so that a way might be found to expand the forces without causing intolerable internal strife.[197]

Even the Party Headquarters felt that it was necessary to exercise more control over the S.A. On 22 January 1934, an article appeared in the *Völkischer Beobachter*, written by Hess, which indicated a desire for more obedience from the party formations.[198] It also suited the Party to yield to Reichswehr pressure for the formation of a Working Committee for the National Defence Council, which was to be under the chairmanship of the leading opponent of the S.A. within the Reichswehr, General von Reichenau.* The response of the S.A. to this was swift. On the evening of the day on which the Working Committee was established, 26 January 1934, the S.A. wrecked the celebrations which were being held by monarchist army officers at the Hotel Kaiserhof in Berlin, in honour of the Kaiser's birthday.[199] This was followed on 1 February by a plan which Röhm placed before Blomberg, which suggested that the whole compass of defence should be placed under the S.A., that the Wehrmacht should be limited to training leaders and men for the S.A., and that all officers were to be placed at the disposal of the S.A. as advisers.[200]

Blomberg called a conference of the Wehrkreis Commanders at the Ministry for 2 and 3 February.[201] Firstly, the Polish question was discussed. Beck blamed Reichenau for making the Army too dependent on the S.A. for frontier protection troops. Fritsch, the new Commander-in-Chief of the Army agreed that this was also giving the S.A. too much opportunity for ideological subversion.[202] Blomberg dismissed these problems by observing that, since the non-aggression pact with Poland,† frontier protection was not so important, and that more time should be devoted to the expansion of the forces. The ensuing debate, in which Fritsch played a major part, brought about a decision to end the policy of compromise with the S.A.[203] Blomberg considered that, in view of Röhm's stated intentions, any further co-operation was out of the question. He said that the decision was then Hitler's affair. Blomberg continued that he did not want a sudden change of policy, as he felt that this would lead to open fighting. A period of adjustment was necessary. A two-sided policy had to be followed: while pressing forward with preparations for a 'Defence Reform' on 1 April 1934, the Reichswehr would have to enter into new negotiations with Röhm which would defeat the proposals of the

---

* This was established on 26 January 1934. Robertson, *Hitler's Pre-War Policy and Military Plans 1933–39*, p. 30. The events of the previous twelve months had caused Reichenau to change from being a keen advocate of the S.A., to one of its sharpest critics. His attitude is illustrated in the events described below, especially p. 47.

† Concluded on 26 January 1934. This pact was received with mixed feelings in Army circles. Besides offering some relief for the Eastern situation, it seemed to be a further reversal of the successful policy of the 'twenties, of close collaboration with Russia.

S.A. Blomberg knew that this would be impossible without the support of Hitler, therefore he ordered the Wehrmacht in February to adopt the Party emblem (Hoheitsabzeichen) as part of its uniform, and to allow the 'Arier-Paragraph' of the regulations for the appointment of officials to be applied to military appointments.* While the discussion was going on, a letter from Röhm was brought in to Reichenau. Reichenau read it through, and then asked Fritsch for permission to read part of it out aloud. Fritsch assented, and Reichenau read:

I regard the Reichswehr now only as a training school for the German people. The conduct of war, and therefore of mobilization as well, in future is the task of the S.A.[204]

Such was the conceit of Röhm at that time that he dared to inform the Reichswehr directly that it was, as far as he was concerned, to play only a minor role in the future military development of Germany. If any confirmation was needed that the time for mutual agreement had passed, this letter must have provided it.

It is difficult to imagine how men of the character of Fritsch and Beck were able to tolerate the addition of the symbol of the Nazi Party to the uniform of the German Army, unless they felt to be under great duress to prove to the government that the Army was, first and foremost loyal to its political superiors, and that there was no need to do as Röhm suggested, at least from the point of view of the security of Germany. Fritsch did remark at the conference which followed on 27 February 1934 that the introduction of the Party badge† would give the necessary impetus to the Reichs Chancellor to deal with the S.A.‡

The permitting of the application of the 'Arier-Paragraph' was much more than the introduction of an outward formality of the nature of the Party badge. This was a *de facto* recognition of the extreme discriminatory doctrines of the Nazi movement. Possibly it was thought by the participants in this conference that this was justified by the large influence that this would have on Hitler, compared with the relatively few Jewish soldiers who were to be dismissed from the Army. Blomberg had stressed that because of the escape clause which enabled war veterans to remain in

---

* Liebmann, *Notizen*, p. 69. The Aryan paragraph had first appeared on 7 April 1933, in the *Gesetz von Wiederherstellung des Berufsbeamtentums*, to be found in WK VII file 2306. It ran:
   3. 1. Officials who are not of Aryan descent are to be retired. In cases of honorary officials, they are to be dismissed from their official positions.
   2. 1. does not apply to officials who have been officials since 1 August 1914, or who served at the front for Germany or her allies in the Great War, or whose father or sons fell in the war. The condition for Aryan descent was:
Non-Aryan if one grandparent or one parent was non-Aryan—especially if they were Jewish. The onus of proof was on individuals, who had to show by documents that they were of true Aryan descent.
† 'der Vogel' or 'the bird', as it was nick-named by the Army.
‡ Liebmann, *op. cit.*, pp. 76, 79. The official announcement of its appearance came out in *Militär-Wochenblatt*, Nr. 32, of 25 February 1934. The badge was being worn in March. Foertsch, *Schuld und Verhängnis*, p. 39. Hindenberg signed the order for the introduction of the badge on 21 February 1934. See Schultheiss' *Europäischer Geschichtskalendar 1934*, Munich 1935, p. 73.

the service, very few soldiers would be affected.* The orders for the application of the racial restrictions were promulgated on 28 February 1934.[205] They stressed speed, difficult cases were to be handled by the Ministry, reports on those who were to be dismissed were to be at the Ministry by 31 May, and interim reports were to be submitted by 1 April.

The execution of this order was not as precise as the order itself would seem to infer. It was used for getting rid of trouble makers who happened to have a Jewish streak in their ancestry, and all checking of ancestry was done within the Reichswehr.[206] One officer, the then Oberst von Manstein, wrote to Reichenau that it was cowardice that the Army was surrendering to the Party by discrimination against a few soldiers, who had demonstrated by their voluntary enlistment that they were ready to give their lives for Germany. Reichenau showed this letter to Blomberg, who demanded of Fritsch that he took disciplinary action against Manstein. Fritsch took the letter with the remark that this was his affair, and did nothing more about it.[207]

Röhm continued to press for the adoption of his plan for the relegation of the Reichswehr to the position of training branch of the S.A. At a Cabinet meeting in mid-February he produced a scheme for the co-ordination of the Wehrmacht, the S.A., the S.S., and the veterans' organizations, the Stahlhelm, the Kyffhäuser Bund, etc., under one ministry, and implied that he was to become the head of this ministry.[208] Hitler's reaction to this proposal might have been the opposition to Röhm implied by his offer to Eden on 21 February to reduce the S.A. by two-thirds, and to see that the remainder had no military training.[209] It is interesting that the Reichswehr Ministry issued a decree on the same day, 21 February, which was circulated to all ministries and throughout the Army, drawing attention to the fact that 'many private persons and organizations are exploiting the term "National Defence" for their own individual interests'.[210]

Hitler called a conference of the heads of the S.A. and the Reichswehr for the morning of Wednesday, 28 February 1934, to be held in the Great Hall of the Bendlerstrasse buildings.† The date was the 101st anniversary[211] of the birth of Schlieffen, and the day on which the Association of

---

* Liebmann, *op. cit.*, p. 69. Those affected were:
>   Army: 5 Officers,
>   2 Officer Cadets,
>   1 Medical Officer Cadet,
>   31 N.C.O.s and men.
>   Navy: 2 Officers,
>   4 Officer Cadets,
>   5 N.C.O.s and men.

Das Archiv, April 1934, p. 42.

† The details of this conference are taken from the memoirs of Field-Marshal von Weichs, and confirmed in conversation with two participants, Field-Marshal von Manstein and General-oberst Heinrici, in February and March 1964. Weichs's account was taken down in shorthand at the time. He kept the record and showed it to Blomberg when they were both under interrogation at Nuremberg in 1945. Blomberg confirmed its accuracy. Weichs then re-wrote these rough notes into a connected, readable report after his release from detention in 1949, as part of his memoirs. The other accounts of this conference which remain all concern themselves with the problem of the S.A., and make no mention of Hitler's plans for eastern expansion.

General Staff Officers held its annual dinner, and so the Army was well represented in Berlin at that time. Those present included the Wehrkreis Commanders,* heads of the S.A. and S.S., Göring and Hitler.

Because of its special importance, the account given of the conference by Field-Marshal von Weichs in his unpublished memoirs is reproduced in full:

The purpose of this address was to state his [Hitler's] decision to reject the suggestion of Röhm to form an S.A. militia and to affirm his resolution to build a people's army on the lines of the old army out of the Reichswehr. He based this on examples from military history, to prove that a militia, such as Röhm suggested, was not sufficient for national defence.

The S.A. would have to limit itself to political tasks. For the transitional period, he declared himself to be in agreement with the suggestion of the War Minister [sic] to employ the S.A. for tasks of frontier protection and for pre-military training.†

I have taken down part of this speech in shorthand, and can quote its content fairly exactly. He began:

'The German people is going to face frightful destitution.' This opinion had been shouted down by Hitler's own mouth, as indeed we had always heard from him and from Goebbels that everything in the Third Reich would be so wonderful. This prophecy was not related to circumstances as they actually stood, but he based it on the following reasoning: the N.S.D.A.P. had overcome the unemployment. These blossoms would only last for about eight years, however, as then an economic recession must ensue. This evil could be remedied only by creating living space for the surplus population. However, the Western Powers would not let us do this. Therefore, short, decisive blows to the West

---

Manstein, *Aus einem Soldatenleben*, p. 185, makes a vague reference to Hitler's 'idea of the necessity for sufficient living space' being mentioned. The best alternative accounts are: Liebmann, *op. cit.*, p. 79, and his notes for a Wehrkreis conference, 9–15 March 1934, and Heinrici, *Zeugenschrifttum Nr.* 66, II, p. 166, held at the Institut für Zeitgeschichte, Munich.

* As far as I have been able to deduce, the following were the military participants in the conference of 28 February 1934:

Reichswehr Ministry
Blomberg   Minister
Reichenau   Wehrmachtsamt

Heeresleitung
Fritsch   Commander-in-Chief
Beck   Chief of General Staff
Fromm   General Army Office
Heinrici   Central Department, General Army Office
Schwedler   Army Personnel Office

Gruppenkommando I		*Gruppenkommando II*	
Rundstedt	Commander	Leeb	Commander
Kress	Chief of Staff	Geyer	Chief of Staff
Brauchitsch	WK I, 1 Inf. Div.	Liebmann	Wk V, 5 Inf. Div.
Bock	WK II, 2 Inf. Div.	Fleck	Wk VI, 6 Inf. Div.
Witzleben	WK III, 3 Inf. Div.	Adam	WK VII, 7 Inf. Div.
Manstein	C. of S., WK III	Weichs	3 Kav. Div.
Feige	1 Kav. Div.		
Kleist	2 Kav. Div.		

Total: Approx. 30 officers.

† Evidently Blomberg had modified his views since 2 February, when he had been opposed to the use of S.A. personnel in the Grenzschutz. See above, p. 37.

and then to the East could be necessary. A militia, as Röhm suggested, would not be the least bit suitable for national defence. He sought to establish this by examples from military history. In the course of this, he came to his own experience. The hastily and superficially trained division, to which he belonged in 1914 as a private, had come to grief at Langemarck with the most heavy losses. Therefore he was resolved to raise a people's army, built up on the Reichswehr, rigorously trained and equipped with the most modern weapons. He also rejected a Fascist Militia on the Italian pattern. This new army would have to be ready for any defence purposes after five years, and after eight years suitable also for attacking. The S.A. must confine itself to internal political tasks. One must be loyal in an internal political sense, while externally one could break one's word. In this connection, he referred to Bismarck, who once said that treaties only apply as long as they are of use to both partners. He would there-fore demand of the S.A. that it submit to his instructions. For the transitional period until the establishment of the planned armed forces, he would consent to the suggestion of the War Minister [sic] to employ the S.A. for the task of frontier protection and pre-military training. Otherwise the Wehrmacht must be the only bearer of the arms of the nation.

On reflection, one can say that Hitler had set forth his complete foreign policy programme and had already intimated the probability of aggressive war. Con-sidering the great number of listeners, it is almost miraculous that this prophecy of 1934 has never become known. The only detail which did not correspond to later developments was the actual timing of the predicted entanglements of war. The war came much earlier than the training programme which had been speci-fied here for the future armed forces allowed. However, one did not take at face value these warlike prophecies which were certainly in sharp contradiction to the protestations of peace which otherwise filled the air. The soldier was accus-tomed never to take the words of politicians too seriously. They often chose points of view which did not have to correspond with their true intentions, in order to achieve political ends. Thus these gloomy prognostications were probably soon forgotten.

Of his policies to be internally loyal, and externally perfidious when necessary, he kept only to the latter. No one can maintain today that he pursued a policy of loyalty in internal affairs. When he referred to Bismarck in the matter of break-ing one's word, that was either a miscomprehension or a deliberate misinter-pretation of one of Bismarck's sayings. If Bismarck did say something similar, then he certainly did not mean that one could break treaties without the declara-tion of a specified time of expiry.

When Hitler then designated the Wehrmacht as the sole bearer of the arms of the nation, as he was to reaffirm later, even he himself did not hold to this apparent intention, for after the elimination of the S.A., a new and more success-ful rival to the Wehrmacht arose in Himmler and his S.S. This fact alone shows that he did not honour his policy of internal loyalty.

After this address, the feeling of contentment reigned amongst the military audience that the Army High Command had scored a notable success over the Party organization and that it appeared as if Hitler wished to rely first and fore-most on the Army. Following on the conference, Röhm had invited us to his later notorious house in the Standartenstrasse to a luncheon of reconciliation. Hitler did not take part. The food was good—the atmosphere frosty. At any rate it seemed as if the peace was restored. One certainly believed that the authority of Hitler in the Party was so great that his decision would remain binding on the S.A.

Before the conference broke up and adjourned to Röhm's house, Hitler called forward Blomberg and Röhm, and presented them with an agreement to sign. This agreement stated that the Reichswehr Minister bore sole responsibility for national defence and that any war preparations and the conduct of war were totally the task of the Reichswehr. The S.A. was to take over the pre-military training of youths aged from 18 to 21, it was to train those from 21 to 26 who were not serving in the Reichswehr in 'S.A. sport',* and it was to maintain the military skills of those who were discharged from the Reichswehr on completion of their period of service. The S.A. was to take direction in all these matters from the Reichswehr Minister. When required, it was to make units available to be placed under the command of Grenzschutz Ost, the organization which assisted the Army with the defence of Germany's eastern frontier.†

The Army leaders did not remain longer than strictly necessary at Röhm's house. When they had departed, Röhm called his followers to a private conclave. He was extremely annoyed. He said that this agreement which he had been forced to sign was a new 'Versailler Diktat', and referred to Hitler as the 'ignoranter Gefreiter des Weltkriegs' (ignorant corporal of the World War). Furthermore, he could not possibly accede to this agreement, and if he could not go with Hitler, then he must go against him.‡

These strong sentiments were not shared by all of the senior S.A. leaders. Obergruppenführer Lutze, the eventual successor to Röhm, went to Hess and informed him of the dangers which were threatening the Party from the inside. Hess said that he had no desire to become involved. Lutze deliberated on the problem and then decided that he was obliged to inform Hitler himself. He went to the Berghof shortly afterwards and spoke to Hitler in secrecy. At the close of this conversation, Hitler said, 'We must allow the affair to ripen fully.'[212]

This conference of 28 February 1934 has significance both from the point of view of Hitler's war policy and from his public subjugation of the S.A. to the Reichswehr. Although the two aspects are obviously closely connected, discussion of matters relating to the possibility of war will be dealt with below (Chapter 10), except in so far as they relate directly to

---

* This was a code name for the organized military training conducted by the Ausbildungswesen. Hitler had instituted a special S.A. Sport award on 28 November 1933, which required proficiency in the following:

Physical Training. 100 metre sprint, long jump, weight putting, grenade throwing, 3000 metres run.

'*Defence Sport*'. 25 kilometre march with full kit, small bore shooting, grenade throwing at a target, obstacle course (in a gas mask), swimming or cycling, first aid.

Fieldcraft. Orientation, observation, topography, distance estimation, camouflage, observing and reporting.

Bennecke, *Die Reichswehr und der Röhm-Putsch*, p. 27.

† The wording of this agreement appears partly in Liebmann, *op. cit.*, p. 76, and partly in the papers of Krüger, the Chief of the Ausbildungswesen, in I.M.T., Vol. XXVIII, p. 538 and fol. This wording was passed on by Fritsch to the Wehrkreis Commanders, etc., at a separate conference. Liebmann quotes the date of this conference as 27 February 1934; either this is a mistake, or Fritsch conducted a special conference prior to the main one. Sauer, *op. cit.*, p. 943.

‡ These events of the afternoon of 28 February 1934 were related to Weichs by Lutze. Lutze and Weichs were on good terms with each other, if not actually friends. Weichs, *op. cit.*

the treatment of the S.A. problem. On the surface, Hitler's speech of 28 February seems to be a clear, reasoned statement of his policy towards the S.A. The time of internal revolution was over, as far as he was concerned, while the time of external strife was approaching. Therefore, the Army had to be supported. The possibility remains that Hitler was attempting to deceive one party or the other. It is difficult to imagine what end the public humiliation of Röhm in such a manner could have served as a means of deceit. Hitler was clearly making no attempt to deceive the S.A. Hitler's forcing of Röhm to sign such an agreement in front of the Reichswehr itself was not the sort of act which can be used for underhand purposes, as is emphasized by the strong reaction of Röhm to this treatment. Therefore it is extremely likely that this conference was a true statement of Hitler's policy in Army-S.A. relations, and is thus the clearest indication of a turning point in Hitler's policy towards the S.A.

This is how the Army viewed Hitler's statements.[213] The senior officers felt that Röhm had seriously threatened the position of the Army as the principal means of defence. This threat had been very worrying in view of the small size of the Army, and in view of the nature of the National-Socialist State, for the threat came from the strongest support of Hitler, to which he might have been thought to owe a special debt of gratitude. It was not to be expected that Hitler would have made such a decision in favour of an organization which had played a large part in preventing his coming to power by force, without some sacrifices on the part of the Army as well. It might even have been thought by the Army at the time that by far the biggest sacrifice had been made by Hitler, and therefore he was entitled to specially loyal service, and that in future, he was also entitled to more trust than had been extended to him in the past by the Army.

Unfortunately, the Army leaders do not appear to have been aware of the subtle insidious effects which such sacrifices in matters of principle can carry with them. Had it been foreseen that eventually the Army would have to act against Hitler, then its leaders might have shown more caution in advertising their support for Hitler and the Nazi Party by wearing the Party emblem in a prominent place on their uniform, and by subscribing to one of the most radical of the doctrines of the Party, even in a symbolic sense. These measures must have had a great effect on the minds of the men in the ranks who never gave serious or critical thought to the political situation, and who were content to be guided in their inner beliefs by such superficial features.

The balance seemed to continue to swing in favour of the Army during March 1934. Goebbels launched a propaganda campaign against malcontents and critics of the movement,[214] Blomberg reported military activities of the S.A. which had been discovered by the Reichswehr, to Hitler,[215] long lists of people who were not to be accepted into the Reichswehr were given special emphasis,[216] and Röhm published a statement that he had promised the obedience of the S.A. to the Reichswehr.[217]

The Army did not become complacent about this situation, however, and the Commander of Wehrkreis V, Stuttgart, General Liebmann, told his staff that the military value of the Röhm-Blomberg agreement was 'exactly nothing'. He added that a smooth delineation between the Army and the S.A. was simply not possible, as the Army was too weak to be able to hold its own against the S.A. in all aspects.[218]

This weakness was illustrated by an instruction promulgated by Blomberg on 10 March 1934, governing the membership of service volunteers to Party organizations. This specified that no ultimate decision had been reached on this difficult point, and until one was obtained, the old regulations forbidding membership of political organizations were to be ignored in this regard.*

A major incident was created on 29 March by a group of Austrian S.A. men, numbering some 1,500 who had fled from the Dollfuss régime into Bavaria. They had threatened to sack the small town of Weiden, after a series of clashes with the local inhabitants. There was no Army detachment closer than Regensburg, and this was far too small to quell such a disturbance. Fortunately, the local relations between the S.A. and the Army were good, and the situation was brought under control by the joint action of the S.A., the S.S. and the Reichswehr.†

In early April, another disturbance was made by S.A. Gruppenführer Lasch, who addressed the Thüringer S.A. at Jena, telling them, 'The revolution is not yet over. This will only happen when the S.A. State is founded.'‡ Röhm followed this up by spending a record amount of money on the S.A. for any one month, 12·5 million Reichsmarks.[219] But he attempted to maintain relations with the Army by attending the staff exercise held for higher commanders in late April.[220]

Blomberg continued to stress that the position of the Reichswehr was not to be challenged. On 21 April 1934, he issued an appeal to the Wehrmacht to conduct themselves in public to stress that:

1. The Wehrmacht was the only bearer of the arms of the nation.

2. The Wehrmacht was completely loyal to the National-Socialist régime.

3. The Wehrmacht had been systematically educated in National-Socialist thought.[221]

The tenseness of the situation at the end of April was shown by the urgent instruction issued by Wehrkreis VII on 25 April to all units within its command, that all preparations to meet an emergency were to be carried out, and complete readiness was to be reported by 15 May.[222]

On Sunday, 6 May 1934, the senior officers of the Reichswehr assembled at Bad Nauheim for ten days of discussion.[223] On the following day, Fritsch addressed the conference on the possible danger of a putsch

---

* OKH file H 24/6. On the copy which Fritsch initialled, he placed a heavy exclamation mark alongside the suspension of the old order.

† WK XIII file 754 contains the full details of the Weiden incident. In 1933 no rigid distinction was observed between the S.A. and the S.S. The S.S. was regarded as an élite guard of the S.A. and drew its recruits from the ranks of the latter. Divisions between the S.A. and the S.S. began in 1934 and were made permanent during the period of crisis in June. Conversation with Dr Heinrich Bennecke, February 1964.

‡ Weichs, op. cit. Weichs was at Weimar at that time and investigated the incident by interrogating the local Gauleiter, who attended Lasch's address. When Weichs asked the Gauleiter what was meant by 'the S.A. State', the only reply was a shrug of the shoulders.

by the S.A., and instructed those present to maintain a close watch on Röhm and his bands to see that the S.A. did not break the agreement which they had made.* On the last day of the conference, Blomberg had invited Röhm to appear. Unfortunately the arrival of these two together attracted so much publicity that the course of the conference was disrupted, and nothing more was achieved.

On 22 May Fritsch attempted to minimize the friction between the Army and the S.A. by issuing an order, which reminded the Army of Blomberg's instruction of 19 September 1933,[†] which stated that saluting between the Army and the S.A. was a matter of comradely duty. Fritsch concluded 'whoever neglects this damages the appearance of the Wehrmacht'.[224] Blomberg went further to demonstrate the loyalty of the Wehrmacht, by publishing a directive, 'Wehrmacht and National-Socialism', on 25 May. Although the content of this concerned the relationship between the Wehrmacht and National-Socialist ideology, and is therefore dealt with below,[‡] it is significant that this directive appeared at this time, as if to convince Hitler that he had nothing to fear from the Armed Forces, and therefore no need to retain the troublesome and disobedient S.A.

On 3 June Hitler called Röhm to a conference of five hours' duration. Röhm did not allow himself to be trapped into openly opposing Hitler,[225] but he kept up a policy of friction with the Reichswehr, particularly in Silesia.[226] Within the Reichswehr, reaction was becoming stronger. Reichenau placed confidence men in the Ausbildungswesen, and obtained reports on all phases of S.A. activity. He even went as far as to commence negotiations with Himmler, with whom he conferred on several occasions during the period of tension.[227]

Röhm continued to co-operate with Hitler, and on 7 June 1934 he agreed to send the S.A. on leave for one month, from 1 July, at Hitler's behest.[§] Röhm's willingness to do this would seem to refute any accusation that he was planning a putsch to take place within this period. He did not neglect to find out what was happening within the Wehrmacht. He had spies in several places, including the Kriegsakademie.[228] His informant there was Hauptmann Höfle, who committed the further offence of being an S.A. leader while on active military service. On 12 June Höfle wrote to Röhm, stating that, *inter alia*, the Army was the main enemy of the S.A. and that General von Schleicher was engaged in anti-Nazi activity.[229]

Hitler, still not content with the course which Röhm was pursuing, called another meeting of the senior Army commanders and the S.A. leaders on 16 June 1934.[230] Here he stressed the primacy of the Wehrmacht in defence matters, and this gave rise to expressions of dissatisfaction from

---

* Liebmann, *op. cit.*, p. 83, and OKW file 867. Fritsch did not stay at the conference very long. He went on a long journey through the Harz to Bavaria until 16 May 1934. His movements on that day are uncertain, but it is probable that he returned to Nauheim for the last day of the conference.

† See above, p. 35.

‡ See below, Chapter 5.

§ The order was published in the *Völkischer Beobachter*, of 9 June 1934. It mentions that the S.A. was going to return from its leave, as a threat to its 'enemies'.

the S.A. leaders.[231] Further tension was created by the address in which Papen protested against Nazi extremism, delivered at Marburg on Sunday, 17 June,[232] and Hitler went to confer with President Hindenburg at Neudeck, the President's estate in East Prussia on 21 June.[233] Hitler may have been impressed by the seriousness of the President's decline in health and his growing inability to cope with affairs of state, for after Hitler's return, a full scale Party campaign was launched against Röhm, by Hess, Göring and Goebbels, which was followed up by co-ordinated action on the lower levels of the Party.[234]

Tension continued to mount, and senior S.S. and S.D. (Sicherheitsdienst) leaders were called to Berlin, where they were told by Himmler and Heydrich that an S.A. revolt was imminent. The S.S. was ordered to negotiate with the Army at a local level and weapons and quarters were to be made available by the Army for the S.S. in the case of an emergency. The Reichswehr Ministry also was informed of the imminent danger, but in the instructions given to Staff Officers within the Ministry, it was stated that the S.A. revolt might not occur until autumn.[235] These same officers were told that the S.S. and the police stood on the side of the Army, and that, if necessary, they were to be armed by disarming the S.A. Grenzschutz units where possible.[236]

The Army made most of its preparations to resist revolt on 24 and 25 June. Infanterie Regiment 5 was held ready at Döberitz for instant movement,[237] and Wehrkreis Commanders were ordered to have spare equipment for one full regiment on hand,[238] apparently should Infanterie Regiment 5 have been rushed to the area. The Bendler Block was to be guarded by a company from the Wachregiment Berlin. All preparations were to be made as unobtrusively as possible. Even the courses which provided the S.A. with military training from the Army under the Ausbildungswesen were not to be interfered with.[239] Around 24 June Fritsch sent warning to the Area Commander in Silesia that a putsch was expected in his area.

On 27 June Kurt Daluege of the S.S. appeared at the Reichswehr Ministry, masquerading under the title of 'Ministerial Director for Police Affairs in the Ministry of the Interior', and told officials that the Berlin leaders of the S.A. had just finished conferring on the outlines of a putsch.[240] This story has been shown to be false, but it did cause serious apprehension within the Reichswehr Ministry at the time.[241] It is typical of a number of subterfuges which the S.S. and S.D. employed at that critical time to heighten the tension within the Reichswehr, and possibly to force the Reichswehr into some precipitate action.[242] It is significant that all the instructions issued by the S.S. and S.D. were to deal with an imminent putsch, while those of the Army did not recognize this degree of urgency, stating that it might be some months before the S.A. took action.[243] Either the S.S. was aware of information relating to Röhm's fate, or they were trying to force the hands of people who could be used to aid their own struggle for power with the S.A.

Daluege's visit to the Ministry was followed by a stream of precautionary orders. All officers who worked in the Bendler Block were to work with weapons ready to hand at all times.[244] Fritsch issued orders to the whole Army, covering all matters of security, but only in so far as an attack by the S.A. on the Wehrmacht in its barracks was concerned.[245] On 28 June Fritsch went to Hindenburg, possibly to discuss the role of the Army in any possible civil strife.[246] He found the President in such poor condition that little could have been achieved.[247]

On the following day, 29 June, Blomberg published a long article in the *Völkischer Beobachter*, which included:

The Wehrmacht stands in close unity with the whole nation, wearing with pride the symbol of the rebirth of Germany on helmet and uniform, standing in discipline and loyalty behind the leadership of the State—the Field-Marshal of the Great War, Reichs President von Hindenburg, its Supreme Commander, and the Führer of the Reich, Adolf Hitler, who once came out of our ranks and who will always remain one of ours.[248]

Thus he made it clear to the whole nation that the Wehrmacht was as strongly opposed to any attack on Hitler as it would have been to any attack on Hindenburg himself.

Further signs of apprehension were shown by some of the orders issued within Wehrkreis VII on 29 June, cancelling movements and training due for the following day.[249] These were followed in the evening by reports which came into the Command Headquarters in Munich that the alarm order had been given to the S.A. by its leaders, and that weapons, including two heavy machine-guns, and ammunition had been distributed amongst local S.A. men.[250]

The nature of the surviving records of these days indicates that an escalation process was going on. The Army received a report that the S.A. was making certain preparations, and orders would then be issued to the Army. The S.A. would then notice these, and would take counter measures, which could have had an entirely defensive purpose. The dangers of this were seen by the Area Commander of Silesia, Generalleutnant von Kleist. Silesia had been one of the areas where much friction had been reported. Kleist made a direct approach to the local S.A. leader, Obergruppenführer Heines, and invited him to the Army Headquarters for talks. Heines called on Kleist on 28 June, and both discovered that the measures which each was taking against the other were prompted solely by the fear of an attack, and that neither had any intention of being the first to commence hostilities. During the night of 28–29 June, Heines telephoned Kleist to say that this situation was occurring everywhere in Germany, and that he would fly to Röhm in the morning to set a *détente* in motion. Thereupon, Kleist flew to Berlin and reported to Fritsch, with similar aims. Kleist thought that this friction could all have been the work of Himmler. After he had conferred with Fritsch and Beck, Fritsch sent for Reichenau and made Kleist repeat what he had said. Reichenau's reply was: 'That may well be right, but it is too late now.'[251]

Reichenau showed by this statement a complete disregard for any means of attempting to avoid a final clash. He may have been privy to plans of Hitler which he knew could not be altered, but his words show that he was intent on a final clash, irrespective of whether the S.A. leaders were planning an open revolt, or whether they were acting out of fear of some blow directed against them from the less radical section of political opinion. Although direct evidence of Reichenau's part in the planning of the action against the S.A. is lacking, there is sufficient to show that he was well informed of what was about to happen, that he had been in communication with Himmler, and that he was amongst those who believed that the end justified the means.[252]

Unfortunately little evidence remains of the reactions of Fritsch and Beck to this statement made by Reichenau. Their concern to avoid all needless conflict is shown by their reaction to Kleist's information, and by Fritsch's summoning of Reichenau. Fritsch could have interpreted the words of Reichenau to mean simply that the escalation process had passed the point of no return, and Reichenau may have fostered the growth of this view in his later remarks. Fritsch may have made protests and given warnings to Blomberg, and been rebuffed, or he may have regarded the clash with the S.A. as inevitable, and thus he might have felt that it was pointless to do anything else except remain on the alert against any sudden revolt. No extra measures were taken by the Army after this conference. No new orders were issued by Fritsch for the situation as a whole until after 30 June. So it is likely that Fritsch, mindful of his responsibilities for the Army, decided that he was not justified in decreasing the state of alertness of the Army, until some new signs appeared from S.A. headquarters in Munich; as no aggressive moves had been planned by the Army it was not his business to interfere in any action which now took place.

At the same time as these events were taking place, another incident with far-reaching consequences for Army-Party relationships was developing. Since his resignation from the Chancellorship, General von Schleicher had lived in retirement. At 7 p.m. on the evening of 29 June 1934, Herr Arno Moysischewitz called at Schleicher's villa in Neubabelsberg, Berlin, in answer to an urgent summons from the General.[253] Moysischewitz was an old confidant of Schleicher, and was also a friend of Beck. As a result of a visit to Beck on 14 June, he had warned Schleicher on 15 or 16 June to be scrupulously careful to avoid any further political activity. Schleicher had expressed indignation at this, stating that he had been approached by politicians from all sides, including the Nazis, for his support, and that he had refused to have anything to do with any of them. Moysischewitz mentioned a current rumour about Schleicher's supposed association with Röhm. Schleicher rejected this flatly. He had seen Röhm only once since January 1933, and had had absolutely no contact with him, although Röhm had sent a man to see Schleicher a few weeks previously, whom Schleicher had refused to see.

Schleicher appeared very glad to see Moysischewitz, as he was worried by several repetitions of Beck's warning which had reached him during the previous few days. He added that the most incredible rumours had been circulating through the Reichswehr Ministry about his political activities. In order to defend himself, he wanted Moysischewitz to pass a message to Blomberg, via Beck. Blomberg was to be reminded of his promise to

Schleicher, made in summer 1933, that he would not tolerate any bad reports concerning Schleicher, within the Ministry, without giving Schleicher a personal hearing on the matter. Schleicher now requested the fulfilment of this promise.

Despite all the efforts of Moysischewitz on 30 June to telephone Beck, he was not allowed to speak to Beck in person, until it was too late, on 1 July 1934.

After making this request, Schleicher went on to discuss his activities in great detail. He said that it was true that he was friendly with the French Ambassador, François-Poncet. He had dined with him two or three times during the previous months, but these had been purely social occasions, at which each had been at the greatest pains to avoid any mention of politics. Around 11 p.m., Schleicher took Moysischewitz out into the garden to a secluded corner, where he had had two deck chairs placed, and began a very intimate conversation with Moysischewitz.

Moysischewitz was surprised by the depth of religious feeling which Schleicher expressed. Only once before, in 1919, had Schleicher revealed this side of his nature to Moysischewitz. He went on to discuss divine pre-determination and Christ, and spoke of the connection between divine ordination and politics. He felt that he had been called by God in the Great War, and in the 'twenties to do crucial work, and that God had decided that he was to be His implement no longer in January 1933. Nothing could tempt him to re-enter politics unless God gave him a most unexpected recall.

At approximately 12.30 on the following day, Schleicher's cook, Marie Guntel, went to the garden door in answer to a knock.[254] Without thinking, she switched the electric locking device off and let the callers in. They stormed through the house, found Schleicher seated at his desk, inquired if he was General von Schleicher, and shot him. His wife was shot down a few seconds later as she entered the room The cook ran off into the garden and the two corpses were left for Schleicher's young stepdaughter to discover shortly afterwards.

In the meantime, shooting had broken out in many other parts of Germany. Hitler had flown to Munich in the early hours of the morning and had arrested Röhm and several other leaders of the S.A. who were with him at Bad Wiessee. Suspects were being rounded up all over Germany. Munich was one of the central points of the crisis. At 7.15 a.m., Wehrkreis VII was informed that Army units under its command had issued 12,000 rounds of rifle ammunition to the local S.S. Five minutes later, 1,000 rifles had also been issued to the S.S.[255] Exact instructions went out to all Army units.[256] S.S. units sought refuge in the Army barracks.* Units in training camps were ordered to return to their barracks on the following day.[257] Soldiers were sent out to disarm the S.A., but they found some S.A. units to be uncooperative.[258] Some S.A. units had even attempted to obtain more weapons from the Army by

* See the photograph of the S.S. unit which sought refuge in the Army barracks at Magdeburg taken by General Flörke.

trickery.[259] Others had gone so far as to force their way into small Army Headquarters and to arrest the officers.[260] The air of tension was relieved for the Army by listening to radio reports of the situation as they came to hand. In at least one officers' mess, bottles of champagne were opened to celebrate the announcement of the arrest of each of the S.A. leaders who were imprisoned.[261] On one station, Fritsch's name was given as one of those who had been shot by the S.S.[262] Startled and bewildered S.A. units which had fled into the countryside began to come back in the afternoon, as they realized that they were not in the midst of a civil war.[263] Some sections of the S.A. marched to Army barracks and placed themselves at the disposal of the Army garrison commander.[264] Others showed a little fight, in a half-hearted fashion, until they saw that the police were not interested in them as individuals.[265] Police filled the streets, patrolling with weapons and setting up machine-gun posts.[266] The S.A. was finally disarmed of 177,000 rifles, 651 heavy machine-guns, and 1,250 light machine-guns.[267] The final losses of the S.A. as a result of the 'Night of the Long Knives', numbered nearly fifty leaders killed, including Röhm himself.[268]

The first official reaction to this day of bloodshed was an order of the day from Blomberg on 1 July, in which he praised Hitler for his courage in breaking the revolt personally. This was followed by a similar message from Hindenburg. In the Cabinet meeting of 3 July 1934, Blomberg declared his utmost gratitude to Hitler for his actions. Here was a case where the tensions of the past few days may well have combined with Blomberg's emotional nature to produce an outburst of adulation for a series of acts which had been inspired, not because Röhm had been planning a mutiny, but by Hitler's intolerance of any opposition and the effect on this of the machinations of other Party leaders who aspired to Röhm's power.

To recognize the blood purge of 30 June 1934 as a naked act of power politics without justification for the killing of eighty-three persons, must have been very difficult for all who depended on the officially controlled sources for their information. There had been trouble with Röhm and the S.A., and Röhm had not disguised his antipathy towards Hitler's policy regarding the S.A. The building up of this into a full scale revolt was not difficult for Goebbels's Ministry of Propaganda. However, the evidence has shown that some of the senior leaders of the Army had reason to doubt the official explanation. This incident marked a sharp turning point in the attitude of Beck towards the Nazi Party, and from then onwards, he became steadily more opposed to Nazi policies.[269] Fritsch made protests to Hindenburg when he had found out a little more about the shootings, particularly that Schleicher had also been shot, but this met with no response from the failing old man, and Fritsch did not regard it as his affair to take any further steps on behalf of the S.A., his former enemies.[270]

Fritsch considered that some alterations were necessary in the system of reporting political incidents involving the Army. He ordered that, in future, all political incidents were to be reported directly to him, with a copy of the report for the Wehrmachtsamt, Reichenau's department, instead of the old system, by which all political reports by-passed him.

Reichenau was not satisfied with this, but Fritsch had his own way.[271]

During the following week, measures were taken to end the armed independence of the S.A. Hitler ordered that the S.A. were to surrender their weapons.[272] The state of emergency was raised.[273] Blomberg decreed that the civilians serving with the Wehrmacht must not belong to the S.A., and ordered any who were S.A. members to leave the S.A. before 20 July.[274] Finally, in view of the large amount of reorganization to be done, autumn manœuvres were cancelled.[275] On 13 July, the affair was closed by Hitler's speech in the Reichstag, explaining the actions which he had taken during the period of crisis. Part of his justification was given as:

My promise to him [Hindenburg] to preserve the Army as a non-political instrument of the nation is as binding for me from innermost conviction as from my pledged word.[276]

From this time on, relations between the Army and the S.A. remained smooth. The S.A. ceased to have any important function within the state, apart from tasks of local administration, propaganda, and administration of ex-servicemen. Co-operation between the Army and the S.A. in training matters continued, but on a greatly reduced scale. The Ausbildungswesen was removed from the S.A., and finally dissolved on 1 February 1935.[277] As a result of the events of 30 June 1934, the Army was able to proceed with making its plans for rearmament without fear of competition and interference.

However, the consequences of 30 June went further than this. While the shootings of S.A. leaders were not strongly disapproved of by the Army, the murdering of two retired Generals, von Schleicher, and his assistant, von Bredow, had provoked much opposition to Hitler, and had led to several demands for a rehabilitation of the two officers. Blomberg banned any discussion of the deaths of the two generals, but this had little effect.[278] He also forbade the attendance of any Wehrmacht personnel at Schleicher's funeral. This was defied by one prominent soldier who was still on the active list—Generaloberst von Hammerstein, who attended in full uniform, attended by an Adjutant, and insisted on carrying Schleicher's decorations.[279]

While Schleicher had always been an unpopular figure within the Reichswehr,[280] he had sufficient admirers to cause concern to the Nazi administration. One of these admirers, the then Oberstleutnant (later General der Infanterie) Ludwig Crüwell, had been the subject of a Gestapo inquiry for speaking out in Schleicher's defence in February 1933.[281] On 22 August 1934, the Gestapo reported the incident to Blomberg. Blomberg passed the matter to Fritsch for comment. After making inquiries, Fritsch held that Crüwell was quite justified in his remarks, and closed the case without taking any action against Crüwell.

During the first months after the death of Schleicher, his old comrades, Hammerstein and Field-Marshal von Mackensen, agitated constantly for his rehabilitation. They had submitted a long memorandum to Hindenburg, setting out the full details of the two killings, and asking for rehabilitation for the dead men, and punishment for the killers.[282] Whether

Hindenburg ever received the document or not is not known. However, it had a wide circulation, and Hitler realized that some concession towards the murdered generals was necessary.[283] He called the senior officers of the Army together at the Kroll Opera, on 3 January 1935. At the end of his speech, he added an 'off the record' statement to the effect that the shootings of the two generals had been 'in error'. He said that the statements made later by Göring and himself had been based on incorrect information, and that the names of the two innocent officers were to be restored to the honour rolls of their regiments.[284]

Six days later, a fresh incident arose.[285] A young Army officer, Oberleutnant Engel had overheard an S.A. man and an S.S. man discussing Schleicher as 'rogue, reactionary, thank God he was shot'. Engel had objected to this, and had become involved in a heated argument. The matter was eventually smoothed over after negotiations between the Army, the S.A. and the S.S.

Mackensen chose the annual meeting of the 'Association of Former General Staff Officers' (Verein Graf Schlieffen) to announce Hitler's admission of the innocence of Schleicher and Bredow.[286] This association met on the anniversary of Schlieffen's birthday, 28 February. Towards the close of the meeting, Mackensen rose to his feet, and called upon the members to remember the comrades who had died during the course of the previous year, particularly the Generals von Schleicher and von Bredow. He said:

Concerning the death of the generals in question, it has been established that in the purely political struggles for power which occurred at that time, the personal honour of the two officers concerned has not been touched, but that they chose paths which were regarded as hostile to the Government and thereby led to fateful consequences.

I cannot permit discussion of this question, as the Reich Government has explained in a document which has the force of law, that the deaths of those men on 30 June and on 1 July, are to be regarded as having occurred in the interests of the State. By further examination of the matter, we will be stepping on to political ground, which is forbidden under the constitution of the Verein Graf Schlieffen.

He then raised his voice:

According to this therefore, our fallen comrades, the Generals von Schleicher and von Bredow, died in all honour and have fallen on the field of honour.*

* Two records of this speech exist. One is an unsigned account in the Schleicher Papers, *op. cit.*, written on the day afterwards by a member of the audience. The other is given in the instruction on the matter published by Blomberg on 2 April 1935, to be found in WK IX file 134. Considering that the published version was probably provided by Mackensen himself, there is remarkably close agreement between the two, except that the final paragraph, for which Mackensen raised his voice, was not published by Blomberg. In view of the exact nature of the anonymous account and of the rumours to this effect which were circulated afterwards by the Gestapo, it is highly probable that this final paragraph was spoken by Mackensen. Its omission from the published account then, was probably deliberate suppression by either Mackensen, or Blomberg. As Blomberg had probably heard the rumours himself through the Gestapo reports, and also received accounts of the meeting from senior officers on his staff, it is unlikely that the suppression of this paragraph was entirely due to Mackensen. Therefore the responsibility for the withholding of this most important part of the proceedings probably rests with Blomberg.

This speech was warmly received in Reichswehr circles.[287] It provoked so much discussion that Blomberg issued an order on 2 April 1935, stating:

The internal conduct of the matter by the Verein Graf Schlieffen as to whether the Generals von Schleicher and von Bredow should be struck off the rolls and an ill-considered statement by the President, Field-Marshal von Mackensen, have awoken the impression that a rehabilitation of the two generals is intended, or is actually in effect. This is a misunderstanding.

The following statement was made to the Schlieffen-Verein, purely for its own purposes:

[then followed the account given above, except for the last paragraph of Mackensen's speech]

No alteration of the standpoint of the Government and of the view held up until now by the officer corps on this question has taken place, and, further-more, this is impossible.[288]

Thus the aftermath of 30 June 1934 came to an end. The Army was once again able to carry out its tasks without fear of intolerable interfer-ence, at the price of appearing to condone violent methods. This gave the Nazi movement further opportunity to take charge of the minds of those in, or shortly to be in, the lower ranks of the Army, and so rendered the difficulties of resisting the power of the dictatorship even greater. It appears that the price in relation to the benefits derived was under-estimated by the Army at the time, but the costs of any alternative course of action may well have been far greater, and unless the disasters which were to befall Germany and the world in later years were seen in 1934, it is difficult to see what else the Army should have done to prevent the entire defence structure of Germany from falling into the most radical hands.

4

Hitler Assumes Absolute Power

THE coming of August 1934 caused the German High Command to divert its attention from the aftermath of the recent internal struggles within the nation, in order to commemorate the twentieth anniversary of the outbreak of the First World War. Accordingly, orders were given in late July that parades were to be held by units on 2 August, the anniversary of the first day of the German mobilization, and rehearsals were held during the last days of that month. Suddenly, in the early hours of the morning of 2 August 1934, the death of Hindenburg was announced. New orders for the parades of remembrance had to be issued at great speed.

The Reichswehr Ministry was not unprepared to meet this situation, for Reichenau had been planning for it, by preparing an oath of allegiance for the Reichswehr to swear to the person of Adolf Hitler. Reichenau disliked the form of the oath of the Weimar Republic,[289] which had been sworn to the Constitution, not to the Head of State, and represented a break with German military tradition. Reichenau's readiness may be partly explained by a desire to exploit the old German military tradition of taking the oath to a new monarch immediately after the death of the old. The oath had been composed by Reichenau on his own initiative, without any suggestion from Hitler,[290] although presumably Hitler had agreed to the idea in principle some time before Hindenburg's death.

The orders went out during the morning of 2 August, but in some cases it was several hours before the wording of the oath had reached unit commanders, and the parades were postponed until the early evening. The main part of the parades was still the service of remembrance, which was conducted by Chaplains, and which lasted approximately half an hour. The ceremony of the swearing of the oath took only a few minutes, and then the troops were marched back to their quarters, through silent crowds, to prepare for the duties of the following day.

However, there was another event on 2 August 1934, with even greater consequences than the oath for the course of German political-military relations.

This was the amalgamation of the offices of Chancellor and President to place all executive power in the hands of Hitler. He was not able to be checked from above, because there was no one superior to him, and the restraining influence which the Reichstag could have exercised had been largely swept away by the Enabling Law.

This meant that the leader of the Nazi Party became the Supreme Commander of the Armed Forces. The highest military office in Germany was occupied by a Nazi, and the distinction between State and Party was blurred, in some cases, into non-existence. Hitler was thereby enabled to order the Army to do whatever he liked without fear of any legal or constitutional check. No means was provided for judging when Hitler's commands were legitimate, by virtue of his State offices, or illegal through his using the Army for the ends of the Nazi Party alone. Indeed, the oath had removed any means of legally defying Hitler, as the Armed Forces had promised obedience to Hitler as a person, without any limits.

There is little evidence to show that the dangers of this situation had been appreciated by the Army leaders. Beck, speaking on the evening of 2 August 1934, described the day as 'the blackest of my life'. He could see the drastic consequences of such an oath to a man like Hitler and even talked to Fritsch about resigning. Fritsch dissuaded Beck on the grounds that he could not be replaced and that the Army would not understand the reasons for his resignation. Beck continued to have grave conflicts of conscience concerning the oath for several years.[291]

There were several reasons for the Army's failure to perceive the dangers of the concentration of power and of the oath. Some officers still viewed Hitler as Germany's salvation, by virtue of the economic and foreign policy achievements of the Nazi government, and they might have believed that the more power he had in his hands, the quicker Germany would regain her strength. Others argued that as Hitler was able to avoid censure in matters such as the Enabling Law, and his treatment of the S.A. leaders, he already had absolute power, and so his assumption of Hindenburg's office was a mere formality. Yet others, possibly the majority, read the newspapers, made one or two very general and unoriginal comments, and promptly reimmersed themselves in their very demanding work.

If the dangers were seen, there were other reasons for doing nothing. Some may have regarded the matter as a gamble. Because there was no real alternative leader to Hitler, and no party with anything like the amount of popular support which the Nazi Party had, it may have seemed better to take a risk on Hitler's qualities as a statesman, than to have him replaced by some ineffective figure, who might have been the cause of further internal strife. Others, who disapproved of Nazism, may have regarded the concentration of powers as a bad move, but did not consider it their duty to attempt to rectify the situation.

One matter which has given rise to much comment has been the wording of the oath. The text of this was:

I swear by God this holy oath, that I will render to Adolf Hitler, Leader of the German nation and people, Supreme Commander of the Armed Forces, unconditional obedience, and I am ready as a brave soldier to risk my life at any time for this oath.

The chief criticism has been that this oath was sworn, not to a government, not to a constitution, nor to any particular bearer of official office, but to one specific individual. Much of this criticism has been made after observation of the tremendous conflicts of loyalty which it caused later within the higher ranks of the Army, when one group of individuals held that a man's word was his bond, while another group held that the purpose of an oath was to maintain the discipline of the fighting forces, not to be an active agent in the destruction of Germany.

Certainly this was the major difference between the oath of the Weimar period, and that of the Nazi period. The Weimar oath ran simply:

I swear loyalty to the Constitution and vow that I will protect the German nation and its lawful establishments as a brave soldier at any time, and will be obedient to the President and to my superiors.

However, when one looks at the two oaths from the point of view of imparting them, together with a little feeling and real meaning, to recruit soldiers, the Nazi oath has the advantages of clarity, of decisive impressive form, and of establishing the personal link between the Head of State and every one of his or her soldiers. While there may be no legal or constitutional significance to this link, it does have a good effect in terms of morale. Some soldiers hold that it is this personal oath which sets them aside from civil servants, and it is a matter of great pride to them that they have promised to serve their Head of State with their lives, if the need arise. An oath to a constitution means little in countries where the constitution is not given a great deal of importance. Most soldiers do not know what is in the constitution, and from the point of view of administering a system of discipline, there are too many legal loopholes, or subtleties, by which sharp-minded soldiers can plague their officers.

For these and many other reasons, the old form of the British oath has been largely preserved thus:

I, . . . , swear by Almighty God that I will be faithful and bear true allegiance to Her Majesty Queen Elizabeth the Second, Her Heirs and Successors, and that I will, as in duty bound, honestly and faithfully defend Her Majesty, Her Heirs and Successors in Person, Crown and Dignity against all enemies, and will observe and obey all orders of Her Majesty, Her Heirs and Successors, and of the Generals and Officers set over me.

The differences between this and the Nazi oath would seem to be formal. German soldiers promised Hitler unconditional obedience, while British soldiers promise to obey all the orders of Queen Elizabeth the Second. At least the Nazi oath offered no justification for an adolescent successor to Hitler to embarrass the Army when he felt that his dignity had been affronted, and had ordered the Palace Guards to shoot a newspaper reporter. Even the American* and Soviet† oaths, which are sworn

---

* The text of the United States Oath is:
   'I do solemnly swear (or affirm) that I will support and defend the Constitution of the United States against all enemies, foreign and domestic; that I will bear true faith and allegiance to the same; and that I obey the orders of the President of the United States and the orders of the officers appointed over me, according to regulations, and the Uniform Code of Military Justice. So help me God.'

The Cuckoo in the Nest—the Magdeburg S.S. seeking refuge from the
S.A., 30 June 1934 in the Anger-Kaserne, barracks of Infantry
Regiment Halberstadt (I.R.12). The Army did not expect to be
threatened in later years by this motley crew.

The Magdeburg Garrison takes the Oath to Hitler, 2 August 1934.
This parade had been ordered to honour the memory of President
von Hindenburg who had died the night before. The ceremony of
the Führer-Oath was hurriedly and insidiously appended to this
solemn occasion on orders from Berlin. The parade took place on
the Cathedral Square. In the foreground stand representatives of
veterans' organizations with their banners. In the middle of these the
old colours of the regiment's Prussian lineage are borne by soldiers
of the regiment. In the background are the crowds of civilians who
watched the parade. The Oath to Hitler was sworn on the revered
old Prussian colours by representatives of each company of the
regiment.

Hitler saluting a guard of honour provided by the Goslar Jäger Regiment in front of the Kaiserpfalz in Goslar before the Harvest Thanksgiving Festival on the Bückeberg, October 1934. On the extreme left is the then Major Erwin Rommel.

The High Command
free from the threat
of the S.A. showing
Hitler, Göring,
Blomberg, Fritsch
and Raeder. Göring
proudly wore his
general's uniform
after his rapid
promotion from the
rank of Captain
(Retired) on
occasions on which
he wished to
identify himself with
the Armed Forces.

The Oath-taking
Ceremony in 1938—
Recruits laying their
left hands on the
Regimental Colours
on the Königliche
Platz, Munich.

The Reichs Cabinet at the proclamation of
the new Defence Law, 16 March 1935.
From left: back row: Frank, unidentified,
Frick, unidentified, Rust, unidentified,
Neurath, unidentified, Schacht, Meissner.
Darré, front row:
Goebbels, Göring, Hitler, Blomberg,
Schwerin von Krosigk, unidentified, Seldte,
Funk.

Fritsch and Hitler inspecting troops of the
Army and Air Force at the Harvest
Thanksgiving Festival on the Bückeberg.

The Army parading under the banners of the Nazi Party at the Great Tattoo on the evening of 1 May 1935, in the Lustgarten, Berlin.

Blomberg greeting the 88-year-old General Karl Litzmann, a former Nazi member of the Reichstag, and well-known "old-campaigner" for the Party, on the Hauptmarkt before the famous "Schöne Brunnen" in Nuremberg at the Party Rally, 1935.

Blomberg, Göring, Fritsch and Hitler at the Party Rally, Nuremberg, 1935.

Motorized heavy artillery which was forbidden under the Versailles Treaty, parading before Hitler at the Party Rally, Nuremberg, 1935.

The Team of Two—
Fritsch and Beck at
Army exercises,
1935.

The Ceremonial Re-opening of the Kriegsakademie in Berlin on 15
October 1935, the 125th Anniversary of its foundation by
Scharnhorst. This photograph shows Blomberg making the speech
referred to on p. 90 of the text. In the front row of the audience
are, from left: Goebbels, Beck, Göring, Hitler, General Liebmann,
Commandant of the Kriegsakademie, Field-Marshal von Mackensen,
Fritsch and Seeckt.

to the President, and to the Soviet Government, respectively, offer no easy solution to the question of the deposition of the executive head of government by the military forces. Either one has to be able to justify the breaking of an oath sworn at least as solemnly as a marriage vow, or one has to be able to live with the consequences of adhering to one's word.

There has also been much debate about the use of the phrase 'unconditional obedience' in the Wehrmacht oath. This phrase makes it amply clear that German soldiers did promise to obey Hitler's illegal orders as well as his legal ones and it lays these men open to criticism for taking such an oath. However, since the concept of conditional obedience, the alternative to unconditional obedience, has been foreign to military oaths, as shown by the examples quoted, it seems hardly surprising that the German Army was not deeply concerned about the possible implications of swearing unconditional obedience to their head of state. Moreover, it may be argued that conditional obedience is a contradiction in terms and that therefore the word 'unconditional' was a redundancy rather than a matter for intense debate.

Another relevant factor to be considered is the amount of importance attached to an oath by the Army which has taken it. In British and Commonwealth Armies, one seldom hears of the oath after it has been taken. It is administered usually in great haste in the office of an adjutant, before any training has begun. It is not the subject of lectures, and very little explanation has been written about it. British soldiers have fought for their monarch for centuries, and that is taken for granted. There is no need for any further mention of the oath to be made in the British Army. In contrast, the turbulent history of Germany has led to the attachment of a greater degree of significance to the German oath. It was important to know for whom one was fighting, when princes and armies were ranged on one side in one battle, and on the opposite in the next. The German oath was not taken until the end of basic training. It was not taken in the privacy of an office, but as part of a solemn public ceremony, in which a man dedicated himself to his country in the presence of his family and friends, and before the whole regiment, on the most sacred of military objects, the colours. Before and after taking the oath, the German soldier was lectured on its significance, and its legal nature was explained in detail, with many examples of those who had betrayed the honour of their

---

† The text of the Soviet Oath is:
   'I, a citizen of the Union of Socialist Soviet Republics, vow, while I am in the ranks of the Armed Forces, this oath, and solemnly swear to be an honourable, brave, disciplined and vigilant soldier, to guard the military and State secrets strictly, and to execute without any contradiction, all military regulations and the orders of my commanders and superiors. I vow to learn conscientiously the skill of warfare, to care for all military property and the property of the People, with every means, and to remain obedient, unto my last breath, to my People, to my Soviet Homeland, and to the Soviet Government. I am ready at all times to be engaged for the defence of my Homeland—the Union of Socialist Soviet Republics—on the orders of the Soviet Government as a soldier of the Armed Forces. I swear to defend it manfully and skilfully, with all my power and honour, without sparing my blood or my very life itself for the attainment of total victory over the enemy. Should I break my solemn oath, may the severe punishments of the Soviet Law and the universal hatred and the contempt of the labouring masses strike me.'

country, their army, and themselves, by failing to keep their oath. Finally, the effect of the German penchant for written rules and regulations must be added to the balance. The result was that many Germans regarded their oath as the positive embodiment of the essence of their honour. In these circumstances it is reasonable to expect Armies like the German to show greater care about the wording of an oath sworn. This places somewhat greater responsibility on the shoulders of Reichenau and Blomberg than would have been the case in other armies.

Hitler was quick to show his gratitude to Blomberg for the loyalty expressed by the Wehrmacht in this form. His thanks took the most unusual form of a letter, which Hitler wrote shortly after the confirmation of the new wording of the oath by the passing of a new, retroactive law on 20 August 1934. In this letter he said:

After the completed confirmation of the Law of 2 August, I wish to express my thanks to you, and through you, to the Wehrmacht, for the oath of loyalty which has been sworn to me. Just as the officers and men of the Wehrmacht have obligated themselves to the new state in my person, so shall I always regard it as my highest duty to intercede for the existence and inviolability of the Wehrmacht, in fulfilment of the testament of the late Field-Marshal, and in accord with my own will to establish the Army firmly as the sole bearer of the arms of the nation.[292]

The first few days after the oath-taking ceremonies were taken up with the preparations for the funeral of Hindenburg. After preliminary services in Berlin, the body was taken to East Prussia, to the Tannenberg Memorial, for burial on 7 August. Despite all the events of the past few months, the coffin was borne through two guards of honour—the one provided by the Army, the other by the S.A. and S.S.[293] At the ceremony in East Prussia (and while the *Horst Wessel* Song was being sung in St Patrick's Cathedral, Dublin)* Blomberg made further display of his impetuosity by suddenly suggesting to Hitler that the Armed Forces should cease to address Hitler as 'Herr Hitler', and substitute 'Mein Führer' in its stead.[294] Hitler agreed, and another means of confusing the Nazi Party with the State was added to the difficulties of the Wehrmacht.

The new Supreme Commander showed no desire to exert anything other than nominal control over the internal affairs and day-to-day business of the Army.[295] He even dismissed his Wehrmacht Adjutant for a few weeks while he went to Bavaria for a late summer rest.[296] However, some of his subordinates were not content to remain so placid regarding their Führer's interests. A series of inquiries was sent out from the Reichswehr Ministry to all units, to discover if there were any officers who had not yet

---

* A memorial service was held in St Patrick's Cathedral, Dublin, at the same time as the ceremony at the Tannenberg Memorial, which was attended by the Equestrian Team of the German Army which was competing in the Dublin Horse Show. The service ended with the singing of the *Horst Wessel* Song. Afterwards, Mr de Valera said to the leader of the German team, Major von Lenski, 'Germany, beware of England! Don't be deceived by friendly gestures —they are never genuine!' Written report of Major von Lenski to General von Fritsch, 21 August 1934, OKH file H 24/6.

taken the oath. If there were any such officers, their names were to be reported to the Ministry.[297]

On 15 August 1934, Hindenburg's Testament was published on the orders of Hitler.[298] This document, besides extolling the achievements of Hitler and the Nazi Government, stressed the importance of the Reichswehr as a supporting member of the State. 'The guardian of the State, the Reichswehr, must be the symbol of, and firm support for this superstructure (i.e. the new form of state). On the Reichswehr as a firm foundation must rest the old Prussian virtues of self-realized dutifulness, of simplicity, and of comradeship. . . . Always and at all times, the Reichswehr must remain the model of State conduct, so that, unbiased by any internal political development, its high mission for the defence of the country may be put to good account.'[299] How tragically this last sentence was to be mocked by the events of the following years. To several officers, this testament looked too good to be true. Not only were Hitler and the Nazi movement praised, but the status assigned to the Wehrmacht smacked too highly of Nazi propaganda. Whether this Testament was fraudulent or not, is not certain, but it raised many doubts, and caused some schisms within the Reichswehr.[300]

The deep significance of the events following immediately on the death of Hindenburg was illustrated very clearly by the next main task which was assigned to the Army. It was ordered by Hitler to appear at the Party Rally in Nuremberg, to be held in mid-September, and thus to appear as one of the chief supports of Nazism.[301] This was exploited by the Party propaganda machine. In fact the Armed Forces were at the Rally because they were ordered to be. Goebbels, however, published through every means of mass communication which was available to him that the Armed Forces were there because they wanted to publicly demonstrate their support for Nazism. As there was no way of publicly questioning, let alone of denying this, the end result of the obedience of the Armed Forces to what seemed to be a lawful command of the Supreme Commander, was that the Nazi Party was able to transfer a good deal of the respect which was normally accorded by the public to the Armed Forces, to itself.

The actual duties which the Wehrmacht was called upon to perform consisted of large displays of equipment and tactical procedure, marching and drill displays and, at night, spectacular demonstrations of pyrotechnics and searchlights. Most of this took place on a special 'Wehrmacht Day', which was at the end of the week-long rally of speeches and conferences. It was one of the most popular sections of the Party Rally, and became a regular feature until the Rallies ceased at the outbreak of the War. The participation of the Wehrmacht was accompanied by many speeches on various Nazi themes, from the building of the character of the individual to the role of the Wehrmacht in German foreign policy. The strong distaste of the Generals who were ordered to attend was aroused by the Nazi leaders, Himmler, Göring, Goebbels, Ley, and of course, Hitler, who acclaimed to the nation that the Army had become completely National-Socialist, what a strong pillar of the Third Reich the Army was, and how successfully the old class distinctions and similar defects of the

Imperial Army had been eradicated. Hitler boasted of how he had made a 'People's Army' out of the Reichswehr, while the opinions of the Army leaders were kept hidden from the public, except in the cases in which these opinions were of service to the Nazi Party.[302]

All of the senior Generals had been commanded by Hitler to be present at the 1934 Rally. After the great display on the Zeppelin Field, a tattoo was held by the massed bands of the units closest to Nuremberg, in front of the Führer's hotel, the Deutscher Hof, on the broad expanse of the Frauentor Graben, at 10 p.m. The Generals were then invited to dine with Hitler. During the dinner, Hitler made a speech. Weichs claims to have recorded the exact wording of part of this:

I know that you accuse me of many wrong things which exist in the Party. I admit that you are one hundred per cent correct, but you must remember that in the time of struggle, the intelligentsia deserted me, so that I still have to work primarily with personnel of low quality. I am constantly endeavouring to rectify this defect. But just as the construction of the officer corps for the new Armed Forces will take years to complete, so will the creation of a good body of leaders for the Party require even longer time.

Weichs adds:

This was much heeded at the time. . . . We knew Hitler too little at that time to be able to evaluate that sort of speech correctly. Instead of increased confidence, more and more mistrust towards the leaders of the Wehrmacht developed, and the Party leaders went from bad to worse—perhaps out of a mistaken idea of loyalty to old comrades on the part of Hitler, or perhaps because he had poor judgement of people. Or did he want to deceive us, for he knew how to fit his speech to his audience with masterful skill?[303]

Thus we have an indication of the manner in which a representative of the conservative, aristocratic, type of senior officer was thinking. We also have Hitler's own admission that there was noticeable dissatisfaction with the Party on the part of the Generals. The outlook of this type of General to which Weichs belonged, the middle ranking men who did not come into contact with Hitler, or the central organization of the Nazi Party, seemed to be one of limited approval towards the new régime, with Hitler standing much higher in their confidence than the other Nazi leaders. Their trust in Hitler had not apparently been shattered by the events of 30 June 1934. The feeling of relief that the threat of Röhm had been defeated permanently was not tempered by the thought that this might happen to themselves one day, if it suited the convenience of the Führer. Had anybody expressed this view at that moment, he would probably have been branded as an arch-cynic.

Thus, the dreadful significance of the passing of the authority of the Supreme Commander from the hands of Hindenburg to those of Hitler, of the concentration of the major political power of Germany in the hands of one man, and of the obligation of the Army to his will, went largely unnoticed by the senior officers of the German Army. The unification of the offices of President and Chancellor was ratified by the people in a direct vote of apparent enthusiasm. The office of Supreme Commander was filled by a man who had stood up for the true interests of German defence against one of the most powerful proven organizations of the Party. The impreciseness of the Weimar oath had been replaced by one which was in accord with the changed political leadership of Germany and which had the form of the revered oaths which had been sworn to the Kings of the German States, and to the Emperors of Germany. Under these conditions, with the first busy stages of the reconstruction of the Armed Forces in full swing, the Army carried on optimistically, attempting to overcome the bogey of German insecurity from external attack.

5

The Army and Party Ideology

NATIONAL-SOCIALISM attempted to explain all important events and occurrences, from international history to the role of the individual in society, in terms of a unified, coherent, consistent and multifarious set of political beliefs and ideas. The German Army as distinct from a few of its leaders, had shunned the notion of active involvement in politics, in continuance of the traditions of the special relationship between the Head of State and the Army which had existed in Prussia since its formation. This condition had been emphasized throughout the Weimar period, because of the troublesome times, and the small size of the Army, and by the personality of its Commanders, notably Hans von Seeckt. Consequently, the German Army in 1933 stood before National-Socialism like a vacuum about to be unsealed.

The Nazi Party regarded the Army as a target of prime importance. If the Party was to have secure tenure of power and absolute authority it was necessary to convert the Army to Nazism. Long term Nazi policy envisaged German expansion by military conquest and the acceptance of many strategic risks during the development of sufficient military power to achieve the necessary living space. Since the Army was cast in so vital a role for the future of the Third Reich, and was to bear the brunt of the coming struggles, its fidelity to the Party ideology and to the Führer had to be beyond doubt and capable of enduring in the most difficult circumstances.

In addition to the general pressure of Nazism, the Army was the subject of several special notions of Hitler, which probably had their origins in his war experiences. The war was one of the most significant experiences in Hitler's life.[304] He saw it as a glorious life-or-death struggle for the existence of the German people, and regarded the conflict as a good thing in itself. The war taught him nationalism and bravery, ruthlessness and bitterness. He had learnt most of this while in the Army, and he came to regard the Army as a sort of higher school for the whole people, which could teach men the virtues of sacrifice, devotion to a cause, physical courage, toughness and comradeship. He even placed some reliance on this for the prevention of another national collapse of the type which occurred in Germany in 1918-19. He expressed his views in *Mein Kampf*:

Apart from this, this education has to be completed from the point of view of the nation by service in the Army. Thus, in the main, the period of military service shall serve as the conclusion of the normal education of the average German.[305]

The significance of these views for Germany, and for the Army in particular was illustrated by the article on Hitler's birthday in the *Militär-Wochenblatt* of 18 April 1934, which stated:

In National-Socialist Germany, the transfer of the system of values and the decency of the front-soldier to the whole of public life is being completed.[306]

This second line of thought was a very powerful tool. The accompanying dangers are easy to overlook even today when their insidious effects have been so clearly illustrated by recent history. When spoken in conjunction with, or, as often, mixed up inextricably with, a stream of National-Socialist ideology, the result was often a new success for the spreading of National-Socialism throughout the Army. In the early years of his rule, Hitler was able to capture the minds of many soldiers by winning their support in a few military matters and then by exploiting this, he was able to dominate most of their thinking. Hitler worked on the Army as a whole in a similar manner.

The ceremony of the opening of the new Reichstag on 21 March 1933 in the Garrison Church at Potsdam was a symbol of acceptance by the bearers of the traditions of Old Prussia towards the National-Socialist government. For the masses of observers in the lower ranks of the Army, it possibly signified a great deal more—namely acceptance by the old constituted authorities of Nazi ideology in its full extent. It was not known to them that the Commander of Wehrkreis III, Generalleutnant von Fritsch had ordered the Commander of the Potsdam Garrison to see that no salutes were made to the new Chancellor.[307] By appearing to have won the respect of the senior members of the Army, Hitler consolidated his standing in the eyes of the younger soldiers.

The task of the Party was greatly simplified by the keenness of the new Reichswehr Minister. Blomberg had failed to see the difference between the military virtues and National-Socialism. His idealistic outlook on the conduct of warfare was susceptible to expansion into Nazism by the influence of extreme romanticism.[308]

Blomberg's outlook on National-Socialism was described in a speech which he made to the officers of the Sixth Division at the close of autumn exercises, on 15 September 1933. Copies of this speech were printed and sent to all units of the Army and Navy. He began:

I am particularly glad to have the opportunity of speaking to the officers of the Division about the political situation. . . . What is happening today far exceeds the expectations of most people after the Seizure of Power. Many thought of a new political constellation in the same sense as the changes of governments in the past years. Today it is clearly to be seen that the change concerns not only such a political arrangement, but a fundamental transformation of the mind and will of the entire people, and the realization of a new philosophy.

One must always confront the question of what the characteristics of the National-Socialist philosophy are. I see the essentials in the following points:

1. The new concept of the state is founded on the basis of authority. The period of majority decisions, of collecting votes which can combine to achieve political goals is over. The concept of leadership, of the governing of affairs by authority and responsibility alone has taken over completely.

2. An important part of the new philosophy is the doctrine of the subordination of the individual to the whole, expressed by the phrase, 'common good before individual good', or, expressed differently, by the words the totality of the State, which applies right down to the most personal affairs of the individual. The old liberal principle of the predominant freedom of the individual is no longer in force.

3. Sacrifices are bound up with these two requirements, the authority of the leadership, and of the subordination of the individual to the whole. Today, they are made willingly for the most part, but sometimes they are made unwillingly. However, sacrifices are indispensable and must be made out of ready acknowledgement. Then they will prove a blessing to the nation, and thereby to each individual.

He then went on to make several comments with relevance to the rivalry of the S.A., but he did not fail to point out:

On my visits to S.A. camps, I have been convinced of the close personal unity between the leaders and the rankers. Here, the concept of personal administration in the best manner has become a reality. Even we have much to learn here in the field of our never-to-be-questioned concepts of discipline and authority.

In discussing the 'Versailler Diktat', he said that it necessitated close co-operation between the armed forces and the Party. Greater independence of outlook was necessary on the part of commanders in their administrative work, due to the changes of the times. He ended with a comment on the Geneva Disarmament Conference, and an exhortation to patriotic service.*

On 25 May 1934, an important decree entitled 'Wehrmacht and National-Socialism' was issued by Blomberg as an 'Important Political Instruction'. In view of its importance in the conduct of Army-Party relationships in the years which followed its appearance, it is reproduced in full.

WEHRMACHT AND NATIONAL-SOCIALISM

The Wehrmacht since 30 January 1933, has received the place in the National-Socialist State which is its due, on account of its conduct since its foundation, its inner firmness and its unshakeable discipline. The acknowledgement which the Führer, Adolf Hitler, has repeatedly shown to the Wehrmacht, and the respect which the Wehrmacht now enjoys, as great as ever in all informed circles of the German Nation, confirm this view. Of this we wish to be proud.

---

* This speech occurs in several files, due to its wide circulation, e.g. WK VII file 759, and OKH file H 24/6. The copy in the latter file was the copy which Hammerstein read and initialled. This copy has all of the more strongly worded sections sidelined. It is interesting that the speech was printed in the Reichswehr Ministry on 22 September 1933, but it did not reach the 7 (Bavarian) Pioneer Battalion until 10 November 1933.

National thought is the natural basis of all soldierly efforts. However, we do not wish to forget that the philosophy which fills the new state is not only national, but National-Socialist. National-Socialism draws its rule of conduct from the necessities of the life of the whole people, and from the duty to work in concert for the entire nation. It embraces the idea of the fellowship of blood, of the fate of all German people. It is indubitable that this principle is, and also must remain, the foundation of the duty of the German soldier, for the principles of soldierliness and of National-Socialism arise out of the same experiences in the Great War.

However, this principle must not only fill our official labours, but must also dominate our private and social lives. I desire that the officer corps of the Wehrmacht retains the leading position in social conduct, especially in the smaller areas, which it created before the World War and which it has maintained in the difficult years since. For our life in society today, however, this requires a modification and an engagement of wider sections of the community than before. Representative functions are therefore requisite and necessary, where they serve a closer official and comradely connection with authoritative representatives of the new Germany, especially with officials and organizations. They shall be unpretentiously held, and show an individual Wehrmacht style which amalgamates tradition and progress. It can no longer be the task of our officer corps of today to care for society within a certain social class, in accord with the old outlook. The principle of the partnership of the people must pervade all our social conduct. Prejudices which are based on birth and breeding alone have no justification. It may be hard for those individuals, who from a traditional point of view are essential members of society, and who are repelled by this outlook, but nonetheless, it is necessary. Anyone today who does not completely adopt the idea of national partnership, excludes himself. It is not intended, nor is it possible, to define precisely the circle of people who are to be brought into contact, or to give a pattern for social functions. I expect that commanding officers will find the correct path, under the guidance of the above views.

The conducting of social gatherings within the officer corps, and the associated training of junior officers remains as important as ever.

At functions which are attended by N.C.O.s and men, special attention is to be given to see that the officers do not sit apart from the men. They belong, just as much as the N.C.O.s, to their normal formations, or to their guests, according to the nature of the occasion.

I ask that these principles be given the most earnest attention. The reputation of the Wehrmacht amongst the various sections of the German people who cannot observe our official work depends not least upon the execution of these principles.

This order is to be promulgated immediately, word for word, to all officers and is to be made a regular theme for instruction in Wehrmacht schools, and in the corresponding Officers' Training Institutions.[309]

This directive shows the significance of the Socialist part of National-Socialist doctrine, as well as the direction in which Blomberg's political thoughts lay. Once again, the content of this document was a mixture of good and bad. On the one hand, genuine efforts were being made to sweep away the old barriers of class, but on the other, the notion of the identity of the fate of all German people with National-Socialism was subtly propagated throughout the Armed Forces.

The passage of time brought several other general statements of policy such as this from Blomberg. They show a trend towards a stronger National-Socialist line and to a more complete acceptance of the ideas of Hitler. On 16 April 1935, Blomberg issued another long decree, covering many aspects of the Wehrmacht-Party relationship. In the opening he expounded very clearly the full National-Socialist conception of the position of the Armed Forces within the State.

With the introduction of general conscription, the Armed Forces again become the great school of national education. Several times Adolf Hitler has stressed the importance of this task. On 1 May 1934, he gave the Army the task of being, along with the other organizations of the State and the Movement, 'a national and social melting pot for the education of a new German human being'. In his book, *Mein Kampf*, the significance of the Armed Forces for the education of the people is often emphasized. . . . In other places, the Führer designates the completion of military service as the prerequisite for the granting the rights of citizenship. Service in the Armed Forces is therefore the last and highest step in the course of the general education of a young German, from parental home, through school, Hitler Youth, and the Labour Service. *The educational goal of the Wehrmacht is not only the basically trained soldier and the master of a weapon, but also the man who is aware of his nationality and of his general duties towards the State. . . .*
It would be a sign of lack of self control and an absence of political instinct if annoyance over the defects of an individual led to *derogatory criticism and remarks about institutions and organizations which are outside the Wehrmacht.* Careless words in this direction damage the reputation of the Wehrmacht, and decrease the success of its work. *They correspondingly incriminate him who states them.* The Wehrmacht owes its re-birth primarily to the Führer and Reichs Chancellor, and to his political tool, the N.S.D.A.P. The Wehrmacht, S.A., S.S., H.J., Labour Service, Police, etc., are the parts of a whole, which, in separate fields of activity, serve the same aim. Community of purpose and comradeship must link all of these organizations. Every day friction and short-comings, which can never be avoided completely, can easily be magnified to the status of prestige matters, but this is wrong. *The Wehrmacht does not need to pursue prestige politics. Its best propaganda is the successful education of the youth in the spirit of National-Socialism, according to the will of its Supreme Commander.*[310]

Thus, not only was the doctrine that the Army was a part of the general education system of Nazi Germany taught to all soldiers, but they were specifically instructed that they were to be silent about any short-comings of the arrangement. The repression of internal criticism which so often accompanies any large organization was converted from a vice to a virtue, and helped further to prevent the growth of natural forces which would have been able to discard, either wholly or in part, the grip of National-Socialism on German life.
Blomberg continued to issue similar statements of policy until his dismissal in early 1938. They stressed complete trust in the Party on the part of the Wehrmacht, the inseparable nature of the tasks of Party and Wehrmacht, admiration of Hitler, and the undesirability of the small

clashes which were, on Blomberg's own admission, constantly occurring between the Armed Forces and the Party.

While it is perfectly clear that the views of Blomberg, and those of Reichenau and Keitel, who were his chief assistants in the political field, were strongly pro-Nazi, it is difficult to say precisely what the views of those lower down in the military organization were. Certainly there were those who did not see any flaws in what they were told to believe in, and who were ardently National-Socialist in outlook. The new recruits and young officers, who had known little else apart from Nazi philosophy, formed the largest group of National-Socialists within the Army. Older men of a more independent way of thought, such as Fritsch and Beck, comprised a separate group, about which there is but little direct evidence. It is a simple matter to discover who in Nazi Germany were the most active in their support for Hitler, because we have so much documentary evidence of this type. The Third Reich encouraged the production of this material, it disseminated it widely, and preserved it until the collapse in 1945. On the other hand, there are many obvious reasons why opponents of Hitler are difficult to trace by means of documentary evidence.

Yet, in view of the incentives to display Nazi views in the Third Reich, the absence of any such display from the public declarations of anyone who was responsible for leading large numbers of men, is significant. Fritsch did not restrict himself to a purely technical role. From time to time, he issued directives on topics which were very susceptible to treatment in terms of National-Socialist ideology, such as honour, social conduct, duties of an officer, mode of living, etc. Yet his directives were written in terms of his own albeit conservative outlook, avoiding the well-known Nazi dogmas and clichés. These directives were a public indication that the Commander-in-Chief of the Army did not regard National-Socialism as having any great relevance to such topics.[311] As Fritsch was under Gestapo surveillance for most of his term of office,[312] these views must have been known by the Party leaders, who, from 1936 at least were concocting evidence to get rid of Fritsch by one means or another.

After Fritsch had been dismissed, Nazi doctrine became more noticeable in the orders and directives of the Army High Command. His successor, Walter von Brauchitsch,* was a man of a different outlook. While he was not as forceful a character as Blomberg, he was nonetheless able to make his adherence to National-Socialist ideology an influence upon the minds of his subordinates by decrees which were very similar in character to those of Blomberg, with perhaps an additional urgency due to the increase of international tension which occurred in 1938. On 18 December 1938, he issued an order concerning the training of officers. In this he wrote:

Adolf Hitler, our leader of genius, who has recast the great lessons of the front-line soldier in the form of the National-Socialist philosophy, has built and secured for us the new Great-German Reich. Only he who can comprehend the

---

* For a detailed treatment of the character of Brauchitsch, see below, Chapter 11.

yesterday, today and tomorrow in their full difficulty and immensity can appreciate the historic nature of the deeds of this man. The revolution has been stupendous in all fields. A new German being has grown up in the Third Reich, filled with ideas different from those of the generation which went before us. Above and beyond all classes and divisions, a new unique fellowship of the nation has been created, to which we, People, Armed Forces, and Party, all belong.

Our loyalty to the man who has created all this, who by his faith and will has worked this miracle, is unshakeable, our confidence in him is firm.

That National-Socialist thought found more approval amongst the officer corps than anywhere else is obvious. Its basic ideas have always given the Armed Forces guidance. The Armed Forces and National-Socialism are of the same spiritual stem. They will accomplish much for the nation in the future, if they follow the example and teaching of the Führer, who combines in his person the true soldier and National-Socialist.

He then went on to cite a number of points which had been constantly emphasized during the previous years, but which were still offended against from time to time. They included:

1. The officer corps must not be surpassed by anybody in the purity and genuineness of its National-Socialist outlook. It is the banner bearer, and therefore unshakeable, if all else should fail. Naturally, the officer must handle any situation in accordance with the views of the Third Reich, even when such views are not laid down in any instructions, regulations, or official orders. He shall also be the leader of his men with regard to politics. This does not mean that he shall talk a great deal with them over politics, but that he must have command of the basic ideas of National-Socialism, otherwise he cannot answer questions which are put to him, nor can he discuss and correctly explain current affairs matters from this point of view. . . .

3. Social intercourse within the families of officers is necessary for reasons of education. Social life, however, must be kept simple. But it also goes without saying that an officer will seek the company of families outside the officer corps, in which National-Socialist ways of thinking, decency, and good morals prevail. Friendships with people who are outspokenly negatively disposed are to be avoided.[313]

There are many other examples of Brauchitsch's outlook, which are similar in tone to the above extract.[314] It is apparent, then, that the Army was being subjected to a constant stream of indoctrination from the High Command, and that every encouragement was being given by the men of pro-Nazi outlook to those who were in their charge to adopt these views as well. On the other hand, there were those men who did not subscribe to this outlook, and who continued in their own beliefs as isolated individuals, or groups of individuals, for whom it was an offence against orders to express their doubts and criticism, and who would have faced professional and social sanctions for doing so.

Having expressed his support for National-Socialism so clearly, Blomberg had severe difficulties over the question of whether or not soldiers were to be allowed to be Party members, during the time of their military service. This applied particularly to those who came into the Army for short periods, such as the conscripts, who had already been Party members. There was considerable pressure from the officer corps that the old regulations, which forbade membership of political parties to active soldiers, should be upheld.

The first order on the subject came out on 10 March 1934, which stated that in the cases of volunteers who were also members of the Party or its formations, the final decision would be made by the Party. Pending the communication of this decision, the existing regulations which required soldiers to discontinue their membership of such organizations on enlistment were to be ignored.[315] Fritsch indicated his surprise at this ruling by a heavy exclamation mark in the margin of his copy of this order opposite the paragraph which suspended the existing regulations. This matter may not have been decided upon for some time, as the next available order on the subject was issued on 21 June 1935. This stated that 'during military service, membership of the N.S.D.A.P. and its associated organizations shall lapse', but that participation in National-Socialist collections for welfare was 'more than ever desirable', as was membership of the 'Kraft durch Freude' organization.[316] This ruling was extended to Party members while they were on short exercises with the Army, on 30 August 1935, but they were permitted by the same order to continue the payment of their Party dues, so that membership could hardly be said to have ceased at all.[317]

This situation continued to be gradually eroded, despite the efforts of senior non-Nazi soldiers to stem the growth of the privileges of Party members who were in the Army.* Civilian members of the Wehrmacht were permitted to hold Party office under certain conditions, according to an 'Important Political Instruction' from Blomberg on 2 November 1935.[318] On 25 June 1936, Blomberg pointed out that some soldiers' wives had left the National-Socialist Welfare Organization as a result of previous orders. This was not to happen, as the past orders were not applicable to wives, and their membership of the Organization was urgently desired.[319]

The situation went as far as the informing of units that:

It is to be reckoned that the ban on membership of the Party will be relaxed in the foreseeable future. It is in the interests of the Wehrmacht, to induce soldiers who are being discharged to enter the Party.[320]

Despite this, the ban was not lifted, but the degree of 'suspension' of Party membership declined. Leading Party members were permitted, during military service, to participate in Party functions in Army uniform, but not to make speeches, nor to inspect Party formations while wearing Army uniform, as some had been doing.[321]

---

* See for example the instructions imparted to officer cadets in *Richtlinien für den Unterricht im Heerwesen* issued by the Inspekteur der Kriegsschulen as *Nr.* 490/38, In 1 (IIa) of February 1938, p. 27, which state:

All who wear the soldier's coat are to be treated alike, whether they are manual labourers or men who work with their heads, whether Party members or not, rank and class lose all significance, all are recruits with equal rights and duties.

A copy of this instruction is in the possession of its author, Generalleutnant Flörke.

The abuses to which this general situation was open were illustrated by Keitel's order of 27 July 1938, which forbade Party officials from carrying out their military service within the same area in which their particular Party posting lay. The same order stated the Reichsleiter and Gauleiter were no longer to be called upon to attend Army manœuvres.[322] On 15 December 1938, orders were given that young soldiers who were candidates for the Ordensburgen were not to be granted a reduction in their time of military service, but they might be sent on leave. The whole question of Party membership became treated in this way, so that the efforts of those officers in the High Command to stem the influence of Nazism by the application of established regulations with long traditions behind them were largely brought to nought. The reverse sign of the coin was illustrated by the order of 26 May 1936, that politically unreliable soldiers were to be reported to the local Gestapo.[323]

Fourteen months elapsed between the coming to power of the Nazis and the introduction of special instruction in National-Socialist ideology into the Army. Whether the impending crisis regarding the S.A. influenced the Army's readiness to accept such further intrusion of the Nazis on to military ground or not, is not certain, but the introduction came when the crisis was near its height. On 4 April 1934, Blomberg announced the introduction of co-ordinated instruction on current affairs, in an 'Important Political Instruction',[324] which stated:

The first year of the National-Socialist government has laid the foundations for the political and economic reconstruction of the nation. The second year places the emphasis on the spiritual saturation of the nation with the principles of the National-Socialist state. Instruction in accord with this end is therefore an important task for all organizations who support the new state with their will. This applies especially to the Wehrmacht, which is the guardian and protector of National-Socialist Germany and of its territory with respect to the exterior.

I therefore order that in the future, concerning instruction in current political matters in the Wehrmacht, increased significance and greater attention are to be paid to these topics by all units of the Wehrmacht. To facilitate a unified execution of the instruction in current political matters, the content of the teaching will be issued twice monthly by the Reichswehr Ministry as 'Principles for Instruction in Current Political Matters'.

The actual content of these bulletins was simply a condensation of Nazi propaganda, which becomes increasingly boring to read as the years advanced. Initially, they dealt with some really current events, such as the League of Nations, but as these topics became used up, the bulletins became more concerned with the well-known issues of German history, rewritten with a Nazi bias. Their brevity was such that they could not have been of much use to any except the most uneducated soldiers. It is therefore not surprising that Blomberg had to issue the following order on 17 April 1935:

It has come to my attention that the 'Principles for Instruction in Current

Political Matters' are not being given the attention which should be given to them.

I determine and authorize their contents, and they are just as binding as any other official instructions.[325]

An interesting comment on this matter is provided by a Communist propaganda sheet which was intercepted by the Army, and distributed to the troops. It stated:

Of National-Socialism, there is little to be traced in the barracks. Now and then the troops are broken off to hear a speech of the Führer—it is a welcome interruption. In instructional time, there is no mention of National-Socialist philosophy and of the building of the Third Reich—but much is made of the rank structure of the Army.*

Matters became more thoroughly organized at the beginning of 1936. On 30 January, Blomberg ordered the introduction of special political instruction for all officer training schools, for the Staff Colleges, and for the Wehrmacht Academy.[326] The efficient execution of this programme was provided for by the establishment of central political training courses, to be held in Berlin, and run by Party specialists, which were to be attended by all officers who were to become political instructors. The officers who were not at the various academies were provided for by special local courses, conducted within each Wehrkreis, for officers from the appointments of Company Commander to Regimental Commander. The officers who were to conduct these courses were also to attend the central courses in Berlin.

The first of these combined central political training courses took place in Berlin in January 1937.[327] It was well exploited by the Party, and was, according to Blomberg, most fruitful. He liked the idea so much that he set about organizing similar courses throughout the Wehrkreise, in which the instruction was to be carried out by the local Party headquarters, thus further increasing the opportunities for direct penetration of the Army by National-Socialism.[328] A book containing the lectures given at the first Berlin course was produced, and distributed to all sub-units of company strength. From this book regular instruction once weekly was to be given to N.C.O.s and men.[329] Special use was to be made of the summer for units to have visits at the conclusion of exercises, so that they would see more of the strong points of the National-Socialist state in action.[330]

Thus political indoctrination became steadily, year by year, more organized and far-reaching, so that in March 1939, the 17th Division reported a shortage of clothing, but that everyone had been issued with a

---

* This was taken from a long article in the KPD publication *Hammer and Sickle* for June 1935. It was promulgated to all branches of the Wehrmacht by order of Blomberg. 6,986 copies were distributed to the Army, so that every sub-unit of company strength would have one. This was an interesting gesture of confidence on the part of the High Command, as the article made sharp attacks on many matters which may well have deserved criticism, viz: administration, brutal treatment of recruits, attitude of the Generals to the three changes of the form of state since 1918, etc. WK VII file 2196.

copy of an instructional book on Nazism.[331] An entire organization for the systematic indoctrination of the Army into the principles of National-Socialism had been set up, and was working at high pressure. The administration of this system was in the hands of the 1(c) Staff Officers, who usually handled intelligence and other political matters on divisional headquarters and higher levels. This was a subtle system, free of the defects of the Soviet system of Political Commissars. Naturally, the 1(c) men were not called upon to perform tasks of the same nature as the Commissars, but they had much more chance of successfully carrying out the tasks which they were given, because they were primarily soldiers, who had spent most of their lives in the Army, and who had friends throughout it.

Besides formal instruction in the principles of National-Socialism, the Army was subjected to many other forms of indoctrination. Blomberg even went so far as to write National-Socialism into a new directive, describing the 'Duties of the German Soldier', which was issued above Hindenburg's signature, as well as his own, on 25 May 1934.[332] In this, the task of the Wehrmacht was defined as:

The Wehrmacht is the bearer of the arms of the German nation. It protects the German Reich and Fatherland, the people united in National-Socialism, and their living-space.

The Propaganda Ministry began to take some responsibility for conveying the picture of the new, National-Socialist Army to the public. On 9 November 1933, a manual entitled *Instructions for Military Propaganda* was introduced.[333] This gave rise to some disputes as to the degree of control which the Propaganda Ministry was to be allowed to exert over press reports relating to the Army. In the past, the Army had had sole control over what was released to the press, and what was to be kept secret. The situation was temporarily resolved in March 1934, when Reichenau announced that the control of the Propaganda Ministry was only to cover technical naval and army matters. General defence matters, and statements on defence policy were to be released by the Reichswehr Ministry and by its authorized subordinate agencies.[334]

This ruling did not prevent the Propaganda Ministry from giving to the public its own view of the Army and of the stages of its development. At various times, the Army was warned that for the coming few weeks, it would be in the forefront of the output of the Propaganda Ministry, and that the national press had been co-ordinated to give leading articles on such topics as the saturation of the Wehrmacht with National-Socialist thought, and the battle of the Army against the Communists in the early 'twenties.[335]

In practice, it mattered little that the Reichswehr Ministry had retained control of publicity in general defence topics. This control was placed in the charge of the Wehrmachtsamt, and its various successors, which were controlled by Reichenau till October 1935, and then by Keitel. A special chain of officers was established to administer Army publicity, from the Ministry, to local units, which significantly by-passed Fritsch, by going straight from the Ministry to the Wehrkreis headquarters.[336] The type of material issued by this publicity controlling system was little different in political content to that issued by the Propaganda Ministry. Confidential instructions from the War Ministry, as the Reichswehr Ministry was known from 21 May 1935, issued on 8 January 1936, stressed that the inner unity of the Army with National-Socialism was to be publicized by measures such as press reports of Army assistance for charity, and the *Winterhilfe*, and of Army officers giving lectures at Nazi Party schools.[337]

Simultaneously, the Propaganda Ministry was actively disseminating instructional material of a political nature throughout the Armed Forces. The prime means employed was through newspapers, such as the *Völkischer Beobachter*, the main Nazi Party paper. All units of the Armed Forces were given state funds for the purchase of this, and other approved papers.[338] Also, large numbers of books and pamphlets which had been produced by the Propaganda Ministry, were made available free, or perhaps more effectively, at very low prices. Reading rooms were provided for the troops, and naturally they contained mainly propaganda material.[339] Restrictions were placed on the newspapers which the Armed Forces were permitted to take, particularly those which were distributed free, except those which had been approved of by the War Ministry.[340] However, approval was not given to all Nazi publications. In October 1938, it was stated by OKW that it was not necessary for units of the Army to purchase Streicher's notorious *Der Stürmer*, and that Streicher's speeches were not to be classed as 'training literature'.[341]

A major onslaught was made by the Party on religion. Christianity had been established as an integral part of the Army for many years. Official chaplains were provided for, regular hours were allotted for religious instruction, and church parades were normally attended by most soldiers on Sundays. The nationalistic religious movement called the Deutsche Glaubensbewegung which had grown up during the late 'twenties and early 'thirties was strongly anti-Christian in outlook, and strife was introduced into the religious life of the Army as a result. The Deutsche Glaubensbewegung had been encouraging Germans to withdraw from whatever Christian church they belonged to. On 1 September 1934, Blomberg promulgated to the Army a letter which he had written to the Minister for the Interior on this topic. In this he wrote:

The Führer has declared in his speech in Hamburg: 'The National-Socialist state confesses itself to positive Christianity. It will be my honourable task to protect the two great Christian denominations in their rights, to guard their teachings from attacks, and to establish harmony between their duties and the beliefs and necessities of the present-day state.'
I see a danger to the discipline and battle-readiness of the Wehrmacht in the discussion of religious controversies, and therefore hold even withdrawal from the church to be undesirable.[342]

This illustrates the position of relative strength of Christianity within the Wehrmacht in the early years of Nazi rule. This position was gradually eroded. Officially in the Weimar Republic religious matters had been left as a voluntary matter for the individual soldier. In particular, this meant that soldiers could not be ordered to attend church parades. Seeckt had administered religious matters largely in accordance with the customs of the old Prussian Army, however, and this meant that church attendance was regarded as a good thing in itself, and that officers were permitted to exhort their soldiers to attend.[343] This state of affairs was still in force in the early days of the Third Reich.[344] On 29 May 1935, Blomberg issued new principles in an 'Important Political Instruction', to make it quite clear to every soldier that any form of coercion was illegal. Blomberg stated that:

1. Participation of soldiers in Sunday church parades was desired, but left voluntary. The commanding of soldiers to attend church was forbidden.

and

4. Military ceremonies with religious dedications as a part of them, were to be regarded as normal duty.[345]

In April, 1937, Blomberg issued a revised form of this instruction, with two additional points, viz:

5. The participation of soldiers in 'Barrack Evening Hours' (religious instruction conducted by Army Chaplains) was now voluntary, instead of obligatory.
6. 'Barrack Evening Hours' were no longer to take place for reserve troops.[346]

Thus, despite the passage of four years, the Nazi régime had done little to alter the status of religion for the Army, beyond the addition of a few minor restrictions.

In the interval between these two instructions, three other directives on religious affairs, classified as 'Important Political Instructions' appeared. On 3 December 1935, Blomberg stated specifically that chaplains were to use absolutely no form of compulsion, direct or indirect, to influence non-believers.[347] On 14 February 1936, he ordered that only the nominated unit chaplain was to be permitted to minister to the spiritual needs of the soldiers, and as a consequence, he ordered that the distribution of religious magazines and tracts within the Wehrmacht was to be forbidden.[348] Finally, on 3 March 1936, Blomberg ordered that the collection of votes on the 'question of the Evangelical Church' was not to be carried out within the Wehrmacht, 'because it is not in accordance with the strong reserve and impartiality of the Wehrmacht in religious matters'.[349]

These directives, plus the evidence given by the personal correspondence of General der Artillerie Dollmann[350] indicate grave concern on the part of some senior officers that more accommodation was necessary from the Party in order to avoid a break between Church and State. They also show that during these years, a series of small battles was being fought by clergymen, chaplains, and some officers, to maintain the independence of the churches, and to keep the relations between Church and State as harmonious as possible. From 1 October 1935, these matters had to go through Keitel, who had succeeded Reichenau as head of the Wehr-machtsamt.* Keitel's views on the subject were given in one of his letters to Dollmann thus:

Church matters are so difficult that we do any good only if we leave them entirely alone. . . .
It is necessary that we confine ourselves to our own sphere of work.[351]

Dollmann must have come to accept the notion of the primacy of the state over the church in fields in which the state was vitally concerned. The notes of a talk which he gave to the Catholic chaplains of Wehrkreis IX, probably in 1937,[352] illustrate his outlook. In this talk, he said:

You may not introduce any political strife into the Wehrmacht. You may attend only to those soldiers who approach you voluntarily.
The soldier must never be placed in a dilemma internally by the fulfilment of voluntary religious duties. The Oath which he has taken to the Führer and Supreme Commander of the Wehrmacht, binds him unto the sacrifice of his own life to National-Socialism, the concept of the new Reich. It follows then, that no doubts may be permitted to arise out of your attitudes towards National-Socialism. The Wehrmacht, as one of the bearers of the National-Socialist state, demands of you as chaplains, at all times, a clear and unreserved acknowledgement of the Führer, State, and People.

To what extent these views of Dollmann are typical of the outlook of senior officers, is not known. Certainly at that time, Fritsch was fighting for freedom from National-Socialist interference in religious matters.[353] But Dollmann is not known to have been particularly strong in his admiration for Nazism, so there were probably other Generals who were influenced similarly by the growth of the power of Nazism, to change their ideas from those of Prussian tradition to ones which were more in agreement with those of the Third Reich.

Reichenau's outlook was shown in a list of discussion points, compiled for the division commanders of Wehrkreis VII, in December 1936.[354] This stated that chaplains who used the allotted hours of religious instruction for expressing disagreement with the teachings of Nazism, were to be replaced by more suitable men.

By 1938, the situation had declined to a point where a local administrator, Kreisleiter Bohl, was able to denounce an army chaplain before an audience of 130 women in Hofgeismar on 25 January, for the commission

---

* The date of Reichenau's transfer to the command of Wehrkreis VII, Munich, is given in Weichs, *op. cit.*, and by Berthold Jakob, *Das Neue Deutsche Heer und seine Führer*, Paris, 1936, p. 115, as 1 October 1935. The former Commander of Wehrkreis VII, General Wilhelm Adam, a former Chief of the General Staff himself, dismissed in 1933, probably for his association with groups who were hostile to Hitler, was posted to Berlin as Commandant of the new Wehrmacht Akademie, on 1 October 1935. An article in *The Times* of 28 August 1937, states that Reichenau was transferred to Munich in August 1935. The main force behind Reichenau's departure from Berlin, it went on, was Fritsch. Blomberg did not want to fight Fritsch on the issue, and Hitler would not intervene on Reichenau's behalf. The report purports to have been written by an officer from the Reichskriegsministerium who had just fled to England.

of high treason, because he was anti-Nazi. Bohl added that the chaplain would not be forgotten, but dealt with at the right time. In Bohl's opinion, all chaplains were blackguards—Christianity and Judaism were one, and whoever based his life on the Bible was not a citizen of Germany, but of Palestine.[355] Although Army demands for an investigation of this address were made to Gauleiter Weinrich of Kassel, no result has been shown by the remaining documents.

It is possible that the attack on the Christian religion in the Army was weakened by the emphasis on the Jewish question. The matter of soldiers shopping in Jewish businesses was raised in conjunction with the doctrine of the S.A.,* and Blomberg advised that this was an undesirable practice. In February 1934, the 'Aryan paragraph' was applied to the Wehrmacht, ten months after its application to the Civil Service.† Although the immediate casualties of this were few in number, the effect on the mental attitudes of soldiers must have been considerable, and very few further instructions on the matter were necessary for the Wehrmacht.

The consequences of the application of Nazi racial policy to the Army were varied. While there were many officers who did not hate Jews fervently, there were also many who did not think that the matter was worth provoking trouble over. Recorded incidents of resistance to the application of the Party racial doctrine are few, but there are sufficient to show that this was a cause of Army-Party friction throughout the life of the Third Reich.[356] One of those who attempted to assist the Jewish officers and soldiers who were dismissed from the Army was Beck. On 16 May 1934, he gave a dinner for the foreign military attachés at the Hotel Kaiserhof in Berlin. At this dinner, one of Beck's staff officers spoke with the Chinese attaché, about finding appointments for the dismissed Jewish soldiers and officers with the German mission in China. The Chinese attaché replied that he did not think that this would be possible, as relations between the Chinese Government and the Nazi Party were too close to permit such a loophole to be made.

The views of Fritsch on the Jewish question, while not necessarily contradictory to those of Beck, show a marked anti-Jewish prejudice in the matter of officers' wives. On 21 December 1934, as part of a long decree on general ethical matters, he wrote:

It must be a matter of course that an officer seeks his wife only in the Aryan groups of the nation.[357]

On the other hand, an order of Fritsch's of 15 January 1936 showed that he did not want the Jewish question to be a source of disharmony within the Army, and it may even have been issued with the aim of ameliorating conditions for non-Aryan officers or the non-Aryan wives of officers. This order stated:

I expect from the spirit of comradeship of the officer corps that officers will

* See above, p. 36.
† See above, p. 38.

refrain absolutely from any conjectures or spreading of rumours about the non-Aryan ancestry of a comrade or of his wife.

and

Any correspondence on the non-Aryan ancestry of an officer is to be treated as a secret matter.[358]

The question of soldiers frequenting Jewish shops was finally decided by an order from Blomberg on 15 July 1935. This stated that:

It conflicts with the duty of the Wehrmacht as one of the responsible schools of the new state when soldiers shop in non-Aryan businesses.
I ask that commanders will take care, by means of oral instruction in suitable form, that the basic National-Socialist attitude in this regard also becomes generally current in the Wehrmacht, and that violations of this will be avoided in the future.[359]

Blomberg also expressed his views on the subject of marriage in an order of 1 April 1936, which said that a soldier's bride must be of German, or similar blood. If one grandparent was Jewish, then a woman was not of the correct blood.[360]

However, it must have seemed necessary to Hitler that he emphasize the racial policy within the Wehrmacht himself. On 13 May 1936, he issued the following decree:

The National-Socialist concept of state demands the nurturing of the idea of race, and of a specially selected group of leaders from people of pure German, or similar blood.
It is therefore a natural obligation for the Wehrmacht to select its professional soldiers, hence its leaders, in accordance with the strictest racial criteria above and beyond the legal regulations, and so to obtain a selection of the best of the German people in the military school of the nation.
I require that the Wehrmacht is aware of this responsibility to People and to Fatherland.
The Minister for War will ensure the unified application of this within the Wehrmacht.[361]

This was followed by a detailed instruction, describing how professional soldiers were to be selected for their racial background, and expressly forbidding the marriage of professional soldiers with women of non-Aryan stock. But as these principles were already in application, by virtue of the application of the 'Aryan paragraph', this is more interesting from the point of view of Hitler's attitude towards the Wehrmacht, than for any effect which it achieved. After this order, the Jewish problem took the form of a myriad of small incidents, involving soldiers who patronized Jewish shops, and the protests of the many officers who objected to the content of Streicher's *Stürmer*. Although the campaign against Jews was strongly stressed by Nazi propaganda, and made much of in the press, the effects of it within the Army were small. There were not many Jewish soldiers to begin with, it was possible to hide some of these within the Army, while the main battle was conducted in German civilian life by the full power of the Party and its associated propaganda and terror media.

Another part of the ideological programme of the Nazi Party was the eradication of Freemasonry. The Craft of Frederick the Great and Kaiser Wilhelm I was strongly represented amongst the officers whose families had a tradition of Freemasonry running through them. On 26 May 1934, Blomberg ordered that no member of the Armed Forces might belong to a Masonic Lodge, any who did belong were to leave their lodges at once, and any infringement of the order was to be punished by instant dismissal from the Services.[362] On 7 October 1935, in an 'Important Political Instruction', Blomberg laid down that amongst the principles which were to be applied to the selection of officers, the following were to be included:

1. Former Freemasons were not to be considered for appointment.

2. Applicants who were Freemasons, but who had resigned from their lodges before 1 October 1932, and who had not taken the Third Degree, might be considered, after the following points had been investigated:

    (a) the reputation of the lodge
    (b) the period of membership
    (c) the individual political background of the applicant.[363]

Eleven days later, Blomberg ordered that all officer-candidates were to sign an affidavit to the effect that they had never been Freemasons.[364] He was forced to modify this position, however, by the pressure of numbers, and on 18 March 1936, he ordered:

In view of the large number of Freemasons who wish to join the Wehrmacht, I am inclined to allow individual cases on their merits, where men have taken the Third Degree, especially if they have fought in the World War.[365]

It is almost impossible to tell what effect the attempts to suppress Freemasonry within the Army had. The question did not rise to the surface again after this decree, except in inquiries by the Gestapo concerning the background of suspected Freemasons.[366] In view of one of the statements contained in a Gestapo communication to the War Minister, of July 1936, viz.:

. . . there have been no lodges who have not been more or less hostile to the concept of National-Socialism.[367]

it would not be surprising if several small groups of resistance grew out of the convenient secrecy provided by Masonry.

The next ideological thrust of the Party was in the direction of family life. On 6 September 1936, Blomberg issued a decree entitled 'Administration by Block and Cell Directors'. This described the way in which the whole of Germany was being divided up into groups of from 40 to 60 households, which were to be formed into 'Blocks', while 6 to 8 Blocks were to be administered as a 'Cell'. The Directors of the Blocks and Cells were charged with the duties of propagating National-Socialism, recruiting for the various Party organizations covering every age-group and both sexes, and handling general questions, investigations and complaints Some attempt to guarantee personal privacy and security of information was made, but only in a very loose form.

Blomberg declared that he regarded the formation of this system as the most timely opportunity 'to confirm the German people in National-Socialist thought, and to weld them together in an unshatterable unity'. He went on to state that he had informed the Government that he had no objections to the administration of the families of soldiers, as long as the Party confined its attentions to these, and not to the soldiers themselves. As far as married soldiers were concerned, he had agreed to contact being made with them by the Party on a personal basis, and to occasional discussions of views, as long as official military matters were not touched upon.[368]

By these means, Blomberg had opened the way for Nazism to penetrate into the home and family life of most members of the Army. Nazi Party officials were given access to the private lives of Army members and their dependents, for the purposes of soliciting 'voluntary' labour, selling tickets, badges, books and propaganda material of all kinds. The Block and Cell Directors were officially restrained from using coercion as part of their work, but many incidents showed that this regulation had no effect. In some cases, the wives of the soldiers were subjected to various pressures, in order to extract money for this or that charity or Party fund. In others, soldiers themselves were asked to fill in long questionnaires, or to tolerate exhaustive cross-examination on the subject of their political views and what they knew of orthodox Nazism. The OKH files dealing with friction between the Army and the Party are full of details of this kind from this time onwards. There must have been many soldiers who felt that they had been betrayed by Blomberg for allowing the privacy of their home life to be shattered.

The steady infiltration of Nazism into the Army was continued by many other means. Party leaders had to be invited to social functions,[369] politically unreliable soldiers had to be reported upon to the Gestapo[370] and barracks had to be named 'after the members of the N.S.D.A.P. who had fallen for the freedom of Germany'.[371] All this contact between the Army and the Party resulted in a steady growth of friction on all levels. The Army felt often that it was being encroached upon by political matters, while many members of the Party felt that the Army was not pulling its weight in the new Germany and that it was becoming a harbour for reactionary views.

On 28 January 1936, the Commander of Wehrkreis IX, General Dollmann, issued a directive, stressing the following points:

1. In the Party, particularly in the lower ranks, some mistrust of the inner attitude and conduct of the officer corps exists.

This mistrust is based on a series of incidents which are inclined to give the picture that the officer corps stood in opposition towards the concept of state and outlook, represented by the Party. They believe that the officer corps inclines more to the circles who reject the present state, and hence are of the opinion that these circles regard the officer corps as their ultimate support. This is undesirable.

2. It must be clearly recognized that the Party is deliberately intolerant (Principle of Totality), in order to achieve its goals.

With this consciously subjective, fighting attitude, particular utterances and incidents can occur which do not always quite withstand a purely rational and objective examination. This must be accepted. We must share a common front with the Party.

3. The officer corps must have confidence in the representatives of the Party. Party opinions should not be examined or rejected. By doing this, the officer corps has given rise to the impression, that, in many cases, it is the attorney of people and views against whom the Party is fighting politically.

Decisions from higher Party Headquarters are *official* and therefore are *binding* for us.

5. In order to show outwardly a positive attitude towards the Party, I want attention paid to the following points:

(a) In every officers' mess, etc., *worthy* pictures of the Führer and Supreme Commander, as well as of Field-Marshal von Hindenburg, are to be displayed in a *prominent* place. Finance is available. Pictures and busts of the Kaiser and of other Royal personages are to be put into a special 'tradition room'.

(b) No functions are to be held in officers' messes by groups which are disapproved of by the Party. No Kaiser's Birthday celebrations are to take place.

(c) Talks may be given only by people without political bias, and who will speak in a National-Socialist sense.

(d) It is desired that the wives of officers take an active part in the National-Socialist League of Women.

(g) Social contacts with the Party, and not only with leaders, are to be built up.

In conversations off-duty, officers must always show a positive attitude towards National-Socialism.

(i) Regarding the selection of officers, Party circles have reported discrimination against them. This is to cease. Only military proficiency is to be considered.

It lies in our own interests that as many members of the Party as possible come into more friendly contact with the officer corps, through their appointment to reserve commissions.

(k) Military Chaplains must show a positive acknowledgement towards National-Socialism.

In conclusion, I make it the urgent duty of all Commanders to ensure, by example and by education, that the conduct of every single officer, in every case becomes positively National-Socialist. The Wehrmacht must be exemplary in its thought and inner conduct, in order to be able to reject any doubts as irrelevant and unjustified from the outset.[372]

Whether this instruction originated with Dollmann, or was transmitted by some confidential means from the War Ministry, is not known. However, there is ample evidence, from photographs and from the memories of those who experienced this phase, that similar things were occurring throughout the German Army. After the dangers of 1934 had passed away, and the rate of Nazi indoctrination had increased, tension mounted, leading to many measures similar to the ones outlined above by Dollmann.

By mid-1937, it was necessary for a special directive to be produced, in Wehrkreis VII, Munich, at least, on the subject of insults to the Wehrmacht and to its members.[373] This directive went as far as to outline the exact procedure which was to be followed in cases in which the insults were made by members of the Party.

On 4 November 1937, Blomberg issued a directive entitled 'Incidents involving the Wehrmacht and the Party'.[374] The basis of settlement in all cases was to be confidential personal contact between the divisional commander of the soldier or soldiers concerned, and the local Kreisleiter. If this failed to produce results, then the matter was to be taken to the next highest level, on both sides, and so on. How effective this procedure was from the point of view of the Army is unknown, but in view of all the physical and ideological sanctions which Party leaders could exert, both over any soldier who had got into trouble with the Party, and over the Army officer who had to carry out the negotiations on behalf of the Army, it is likely that this procedure made it easier still for the Party to shape the political thought and conduct of the Army as a whole.

On 3 December 1937, another chain of frictional incidents was brought to a formal settlement. Since the first Party members had begun military training under the Army, a series of complaints about the Army had been made to Party Headquarters by Party members who were serving with the Army. These complaints ranged over topics from the political outlooks of individual officers, to questions of administration and welfare. The general character of these complaints was vindictive, and Blomberg attempted to stop the practice by an 'Important Political Instruction' of 28 May 1934.[375]

This order was impossible to put into effect without the close co-operation of the Party in reporting offenders to the Army. Apparently, this was not done—in some cases, it was actively undermined by Party organizations such as the S.A. and S.S., who encouraged their members to report on their superiors while on military service. This had become such an accepted thing in some Party circles, that incidents occurred in which the Party member sent a copy of his report to his Company Commander, if the report was a favourable one.[376] Blomberg immediately protested about this to Hess,[377] but the result does not appear to have been complete victory for Blomberg, as these incidents continued. This is not surprising, considering the activities of Hess. Hess was striving for the establishment of a Party Complaint Centre, to be set up within the Wehrmacht, so that soldiers could make complaints directly to the Party organization.[378] Hess approached Fritsch, for the services of Hitler's military adjutant, Hossbach, to run the Centre, so that it would have been directly under Hitler. Hossbach and Fritsch were agreed that such a step would have been disastrous for the maintenance of discipline and efficiency, and the matter was strongly opposed by the Army. Whether Hess took this matter to Hitler or not, is unknown, but the Complaint Centre was never set up.

Finally, Hess's directive of 3 December 1937 laid down that no Party members would be permitted to make reports on the Wehrmacht, during their period of service.[379] This directive is also interesting on account of its tone. Throughout its length, it talks down to the Wehrmacht High Command, and shows quite clearly to all who read it that its author regarded or at least wished his readers to regard the Wehrmacht as being under the control of the 'Movement', as well as of Hitler.

These, then, were the major steps by which the Nazi Party came to exercise control over the political outlook of the members of the Army. Nazi ideology cast the Army in the role of a school of patriotic education for the whole German people. This may have coincided with the views of the senior Army leaders—almost certainly they saw nothing in this to oppose. In a western democratic state, this spirit is often combined with the various other justifications which are given for National Service. In Nazi Germany, this outlook was exploited deeply and widely by the Party for the purposes of gaining control over the greater part of the mental activity of the Armed Forces. The concept of educating the 'whole man' was used to support the introduction of National-Socialist indoctrination on a wide scale.

At the same time, the other main features of intellectual and moral life, such as the press, religion, and family life, were also being brought under the influence of National-Socialism. Everywhere a German soldier turned, after 1935, he became subject to some Party influence or other. Some of this was introduced through the active desire of Blomberg to see the whole Wehrmacht united behind Hitler and the new Germany. Other parts were brought about by his passive consent. There is much evidence of his active co-operation with the Party, and little of any resistance. In many ways he bears the prime responsibility for the inability of the Wehrmacht to offer more resistance to Hitler than it did. In this he was greatly assisted by both Reichenau and Keitel, the two heads of the Wehrmachtsamt during this period.

But this is not to absolve automatically the senior Army leaders, such as Fritsch, Beck, and the Wehrkreis Commanders. This question is complicated by a lack of specific evidence. Men who knew Fritsch well during this period, such as Manstein, Heinrici, Viebahn, Hossbach, Halder, Erfurth and Foertsch have all reported his opposition to these measures, and that he protested frequently to Blomberg about their introduction, but how these protests finished up, and their exact nature is unknown, except in the broadest outlines. We do know that Fritsch was becoming increasingly anxious in 1937, and that his health had begun to deteriorate.[380] There is also evidence of weariness and resignation in his letters to the Baroness von Schutzbar-Milchling. It is possible that, as he was under the direct command of Blomberg and Hitler, he made protests as a matter of course, believing himself obliged to carry out the orders of his superiors when the protests met with no response. He may also have been haunted by fears of the consequences of his being replaced by his old rival, Reichenau, and have believed it to have been his duty to carry on, despite everything, in the hope that at least Germany's military security from outside attack would be guaranteed by the reconstruction of the Armed Forces. Consequently, there may have been justification for

Fritsch's behaviour, but until more evidence is discovered on this specific issue, it is possible neither to free Fritsch completely from responsibility for the dissemination of a powerful political ideology throughout the Army, nor to condemn him for it.

The reactions of the other generals followed on from those of Blomberg and Fritsch. On the one hand, there were those who regarded the dissemination of Nazism within the Army with favour, or equanimity, as did Brauchitsch, Reichenau and Dollmann. On the other, there were those who opposed the political indoctrination of the Army, such as Beck, Weichs and Ulex. They saw that Fritsch was able to achieve little against this, and that the only thing to be done was to cut their losses in the political fight, and set about their actual military duty, leaving politics to the politicians. This suited the Party admirably. Its co-ordinated policy of indoctrination was able to gather gradual momentum, assisted by the successes of Hitler's foreign policy. The effectiveness of this policy was to be shown by the hesitation which was induced in the minds of those generals who considered armed revolt in 1938 and 1939, and by the tenacity with which many soldiers clung to Nazi beliefs throughout the war. The predominant mood was appropriately summed up by the commander of the Seventeenth Division, Generalleutnant Friderici, in his farewell address to the division before his re-posting, on 30 March 1939, thus:[381]

The Führer Adolf Hitler gives us the example. We will follow him gladly into the German future—come what will!

6

Rearmament and its Political Effects on the Army

THE relative weakness of the German Army after the First World War with respect to the armies of the other large nations of Europe had bound it together, unified under the leadership of Seeckt, in an attempt to win back sufficient military strength to ensure the security of Germany from outside attack. From the early 'twenties, the Reichswehr had been planned and administered as a cadre for expansion. Despite the immediate political difficulties, Seeckt never lost sight of the ultimate aim of an Army which would be able to prevent a foe from crossing Germany's borders. When Seeckt went into retirement, his aims were continued under the direction of Heye. In the years 1927-30, great use was made of Russian facilities for the development of weapons such as the tank and the aircraft, and for the training of men in the techniques of their use.[382] When Hammerstein succeeded Heye in 1930, the same policy of preparation for an eventual re-expansion of the Army was continued in greater detail.

Throughout these years, the demand for rearmament had been led by the parties of the right wing. As National-Socialism gained in strength, so the leadership of this demand passed into the hands of Adolf Hitler. One of the avowed aims of the Nazi Party was the destruction of the system laid down by the Treaty of Versailles. This aim was proclaimed in *Mein Kampf*, in speeches, Party literature, election campaigns, and on the several occasions, such as the trial of Scheringer, Ludin and Wendt, at Leipzig in September 1930,* at which Hitler had the chance to speak his message directly to the Army itself. As the fortunes of Nazism rose, so did the optimism of many anxious officers. By 1932, Hitler was not the only German political leader who was working for the restoration of equal rights for Germany in the military field. Brüning had made deliberate efforts to prepare the way for the international acceptance of a rearmed Germany during his last year of office, but his lack of success led to greater coincidence of views between the Army and the Nazi Party.

Thus, the Nazis had created a favourable disposition towards themselves within the Reichswehr. On coming to office, they lost no time in proclaiming that rearmament was still their policy, and they set about bringing it into reality. The question of rearmament was one of the

* See above, p. 4.

strongest links between the Nazi Party and the German Army, both in the days of speculating during the Weimar Period, and in the time of application in the Third Reich. Earlier chapters have described how the Nazis exploited the position of the Army for internal ends. The manner in which the Nazis honoured the promises which had made political domination significantly easier remains to be investigated.

Army plans for increasing its manpower had been prepared before Hitler came to power, but only the smallest attempts had been made at putting them into effect. As a result of the 'Five Power Declaration' of 11 December 1932, by which the disarmament clauses of the Treaty of Versailles were to be replaced by a convention, in which Germany should possess 'equality of rights in a system which would provide security for all nations',[383] the Reichswehr Ministry ordered that a small increase of the strength of the Army was to take place after 1 April 1933. Normally, the Reichswehr had two annual intakes of men, in April and October, to replace the men who had been discharged during the previous six months. In this case, the April intake was also to provide sufficient cover for those who were due to be discharged during the following three months. This raised the strength of the Army from approximately 100,000 to 102,500.[384]

Until this time, the Reichswehr Ministry had borne the burden of defence planning alone. A Cabinet decision of 4 April 1933, made defence the concern of all relevant Ministries, by the formation of the Reichs Defence Council.[385] This Council was chiefly concerned with the wider aspects of defence, such as the provision of equipment, the co-ordination of industry, and the planning of full civilian mobilization. Apart from this, not a great deal more was done to strengthen German defences during 1933. In the latter part of the year, after Beck had become Chief of the General Staff, plans were made for the number of infantry divisions to be increased in the near future from seven to eleven.[386] During this time, the actual strength of the Army had been increased by between ten and twenty thousand without actually increasing the number of men officially employed. This was achieved by deceptive moves, such as making men auxiliary personnel after their basic training, so that their places might be occupied by additional recruits.[387]

During this time the much discussed trebling of the strength of the Army became the subject of disputation and trials. Beck was not in favour of as rapid an increase as the sponsors of the idea suggested, and it was another year before the original plan was put into effect.[388] However, this did not prevent experiments in this direction. In the autumn of 1933, the third battalion of Infanterie Regiment 9 was expanded into a regiment under its old commander, Oberstleutnant von Gablenz. Confirmatory exercises were then conducted for three days, against two battalions of the Potsdam garrison, under the command of Oberst von Weichs. The new Regiment Gablenz proved to be surprisingly good.[389]

Exactly when the decision was taken to go ahead with the plan for trebling the Army is not certain. Meinck[390] mentions as a possible beginning the demand of the German Government of 11 December 1933, which called for expansion of the Army to 300,000 men. However, it should not be forgotten that Hitler had spoken to Sir Eric Phipps, the new British Ambassador to Germany, on 24 October 1933, and had asked for a convention to permit Germany to raise an army of 300,000 men. The convention was to run for eight years. Whether the correspondence between the time of expiry of this convention, Hitler's estimate of the life of the current German prosperity, and the date by which the Army was to be ready for attacking, according to Hitler's speech of 28 February 1934,[391] is purely coincidental, is not known. What is important is that the intention to treble the size of the Army was passed on to the officers of the staff of Wehrkreis V, Stuttgart, by Generalleutnant Liebmann on 15 January 1934.[392] From this it may be deduced that the firm decision to treble the Army was made not later than the end of 1933.

At the same time, the Luftwaffe was being formed. This required the transfer of some thousands of men from the Army to the Air Force. The Army was informed of this on 1 April 1934, when the Wehrkreise were called upon to supply quotas of N.C.O.s and men for the Luftwaffe.[393] These losses were more than counterbalanced by the inflow of recruits which resulted from a recruiting drive held in the first months of 1934. For this, recruiting offices and staffs had been set up by the Army throughout Germany.[394] Results were good, and between 50,000 and 60,000 men entered the Army on 1 April 1934.[395] These men were absorbed into the existing organization by the creation of special training battalions.[396]

The summer of 1934 was devoted to planning for expansion to 21 divisions of infantry, apart from the demands made on the Army's time by the S.A. crisis. On 1 October a new organization was introduced. This provided for 21 divisions of infantry, three of cavalry, the enlargement of the Wehrkreis headquarters to approximately the size of corps headquarters, and the establishment of 23 Wehrgauleitungen, distributed throughout the Wehrkreise in a manner corresponding to the 21 former infantry regiments, apart from Berlin and Hamburg.[397] On the same day, an additional 70,000 recruits entered the Army, bringing the total strength to 240,000.[398] The defence budget was increased by 172 million Reichsmarks to 654 million.[399]

This was a staggeringly rapid increase in strength for peace-time conditions, and it did not proceed without objections being raised from within the Army. The leader of the protest was Generalleutnant Beck. In reply to a memorandum from the Allgemeines Heeresamt, he wrote on 20 May 1934, that the trebling of the Army was:

. . . not a building up of a peace-time army, but a mobilization.[400]

However, Beck's views did not prevail, and the resources of the Army were forced to extend themselves to train three times the number of men for which they had been designed.

The recruits who had entered the Army before the end of 1934 had all been volunteers. However, the High Command had realized that volunteers could not supply the whole of Germany's needs, and that conscription was necessary. This had been supported by Hitler from the very beginning of his period of office,* and so the main expansion plans of the Army had been made on the basis of conscription from the outset. What a difference this must have seemed to the atmosphere of extreme caution and fear which had so often accompanied the approach of the various governments of the Weimar period!

The Army was still not inclined to throw caution completely aside, and it kept a close watch on the state of public opinion in the most important foreign countries. A large collection of foreign press accounts of German infringements of the Treaty of Versailles was completed on 13 October 1934,[401] and special attention was paid to Czech press reports of late November 1934, to the effect that Fritsch had written a long memorandum to Hitler, on the reorganization of the Army.[402]

The question of conscription soon attracted the attention of other organizations which had been hoping to benefit from the services of the youth of Germany. The Reichs Arbeits Dienst had plans for the construction of public works which called for the entire youth of Germany to serve in its ranks for two years. The Army was aware at this stage that the minimum period for which it would require men to serve was one year, while there were strong grounds for holding that a two-year period of service would be necessary. If the ambitions of the Arbeits Dienst were to be met at the same time, then each young man would have been required to give four years of service to the state. The Army held that this was quite unreasonable, and a sharp struggle for Hitler's favour ensued between the Reichs Arbeits Dienst on the one hand, and the Army on the other. Reichenau's leadership of the Army's campaign was successful, and Hitler decided that six months' service would have to content the R.A.D.[403] However, this clash had other and more immediate repercussions. It was necessary for Fritsch to order that voluntary recruits could be taken from the Reichs Arbeits Dienst only after they had completed six months of service with the R.A.D., and that Army recruiting staffs were to stay clear of the R.A.D., allowing any necessary liaison to be conducted by the local Gauleitung.[404]

For the following few months, the rearmament question was dominated by considerations of foreign policy.[405] The matter was brought to a head by Hitler's announcement of the existence of the Luftwaffe, on 9 March 1935. The announcement was received by France and Britain without formal protest.[406] On the following day, an extension of the French period of military service was proposed by the French War Minister. Whether this combination of circumstances seemed to Hitler to be too favourable to be allowed to pass, is uncertain, but during the days immediately following he made up his mind to announce the re-introduction of conscription for the German Armed Forces. During that week he had been at Berchtesgaden, accompanied by Ribbentrop.[407] On 13 March he ordered Hossbach to meet him in Munich on the following day, at the Hotel Vier Jahreszeiten.[408] Hossbach reported to Hitler on the morning of 14 March, and Hitler told him that he intended to announce the

---

* See Hitler's speech to senior officers of the Army on 3 February 1933, in Chapter 10.

reintroduction of conscription and new limits for the size of the Armed Forces. Hitler wished this announcement to coincide with the conclusion of the debate in the French Chamber. Hossbach then told him the number of divisions for which the Army High Command was planning. Hossbach was personally familiar with these figures, since he was, at the same time, a department head within the General Staff. The plan which Hossbach gave Hitler was for an army of twelve corps of infantry, i.e. thirty-six divisions. Hitler accepted this proposal and permitted Hossbach to return to Berlin, in order to prepare Blomberg and Fritsch for the announcement, and to convene a meeting of the Reichs Defence Council for the evening of 15 March 1935.[409]

Blomberg's reaction was one of grave concern about the possible objections of the other major powers. At the meeting of the Defence Council, Ribbentrop told Blomberg not to worry about them. Blomberg's tension was revealed in his reply: 'What you say is all stuff and nonsense!'[410] Blomberg continued throughout the meeting to oppose the new measures. Hossbach thought that this opposition could have been decisive, had it not been expected that Blomberg would surrender at the last minute. The details of the proclamation were worked out in the late hours of that night. Blomberg and Fritsch reported to Hitler on the following morning. By then, Blomberg had let his objections drop. Fritsch stressed that this plan could be completed only over the course of several years, and that over-straining of the whole armaments system had to be avoided.[411]

Within the Army itself, the announcement caused great surprise. Even Reichenau was visibly amazed.[412] Local commanders, such as General-leutnant von Witzleben, Commander of Wehrkreis III, first heard of the new increases over the radio.[413] It must be remembered that this came at a time when the Army was fully extended in increasing its strength three-fold and the announcement of what amounted to a greater than five-fold expansion was far beyond the bounds of the expectations of most soldiers. The cause of the surprise appears to have been the timing of the announcement. Weichs relates that the senior officers all knew that an army of this size was in the Party's programme, but that the announcement came at a most unexpected time.[414] Hossbach's account confirms this, but the surprise exhibited by Reichenau, according to Foertsch[415] who was with Reichenau at the time of the announcement, indicated that the planned total of thirty-six divisions was not known to him, and therefore it could not have received a very wide circulation.

The full burden of the rearmament programme was not placed on the Army alone. For many years, the Landespolizei (or Schutzpolizei in Prussia and Thüringen) had been receiving military training, to enable them to cope with the serious disturbances of the 'twenties, and to act as an auxiliary force for national defence. The coming strains of rearmament were foreseen by the Reichswehr in 1933, and it instituted a type of pre-military training for the Landespolizei. In 1934, army officers were assigned to the Landespolizei, so that the training of the police would fit as smoothly as possible with that of the Army. At the Cabinet meeting on the afternoon of 16 March 1935, the transfer of the Landespolizei to the Army was discussed. Göring, as Minister Präsident of Prussia, was reluctant to surrender complete control of any of his forces. Blomberg argued with him and a compromise was reached which enabled Göring to retain command over the police regiment *Hermann Göring*, and which gave control of the remainder of the Landespolizei to the Army.

On 21 March 1935, Hitler announced that the central staff of the Landespolizei, the Reichsstab, was to pass from the command of the Minister for the Interior to the Commander-in-Chief of the Army, and that the various units of police were to pass into the Army, while their police functions were to be taken over by the local police. An important exception to this transfer, besides the regiment *Hermann Göring*, was the Landespolizei force which was stationed in the Demilitarized Zone, i.e. the Rhineland and the Fifty Kilometre strip on the eastern bank of the Rhine. On 1 August 1935, the officers of the Landespolizei were transferred directly into the Army, and on 1 October 1935, the various units of the Landespolizei were completely incorporated into the Army. This increased the strength of the Army by 58 battalions of police, leaving a further 28 battalions under the control of the Minister for the Interior, which were almost all stationed in the Demilitarized Zone.[416]

The introduction of conscription also served to free the Armed Forces from one particular form of Nazi supervision. It was promulgated on 19 March 1935 that the Defence Policy Office of the Party (Wehrpolitisches Amt) was to be disbanded, since its objectives had been achieved.[417]

Shortly after the announcement by Hitler of the reintroduction of conscription, details of a complete reorganization of the command structure of the Armed Forces were announced. The means chosen to express these were two laws, the one secret, the other public, and passed by the Reichstag on 21 May 1935. The law which was published was the Wehrgesetz (Defence Law) which covered general questions of organization, laid down specific conditions governing the duration and size of the conscription programme, and determined the liability of individuals for service.[418] The nomenclature of the High Command was reorganized by the substitution of Reichskriegsminister (War Minister) for Reichswehrminister, Oberbefehlshaber des Heeres (Commander-in-Chief of the Army) for Chef der Heeresleitung, Chef des Generalstabs des Heeres (Chief of the General Staff of the Army) for Chef des Truppenamts, Oberkommando des Heeres for Heeresleitung, and Generalstab des Heeres for Truppenamt.[419] These alterations in nomenclature came into effect on 1 June 1935, but their significance lay in a change of name, rather than in any change of function, since the former names had been almost entirely camouflage titles, to satisfy various points of the Treaty of Versailles.[420]

The secret law was the Reichsverteidigungsgesetz. It conferred upon Hitler the powers of declaration of war, mobilization, and a 'state of defence'. Upon the declaration of a 'state of defence', all powers of administration in the area of operations designated were transferred to the Commander-in-Chief of the Army, and could be delegated to his subordinate commanders. The highest branches of the government were to be reorganized on the declaration of this state so that the different ministries became grouped under a Commissioner for National Administration and a Commissioner for Economics. Special facilities for the control of these agencies were granted to the Minister for War. On the declaration of war, martial law was to come into effect.[421] An interesting minor point of this law was the cancellation of the law of 27 March 1930, by which the Reichswehr Minister was not permitted to be a soldier.[422]

Hossbach records that these laws contained much less of the Party policy than the original drafts compiled in the Wehrmachtsamt under the direction of Reichenau. Fritsch had taken exception to several of the proposed points and had used Hossbach to insert a few ideas of his own. Hossbach was sent by Blomberg to Hitler in order to obtain the approval of the Führer before Blomberg made his final statement within the War Ministry. During the discussion of the drafts with Hitler, Hossbach was able to achieve some improvement in the status of the Wehrmacht with respect to the Party organizations, particularly the S.S., by the maintenance of the Armed Forces as the military training school of the state.[423]

Shortly before the first batch of conscripts marched into their units, an event of considerable traditional importance took place in Berlin. Under the conditions of the Treaty of Versailles, the Kriegsakademie, the school of the General Staff, had been closed. The training of General Staff officers had had to be conducted by the Wehrkreise, under the direction of the Truppenamt until 1932. On 1 October 1932, all General Staff trainees were gathered together in the 'Offizierslehrgang Berlin',[424] and centralized General Staff training commenced again in the Court Building in the Lehrterstrasse.[425] 15 October 1935 was the 125th anniversary of the founding of the Kriegsakademie by Scharnhorst. This occasion was celebrated by the reopening of the Kriegsakademie in new buildings in the Kruppestrasse on the site of the old academy.

The guests of honour at the ceremony were Hitler, Göring, Goebbels, Frick, Mackensen, Seeckt, the Rector of the University of Berlin, and the Rector of the Technical University, Charlottenburg.[426] Blomberg conducted the main part of the ceremony, and made a long speech in which he extolled Scharnhorst as a revolutionary, one who had freed the Army from the prejudices of a bygone age, 'who tore down barriers for the sake of establishing the unity of the People, the State and the Armed Forces'. He made a passing cut at the independence of the Army by stressing the primacy of the Wehrmacht. As part of the development of his favourite theme of the subjugation of the particular to the general,* he said that it was part of an officer's duty to acknowledge freely the philosophy of National-Socialism.[427]

Blomberg was followed by Beck, who spoke for twice as long,† without mentioning Hitler once. His speech was of purely military content, based on the dictum of Moltke, 'genius is work'. It is difficult to imagine anything less applicable to the methods of Hitler. Blomberg had just stated

---

* See above, pp. 63–64 for Blomberg's speech to the officers of 6 Division, September 1933.
† Beck's speech was approximately 3,000 words—Blomberg's was approximately 1,500.

that genius was much more, as it also embraced 'fate'.* General Liebmann, the Commandant of the Academy, dwelt in his speech on the
successes of Hitler's policy regarding the Treaty of Versailles.[428] After the
ceremony at the Academy, a dinner was held at the Hotel Kaiserhof, which
was attended by the senior generals, without any representatives of the
Party, or the War Ministers.[429] Seeckt and Fritsch gave small speeches,
with an interesting difference between them. Seeckt made no reference to
Hitler, and ignored the recent order of Blomberg that speeches were to be
closed with a toast to the Führer.[430] Fritsch made a more conventional
ending, thus:

> And then our thoughts turn to the man who has given us examples, probably
> in a unique fashion, of boldness, initiative, and readiness to take decisions, who
> has taught us soldiers and who daily teaches us more of what it means to dictate
> the rules of conduct to opponents by resolute deeds.
> I ask you, gentlemen, to shout with me: the Führer and Reichs Chancellor,
> the Supreme Commander of the Armed Forces, Adolf Hitler! Sieg Heil![431]

Thus, the initial stages of the rearmament had begun smoothly and the
process was rapidly gathering momentum. But the pace was not allowed
to settle at a constant rate. The demands of Hitler for greater and greater
efforts fell frequently on the High Command throughout the following
years, so that the number of recruits taken into the forces each year
mounted. The growth of the size of the German Army is shown by the
table below:[432]

Unit	1933	1934	1935	1936	1937	1938	1939 Peace	1939 War
Army Group H.Q.	2	2	3	3	4	6	6	11
Corps H.Q.	—	10	10	12	13	19	22	26
Division H.Q.	10	24	29	39	39	51	51	102
Battalions:								
Infantry	84	166	287	334	352	476	476	906
Artillery	24	95	116	148	187	228	228	482
Panzer	—	6	12	16	24	34	34	34

Figures of the numbers of men in the Army at each stage are not available
for the whole period. However, the following are the establishment totals
for the years shown:[433]

	1937–38	1939–40
Field Army Total	2,104,355	2,758,064
Replacement Army Total	1,239,121	996,040
Combined total	3,343,476	3,754,104

* One significant comment in Beck's speech which may have been intended to have wider
interpretations, was made in connection with a condemnation of 'lightning appreciations'.
    'Otherwise the danger threatens that the leader or his auxiliary does not see things as
they really are, but as he wishes to see them.'

To meet this requirement in men, the following numbers of trained soldiers were available:

	1937–38	1939–40
Men on active service	550,000	730,000
Reservists I	200,000	500,000
Reservists II	250,000	600,000
Total	1,000,000	1,830,000

The enormous gap between the strengths of the Army and its different establishments for each mobilization year provide a measure of Hitler's lack of satisfaction with the progress made. On the other hand, comparison of the final figures of trained men with the original strength of the Army in 1933, viz. 100,000,[434] indicates the staggering amount of work which must have been performed by the officers of the old Army during the pre-war years of the Third Reich. To have trained a force of men eighteen times the size of the original trained body in seven years and to such a degree of efficiency that this force was able to occupy the greater part of Europe within two further years was an unparalleled achievement.

This in itself is of notable significance in terms of the political-military relationship. If a group of professional men are given huge amounts of resources with which to develop their ideas, they are likely to throw themselves into the work with enthusiasm. If the work required of them is constantly increased, and their moments of relaxation are partly occupied by propaganda which glorifies the creator of all this activity, then they are not likely to develop a detached, critical approach towards the consequences of what they are doing. Unless the propaganda is hopelessly exaggerated, all the essential features of their relationship with the government are cooperative in essence, in the short term in particular. Thus the sheer pace of the rearmament was a most important factor in maintaining the allegiance of officers of the lower and middle ranks to Hitler.

The size of the whole rearmament programme had been troubling Fritsch, however, and on 4 June 1936, he ordered Generalmajor Fromm, head of the Allgemeines Heeresamt to prepare a study of the financial, material, and manpower requirements of the rearmament programme as it then stood. Fromm completed this study on 1 August. The main part of it dealt with financial aspects. Fromm set out the costs of the programme thus:[435]

Budget Requirements in Millions of Reichmarks

Year	1937	1938	1939	1940	1941	1942	1943	1944	1945
New Requirement	8,882	8,979	8,885	4,669	4,294	3,499	3,469	3,469	3,169
Former ,,		3,575	3,675	3,859	3,439	2,584	2,584	2,584	2,584	2,584
Increase		5,307	5,304	5,026	1,230	1,710	0,915	0,885	0,885	0,585

It is doubtful whether this amount of money is available. To maintain the armaments industry in good order after 1940 will require:

1940	7,570	1943	7,650
1941	7,620	1944	8,070
1942	7,230	1945	7,770

For a long period, this would be intolerable. Therefore, either the Armed

Forces must be put into action at the end of the rearmament period, or an amelioration of the situation obtained, so that the requirements of the degree of preparedness for war can be reduced.

The whole position depends on many questions outside our jurisdiction, such as the possibility of easing the situation by huge imports from foreign countries.

As a result,

    1. The General Staff should review the situation with a view to making reductions, and

    2. So should the Minister for War.

Attached to this study were several appendices, mainly concerned with the strength of the Army as on 1 October 1939. Appendix 1 estimated the strength of the peace-time Army at 43 divisions. Appendix 2 put the strength of a war-time Army at 101 divisions. Appendix 3 gave the strengths of the peace- and war-time Armies as 830,000 and 4,620,600 (3,113,600 without reservists) respectively. The estimates of the number of divisions were close to what was achieved, particularly in the case of the war-time Army,* but the manpower estimates were rather high. In order to maintain this number of men, Fromm thought that it would be necessary for the Field Army to receive 387,000 recruits per annum, while the Replacement Army should have a yearly intake of 178,000 men. This meant that all men born in the years 1914–19 would have to serve in the forces, and all of those born in 1913 would have to enter the Replacement Army.

Fromm then went on to calculate the endurance powers of Germany in a war. There were 14 million men who were born between the years 1894 and 1919 (i.e. men who, in 1937 would be between the ages of 18 and 43). Of these, 30% were unfit, leaving 10 million for active service. Of these, the national economy would require 3 million normally, but with the demands of armaments, 4 to 5 million should be allowed for, leaving 5 to 6 million for the forces. The forces needed 3·1 million (Army), plus 0·09 million (Navy), plus 0·3 million (Air Force), i.e. 3·5 million in all, leaving 1·5 to 2·5 million at the disposal of the forces for replacement of losses. Losses in the First World War were three-quarters of the field army per annum, therefore the German Army had just enough reserves of manpower to fight a war for one year. However, manpower was not the most critical factor. Consideration of the oil fuel needs of the German Armed Forces showed that it would be necessary to supply 246,000 tons per month. German storage capacity was 1,100,000 tons, therefore a reserve of $4\frac{1}{4}$ months could be built up. Synthetic processes were capable of producing 100,000 tons per month, so that if Germany had all fuel storages full at the beginning of a war, there would be enough fuel from all resources, assuming that deliveries from abroad were cut off, for Germany to fight for 7 months. These points served to emphasize the original conclusions that the whole situation was in need of review, either by the General Staff, or by the Minister for War, for what was the point of

* See above, p. 91.

making such crippling financial outlays on a large army, when it could only fight for seven months?

Thus Fritsch had precise evidence that rearmament was being driven at such a pace that efficiency had begun to decline. To what use he put it is not known. However, within three weeks of receiving the report, he and Beck proposed to Hitler that the period of service ought to be increased to two years.[436] This was decreed in *Reichsgesetzblatt 1936*, page 609, on 24 August 1936. One of the effects of this was to reduce the rate of increase of reserves. Fritsch considered that this had to be tolerated in the interests of better training. He also hoped that, through this better training, the Army would gain a stronger influence within the national life of Germany, with respect to the Nazi Party, thus exercising a moderating influence on the development of German youth.[437] But since by 1936 the Army was simply one of the organizations in the stream:

> Deutsches Jungvolk
> Hitler Jugend
> Reichs Arbeit Dienst
> Wehrmacht
> S.S., S.A., or N.S.K.K.

this policy was not likely to have had any great effect.

Apart from the sheer size of the rearmament activity, it provided great scope for new ideas and techniques. This was a period when great revolutionary changes in strategy and tactics were taking place, consequent to the deadlock of the trenches in the First World War, and the development of the tank. The German Army had been active in conducting small experiments in the new techniques, especially in Russia, but until the advent of Hitler, there had been no means for following up these experiments with the development of large mechanized forces. This was a subject which interested Hitler personally, and he did much to encourage the work which was being done to restore mobility to warfare. He became the first German Chancellor since Bismarck to visit the weapons proving establishment at Kummersdorf. In 1933 he attended a demonstration of the earliest Mark I tanks there. He was greatly impressed by the speed and precision with which the tanks manœuvred, and said repeatedly to Oberstleutnant Guderian, 'That's what I need! That's what I want to have!'[438] Throughout the pre-war period, he was active in giving support to new methods where it seemed necessary, in order to overcome excess conservatism. In the autumn of 1938, he attended a demonstration of the new 88 mm. anti-aircraft gun. During the demonstration, he suggested to the Director of Army Ordnance, General Becker, that the gun ought to be mounted horizontally, for use against tanks, and also placed in tanks.[439] Thus the most deadly anti-tank gun of the Second World War was conceived. It may be imagined that the progress due to Hitler's interest also had a big influence on the development of the attitudes of officers towards Hitler himself, if not towards the Nazi movement as a whole, for the potential of these new weapons provided an important element of high morale.

During the pre-war period, Hitler gave the German Army one of the best opportunities any army could have had at that time to recoup its strength, and to increase its efficiency through the pursuit of the most modern methods. The Army had been taught to look forward to this day by Seeckt and his successors throughout the confining duration of the Weimar Republic, and greeted its arrival with great enthusiasm. It was most unfortunate that some of this enthusiasm should have been attached to Hitler personally for providing this opportunity, but when viewed from the position of a junior or middle-ranking officer who knew no more of Nazism than the Movement itself taught him, this transference was not unnatural.

The situation was different for men at the summit of the German military structure, for they were in a position to see that the pace of rearmament was being forced along at too great a rate. Blomberg remained blindly faithful to Hitler. When objections to this effect were made to him on many occasions by General Joachim von Stülpnagel, his reply again and again was:

The Führer is cleverer than we are, he will plan and do everything correctly.[440]

Fritsch was well aware of the dangers, and those who knew him affirm that he made frequent protests to Blomberg, but to no avail.[441] He may have also been influenced by a desire to have a strong army, believing German security to be permanently in jeopardy until this was achieved, without believing that this army could be made the tool of aggression. Beck also saw many dangers and disadvantages in the rearmament, and left ample evidence in his writings, but both Beck and Fritsch apparently saw their duty as to remain in office, exerting as much moderation as possible, until something else became feasible.

Unfortunately, the longer they waited, the less chance they had of exercising restraint on the military policies of the Third Reich, since the Army was being filled beneath them with the spirit of Nazism, transferred from the Hitler Youth, from the schools, and from the other Party organizations, by the thousands of youths who, from 1935 onwards made up the mass of the striking power of the Army. Thus the process of German rearmament took place under circumstances which resulted in the steady tightening of the influence of the Nazi Party upon the Army, while making it increasingly difficult for the Army to exercise control over its own fortunes.

7

The Army and the S.S.

THE German Army in the Third Reich was in the most unusual position of facing active competition from two of the major organizations of the Nazi Party. The danger presented by the first, the S.A., was of significance only until 30 June 1934. The jealous and active competition of the S.S. under Heinrich Himmler was not overcome until the overthrow of the Nazi State itself in 1945. The relationship between the Army and the S.S. may be considered from two main viewpoints—that of the Army and the S.S. as a whole, and that of the Army and the armed military forces of the S.S., the S.S. Verfügungstruppen (the S.S. Military Reserve).

Relations between the Army and the S.S. as a whole were not greatly different from the relationship between the S.S. and any other individuals or groups who sought to preserve a degree of independence from the more extreme forms of Nazism. The S.S. had no authority over the Army as of constitutional right, but as the élite formation of the Party, under the command of a man who was one of the most important of Hitler's associates, the S.S. was able to exercise an influence on the conduct of political-military relations which was beyond the power of the Army to ignore. The essence of the role of the S.S. in this field was that of a vicious watchdog which was guarding the interests of doctrinaire Nazism. That this was to be the case, however, was not obvious in the early days of the Third Reich.

Initially, the S.S. was treated almost as a part of the much larger S.A. Throughout 1933, Army orders relating to the S.S. lumped the two organizations together.[442] Until 1933, it had been quite usual for men to pass from membership of the one organization to membership of the other without the slightest difficulty.[443] But by the time the S.A. had reached the stage of challenging the position of the Army within the state, Himmler had perceived that such a policy was not favourable to Hitler, and a gradual dissolution of the partnership between the two armed forces of the Nazi Party occurred, so that during the anxious days of June 1934, the S.S. was sheltered inside the barracks of the Army, and provided with weapons in order to overcome any open rebellion on the part of the S.A.

After the subsidence of the Röhm crisis, the ways of the S.S. and the Army diverged as the S.S. grew in size, power and independence. As late as 30 July 1934, S.S. troops were being quartered within barracks of the Army,[444] but this relationship led to friction and was terminated swiftly.

This did not bring about a complete severance between the Army and the S.S., because the S.S. was attempting, as late as 15 November 1934, to have complete S.S. units enrolled in the Grenzschutz.[445] The reluctance of the Army to train another possible replacement for itself was illustrated by the reply of the local commander at Regensburg to Wehrkreis VII, which stated that it was not in the interests of the Army to train the S.S. for Grenzschutz employment, unless there was complete certainty that the S.S. really was at the disposal of the Army for this work. A final ruling was given by Wehrkreis VII on 13 December, possibly after consultation with Berlin, that there were no objections to individual S.S. men who volunteered for the frontier protection service receiving training, but S.S. units were neither to be trained, nor to be used for such work.[446]

During the autumn, a major crisis in relations between the Army and the S.S. occurred. Rumours circulated that the S.S. anticipated that the Army was about to make a putsch, under the leadership of Fritsch.[447] A planned campaign of hatred was implemented against Fritsch, led by the Gestapo. Various alarms were given by the Wehrkreise, culminating in reports from all Wehrkreise that the S.S. was planning a great blow. At this stage Hitler decided to intervene, in order to prevent the situation from becoming too dangerous to control. He addressed a meeting of senior Army officers and Party officials at the Kroll Opera, on 3 January 1935.* In his speech he gave special emphasis to the loyalty of the Army and of its leaders. He said:

> The Army and the Party are the two pillars of the State. Perhaps then one of the Party will say to me:
> 'That is all very well, my Führer, but General So-and-So speaks and works against you!'
> Then I would reply to him:
> 'I do not believe it.'
> and if the other replies:
> 'I will bring you the written evidence!'
> then I would tear the scrap of paper up, for my faith in the Wehrmacht is unshakeable.[448]

This speech had its desired effect, and the tension eased, although only for a few months. Fritsch also noticed that the attacks which had been made on him in the foreign press in late 1934 stopped suddenly after this speech.[449] Fritsch thought that these attacks were also co-ordinated by the S.S.

In January 1935, the Gestapo published a special report, entitled *The Poisoning of the Relationship between the Bearer of the Arms of the Nation and the Bearer of the Philosophy in the State and the Party*. This report included a list of rumours which were being circulated at the time. These rumours throw some more light on the special difficulties of the Army in January 1935. They included the following:

---

* This was also the meeting at which Hitler stated that the shootings of Schleicher and Bredow had been in error. See above, p. 52.

Himmler was poisoning Blomberg.
A Reichswehr putsch was imminent.
Blomberg and Göring were at loggerheads.
Goebbels had demanded Fritsch's resignation.
Blomberg was going to break finally with Hitler.
Schleicher's daughter had attempted to kill Hitler with a revolver.
Fritsch and Schacht were always at loggerheads.
Fritsch wanted to oust Göring from the Air Ministry.
Rundstedt was about to replace Fritsch.

A list describing the contents of the rumours in circulation gave first place to the Reichswehr amongst the affected parties, and second place to Fritsch. There were many references to hostility between Fritsch and the Party, and between Fritsch and Reichenau. This report included the *Blue Book of the Reichswehr*, which was supposed to have been submitted to Hindenburg by Army officers after the shootings of 30 June 1934, calling for a change in the government, with Fritsch as Vice-Chancellor, Hammerstein as Reichswehr Minister, and Nadolny as Foreign Minister.

It is most interesting that such a report should have been published, not only for the Gestapo, but for the Army as a whole to read at such a time,[450] for it does raise the thought that Fritsch in particular was a most reluctant servant of the Nazi régime. However, the publicity may have been an attempt to show this idea to be utterly ridiculous. It may also have been an attempt to exercise a constraint on Fritsch.

Before Hitler made his speech of 3 January 1935, Himmler had gone so far as to designate a day on which Fritsch was going to attempt a putsch against the Nazi government.[451] Fritsch recorded that he thought that this day was 10 January 1935, but other evidence suggests that this day was 13 January.* Blomberg was informed of this, although it is not known from which side the warning came. Accordingly, he called a meeting of the senior officers of the Army for the night in question, in Berlin. His motivation for this action would have depended upon the source of his information. Blomberg invited Himmler to address this meeting. Fritsch related in his memorandum of 1 February 1938:

In this speech I was accused of inviting a Professor, who was also a senior legal adviser to the Government, I think his name was Schmidt, to give an address one Thursday at the Tirpitz Ufer. Göring held that it would be shown in this address that a putsch was permissible, according to constitutional law.

* A directive issued by Blomberg in early 1935, *Richtlinien für den Unterricht über politische Tagesfragen* Nr. 2, 1935, contained a speech made by Himmler at a gathering of senior Army officers, called by Blomberg on 13 January 1935. Himmler's subject was 'The Tasks of the S.S.'. WK XIII file 342. The coincidence between the content of this speech, and the description given by Fritsch, together with Fritsch's own admission that he was not certain that the meeting took place on 10 January 1935, makes it extremely likely that the occasion to which he referred was the one described above, which took place on 13 January 1935. Further confirmation is provided by a notice paper circulated within the Army High Command, stating that Himmler was to address 'the same group of Generals as yesterday' at the Militärärztliche Akademie, Scharnhorststrasse 35, on 'The Tasks of the S.S.', at the request of the Reichswehr Minister. OKH file H 24/6.

This, in the presence of the Minister and many officers! The invitation had been issued by the Training Branch of the General Staff. The man was and is totally unknown to me. The address was cancelled.

I bring this episode in, only to demonstrate that nothing is too ridiculous to be used against me.

It is surprising, in view of Fritsch's own words, that he tolerated such treatment in front of his own subordinates, and continued to carry out his functions in loyal obedience to Hitler. However, there are a number of factors which may account for Fritsch's failure to perceive at the beginning of 1935 that he was being exploited for as long as he was co-operative, by a movement which was basically evil. First, Hitler was his Supreme Commander, not Himmler. Hitler had, only a few days previously, reaffirmed his faith in the leaders of the forces, and brought about a relaxation of the tension between the Army and the S.S. It was only six months since Hitler had made an example of the leaders of the S.A., and so Fritsch may have continued to regard Hitler as a capable, respectable leader. Secondly, the process of building up the Army, and thereby of restoring national security, was in full swing. Fritsch may have regarded the magnitude of this task as justification for the toleration of all sorts of personal attacks and insults from the onlooking group of lesser Party leaders, until the security of Germany had been re-established.

The hatred of the S.S. for the Army did not abate for long, however, for in summer 1935, the S.S. units quartered at the exercise range, Altengrabow, carried out the vilest cursing of the Army in general, and of Fritsch in particular.[452] Fritsch summed up the ensuing trend in relations with the S.S. thus:

While it was possible in the following period to achieve a good, in many cases even confidential relationship with all of the officers of the Party, this was not the case with the S.S. This may be, when seen from our side, because there was scarcely a single senior officer who did not feel that he was being spied upon by the S.S. Also, it became known again and again that, contrary to the expressed orders of the Deputy to the Führer, S.S. men who were serving in the Army had orders to report on their superiors. Unfortunately, these matters came to my attention only in such a manner that I could not pursue them.

Fritsch's summary is well supported by the available documentary evidence. The story of the relationship between the S.S. as a whole and the Army was a series of clashes, usually of a minor nature, but sufficiently severe to indicate that there was much bitterness beneath the surface on both sides. The following incidents are cited as examples.

On 9 January 1935, an officer objected to an S.S. man describing Schleicher as 'Blackguard, reactionary, thank the Lord that he was shot'. The S.S. man then accused the whole officer corps, especially staff officers and above, of being reactionaries, and added: 'What the Führer tells us is true. What he says to you need not be.'[453]

In April and May 1935, listening devices were discovered which had been clandestinely inserted into Army telephones,[454] and even into the offices of Admiral Canaris and the Abwehr.[455] This brought protests from Blomberg and Fritsch, and Hitler limited Gestapo authority to exclude the headquarters of the Armed Forces.[456]

On the night of 31 August 1935, two corporals were insulted, threatened with daggers, and physically attacked by S.S. men.[457] On 21 October, some officers were struck by S.S. leaders in a bar.[458] On 1 December 1935, an Army civilian official was beaten up by the S.S. on the Kurfürsten-damm, Berlin, before many onlookers.[459] On 28 December 1935, an officer cadet was drinking in a bar, when an S.S. man entered and ordered him to leave at once. The officer cadet replied that the S.S. man had no authority over him. The S.S. man then said: 'I have police authority over all Germans, and that includes soldiers.'[460] A New Year party at Oranien-burg, on 31 December 1935, turned into a massive brawl between local Army and S.S. units.[461]

This series of incidents grew steadily throughout the following years, and it was necessary in early 1938 for a special directive to be issued by Blomberg on the handling of incidents between the S.S. and the Armed Forces. The S.S. was the only individual Party body so to be distinguished. It is also interesting that Blomberg signed this directive on 25 January 1938, just prior to his dismissal. It is possible, therefore, that he worded this directive in such a manner as to stress his indispensability to Hitler and to the Party. The directive began with a general introduction by Blomberg. This contained:

Public court proceedings concerning incidents between the Armed Forces and the S.S. are not desired. They damage the appearance of both, and they undermine the confidence of the people in the unity of the nation. . . .

I expect that . . . with all incidents, a settlement will be found outside of the courts.

I stress particularly that the relationship to the S.S. is, like that towards the other organizations of the movement, one of conscious comradeship. Short-comings in this regard not only damage the appearance of the Armed Forces, but at the same time constitute a severe infringement of my expressed will. I request that attention be given to this thought in the allocation of punishment.

The fact that prosecutions will no longer be made by the S.S., and that thereby court sentences will be avoided, represents an appreciable reduction of the size of punishments.[462]

The actual orders governing the handling of these incidents were signed by both Blomberg and Hitler. They laid down that negotiations were to be carried out initially by the battalion commander of the soldiers involved and by the Standartenführer of the S.S. men who were concerned. Higher commanders were to be called in only if these men were unable to agree on a solution.[463]

It is interesting that on 8 April 1938, Fritsch's successor, Brauchitsch, issued another order[464] stating that the above directive was to be applied only in cases where there had been infringements of military discipline but not of military law. In all cases in which military law had been broken, the directive was not to be applied. This ruling must have robbed the original directive of much of the power which Blomberg had intended it to have.

This directive and its amendment appear to have been the last landmarks in the pre-war relationship between the Army and the S.S. The flow of small incidents and clashes continued, while both sides attempted to keep matters as secret as possible. Himmler even went to the trouble of sending annual Christmas gifts, such as boxes of cigars, to senior officers,[465] but a real reconciliation between the Army and the S.S. was never made. The Army remained in the hands of officers of the old school, most of whom tended towards conservatism in political matters, while the S.S. embodied the most fanatical groups within the Nazi Party. The older officers of the Army were vital to the rearmament, and so from the point of view of the Head of the German State, this situation had to be tolerated.

These conditions, however, did not prevent the growth of another armed military force within Germany. This force was the private army of the Nazi Party, also directed by Himmler—the S.S. Verfügungstruppe, or the forerunner of the Waffen S.S. This organization grew under the care and guidance of Himmler, and by the exploitation of favourable circumstances, from a bodyguard of 120 men in 1933 to a force of 38 divisions in 1944.[466]

Hitler's bodyguard of 120 men was formed on 17 March 1933. This was enlarged to approximately the size of a battalion on 8 November 1933. At the Nuremberg Rally in 1933, this bodyguard had been given the title 'Leibstandarte *Adolf Hitler*'. It took the following oath on 9 November 1933:

I swear to you, Adolf Hitler, as Führer and Reichs Chancellor, loyalty and bravery. I vow to you, and to those whom you have named to command me, obedience unto death, so help me God.

Thus, these troops were purely Party troops through the period of Hindenburg's term of office as Head of State.

In mid-1934, at the time of preparation of the main stages of the rearmament process, Himmler urged that this small force ought to be expanded. The threat of the S.A. may have made it easier for him to obtain the consent of Hitler. The Army High Command reacted in the reverse manner. They regarded the expansion of such forces as a serious danger, and Fritsch made protests to Blomberg and Reichenau to this effect.[467] These two, however, did not share Fritsch's views, and so the protest came to nothing, but Hitler did agree that this force was not to enter the Army as an integral unit in time of war, and granted the Army the right of inspection.[468] These conditions were annulled by Hitler in February 1935.[469]

The minutes of a conference held by the commander of 7 Division on 17 October 1934, relate that an S.S. Verfügungstruppe with the strength of a division was to be raised for a 'purpose not yet quite clear'.[470] On 17 January 1935, the same commander told his officers the outline organization of the S.S. and the new Verfügungstruppe. This was:

(a) The S.S. in general
   Geheime Staatspolizei
   S.S. Verfügungstruppe
   Allgemeine S.S.
(b) The S.S. Verfügungstruppe
   One Division, consisting of
      Three infantry regiments
      One reconnaissance battalion
      One engineer battalion
      Artillery

These troops were to be permitted weapons, plus enough weapons for 25,000 emergency police.[471]

At the end of 1934, an officer training school for the Verfügungstruppe was set up at Brunswick, under the retired Reichswehr General, Hausser.

These new units were brought in to official contact with the Army by Blomberg's directive of 21 January 1935, on the inclusion of the S.A. and the S.S. in the mobilization preparations of the Wehrmacht. This defined the tasks of the S.A. and S.S. as the unarmed troops of the Party for political purposes, and described the organization of the S.S. Verfügungstruppe as above, except that the various battalions were to be kept separate, and not grouped into independent regiments, apart from the Leibstandarte. The mobilization requirements to be met by the S.A. and the S.S. were to be assigned by the Wehrmacht. The S.A. and S.S. were only to see that enough men were provided to meet the demands of the Wehrmacht. Although the Wehrmacht was not permitted to call up members of the Verfügungstruppe, all other S.A. and S.S. men were placed unconditionally at the Wehrmacht's disposal for mobilization purposes.[472]

The existence of the S.S. Verfügungstruppe was officially announced by Hitler during his speech to the Reichstag on 16 March 1935. After Hitler had revealed the new limits of the Wehrmacht, he added that an S.S. division would also be formed, although this was not included in the official account of Hitler's speech.[473] By May 1935, this unit had 8,459 men, two officer training schools were operating at Brunswick and at Bad Tölz, and the elements of nine battalions had been formed.[474]

The training of these troops had advanced sufficiently for some of them to be employed during the march into the Rhineland in March 1936. In the summer of 1936, an Inspectorate of the Verfügungstruppe was established, under the direction of Hausser. By this stage, the S.S. had been successful in attracting numbers of retired Army officers back to service as instructors, so that the Verfügungstruppe did not lack direct contacts with the Army itself. Hausser relates that this was of great assistance in overcoming shortages of equipment and other training needs.

However, the original plan of keeping the battalions as separate entities did not remain in force for long. In summer 1936, the Verfügungstruppe comprised three regiments: the Leibstandarte *Adolf Hitler* in Berlin, the Regiment *Deutschland* in Munich, and the Regiment *Germania* in

Hamburg. This was due to Hausser himself, through his introduction of complete regimental staffs for the various collections of battalions.

While Fritsch remained in office, he kept up a continuous pressure to restrain the growth of the S.S. Verfügungstruppe.[475] Fritsch's views regarding these troops were set out in his memorandum of 1 February 1938:

Finally, it is the S.S. Verfügungstruppe, which, expanded further and further, must create an opposition to the Army, simply through its existence.

Even though the Army does have a certain right of inspection with regard to the training of the S.S. Verfügungstruppe, this S.S. unit develops itself totally apart, and, it appears to me, in deliberate opposition to the Army. All units report unanimously that the relationship of the S.S. Verfügungstruppe to the Army is very cool, if not hostile. One cannot help forming the impression that the hostile attitude towards the Army is blatantly encouraged within the S.S. Verfügungstruppe. This hostility finds its outward expression in the failure of many S.S. men to salute officers.[476]

After the dismissal of Fritsch and the Anschluss, another S.S. regiment was formed, the Austrian Regiment *Der Führer*. It is also apparent from a mobilization order of 18 March 1938, that Army officers had been attached to some of the S.S. Standarten as training advisers.[477]

A new ruling on the relationship between the S.S. Verfügungstruppe and the Army was given by Hitler on 17 August 1938. This stated that any parts of the S.S. which were assigned for duty with the Army were to be completely under the control of the Army High Command. Members of the S.S. on military service were to have exactly the same rights and duties as the members of the Army. S.S. units which were serving with the Army were to wear the field grey uniform, with Army badges of rank, corresponding to their S.S. ranks.[478] This was a final break with the notion that the S.S. was not to be permitted to form a bridgehead within the Army by entering it as formed units.

Shortly afterwards, on 19 September 1938, further orders of Hitler governing the organization and functions of the S.S. as a whole were promulgated by the Army High Command. These stated that the S.S. Verfügungstruppe was a special unit, at the disposal of Hitler alone. Men who completed two years' service with this unit were regarded as having completed their military service in accordance with the conscription law. The organization of the S.S. Verfügungstruppe was to be thus:

1 Command Staff
The Leibstandarte *Adolf Hitler* (motorized)
3 Standarten (or regiments)
2 motor cycle battalions, under a regimental staff
1 engineer battalion (motorized)
1 signals battalion (motorized)
1 ambulance unit

These units were all to be organized and equipped in accordance with

Army regulations. The ultimate aim, it was stated, was the complete mechanization of all units within the S.S. Verfügungstruppe.

For the purposes of mobilization, this force was to be incorporated into the Army as a motorized infantry division. It was to be subject to all military regulations and orders, but it was to remain politically an organization of the N.S.D.A.P. The Commander-in-Chief of the Army was to prepare the Verfügungstruppe for military service in time of war by assisting with the training of these units, and by the provision of appropriate regulations. Officers of the Army were to be exchanged for short periods with officers of the S.S. units as soon as the officer situation within the Army permitted.

This regulation also described the functions and organization of the S.S. *Totenkopf* units. These were neither a part of the Wehrmacht, nor of the police, but they were to be armed and used for special police duties. Himmler was given authority to recruit men from the Wehrmacht, before they had been discharged from military service. The *Totenkopf* units were to be organized thus:

> 1 Command Staff with communications unit
> 4 regiments, each with
>   3 battalions of 3 companies of infantry and 1 machine-gun company
> 1 ambulance unit[479]

By the summer of 1939 the S.S. Verfügungstruppe had completed expansion to the strength of a full division comprising 18,000 men, by the formation of its own artillery units. This growth necessitated new instructions to enable the complete division to obtain exercise training with the Army. On 20 June 1939, Brauchitsch issued a directive, entitled 'Co-operation of the Army with the S.S. Verfügungstruppe'.

This directive stressed the need for closer co-operation than before. Because the Verfügungstruppe was to be used as a part of the Army in the event of war, it was necessary for 'a mutual relationship of trust and comradeship to be developed, which is the prerequisite for partnership in battle, shoulder to shoulder'. Brauchitsch then went on to order the closest co-operation by all means, both official and unofficial. In particular, local S.S. units were to be notified of exercises, and invited to participate, S.S. officers were to be invited to attend courses conducted by the Army for its own officers, sporting competitions were to be held with the S.S., social connections were to be established between the officers of both forces by regular invitations, and publicity was to be given to this co-operation in the national press, particularly in the newspapers *Die Wehrmacht* and *Das Schwarze Korps*.[480]

Thus the S.S. Verfügungstruppe came to acquire all the advantages of the Army, while remaining an élite political force of the Party. The successful rise of this private force, and the subsequent close contact which was compelled between it and the Army must have helped to complete the process of surrounding the common soldier with clear evidence both of the universality of the Nazi ideology, and of the might of the Nazi system. The growth of the Verfügungstruppe had been viewed with disapproval by those officers who still adhered to conservative views, but they were rendered ineffective by the influence of convinced Nazis such as Blomberg and Reichenau, as well as by the growing strength of Himmler. A possible exception to this ineffectiveness would be Fritsch. During his period of office, the Verfügungstruppe was kept within its initial establishment, while after his departure it blossomed out to become an independent fighting formation, armed and equipped with the most modern material, in many cases superior to the equipment of the Army itself, and trained by the Army on the orders of Brauchitsch himself.

But it is doubtful whether Fritsch's role was of more than minor significance. His influence on Hitler was small, and his opportunity for direct contact was extremely limited due to the zeal of Blomberg. Much more important was the influence of Himmler. He probably saw that he would have to proceed cautiously at the beginning, both from political and from technical considerations, until the growth of international tension enabled him to accelerate with safety. Furthermore, since Himmler was involved in the plot which caused Fritsch's dismissal, he may have decided to wait until this had come to fruition before taking further steps to increase his own power.

The essence of the relationship between the S.S. as a whole and the Army was that of an attack on the old Prussian conservatism which, before the coming to power of Hitler, had dominated thought and behaviour within the Army. This was a political battle in which the Army was denied the initiative by its own outlook as much as by its position within the state. Consequently, it was a battle in which all the Army could hope for was the successful defence of its own ground. But, given the number of influential soldiers who had embraced Nazism and opened the way to Himmler's infiltration, it is scarcely surprising that the defence, although avoiding collapse, was overcome at the most significant points.

8

Internal Disputes concerning the Organization of the High Command

DURING the pre-war years of the Third Reich, the High Command was faced by a multitude of problems, both political and military. The above chapters have described the major political problems which confronted the High Command from outside, together with some of those which tended to split it internally. It must not be imagined that this was the full extent of the worries of men such as Fritsch and Beck, for, throughout these years, there were a series of disputes within the High Command about its organizational structure. Although the essence of these disputes was military, they had political significance for two reasons. First, at the level of the highest military command, it is very rare that any problem is purely military, or purely political. In the case of Nazi Germany, the question of the growth of the personal power of Hitler and Göring became an important factor in determining the manner in which duties and responsibilities were allocated within the High Command. Secondly, the splits which occurred through differences in outlook in organizational matters tended to reinforce those which had resulted from differences in political views.

The first matter of contention was the question of the allocation of duties amongst the Commander-in-Chief of the Armed Forces, the Commander-in-Chief of the Army, and the Chief of the General Staff. The initial views of the Organizations Branch of the General Staff on this problem were given by Oberst (E) von Belli, in a lecture to staff officers undergoing training in September 1933.[481] Belli held that there had to be a single chief for all the Armed Forces, who was to be directly responsible to the Chancellor and to the Cabinet. There was to be no intermediary between this commander and the head of the government. If there had to be a Defence Minister, he was to be restricted to the control of administrative matters. The Commander-in-Chief of the Armed Forces was to be the operational chief for all land, sea and air warfare.

This was attacked by Oberst Fromm in late 1933, when he was Chief of the Defence Office.[482] Fromm held that this was going too far, because it would have been beyond the powers of the Commander-in-Chief of the Armed Forces to conduct the field operations of the Army directly. Fromm's point was taken up by Beck, in early 1934, when he insisted that the Commander-in-Chief of the Army become the Commander-in-Chief of the Armed Forces in war.[483] Reichenau responded to this by declaring that mobilization plans would no longer give command over the Armed Forces to the Commander-in-Chief of the Army, and that several of the departments which were under the control of the Army commander in peace were to pass to the Armed Forces commander in the event of war.[484]

The position of the Chief of the General Staff also came under attack by Fromm. He wrote in late 1933 that the whole organization of the Army High Command ought to be replaced by a simple two branch system of Operations and Armaments.[485] Under the old system, which had divided the functions of the High Command into five groups, the Chief of the General Staff was in a pre-eminent position with regard to the other heads of departments, and acted as the personal adviser of the Army commander. Fromm wished in particular to abolish this special position. The General Staff replied to Fromm, criticizing him for interpreting the functions of the Army High Command too literally, and for creating command difficulties for the Army commander by taking away his best adviser and replacing him with two separate sources of advice, neither of whom was likely to have had the breadth of view of the Chief of the General Staff.[486]

The developments in land, sea and air warfare which had taken place since the Great War led to the notion of a combined Armed Forces General Staff (OKW). This issue became hotly contested in a dispute which lasted until just such a staff was set up, in February 1938. The strongest opponents of this proposal were the senior officers of the General Staff itself. Not only was this a direct threat to the status of the General Staff, but the establishment of a higher General Staff under the direction of Blomberg and Reichenau would have implied a growth in the power of the group who admired Hitler, at the expense of the conservatives and moderates.

However, there were some officers within the General Staff who did not object to this, and the first proposals for the OKW came from the Organizations Branch of the General Staff itself. In a memorandum of 7 December 1933, it was suggested that until the OKW was set up, the Chief of the General Staff should act in the capacity of Economic General Staff Officer to the Armed Forces commander, while two other General Staff officers were to be allocated to assist the Armed Forces commander with more general aspects of planning.[487]

The Operations Branch of the General Staff replied to this on 14 December, indicating their concept of the OKW by stating that it ought to include the Budget Branch of the Ministerial Office.[488] A crystallization of resistance was shown in the reply of the Training Branch of the General Staff, on 16 December 1933, when it stressed that the OKW ought to be kept small, so that it could neither duplicate, nor interfere with the functions of the Army General Staff.[489]

Beck indicated his growing concern at the prospect of an OKW with wide powers in a memorandum which he wrote on 15 January 1934. In this he stated that the Chief of the OKW was not to concern himself with the direct conduct of operations.[490] In another memorandum of early 1934,

Beck wrote that there was an acute danger that the Armed Forces commander would attempt to set up an Armed Forces Operations Staff, thereby jeopardizing both the Army commander and the General Staff. This work had to be retained by the Army.[491]

Reichenau replied to this on 9 May 1934 with a full set of proposals for the establishment of the OKW and for the subordination of the Commander-in-Chief of the Army to an Armed Forces commander, thus making a frontal attack on the two most strongly held organizational views of the Army.[492] His proposal for the OKW included Operations, Organization and Intelligence Branches, so this was in direct opposition to the warnings of Beck. This was the most significant single proposal of the whole period, and it became the subject of much subsequent correspondence, in which the various agencies of the Army progressively rejected one feature after another of Reichenau's plan.

Offices which came directly under the Army commander, such as the Army Administration Office, and the Army Ordnance Office said that they presumed that Reichenau intended that they were to become the respective Administrative and Ordnance Departments of the Armed Forces. The placing of the Armed Forces Budget Office under the OKW aroused the opposition of the Organizations Branch of the Army General Staff. It was claimed that this would give the Internal Affairs Department of the OKW an unfair advantage in the settlement of financial disputes. The Operations Branch objected that the proposal for a Chief of Armed Forces Signal Communications did not remove the need for a similar post for the Army itself. The Organizations Branch said that since this Armed Forces Communications Chief would have to be a high ranking General, it would not be possible to place him under the Operations Branch of the OKW, but that he should be placed directly under the Armed Forces Commander.[493]

This battle was continued between the General Staff of the Army and the Armed Forces Office. The chief protagonists for each side were Beck and Reichenau, and after Reichenau's transfer to the command of Wehrkreis VII, Keitel.[494] Reichenau was supported by Blomberg and Beck was assisted by Fritsch, so that although Fritsch and Blomberg did not enter directly into the details of the argument in the early years, this basic difference in their outlook had come to the surface, and widened the gap which existed through political differences between them.

In order to provide a number of suitably trained officers for an OKW, an Armed Forces Academy was set up in 1935. However, the resistance to the notion of an OKW was so great on the part of all three services that the Academy had to be closed down after only two years.[495]

But before dealing with the final phases of the disputes over the OKW, another point of contention ought to be examined. This was the question of the procurement of armaments. In this case, the dispute was centred on the Army Ordnance Office and Göring. The Army Ordnance wanted to establish a centralized system for the three services, while Göring saw this as a limitation on his expansion of the Air Force, and insisted on having complete control over the armaments of the Air Force himself.

As a result of the Reichenau proposals for an OKW, the Army Ordnance Office had suggested that if any co-ordination was to be done, it should be in the matter of armaments. The Ordnance Office wanted the establishment of an office directly under the Commander-in-Chief of the Armed Forces, responsible for the development, procurement, and acceptance of all equipment except certain specified air and naval items, and with the power of recommending adjustments in the demands of the three services to the Commander-in-Chief of the Armed Forces.[496] In a later memorandum the Army Ordnance Office amplified these proposals, and added that it did not want certain specialized equipment of the Navy and Air Force included within its general field of responsibility, but that there should be close consultation between the Ordnance Offices of the Navy and Air Force and the central Armed Forces Ordnance Office.[497]

Some few weeks later, Göring replied to these suggestions, rejecting them outright. No air equipment could be placed under the control of any other body. The mobilization of industry in war could only be carried out by those who had worked with it in peace-time.

Therefore, I [Göring] cannot share control of the aeronautical industry with any outside agency, any more than I could share control of my Air Force.[498]

However, Göring did suggest the creation of a commissioner for the allocation of raw materials to the three services.

The Army Ordnance Office replied on 11 July 1934, stating that this suggestion did not go far enough, as co-ordination was needed at stages much later than that of the allocation of raw materials. If a factory making machine-guns for the Air Force were bombed, it would be necessary for a central authority to make the necessary arrangements for the transfer of the manufacture of these guns to other factories, which would probably have been producing guns for the Army or Navy, and this could only be done by a group of experts who did that sort of thing permanently for all services.[499]

The Navy also lent its weight to the proposals of the Army Ordnance Office,[500] but the outcome was a compromise which did not content either the Army Ordnance Office or Göring, and so hostility was maintained which made the working of the new system extremely difficult. This system comprised a Military Economics and Ordnance Group, within the Armed Forces Office, under Oberst Thomas, formerly Chief of Staff in the Army Ordnance Office, and who had written most of the memoranda of the Ordnance Office during the battle with Göring. The personnel for this new department were taken from the Army Ordnance Office in a body. It was to be responsible for co-ordinating development and procurement of equipment by the three services, adjusting their differences and preventing duplication. It was also to plan and control the allocation of raw materials, industrial plant, labour and relations with outside organizations, and to supervise the general organization of the armaments industry and the maintenance of uniform prices. Blomberg ordered that this department was to commence operation on 1 November 1934, so that the big increases in armaments which were taking place as a result of the expansion of the Army to twenty-one divisions, might be brought within a co-ordinated controlling system as soon as possible.[501] This decision aggravated the differences between the Army and Göring, and may have had an influence on Göring's feelings towards Blomberg which would explain his later conduct towards Blomberg at the time of the crisis over Blomberg's marriage.

These various disputes settled down into a number of minor feuds between the affected parties until 1937 under the heavy pressure of the general rearmament. After the successful Army manœuvres of 1936, it was decided to hold combined manœuvres in 1937, involving the participation of all three services. The planning and preparation for these exercises had to be done by the General Staff of the Army, because there was no other body capable.[502] After the planning had been completed, in August 1937, Fritsch wrote a long memorandum to Blomberg, on the subject 'Organization of the Armed Forces High Command and Operational Command of the Armed Forces'.[503]

It had become apparent to Fritsch that there were two major defects within the organizational structure of the German High Command. The first of these concerned the status of the Army with respect to the other services, and the Armed Forces High Command, and the second related to the large number of functions which had to be carried out by the Commander-in-Chief of the Armed Forces under the system then in force.

He outlined his notion of the existing relationship of the three services thus:

A strict separation of the three branches of the Armed Forces with complete independence from each other, and with equal rights.

In his view this equality was an error, since the Army was of greater significance to Germany than were the other two services. He argued by analogy that all three services were not necessarily equal. Britain was dependent on sea power for the sustenance of the Home Islands and for the binding together of the Empire, while the British Army played the minor role of an expeditionary force. For France, the Army was the decisive factor. Italy's Army would be ineffective against Germany, its fleet was powerless, therefore it might attach greatest importance to its Air Force. For Germany, victory depended in the final analysis on the Army. The German Fleet could never defeat any of the major Continental powers. Admittedly England could only be brought to her knees by the combined action of the Navy and Air Force, but in view of the international situation, such a conflict was not to be expected. The Air Force also was not sufficient to inflict defeat on any major power, unless in support of the Army. Only the Army, in conjunction with the other services could defend Germany against enemy conquest, and only the Army could inflict decisive defeat on an enemy by conquering his country.

Furthermore, the question of size played an important role. The Army comprised eight-tenths of the Armed Forces, Fritsch continued, and so it was natural that the Army should have a place of pre-eminence. Also, the Army was more subject to the influence of the overall strategic situation.

The Navy's task of keeping the sea lanes open had to be carried out, irrespective of the operations which actually led to the final military outcome. The Air Force, with its greater mobility could strike an enemy without having to worry about the exact position of the front line. Thus, as far as overall strategy was concerned, the warfare on land was the decisive factor.

Therefore, the structure of the High Command had to allow for this. While the Navy had to fulfil a predetermined mission, and the Air Force carried out a continuous operation, the Army had to conduct operations dependent on the turn of day-to-day events. Even the question of the opening of hostilities would be governed by the speed at which the Army could mobilize and deploy itself. The Army alone could inflict decisive defeat on an enemy, and the Army was the only service whose failure would mean the defeat of Germany.

Therefore, Fritsch continued, a strategic Armed Forces High Command which was independent of the Army Command was unthinkable. Any solution which involved the creation of an OKW over the General Staffs of the three services could not be tolerated. The officers on this staff would not be in close enough touch with the affairs of the Army, unless they placed themselves in the same position as the Army General Staff.

The creation of an OKW would, in time of war, lead to an unbroken chain of conflicts.

As the Navy and the Air Force were so relatively independent of the day-to-day events of a war, the only real function of the OKW would be the conduct of the fighting of the Army, and it was certain that the operations of the Army were better known by the General Staff of the Army than by the OKW, if this latter were a separate body.

Fritsch then went on to consider the personal relations which would be likely to exist between a Commander-in-Chief of the Armed Forces, and a Commander-in-Chief of the Army, in view of the special characteristics of the German situation. He concluded that it would be impossible for the Commander-in-Chief of the Armed Forces, advised by an OKW to order the Army Commander to carry out an operation which was not held to be sound by the Army Commander, because at this level, one could not simply command obedience. However, if an OKW were created, this type of friction would be very likely to produce this result.

Since the commands of the Army and the Armed Forces are inseparable, their separation should not consciously be caused by the creation of an OKW as an independent command staff.

To ensure the essential unity of the Army Command and of the Armed Forces Command in war, there were two means open. Either the Army High Command was to be abolished, or the Army High Command should assume the functions of the OKW as advisory staff to the Armed Forces commander. The first method had the disadvantage of adding to the already too numerous duties of the Armed Forces commander, therefore the second one was preferable. Fritsch's final conclusion was that restoration of complete accord between overall operations and Army operations should be achieved by allotting to the Army High Command the task of making the plans for all Armed Forces operations, without infringing on the special individual tasks of the Navy or Air Force.

He began his treatment of the question of the tasks of the Commander-in-Chief of the Armed Forces in a similar manner to his treatment of the question of inter-service relationships by an examination of the current German situation. This required that the overall military command united in one person, who also was the War Minister. Under him were three independent service commanders who acted as his senior advisers. However, this was only the case in theory because the growth of central agencies, particularly the Armed Forces Office, had altered this situation. He went on to state that the more the union of overall command in one man was practical, the less possible it was that all staff functions could be carried out in one agency, under one chief. The Armed Forces commander had three functions as Fritsch saw them. First, he had to command the forces in war. Secondly, he had to organize the fighting nation in terms of manpower and material resources, i.e. carry out the functions of a War Minister. Thirdly, he had to administer and supervise the whole of the organization of the Armed Forces, in so far as this was not carried out by the individual services, i.e. the functions of the War Ministry.

The great breadth of these functions made it quite impossible for there to be a single office, directly under the War Minister which dealt with everything from the planning of the operations of the Armed Forces in battle to the organization of the military economics of the nation. Even more so, was it impossible for any one man to act as Chief of Staff to the Commander of the Armed Forces, chief adviser to the War Minister, chief of the Armed Forces Economics Organization, and Chief of Staff of a combined services War Ministry, at one and the same time. Even though these difficulties might not be present at the time of writing, Fritsch stressed, that was due partly to the existence of peace, and partly to the small amount of progress which had been made towards absorbing the functions of the War Ministry from the services by the Armed Forces Command. Furthermore, the existence of the Chief of the Armed Forces Office made it much more likely that this man would be the only practical adviser to the War Minister and Commander-in-Chief of the Armed Forces, rather than the commanders of the three individual services.

Fritsch's solution to these problems was to separate the three major functions carried out by the War Minister and Commander-in-Chief. Everything relating to the organization of the whole nation in time of war should be combined in one department, under a Reichs Defence Minister. The Armed Forces High Command should be removed from this ministry, and set up as a wholly separate entity. The organization of the administration of the services, or the functions of the War Ministry had to be reallocated between the services and the Armed Forces High Command.

Fritsch saw no clear boundary line between what should be the administrative functions of the services and what should be those of the High

Command. He examined several matters in detail, and arrived at an empirical result. There were several matters of importance to all three services, such as:

> matters involving internal politics,
> relations between the Party and the Armed Forces,
> personnel welfare,
> uniform training, and
> the War Economics Inspectorates.

These could be attended to by the establishment of a small department. The remaining administrative functions, should be retained by the service commanders, in order to avoid the growth of bureaucracy, and the consequent waste of personnel.

This long and detailed memorandum met with a very cool response from Blomberg. He wrote at the bottom of the last page:

> Conversation with Generaloberst von Fritsch on 1 September 1937. I declined the proposal, but again declared myself willing to do the natural thing: that is to include him, the Commander-in-Chief of the Army, in my command and operational procedure by referring to him and not going over his head. We both agreed that we would see and talk to each other more often than at present, if possible, weekly.

Thus, the Army commander was faced by the probability of the growth of a large and cumbersome Armed Forces High Command, which would present him with the dangers of paying scant attention to the commander of the armies in the field and of placing enormous power in the hands of the man who was to act as the Chief of Staff of this organization.

Fritsch's successor, Brauchitsch, was not content to accept this state of affairs, and set to work, almost immediately after taking office, to prepare another long memorandum, pressing a similar policy.[504] He submitted this memorandum to the newly formed OKW on 7 March 1938.

He introduced his thoughts with a historical analysis of the problem of the command of military forces. This had become a difficulty due to two factors. First, the scope of warfare had extended far beyond the purely military aspects, so that the entire resources of a nation had to be organized and employed, hence the need for an organization which embraced both the political and military conduct of a war. Secondly the importance of air-power had created a third, independent service. Formerly, the Army and the Navy had existed separately, but this had not imposed a special problem of command, because they had only rarely acted in combination, and neither had exerted much influence on the operations of the other. The Air Force was quite different, as it had to be able to act in close support of the Army, and of the Navy, as well as act in an independent, strategic role. Hence, a special organization was needed to fit the use of the Air Force into the operations of the other services, without robbing it of its independent capacity.

These problems had been partially solved within the German Armed Forces by the establishment of an Armed Forces High Command, the

113

I

head of which was both Commander-in-Chief of the Armed Forces, and Minister for War. However, practical experience had shown that this system could not be worked without friction, particularly between the Armed Forces High Command and the Army High Command. Brauchitsch was convinced that this friction was not due just to personalities, but to the nature of the organization of the supreme agency or department.

Experience of the past few years led him to three conclusions. First, it was not feasible to unite at a single point within the supreme agency both military command in war, and the organization of the nation as a whole for war. Secondly, without prejudice to the complete parity of the three services, a single service would have a decisive role in the final outcome of a war, and command of this service must not be separated from overall command. Thirdly, it was not possible in practice to maintain three independent services under their Commanders-in-Chief if they were subordinated not only to a Commander-in-Chief of the Armed Forces, but also to a central agency.

His first conclusion was based on the same reasoning as that used by Fritsch, namely that there was too much to be encompassed by a staff working directly under a Commander-in-Chief of the Armed Forces for this staff to be unified. While it was very desirable to centre supreme command on one individual, it was necessary to split the strategic conduct of operations and the organization of the national war effort into separate organizations. Unifying these two functions in one staff would in effect make the chief of that staff close to being the Supreme Commander himself. Therefore, what was needed was the creation of two special subordinates to the Supreme Commander—a Reichs Secretary of War, and a Reichs Chief of Staff.

Brauchitsch summed up his views on inter-service parity briefly by observing that, from Germany's strategic situation, and from the relative sizes of the three services, the Army was the decisive force. In warfare with the eastern countries, only Czechoslovakia was vulnerable to air attacks. To defeat Russia or Poland, the Army alone could be decisive. The Army was subject to limitations which did not apply to the Navy or to the Air Force, due to the slowness with which it moved, and the large numbers of men involved. Thus the whole rhythm of mobilization and the further conduct of a war had to be governed by the requirements of the Army. Therefore, it was vital to maintain the unity of command between the Army and the Armed Forces as a whole.

The interposition of an OKW between the Armed Forces Commander and the various service commanders was intolerable, because the responsibilities borne by these commanders were so great that they could carry out their functions, only if they could present their problems directly to the Armed Forces Commander. Thus, the position of Chief of the OKW would be redundant. Furthermore, if the functions of a Minister of War were also concentrated in the OKW, it would exercise direct control over the Wehrkreise, etc., since their functions were administrative, and so the service commanders would be reduced to the status of inspectors-general.

The remedies which were suggested by Brauchitsch were simply expressed. First the functions of the Commander-in-Chief of the Armed Forces had to be split into their three separate categories, by the appointment of a Reichs Chief of Staff to exercise command of the forces in war, and of a Reichs Secretary of War to organize the nation. Secondly, an assurance of the unity of the Armed Forces High Command with the Army High Command had to be given, and thirdly, the commanders of the three services should be directly responsible to the Commander-in-Chief of the Armed Forces.

Under the Reichs Secretary for War, there were to be the following departments:

a Reichs Defence Office, to integrate all branches of government for war purposes,
a Military Economics Office,
a Defence Office for inter-service matters,
and in time of war, possibly a Reichs Security Office and a department exercising the functions of Commander-in-Chief of the Interior.

The Reichs Chief of Staff was actually to command the Armed Forces, and to advise the Commander-in-Chief of the Armed Forces on all questions relating to the overall conduct of a war. As there had to be unity between the High Command of the Army and that of the Armed Forces, it was logical that the Reichs Chief of Staff should be the Commander-in-Chief of the Army. There could not be a separate OKW as that would lead to friction and duplication. A Reichs Chief of Staff above the Commander-in-Chief of the Army would either be a nonentity, or a restricting influence on the conduct of the land battle by the Commander-in-Chief of the Army. The few essential centralized Armed Forces agencies were to be placed under the Army commander.

In order to place the service commanders as close as possible to the Commander-in-Chief of the Armed Forces, all functions of the War Ministry should be split up, except for a very few which required uniform handling, and allocated to the individual services. In particular, the following matters were to be handled by the Commander-in-Chief in direct contact with the service commanders:

the organization of the Armed Forces,
allocation of resources and funds,
military-political preparations for war,
the military and political commencement of war, and the setting of the objectives of a war.

The final decision was to rest with the Head of State, as Commander-in-Chief of the Armed Forces, but he was to be advised by the service commanders in a 'Supreme War Council'. If, at any stage during a war, the Führer decided to appoint a Generalissimo who would command the Armed Forces for him, then this could be fitted in to the above plan.

The chain of command which Brauchitsch proposed was as follows

Commander-in-Chief of the Armed Forces—the Führer
Commanders-in-Chief of the Services, with the Army Commander as
Reichs Chief of Staff, and the Reichs Secretary of War.

The service commanders were to have the same authority as Cabinet ministers, but within the Supreme War Council, the Reichs Chief of Staff was to be responsible for questions of the overall conduct of war. He was to be assisted by a small inter-service operations staff, which was to be attached to the Army General Staff.

These proposals of Brauchitsch showed great resemblance to those of Fritsch, and they were probably written with close reference to the Fritsch memorandum. They both show that their authors were aware of the dangers which might have been occasioned by a continued development of the command system which was in force at that time, taking control out of the hands of those who were the most thoroughly trained in its use, and giving it to others who, by virtue of their positions would have been unable and unwilling to check the wildest plans of Hitler. In view of Hitler's expressions at that time of a future policy of warlike nature, the urgency of Fritsch and Brauchitsch must have been very pressing. The situation was also complicated by the positions which Göring occupied. His political influence gave him much greater power than either of the other two service commanders, and thus Fritsch and Brauchitsch were most anxious to convince Hitler that the Army was of much greater significance, perhaps even to the point of consciously understating the role of the Air Force.

However, by early 1938, Hitler had a blindly faithful follower in a position from which opposition to the ideas of Brauchitsch could be made, so leaving the battle to be fought out a little longer within the circle of the service chiefs. Keitel wrote a long reply to the proposals of Brauchitsch on 19 April 1938, to demonstrate that the *status quo* was a much better system.[505]

The first part of Keitel's paper attempted to show that it was contrary to the basic principles of total war, the form of warfare of the future, to believe that the three functions of the Commander-in-Chief of the Armed Forces could be separated. Furthermore, these functions ought to be co-ordinated at a lower level in a staff which would form the Armed Forces High Command. He then went on to turn on its head what Brauchitsch had written about the impossibility of the field commander being able to direct the entire war economy by stating that the field commander could not command his troops without an exact knowledge of all other political and economic factors. Therefore, he needed a staff which would be able to co-ordinate the entire activities of the nation at war.

He went as far as to base this partly on the experience of Göring, who had briefly split the functions of his combined civil and military aviation department into two sections, the one under a State Secretary, the other under a Chief of Staff. After a few weeks, Göring 'recognized the uselessness of this separation, and abolished it'.

This was as deep as Keitel's reasoning went on this topic. He then proceeded to refute Brauchitsch's claim that the Army commander ought to be placed in a position of eminence with regard to the other service commanders. Keitel admitted that the Army could have a decisive effect on the course of a war, but it was possible that this might not always be the case. In a war with Russia, or Britain, the Navy and Air Force would have to play the main part. Moreover, during the course of a war, the relative importance of the three services was likely to change. Therefore, it was impossible to place command of the other two services in the hands of the Army. In addition, the normal human problems of jealousy and favouritism would complicate such a system.

Keitel closed with an appeal for a spirit of sacrifice. There would have been no German Nation, had not the states given up their sovereignty, and there could be no German Armed Forces unless all three services considered themselves as only parts of the whole, and willingly ceded to the Armed Forces High Command whatever was necessary for united organization and command.

The final say in this series of proposal and counter-proposal was had by Hitler himself. Very shortly after Keitel had presented his memorandum, Hitler publicly and emphatically confirmed the existing organization as being the final form which the High Command of the German Armed Forces would take.[506] Thus, by organizational structure, the forces of restraint, particularly the General Staff of the Army under Beck, were confined in power and breadth of responsibility, while new fields were opened up for control by those elements which gave Hitler unquestioned loyalty. In effect, the creation of the OKW under Keitel was a powerful means of transferring the strategic direction of German policy from the hands of the Army to those of Hitler, by default of character on the part of Keitel. But, besides the significant effects of this accumulation of power for Hitler, which showed themselves in the crises of foreign policy which occurred in 1938 and 1939, the division within the senior ranks of the Armed Forces between those who supported Hitler and those who questioned his policies was made clearer to all, including Hitler and his leading colleagues. Thus he was not only able to label this latter group as political reactionaries in Party circles, but he was also able to refer to the same group as ultra-conservative in a military sense amongst his loyal military supporters. Destruction of the powerful bond of professional outlook further weakened the power of Hitler's military advisers to oppose him.

9

The Army's Plans for National Defence

CONTACT between the Army and the Party during the first five years of the Third Reich concerned mainly internal politics. During 1938 and 1939 strategic matters came to play a much greater role in Army-Party relations. In order to examine the effect of the Nazi régime on German strategy in the pre-war years, it is necessary to see what the views of the Army, acting from its own initiative, were.

Fortunately, these views are relatively easy to discover. Until November 1937 Hitler avoided interference with the military conduct of German strategic policy[507] and so the plans made by the General Staff during this period are a true indication of the Army's views during this time.

The basic problem of the security of Germany had not greatly altered between the end of the First World War and the coming to power of Hitler. Surrounded by several powers, she was very vulnerable to the threat of an alliance of powers on opposite sides of her whose strength could be sufficient, if well organized, to offset Germany's natural advantage of interior lines. As a result of the Treaty of Versailles, the forces at Germany's disposal, viz.: seven divisions of infantry and three of cavalry, were considerably less than those of Poland or Czechoslovakia or France.* These circumstances gave rise to the basic concepts of Seeckt, which were:

(a) to avoid war in the west at all costs, until Germany was able to regain her armed strength,

(b) to provide a defensive screen on the eastern frontier, to check the Poles, and to counter Polish strength by good relations with Russia.[508]

---

* Manstein, *Aus einem Soldatenleben*, pp. 116–17. According to Manstein, the following were the strengths of Germany's rivals in the early 1930s:

		Peace	*War*
French Army		30 Divisions	90 Divisions
		600,000 men	1,500,000 men
Polish Army		25 Infantry Divisions,	50 Infantry Divisions,
		plus Cavalry	plus Cavalry
			1,000,000 men
Czech Army		15 Infantry Divisions,	30 Infantry Divisions,
		plus Cavalry	plus Cavalry
			600,000 men

From 1929 to 1931 Manstein was head of the section of the Operations Department which dealt with the disposition of units.

These were the principles which were in force at the time of the Machtübernahme.[509] The chief source of concern was Poland. Polish attacks into East Prussia had been feared to be imminent in early 1933.[510] In March 1933, the situation appeared to have deteriorated. Pilsudski's plans for a preventive war were known in Germany, and were being exploited by Hitler, in order to consolidate all political parties behind him.[511] Polish cavalry forces were concentrated in the Corridor, and near the German-Lithuanian border.[512] On 6 March 1933, Pilsudski broke the Polish-Danzig Agreement of 1921, by increasing the garrison on the Westerplatte Peninsula, near Danzig.[513] The response of Hitler to this danger was the *rapprochement* which culminated in the signing of a ten-year non-aggression treaty between Poland and Germany, on 26 January 1934.[514] Part of this *rapprochement* was to allow the German-Soviet Military Treaty of 1926 to lapse in late 1933,[515] so completing the reorientation of German eastern policy. This helped to solve the immediate problem of national security for the Reichswehr, but such a sweeping change from the policy of the Weimar period was very unpopular within the Army.[516]

However, the removal of this danger from the east gave the High Command a breathing space in which it could develop a more long term policy for national defence instead of having to deal with immediate crises. Hossbach defined the central strategic problem of the years 1934–38 as:

How Germany was to conduct herself in any war, which might be forced upon her either on one front or on several, and what demands were to be put before the political leadership of the nation by the military commander, so that the Armed Forces would not be confronted again by the insoluble problem of the simultaneous conduct of war on all sides.[517]

The situation called for planning, rather than for action, and as such was largely in the hands of Beck, who, as Chief of the General Staff, was responsible for the preparation of any plans which were required by the Commander-in-Chief of the Army. The relationship between Fritsch and Beck was good, and they worked together as a team.[518] They were mainly occupied with the immense task of preparing the large increases in the size of the Army, which began in October 1934, with the expansion from seven to twenty-one divisions of infantry. The further expansions of the organization which took place in 1935–36–37, and the extension of the period of service from one year to two in late 1936 continued to provide the bulk of their work, which was regarded as the foundation of any German military strategy.*

In late 1934, after most of the planning work for the expansion of the Army to twenty-one divisions had been completed, the General Staff again turned its attention to the security of Germany's frontiers. The eastern frontier seemed to be secure for the immediate future and within a

---

* For Fritsch's attitude see Kielmansegg, *Der Fritsch Prozess*, p. 28. The similarity of Beck's attitude is revealed in numerous minutes written by him, which are to be found in Bundesarchiv File HO 8/28/2.

few years the strength of the German Armed Forces was to become so great that Poland was not to be regarded as a long-term threat. This left the General Staff free to consider the problem of French incursions into Western Germany and a defensive plan for the deployment of limited forces in Western Germany was issued on 1 November 1934.[519] However, this plan was in no sense a full deployment as had been planned before 1914.

This trend of events was interrupted on 30 March 1935, when Reichenau produced a memorandum which dealt with the Czechoslovakian problem.[520] Reichenau anticipated that in the event of war, Czechoslovakia would mobilize against Germany. She might even allow herself to be used as a base for Germany's enemies. In this case, a surprise attack might be made against the Czechs. Staff discussions took place in April, and on 2 May, the same day on which the Franco-Russian Treaty was signed, Blomberg issued a directive for an operation *Schulung*.[521] This directive was not an order, but a plan. The objective was not specified but it dealt with a surprise attack on a 'South-Eastern State'. This state was Czechoslovakia.[522] Blomberg ordered Beck to carry out a detailed study of the possibilities of this operation. The answer reached the Reichskriegs Minister on the following day.

Beck was appalled at this prospect. He introduced his remarks with the following reservation:

After thorough consideration, I hold it to be my duty to declare this very day that if the memorandum of the Minister is not solely concerned with the purpose of operational studies, but is aimed at the practical introduction of preparations for war, then I must express the most dutiful request to be removed from my position at the Truppenamt, because I do not feel myself to be fitted for this latter task.[523]

Three weeks prior to this reply, Beck had received a memorandum from his Director of Military Intelligence, the Chief of Abteilung T3, Oberst von Stülpnagel. This set out for him the current balance of power and the relative strengths of the various sectors of the German military economy. The conclusions were:
  (a) Germany must avoid provoking any trouble, especially with respect to Austria and the Demilitarized Zone.
  (b) An improvement in relations with Italy was necessary, in order to avoid encirclement.[524]
Beck gave the substance of this memorandum to Blomberg in his reply, stressing the military impossibility of such an action against Czechoslovakia since the other powers would be able to mobilize and deploy their forces rapidly enough to prevent Germany from achieving any temporary numerical superiority. He also emphasized that the rearmament programme was so little advanced that the Army would be fighting without much essential equipment. He concluded thus:

Thus I can regard such an operation as an act of desperation, an act of desperation by which the German Army, as well as surrendering German soil

The Opening of the
Officer Training School,
Potsdam, on 9 January
1936. From left:
Generals von Küchler, von
Fritsch, von Witzleben, and
Oberst Wetzel, the
Commandant of the
School.

The Army training
members of the
National-Socialist Motor
Corps.

The Army training members of the Hitler Youth in marksmanship, in a special camp for the "premilitary training of the youth".

Two members of the Hitler Youth (bottom left and centre) being taught field craft by an Army instructor.

Schoolboys being taught marksmanship as part of their normal education under the Third Reich.

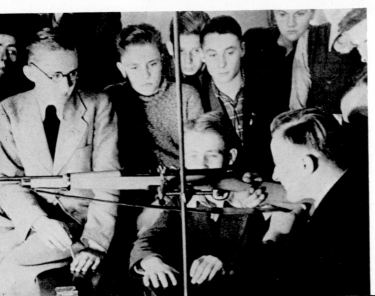

The tanks of the German Army:
  (1) before Hitler came to power
  (2) after Hitler's abrogation of the Versailles Treaty.

Soldiers parading in Potsdam before the Garnisonskirche with the new National War Flag, emblazoned with the swastika, which was issued in time for the autumn oath-taking ceremonies, 1935.

The old colours of the Imperial Army being borne in procession through Nuremberg.

The new colours being paraded before Hitler and Göring (wearing steel helmet) in Berlin.

Newly dedicated colours being paraded before Fritsch and Blomberg in 1936 or 1937.

Motorized units of the Army parade past Hitler at the Party Rally,
Nuremberg 1936. On the tribune are, from left: Raeder, Fritsch,
Göring, Hitler, Blomberg.

Blomberg publicly honours the Hitler-Putsch of 1923 by participating
in the commemorative repetition of the march to the Feldherrnhalle
on 9 November 1936. He identifies himself with fellow marchers (in
the front row) Göring, Hitler, Frick, and Himmler.

Party military propaganda at the exhibition staged in 1937 entitled by the words "Give me four years time!" taken from Hitler's speeches before coming to power. The placard stresses the National-Socialist miracle of the restoration of German power and warns that the future will call for yet greater strength.

Hitler nominating Blomberg to be Colonel-in-Chief of Infantry Regiment 73 on 13 March 1937, the fortieth anniversary of Blomberg's entry into military service. The ceremony took place in the Ministerial Hall of the War Ministry. Behind Hitler are Fritsch, Göring and Raeder. The other officers are departmental heads within the War Ministry.

Hitler presenting Blomberg to Mussolini when the latter visited the
Armed Forces Manœuvres held on the Mecklenburg plain in
October 1937.

itself, excludes itself from the direct defence of the nation, in all likelihood to find an inglorious end in a foreign land, while at home the enemy dictate their own conditions. Such a military High Command will probably not only lose the trust of the homeland, but even earlier the confidence of its own troops, and must expect the severest condemnation, not only of its own age, but also of history.[525]

The Czechoslovakian problem was then allowed to rest. Blomberg ordered that the question would be looked at again during the annual General Staff Exercise.[526] This re-examination was made in 1937,[527] when the General Staff went to Bad Kreuznach.[528] Beck found once more that the plan was militarily unsound.[529]

In the meantime, the problem of the security of Germany's western frontiers had received more attention. During late 1935[530] *Aufmarsch Rot* (Deployment Red) was prepared by the Operations Abteilung of the General Staff, under the direction of Generalmajor von Manstein. This was the first deployment plan to be prepared since the First World War, apart from some small scale operations which had been planned to meet a Polish invasion of the eastern provinces, in the late 1920s.[531]

Aufmarsch Rot was designed to meet a major French attack into Western Germany at a time when the Czechs, although assisting the French, were not playing a strongly offensive role. The automatic hostility of Poland was not counted on, because of the Non-Aggression Treaty. It was thought that Poland would wait to see the course of military operations before committing herself.[532] The two most likely French thrusts were thought to be either through the Kraichgau, between the Black Forest and the Odenwald, with the object of meeting up with the Czech forces to separate Northern Germany from Southern Germany or through the Ruhr, to paralyse the industrial heart of Germany. To meet this situation, the German Army was to be divided into four Armies, three of which were to be deployed in the west, while the fourth, with the Grenzschutz, covered the Czech and Polish frontiers. It was not intended to offer any serious resistance to the French west of the Rhine, but a strong attempt was to be made to bring the French action to a halt on the line of the Rhine itself.[533]

But even if the French were halted without heavy German losses, it was nonetheless a poor guarantee for German security. German security would then have had to depend on the Czechs making the military mistake of remaining on the defensive, instead of exploiting their local superiority, of approximately five to one,* to make a quick thrust over the 120 miles which separated them from Berlin. Therefore Beck was persuaded to authorize the preparation of another plan, *Aufmarsch Grün* (Deployment Green), in 1937.[534] This plan aimed a pre-emptive blow at the Czechs before the French offensive had achieved decisive success. Despite the fact that this plan was prepared within the General Staff, Beck continued to regard it as a military absurdity, as it would bring both Britain and

---

* The Czech Army could put 30 divisions of infantry into the field in time of war. The German Army could raise 21 divisions of infantry, of which five, plus the Grenzschutz were available for the entire eastern front.

France together against Germany just as the Schlieffen Plan's violation of Belgium had done in 1914.[535]

Aufmarsch Grün was to begin with the deployment of the greater part of the Army in the south-east. An attack was to be pressed home from Bavaria, Saxony and Silesia, in converging manner. While this was taking place, a screen was to impede the French advance. The country west of the Rhine was to be sacrificed. As soon as possible, the bulk of the German Army was to be transferred to the west, to fight the decisive battle of the war.[536]

Until the preparation of further actions against Czechoslovakia in 1938, this was the extent of the contingency plans of the General Staff. Blomberg formalized the whole situation in a directive of 24 June 1937, on 'Unified War Preparations of The Armed Forces'.[537] Blomberg introduced his requirements thus:

The general political situation justifies the supposition that Germany does not have to reckon on an attack from any side. This is due mainly to the lack of desire for war on the part of all nations, especially the Western powers. It is also due to the lack of preparedness on the part of a number of states, notably Russia. Germany has just as little intention of unleashing a European war. Nonetheless, the international situation, politically unstable and not exclusive of surprising incidents, requires continuous readiness for war on the part of the German Armed Forces,

(a) so that attacks from any side may be countered;
(b) so that any favourable political opportunities may be militarily exploited.

The directive went on to outline the situations in which Germany could find herself at war, viz.:

1. Two front war with the emphasis in the west (*Rot*).
2. Two front war with the emphasis in the east (*Grün*).

In addition, special preparations were to be made for the following cases:

1. Armed intervention against Austria (*Sonderfall Otto*).
2. Military involvement with Red Spain (*Sonderfall Richard*).
3. British, Polish and Lithuanian participation in a war against Germany (*Sonderfall Erweiterung Rot/Grün*).

The various measures for *Aufmärsche Rot* and *Grün* were outlined, with first priority assigned to *Rot*. *Sonderfall Otto* was aimed at the prevention of a Habsburg restoration. The document concluded with some consideration of the possible roles of Britain, Poland and Lithuania. If these three were to fight against Germany, then 'our military situation would deteriorate to an unbearable extent, even as far as becoming hopeless'. No illusions were felt about Britain, for she will 'employ all her available economic and military resources against us'.

The extent to which Blomberg was responsible for this directive is uncertain, but in all probability its contents were essentially his own views. It is unlikely that it was issued without prior consultation with Hitler, but in mid-1937 Hitler had not begun to immerse himself in the planning activity of the Army. As Hossbach relates:[538]

During this period Hitler adhered strictly to the boundaries of the area of responsibility of his military advisers. There is no substantiated case in which Hitler intervened in military matters on his own authority and without previous consultation with his Minister for War. All directives and orders which required his permission originated in the responsible places within the War Ministry, be it on the initiative of the Ministry or after consultation between Hitler and Blomberg, and were only shown to the former for his signature after counter-signing by Blomberg, and where necessary, by the commanders of the individual services. . . . No military authority, independent from the constitutional advisers, was exercised by the Head of State, until the end of January 1938.

Robertson[539] detects 'an aggressive purpose' in this directive, because:

If Russia was not prepared for war, there could be no object in smashing Czechoslovakia as a Soviet base; if there was no will for war amongst the Western powers, Concentration Red would seem superfluous.

These reasons do not appear to be sufficient. The main point in striking at Czechoslovakia was to protect the rear, and to ensure the security of Berlin. As for *Aufmarsch Rot*, simply because war seems at one instant to be unlikely, a General Staff is not justified in neglecting to make any plans for national defence. Blomberg himself stressed that the international situation could spring surprises.

If aggressive intent is to be recognized in this directive, it is more in the second justification given by Blomberg for the constant readiness of the Armed Forces—the military exploitation of any favourable political circumstances. But even here it does not follow that Blomberg was contemplating the launching of attacks on neighbouring countries. His views may have gone no further than the Sudeten question, Danzig, or right of unrestricted access to East Prussia, via a German strip across the Corridor.

This was the furthest extent of strategic planning by the Wehrmacht, acting from its own initiative. In point of fact, *Aufmarsch Grün* as specified by Blomberg, *Sonderfall Otto* and probably *Sonderfall Erweiterung Rot/Grün* were not prepared by the Army because of Beck's opposition to them.[540] After 1937 all plans for major operations were prepared at the behest of Hitler. A little more light is thrown on the attitudes of the Army by the fortifications which it planned and built as part of the execution of its strategic policy.

In 1933, the borders of Germany were not protected by any fortifications. The only defensive structure to be built was the Heilsberg Triangle in East Prussia, masking Königsberg.[541] In 1934, a strong line was commenced, running across the plains between the Oder and the Warthe. The purpose of this was to force an invading force from the East to split into two, and so to facilitate the defence of the approaches to Berlin, by a method similar to that employed at Tannenberg.[542] The protection of the West was a more difficult matter, for the Treaty of Versailles forbade the construction of any fortifications in the demilitarized zone, inclusive of the Rhine. Nothing was attempted until the Rhineland had been reoccupied when the massive Western Fortifications were commenced.[543] These were intended as a complement to the Maginot Line, although they were built on a different principle. The Maginot Line used the 'hard thin skin' approach, which was valueless, once an initial penetration had been achieved. The German fortifications were built on a 'Milky Way' principle, affording depth with economy of construction, and excellent mutual support for the defending positions.[544] The construction of these fortifications brought some friction with the civil government, since all building materials were under the control of Dr Todt, who was giving priority to the construction of the Autobahnen. These fortifications were still unfinished in 1945.[545]

Thus the plans made by the General Staff between 1933 and 1938 were defensive in character and care was taken to see that there were enough fortifications for these plans to be put into effect.

During the Weimar Republic, the General Staff had been very concerned about the security of Germany. When Hitler came to power, the General Staff was permitted to make strategic plans as it thought fit, without direction from Hitler. Although these plans were never used, they are of great importance for they illustrate the Army's own strategic policy. It now remains to describe how this policy was displaced by designs of conquest.

10

Hitler, the High Command, and the Possibility of War,1933-1938

HAVING considered the role played by the Army on its own initiative in the preparation of plans for war, it now remains to relate the story of its reactions to the war policies which were urged upon it by the National-Socialist Government. A marked change in outlook and circumstances followed the replacement of Fritsch by Brauchitsch on 4 February 1938, so for ease of treatment this chapter will deal with the matter until that date, and the later period will be dealt with below in Chapter 12.

There seems to be little doubt that Hitler believed, from the mid-'twenties onwards, that Germany would eventually have to acquire more living space at the expense of her eastern neighbours, and that this might have to be done by the force of arms. These views were set out at length in *Mein Kampf*,[546] and were repeated in various of his speeches during the following years, as exemplified by his speech before the Düsseldorfer Industrie Klub at the beginning of 1932, in which he listed the 'space problem' as one of the most important of those with which Germany had to deal, and declared that, in order to exist, a nation had to employ its force externally.[547]

Once Hitler had come to power in 1933, he had to overcome the difficulties of putting this policy of eastern conquest into effect. The first essential was the creation of a military force which could occupy and hold the new territory. Accordingly, Hitler wasted little time in making his long range policy clear to the men who would have to create and train this force, and lead it into battle.

Shortly after coming to power, Hitler complained to Blomberg that he did not know the senior officers of the Army and Navy, and he asked Blomberg to arrange an occasion for a meeting. Blomberg had called the Wehrkreis Commanders to Berlin for a conference on Friday, 3 February. He discovered that this was also the sixtieth birthday of von Neurath, the Foreign Minister, and so he arranged a celebration dinner to which the senior generals and admirals, and Hitler were invited. As Schleicher was still living in Blomberg's official residence, the dinner had to be held at Hammerstein's house.[548] After the meal, Hitler arose and began to address the company. It was apparent to some members of his audience that he was under a great strain speaking without the assistance of Goebbels or Hess, who usually helped to arouse his audiences to a suitable pitch before handing over to him, and having to face a silent, undemonstrative and critical group of men whom previously he had been compelled to regard from a distance.[549]

He began his speech with his frequently used technique of deliberate pessimism.* His government was confronted by huge almost insoluble tasks, and as a result he would have to introduce sweeping changes into the internal political scene. He discussed the unemployment problem and the economic crisis. After an unsuccessful attempt to analyse both he began to develop a solution. In his opinion, the false prosperity before 1930 could be traced back to the reparations requirements. After meeting these, there were no more market outlets and thus the present crisis had arisen. The possibility of conquering this crisis by increasing exports offered no prospects of success, as the demand of the world was limited, and production was in surplus everywhere—not least because Germany's traditional export markets had developed their own industries. A new solution which he had mentioned in *Mein Kampf* had to be applied. There remained only the possibility of a policy of colonization to cope with the unemployment. This, however, was only a makeshift measure, because the available living space was too small. Only when this had been enlarged could one reckon on a thorough solution. This could be achieved in two ways—either by obtaining new markets by struggle, or by the conquest of new living space in the East, and its relentless Germanization. It was certain that the present economic conditions could only be changed by struggle.

Reactions to this address were varied. A few officers including Fritsch and Fromm were alarmed by the prospect of a future war, but calmed their fears by an appeal to the realities of the existing balance of power.[550] Others, such as Bussche, Adam, Gienanth and Boehm-Tettelbach regarded the speech as an attempt to win the Army over by bribery, with promises of rearmament.[551] General Ritter von Leeb's reactions were summed up by his remark at the time:

A businessman whose wares are any good, does not need to boost them in the loudest tones of a market crier.[552]

There were some, such as Admiral Raeder, who were very impressed by this speech, and by Hitler's theatrical admiration for Hindenburg, while others including Beck were completely lost in the first hour of general pre-amble, and forgot the speech as soon as it was spoken.[553] The coolness of the response of the generals to this speech could scarcely have escaped

* This account is based on the notes made of this speech by the following participants:
> General Liebmann,
> General von Mellenthin, who was an adjutant of Hammerstein at that time,
> Admiral Raeder.

Sauer has made an excellent compilation of these records which is given in Sauer, *Die National-sozialistische Machtergreifung*, p. 748, together with the following footnote on 'Germanization':

> The meaning of this is given in *Mein Kampf*: 'Germanization can only be applied to ground and never to people'—therefore this signifies at the least driving people off the land, if not extermination of the indigenous inhabitants in order to colonize the land with German peasants.

Hitler. Another year elapsed before he raised the subject of war to his military commanders again.

On 28 February 1934, Hitler addressed a combined gathering of Army and S.A. leaders in the Reichswehr Ministry. A full account of this speech has been given above in Chapter 3, but the details relevant to Hitler's expansion policy are repeated below for the sake of convenience.

According to Weichs, Hitler's address contained the following points:

'The German people is going to face frightful destitution.'

The N.S.D.A.P. had overcome the unemployment. These blossoms would last only for about eight years, however, as then an economic recession must ensue. This evil could be remedied only by creating living space for the surplus population. However, the Western Powers would not let us do this. Therefore, short, decisive blows to the West and then to the East could be necessary.

Therefore, he was resolved to raise a people's army, built up on the Reichswehr, rigorously trained and equipped with the most modern weapons. He also rejected a Fascist militia on the Italian pattern. This new army would have to be ready for any defence purposes in five years, and after eight years, suitable also for attacking. The S.A. must confine itself to internal political tasks. One must be loyal in an internal political sense, while externally, one could break one's word.

The reactions of the Army leaders have been set out by Weichs in his concluding remarks to his description of this speech, as follows:

After this address, the feeling of contentment reigned amongst the military audience that the Army High Command had scored a notable success over the Party organization, and it appeared as if Hitler wished to rely first and foremost on the Army.

On reflection, one can say that Hitler had set forth his complete foreign policy programme, and had already intimated the probability of an aggressive war. Considering the great number of listeners, it is almost miraculous that this prophecy of 1934 has never become known. The only detail which did not correspond to later developments was the actual timing of the predicted entanglements of war. The war came much earlier than the training programme which had been specified here for the future Armed Forces allowed. However, one did not take at face value these warlike prophecies, which were certainly in sharp contradiction to the protestations of peace which otherwise filled the air. The soldier was accustomed to take the words of politicians too seriously. They often chose points of view which did not have to correspond with their true intentions, in order to achieve political ends. Thus these gloomy prognostications were probably soon forgotten.

These words were written by an aristocratic officer of the old school, a devout Christian, who was dismissed by Hitler for refusal to comply with his orders in 1945, and there is no doubt as to the sincerity with which Weichs wrote them. His views at that time were concentrated on the threat of the S.A., and the speech was seen in the context of Hitler's attempts to constrain Röhm and his followers to accept a minor role within the Nazi State. It was not difficult for Weichs to rationalize Hitler's remarks as a façade for political purposes, particularly since at that time, German soldiers had only just ceased to be worried about the threat presented by Poland to German territory. Weichs's views have been corroborated to a degree by the almost complete lack of any mention of Hitler's eastern aims in the other accounts of the address which have survived. While Germany lacked military power, it was thought to be safe to go on with the process of rearmament, and to defer the need for a decision for or against Hitler's plans until the forces were of sufficient size to make any warlike action feasible.

Hitler saw that also this speech had failed to evoke the enthusiasm of the generals which was necessary for the foundation of a vigorous partnership dedicated to the achievement of territorial gains. Instead of a barrage of keen questions and helpful suggestions from the generals, there was silence. Hitler's plans were received not with acclamation but with cynical disbelief.

The next opportunity for the observation of the reactions of the Army High Command when confronted by the possibility of war occurred at the time of the re-entry of the Army into the Rhineland in 1936. The redeployment of military forces in the Rhineland had been a concern both of the Foreign Office and of the General Staff since December 1934.[554] The need for securing the strategically vital area of the Ruhr and for guarding the communications afforded by the Rhine valley was regarded as of the utmost importance for future consideration.

During early February 1936, while on a holiday in Bavaria and far away from his official advisers, Hitler decided that the Rhineland question had to be solved in the near future.[555] On 12 February, he returned to Berlin for a few hours, via Schwerin.* During that afternoon, he summoned Fritsch to the Chancellery.† He was not able to summon Blomberg, as Blomberg had been away at the Winter Olympics since 3 February.[556] Hitler discussed the Rhineland problems with Fritsch, who agreed that its reoccupation was a matter of great importance, but who also stressed that under no conditions must any risk of war be incurred. Hitler declared himself in agreement with this principle[557] and had Blomberg informed on the following day at Garmisch-Partenkirchen.[558]

Hitler then entered into a series of consultations with his advisers, in order to predict the likely reactions of the other Locarno powers, and to set plans in motion for securing the benevolent neutrality of Mussolini.[559] On 27 February 1936, the Franco-Soviet Treaty of Alliance was ratified by the French Chamber of Deputies. On the following day, a high level conference of military officers took place in the War Ministry in Berlin.‡ On 29 February Beck summoned the Chiefs of Staff of the three Gruppenkommandos, the ten Infantry Corps headquarters and the Panzer

---

*Hitler went to Schwerin to participate in the funeral of Landesgruppenleiter Gustloff. Hossbach, *Zwischen Wehrmacht und Hitler*, p. 97.

† Fritsch had returned only recently from a visit to Leipzig, Naumburg and Weissenfels. While in Leipzig, he saw the Oberbürgermeister, Carl Goerdeler, on Monday, 3 February 1936, from 4.15 p.m. to 5.00 p.m. OKH file H 24/39.

‡ The documents relating to this conference do not disclose the topics discussed. OKH file H 24/35. Fritsch had intended to go on leave from 19 February to 7 March. OKH file H 24/39. Presumably this was cancelled. He visited troops at Schwedt an der Oder on 27 February. *Ibid.*

Corps headquarters to a conference in Berlin. Records do not show what the subject of this conference was, but it was also attended by the Director of Operations (Ober Quartiermeister I), the Director of Supply and Transport (Ober Quartiermeister III), and by the Chief of Staff of the Inspectorate of Fortifications.[560] Therefore, it is highly likely that the conference was concerned with a forthcoming operation of major importance, and may have done some confirmation of General Staff planning for the Rhineland reoccupation.

Two days later, on 2 March, Blomberg issued a directive for the operation, called *Winterübung* (Winter Exercise).[561] This directive did not specify a date for the execution of the movement. Blomberg did not release this directive until 5 March, when he ordered that the operation was to take place on 7 March.[562] On 5 March, Hitler began to show signs of nervousness. He summoned Hossbach to him and asked him if the whole operation could still be stopped. Hossbach replied that this was possible, and Hitler then asked to know the latest time at which the troops could be called back.[563] Hitler's first question indicated that Blomberg was issuing the final dates in accordance with a pre-planned programme, rather than getting them from Hitler when the latter felt the moment to be ripe.

The advance of the Army began on the morning of 7 March. Only three battalions were sent off across the Rhine, to Trier, Aachen and Saarbrücken, respectively.[564] However, had the French reacted with strength, they would have had to have dealt with more than this handful of troops, because at noon on 7 March, the Landespolizei of the Demilitarized Zone became four divisions of infantry.[565] Although these divisions had no heavy equipment or artillery, they had received intensive military training which had been organized since 21 July 1935.[566] The estimate of the French Army of the number of German troops in the Rhineland was 265,000[567] so the deception programme carried out by the German Army was a great success.[568]

Unfortunately for the Wehrmacht, Blomberg began to panic after a few days, and he demanded of Hitler that the troops be withdrawn from Aachen, Trier and Saarbrücken, because he feared that the French would make a strong attack if the situation were allowed to continue in its course.[569] Blomberg summoned Hossbach to him three times on the day of his protests, and on each occasion the urgency of his demands mounted. The Army High Command viewed the situation more calmly. Blomberg wanted to see Hitler personally, and gave Hossbach an alarmist telegram from the three military attachés in London to give to Hitler. When Hitler was given this by Hossbach, he put it in his pocket without reading it. Actually, he had been shown a copy of the telegram by Göring a few minutes previously. By the time that Blomberg was allowed to see Hitler, he had regained some confidence, and asked for the telegram back. No changes took place as a result of Blomberg's requests to Hitler. Afterwards, Hitler said that Blomberg had weak nerves.

While the whole of the Rhineland incident fell outside the general theme of Hitler's desire for a drive to the East, it did have a most important effect on the relationship between Hitler and his professional military advisers in the question of the risk of a European war. Hitler had relied on his intuition, and 'superior will', and had proved the cautious advice which he had been given by Blomberg to be wrong. His own opinion of his judgement and leadership went up, while his opinion of Blomberg and of the High Command in general went down. Hence, in the crises which followed in the later years of the pre-war period, the opinions of the Armed Forces counted for less and less, as Hitler dismissed the warnings he was given in 1938 and 1939 by reminding his military commanders of their excess caution in March 1936.[570]

During the months following the re-entry of the Rhineland Hitler's ideas on the future problems of Germany became more definite. In the summer of 1936, probably in August,[571] he prepared a long memorandum on the German war economy. This was produced in triplicate—one copy for each of Göring and Blomberg, while Hitler kept the third which he was to give in 1944 to Albert Speer, by then Armaments Minister.[572] This memorandum included the following:

The military powers of the nation must be raised to the highest possible condition. The urgency of this task permits no gentle scruples of any kind. Even the economy has no other purpose than to provide the basis for the self defence of the German people.

The economic situation is as follows: Germany is overpopulated and cannot feed itself from its own soil. Germany also lacks certain necessary raw materials. To keep on saying this is absolutely pointless. We must now put measures into effect 'which can bring for the future a final solution, and for the interim a temporary relaxation. The final solution lies in expanding the living space or the raw material and food resources of our people. It is the task of the government to solve this question some day'.

'It is better to consider and solve these problems [i.e. shortage of raw materials] in peace, than to wait until the next war before attempting to carry out these economic investigations and experiments in method in the midst of other demands.'

The establishment of a self-sufficient economy was to be dealt with by a multi-year plan, with the following aims:

'I. The German Army must be ready for use in four years' time.

II. The German economy must be ready for war in four years.'[573]

There is no evidence of the reactions of Blomberg or of Fritsch to this memorandum, nor even any to confirm that Blomberg showed it to Fritsch. However, it seems inconceivable that the War Minister would not have informed the Commander-in-Chief of the Army of its contents, particularly because it made specific mention of the Army in the concluding section. The significance of this document is that it told Blomberg, and possibly Fritsch, that Hitler wanted the Army to be ready for an eastern war by 1940. Hitler's preamble stated that this was to be in the nature of a defensive war, but it is interesting that he regarded the nourishment of the German population as a problem only until the outbreak of a war. In view of his earlier statements about the necessity for conquering territories in the East, it is open to assumption that this war with Russia was to provide the means for the execution of these conquests, and thereby the achievement of a permanent solution to the German food problem. It is also significant that the timing of this programme was still in general accord with Hitler's speech of 28 February 1934, when he stated that the Army was to be ready for general defensive purposes in five years, and for an aggressive war in eight years.

An insight into the views of the Army commander was given by a paragraph of the lengthy memorandum which Fritsch had written for Blomberg on the question of the organization of the High Command in August, 1937.* In this, he said as part of his case for establishing the predominant importance of the Army with regard to the other two services:

> Only the Army can defeat an enemy decisively by conquering his country and thereby eliminating it as a hostile power. In the final analysis as a continental power we shall have to win our wars on the ground, as long as the aims of a German victory are only conquests in the East and holding the line in the West—because no eastern nation can be annihilated in the air or on water.†

This shows that Fritsch was aware that there was a possibility of the use of the German Armed Forces to conquer lands in the East. How far he supported or opposed this policy cannot be deduced from this paragraph, as he does not state any personal attitude towards it. It may be that he had come to accept Hitler's Lebensraum programme, and wanted to plan the organization of the High Command to fit this task. It is known, from his later actions,‡ that he was still opposed to a policy of war, but this may have been from grounds of expediency, as much as from grounds of principle. On the other hand, he may still have been firmly opposed to the Lebensraum policy as a matter of principle, but was prepared to use the existence of it as a lever for placing a greater degree of control in the hands of the Army, so that its execution could have been impeded.

Evidence corroborating the latter view has been provided by the written records which we have of Beck's protests about the possibility of an eastern war, which he was making at that time. Beck and Fritsch were the closest of friends, and had known each other for many years. That in these circumstances an Army commander could successfully deceive his Chief of Staff on such a vital matter seems impossible. Beck had threatened to resign in 1935, had Blomberg planned to use Operation *Schulung*, the plans for a surprise attack on Czechoslovakia, for any practical employment.[574] His later memoranda continued to stress that any aggressive war on Germany's part would be a betrayal of both the nation and the Army, and that it would meet with the condemnation of history.[575] His visit to Paris in June 1937 was made in the same spirit.[576] Such a man would not have tolerated service under a commander whom he knew to be ready to cast his highest principles aside when a favourable opportunity presented itself.

* See above, Chapter 8, pp. 110–113.
† Fritsch Memorandum, *op. cit.*, see above, pp. 110–113.
‡ See his reaction to the conference of 5 November 1937, as described below, pp. 133–135.

On 5 November 1937, an important conference assembled at Berchtesgaden. Present were Hitler, Neurath (the Foreign Minister), Blomberg, Fritsch, Raeder and Göring. This conference had been called at the suggestion of Blomberg to iron out differences of opinion between Blomberg and Göring concerning the allocation of raw materials and industrial resources.[577] However, in the meantime, Hitler had altered the theme to include some of his own military ideas.[578] According to the record written down some days afterwards by Oberst Hossbach, Hitler's Military Adjutant, the salient points of Hitler's address were as follows:*

The aim of German policy was the security and preservation of the people, and of their increase. Therefore, it was a question of space.

The only, perhaps dreamlike solution as it appears to us, lies in winning a greater amount of living space, an endeavour which at all times has been the cause of the building of states and of the movements of peoples.

It was not a question of acquiring more people, but of good agricultural land. It was also better to seek raw material resources directly adjoining Germany, than overseas. However, this solution would only assist the next one or two generations—it was up to those who came after to provide for their own needs. History had shown that such expansion could not be achieved without risk, and without the breaking of resistance.

The important question for Germany was where the greatest gains could be made for the least cost. Britain and France would oppose the growth of a strong German colossus in Central Europe, and they would also be against the return of the German colonies.

Germany's problems could be solved only by the use of force, and this was never without risk. The battles of Frederick the Great for Silesia, and of Bismarck against Austria and France involved unheard-of risks. If one accepted the policy of the application of force attended by risk, then it remained only to ask 'when?' and 'how?'. In relation to this, three cases were to be noted:

Case 1. 1943–45

After this period, things could become only worse for Germany. Rearmament would be completed and the other nations would be catching

---

* Hossbach, *Zwischen Wehrmacht und Hitler*, pp. 207–20. It is important to note the qualifications which Hossbach has written in his full account, pp. 217–18.

The record of the conference was compiled by me several days after 5 November 1937, in the War Ministry building and was dated 10 November 1937. I cannot remember whether it took one or several days to complete, and therefore whether it was commenced or finished on 10 November 1937. However, it is certain that the 'record' was a note of the proceedings written after the event, and not official minutes written during the course of the conference. I intentionally avoided the use of the word 'minutes' at the time as inappropriate to the form and to the content of the record. The basis was the notes of the headings which I made during the conference and my memory. Because I have no stenographic skills, I was not able to attempt a complete, word for word reproduction of the conference. Furthermore, from the nature of the conference, I was far more concerned to give as complete a record of Hitler's exposition as possible than of the following discussion, not least because it was not so easy in the excitement to record the content of the thrust and counter thrust by jotting down the main points to enable a completely accurate recapitulation to be made.

up. Germany might suffer food shortages, concurrently with foreign exchange shortages. While the surrounding world fastened itself off, Germany would be compelled to take the offensive. Nobody knew how the situation would be in 1943, but one thing was certain—Germany could not wait any longer. On the one hand were the maintenance of the Armed Forces and the ageing of the Party and of its leaders, and on the other were the prospects of a lowering of the standard of living and of a decrease in the birth rate. Therefore, there was no other choice but to act. Should Hitler remain alive, it was his unalterable decision to solve the German space problem in 1943-45 at the latest. The necessity for action before then was dealt with in Cases 2 and 3.

Case 2
If internal political complications in France should fully absorb the attention of the French Army so that it could not be used for war against Germany, the time would be right for moving against Czechoslovakia.

Case 3
The first essential for Germany in the event of a war would be the defeat of Czechoslovakia and Austria simultaneously in order to prevent a westwards drive against the German flank. Should France become involved in a war with another nation and unable to act against Germany, a third case would arise.

In the event of Case 2, as a result of the incapacity of Germany's most dangerous opponent, such a situation should be exploited wherever it arose for a blow against Czechoslovakia.

Hitler regarded the possibility of Case 3 developing out of the existing tensions in the Mediterranean as strong, and he did not exclude this from happening as early as 1938.

After these expositions, Hitler allowed his hearers to break in and raise objections. Before passing to Hossbach's original account of these objections, it is important to read his later comment on this part of his record.[579]

For the above mentioned reasons* I was compelled unfortunately to omit to record the discussion in its entirety. There is no doubt, however, that it was far more prolonged than I described on 10 November 1937.

The discussion took a very sharp form at times, above all in the differences between Blomberg and Fritsch on the one hand, and Göring on the other, and Hitler participated mainly as an attentive observer. I can no longer remember the exact thrust and parry of the questions at issue. However, I do remember exactly that the sharpness of the opposition, both in content and in form did not fail to make its impression on Hitler, as I could see from his changing expressions. Every detail of the conduct of Blomberg and Fritsch must have made plain to Hitler that his policies had met with only plain impersonal contradictions, instead of applause and agreement. And he knew very well that both generals were opposed to any warlike entanglement provoked from our side.

* See the quotation given in note (*) p. 132 above.

It is a sin of omission before history on my part that the opinions of Blomberg and Fritsch at the conference of 5 November 1937 have not been recorded in greater detail and in the actual sharpness of the argument in my record of 10 November 1937.

The content of Hossbach's original description of the discussion which followed this part of Hitler's address is as follows:[580]

Blomberg and Fritsch urged repeatedly that Britain and France could not be permitted to be cast as Germany's enemies, and stated that the French Army would not be so tied down by an Italian war that it could not take the field with superiority against Germany's western defences. Fritsch estimated that the French would need twenty divisions to secure the Italian frontier in the Alps, while the rest would form a strong French superiority on the western frontier of Germany. According to German thinking, the task of this force would be to march into the Rhineland. Special consideration had to be given to the fact that France would have the lead in mobilization, to the small defensive value of the German fortifications, which Blomberg stressed particularly, and to the useless condition of the four motorized divisions which were intended for the defence of the west.

Blomberg drew attention to the strength of the Czech defences whose construction corresponded to the Maginot Line, and which would have made a German attack extremely difficult. Fritsch stated that, as a result of these circumstances described by Hitler, he would cancel the leave which he had intended to start on 10 November 1937. Hitler rejected this by remarking that the possibility of conflict was not so close.

The Foreign Minister, Neurath, held that an Italian-British-French war was not as close as Hitler would like to accept. Against this, Hitler said that this war could break out in summer 1938. As to the French and British superiority alleged by Blomberg and Fritsch, Hitler repeated that he thought it unlikely that France would attack Germany and that he was convinced that Britain would not participate. Should the Mediterranean conflict lead to general European mobilization, then Germany was to move against Czechoslovakia at once. If the powers which were not involved in the war declared that they were disinterested, Germany would do likewise. Göring added that, in view of Hitler's remarks, operations in Spain ought to be curtailed. Hitler agreed, but reserved the timing of this decision to himself. The second part of the conference then concerned itself with the materials questions for which Blomberg had assembled the meeting.

The reactions of Blomberg and Fritsch showed that they were botsh opposed to Hitler's plans for expansion by war. In view of Hossbach's later comment, this opposition was made with noticeable sharpness, which suggests that Blomberg and Fritsch were fully aware of the grave danger which these plans involved for Germany. The fact that the available evidence gives no direct indication that Blomberg and Fritsch made protests to Hitler on moral grounds about the implications of his policy has been used to infer that Blomberg and Fritsch had no moral objections to

Hitler's aims,[581] that their disagreement with Hitler was limited to purely technical grounds. This explanation ignores other factors, which especially in the case of Fritsch, were likely to have been much more significant.

Fritsch must have been well aware by late 1937 that Hitler was not a man to be impressed by moral considerations when an important matter of policy was at stake. This was in accord with Hitler's method of conducting the government of Germany on absolute lines, on the basis of his personal will. If he was to be dissuaded at all from this policy of aggression, military objections were likely to have been far more effective than moral ones. Furthermore, the nature of a moral objection is so fundamental that it can render two differing parties totally incompatible, and so Fritsch probably realized that if he resorted to moral criticism, he would have been replaced by someone more devoted to obedience to Hitler who would render Germany's situation even more perilous.

The later course of their reactions illustrates clearly the differences of character between Blomberg and Fritsch. Blomberg swung around to the view that the purpose of the conference was much more closely linked to his original purpose in calling it than he had imagined at first. He assured Raeder afterwards that the significance of the first part had been to urge Fritsch and Neurath to accept a faster rate of rearmament.[582] Fritsch continued to be very concerned about the whole question. On 7 November Neurath discussed the gravity of the situation with him and Beck. They agreed that Fritsch was to speak personally to Hitler in order to impress the military impossibilities of his plans on him, while Neurath was to seek another time to present the objections based on foreign policy considerations.[583]

Fritsch saw Hitler on 9 November, at the Berghof.[584] No record of the conversation has survived, but the force of Fritsch's objections was indicated by Hitler's refusal to see Neurath until mid-January 1938.[585] On the same day as his discussion with Hitler, Fritsch wrote to the Baroness von Schutzbar:[586]

Again and again new and difficult matters are brought before me which must be attended to before my departure. I am really very tired and exhausted, far more than you can tell from my appearance.

On the following day Fritsch departed for nearly two months' holiday in Egypt.[587] He had chosen Egypt in order to attempt to cure an attack of bronchial catarrh.[588] Although he might have used this opportunity for making some contact with the British authorities, there is absolutely no evidence to suggest that Fritsch did anything in Egypt but display a mild interest in the Egyptian Army.* He was back in Berlin on 2 January 1938, and on 3 January wrote:[589]

My mistake was to have stayed there much too long.

* The writer has made an exhaustive check of all likely sources for information on Fritsch's stay in Egypt. Apparently, from the paucity of the available evidence, Fritsch did very little bar convalesce and and read official correspondence. A courier service was conducted for him by his adjutants, Major Siewert, and Hauptmann von Both, who flew in Italian aircraft via Rome and Benghazi. OKH file H 24/39.

Despite Blomberg's remarks to Raeder, the former quickly ordered that his staff were to prepare a revision of the plans for *Aufmarsch Grün* so that they would correspond to Hitler's new policy. The revision was placed before Hitler on 13 December 1937, and approved.[590] It altered the degree of probability assigned to the two main plans, so that *Grün* now preceded *Rot*. If one of the greater powers were to attack Germany, and Germany were fully prepared for war, *Grün* would go into immediate effect, with the aim of solving the problem of living space. If France became absorbed in a Mediterranean conflict, and Britain showed no inclination towards participation in a European war, *Grün* was to be put into effect even if Germany were not fully prepared for war.[591] Copies of this instruction were issued to each of the service commanders.

Hossbach showed the contents of his record of the conference to Beck, who recorded his views in a long and critical memorandum.[592] Beck's memorandum was set out in a similar manner to Hossbach's record, and tackled Hitler's points one by one, showing how Hitler had ignored the

military-political, financial, economic, and moral bases.[593]

Hitler's final attempt to win the senior officers of the Army over to his views before he assumed complete control of the Wehrmacht on 4 February 1938, took place on 22 January in the War Ministry. He had assembled the senior generals, and gave them a long, rambling address, which touched on the following matters:[594]

Rome had risen to greatness through strong leadership. The old world was conquered by new nations from the east, seeking space in the west. However, Christianity provided a basis which prevented the onset of complete chaos, and which bound people together. This was the basis of the Holy Roman Empire. It was a sign of great narrow-mindedness in this connection to refer to Charlemagne as the Slaughterer of the Saxons. He was compelled to strike down the opposition because of his policy of Christianity. It simply remained a pity that the best German blood was lost.

In the modern age, millions saw nothing in Christianity. This was the fault of the form, not of the content. Old forms had to go and be replaced by the new.

The basis of the new world was the demand by the masses for a social philosophy. They were less concerned with the improvement of material conditions than with the return of honour to the workers. The revolts of 1918–19 were less about living conditions, which certainly had not been bad—perhaps they were better than in 1938—than about honour. The form of socialism attempted by National-Socialism was the basis for a new structure of the state throughout the world. However, there were two forms of socialism—National-Socialism and Bolshevism. Bolshevism destroyed the existing state of affairs, while National-Socialism removed what already existed and then went on to rebuild and develop.

A government on the basis of a parliament was no longer possible. Only one man could rule, and he carried the entire responsibility.

Believe me, my Generals, I have had sleepless nights at times of difficult decisions. My nerves are shattered, and I no longer sleep because of cares for Germany.

In the new form of government, the question of the relationship between the executive Head of State and the ceremonial Head of State had still to be solved. Theoretically, it was possible for both to exist, side by side, but this could happen only when the two were of the same calibre and were well suited to each other as in the foundation of the Second Reich. In reality this was seldom the case. Therefore Hitler refused to have a king as ceremonial head of state.

The food situation was serious. There was only just enough in a good year. But the population was growing at the rate of 600,000 per annum. How was the German people to be able to feed itself? This would be possible, only if the Germans were to win new space. This space would have to be created by the German people for itself by force.

Germany was in a serious plight, but there was a glimmer of hope when one observed the ruling nations of the earth—Britain, France and America. Only 40–50 million pure-blooded members of the ruling nations dominated millions of other people and huge areas of the earth's surface. There was only one nation which lived in greater unanimity, more unified in race and language, closely pressed together in the heart of Europe. This was the German nation with its 110 million Germans in Central Europe. This comparison made Hitler hopeful and eventually the whole world would and had to belong to this united block of Central Europe.

This address was a direct appeal to the senior officers of the Army, over the head of Fritsch. Coming so soon after Hitler's speech of 5 November 1937, it indicated that Hitler attached urgency to the wider acceptance of his long-term policy within the upper echelons of the Army. This by-passing of Fritsch also indicated that Hitler did not feel able to rely on the Army commander to communicate his policy in the light in which Hitler felt that it ought to be presented.

Documentary evidence of the reactions of the generals to this address is lacking, but several senior officers have described to me their reactions to Hitler's speeches around that time. When making such speeches, Hitler had a habit of wandering far from the point, particularly if the argument was becoming a little involved. Such wanderings took several minutes, after which he would return to the main point, hoping that it would be accepted if it were repeated often enough. He usually took some hours to deliver these speeches, so that the overall effect was one of utter confusion in the minds of his audience. This is one reason why it is so difficult to get a precise description of the content of Hitler's addresses.

This poor technique produced a recognizably negative attitude on the part of his military audiences, and this in its turn produced an effect on Hitler. When he saw that he was making little impression with the logic of his policies, he would abandon the attempt to give a clear, reasoned presentation aimed at convincing his audience by the persuasion of logic, and resort to ranting about his most exasperating difficulties and to covering his audience with abuse for their lack of positiveness and for their conservatism. The easiest way of enduring these ordeals was to sit them out without paying any attention to the speaker.

Within a few days of this speech, Hitler had dismissed both his War Minister and the Commander-in-Chief of the Army, and was planning a reorganization of the upper ranks of the Army. Although the cases of Blomberg and Fritsch were officially caused by other circumstances, as described below in Chapter 11, there is little doubt that the consistent refusal of Fritsch, and, to a lesser extent Blomberg, to enter wholeheartedly into Hitler's plans for aggression played a big part in their dismissal.

For five years Hitler had been proclaiming his warlike aims to the senior officers of the Army. For the first four of these, the Army had regarded Hitler's aims as ludicrous, because Germany lacked the means even of securing its own frontier and because of the possibility that Hitler was making these speeches insincerely as part of a programme of bluff. The aftermath of the conference of 5 November 1937 showed that this less concerned attitude had worn off, as the means for waging war had grown. The crisis in confidence between Hitler and the High Command had increased to the point at which the dictator felt that a sweeping purge of the higher ranks was justified, so that the German Army entered the period of international tension of early 1938 in a state of disunity and confusion.

11

The Fritsch Crisis

BY the end of 1937, it had become clear that the Army was stratified in terms of political opinion. While there were many young soldiers who accepted Hitler and the policies of the Nazi Party, there were the older officers who were opposed to Hitler's plans for foreign conquest. Even Blomberg had questioned their wisdom, and Army-Party relations were moving towards an acute crisis.

The attitude of the High Command towards the possibility of war had disappointed none more than Hitler. For four years he had been taking soundings of Army opinion only to find reluctance towards taking what he considered to be the necessary bold steps for solving the long-term economic problems of Germany. In particular, Hitler knew that Blomberg was likely to panic when it came to gambling on the non-interference of France in the growth of German power, and he also had been aware for some years that Fritsch would remain true to his conservative ideals and continue to view the Nazi government as an unwelcome master.

During the previous five years the Army had become increasingly disliked by Himmler and Heydrich. Himmler had expanded his power via the Gestapo and the S.S. to an extent which gave him control over individual Germans in most fields of activity. An important section of German life which remained outside his direct control was the Army. When he attempted to spread his extreme form of ideas throughout the Armed Forces, he was checked. His efforts to develop a private military force, the S.S. Verfügungstruppe, had met with constant opposition from the Army and this must have annoyed him greatly. The greatest obstacle in his path appeared to be Fritsch. Himmler had recognized this by 1935, as his campaign against Fritsch in the January of that year testified, so by 1938, Himmler's enmity towards Fritsch was several years old.

The outlook of Heydrich was similar. His interests were closely bound up with those of Himmler, while his hostility was sharpened by the memory of his dishonourable discharge from the Navy.[595] Heydrich had acquired much experience in dealing with important figures whom he desired to remove from public life. In October 1934, he had attempted to get rid of one of Papen's oldest and most trusted advisers, Freiherr von Tschirschky, by framing him with a charge of homosexuality. Heydrich had well appreciated Hitler's sensitivity to charges of immorality against members of the Party and of the civil administration. Tschirschky feared

139

that he would not survive the Gestapo inquiry which had been ordered and fled the country at once.[596]

A most obvious target for a repetition of this method was the middle-aged bachelor, Werner von Fritsch. Heydrich set to work, produced documents and a witness incriminating Fritsch for homosexuality, and placed the matter before Hitler in 1936.[597] This attempt failed, for Hitler did not want to have Fritsch replaced at such a critical point in the rearmament process. Hitler ordered that the documents were to be burned and the matter closed. But before these documents were destroyed, the Gestapo made copies of them and retained them for future use.[598]

During 1936 and 1937, Heydrich worked on the problem of decapitating the Russian Army. By triggering off the great purges of 1937–39, he achieved this aim with brilliant success.[599] This success coupled with the continual obstruction presented by the German Army probably encouraged Himmler and Heydrich to make another attempt to get rid of Fritsch.

Himmler and Heydrich were not the only lieutenants of Hitler who were hostile towards the Army in late 1937. For several years Göring had been fighting with the Army to expand the size and role of the Luftwaffe. His chief opponents were Fritsch and Blomberg. However Göring's ambitions did not stop at command of the Luftwaffe. He was junior only to Blomberg, Fritsch and Raeder in the defence hierarchy, and it was most unlikely that a sailor would have been placed in command of the Wehrmacht in 1938. If Blomberg and Fritsch were to be suddenly removed from their positions, then the path seemed to be open for Göring to advance to Commander-in-Chief of the Armed Forces.

Thus the hostility of the three most powerful Nazis, Hitler, Himmler and Göring, was concentrated in early 1938 on Blomberg and Fritsch, while these two men, fundamentally different in their outlooks, remained isolated from each other. It was into this atmosphere that rumours began to spread in late January 1938 that Blomberg had married a prostitute. By the favour of fortune the documents which confirmed that the new Frau von Blomberg had been convicted for posing for obscene photographs came into the hands of Blomberg's arch-rival, Göring.

Blomberg had married Fräulein Erna Gruhn after a brief acquaintance on 12 January 1938. Fräulein Gruhn had been a typist in his office. Blomberg's first wife had died in 1932,[600] and after five years of widowerhood, he asked Hitler for permission to marry Fräulein Gruhn. Hitler consented and he and Göring were the only witnesses at a private wedding ceremony. Only Fritsch was told about it, and he only at the last hour.[601] The documents which testified to the true background of Fräulein Gruhn were discovered by the police shortly afterwards and taken to Keitel to see if the situation could be dealt with without the knowledge of Himmler.[602] Keitel refused to have anything to do with them, and stabbed Blomberg in the back by recommending that they ought to be given to Göring.[603]

However, Himmler had already heard the scandal which was going about Berlin and, with Heydrich, decided that the time was ripe for striking a doubly effective blow at the Armed Forces. The Fritsch file, alleging homosexuality, was enlarged and given to Göring. This placed both of his rivals in his hands and Göring began to make the most of the damning evidence. He placed both sets of papers before Hitler on 24 January.[604]

The scandal about Blomberg had also reached the ears of the Army, and Beck urged that demands should be made to Hitler for Blomberg's resignation.[605] Fritsch refused for the time being to take the matter to Hitler because he did not accept on the available evidence that Blomberg was guilty.[606] However, Fritsch's efforts to preserve some unity within the High Command were sabotaged by Göring who went to Blomberg on either 24 or 25 January and told him that he could no longer remain as War Minister. Göring told Blomberg that it did not matter if he divorced his wife—he had to go because by simply marrying such a woman he had become intolerable for the generals.[607]

Hitler found no great difficulty in making up his mind about Blomberg. He had to go, and a successor had to be found. At this stage, Göring's plans began to miscarry. Hitler discussed nominations for Blomberg's position with Hossbach and when Hossbach said that the successor ought to be another general but not Göring, Hitler agreed emphatically.[608]

Fritsch presented Hitler with a more complicated problem. It was not contested that Blomberg's wife had posed for obscene photographs but Hossbach insisted to Hitler that the evidence against Fritsch must be false. Göring re-intervened and insisted with equal firmness that he had examined the documents personally on several occasions and was convinced of Fritsch's guilt. Hitler was also under the shadow of the previous attempt by Himmler and Heydrich to make him take action against Fritsch for the same reasons. They argued on until late in the evening of 25 January. Before departing, Hossbach asked Hitler for permission to inform Fritsch of the evidence against him. Hitler forbade this and stressed that Hossbach was to obey him.[609]

Hossbach went straight to Fritsch's apartment where he found Fritsch in a troubled mood. Fritsch had just learned that Blomberg was to resign and said that under no conditions did he wish to succeed to the War Ministry. When Hossbach informed him of the evidence which Göring had given Hitler, Fritsch denounced the Nazis' conduct and added:

> If Hitler wants to get rid of me then he has only to say the word and I will resign!

Fritsch suspected that either Göring or Himmler was behind the accusation, but his faith in Hitler was still sufficient to make him confident that Hitler would bring the intriguers to book as soon as he was informed that the documents were false.[610]

Hossbach informed Hitler on the following morning of his disobedience and of Fritsch's rejection of the accusation. Hitler received this news with calmness and self-control. He told Hossbach that as far as Fritsch was concerned, everything was then in order and he could become War Minister. He added that he valued Fritsch greatly and would not willingly part with him. The insincerity of these remarks was shown up when Hitler's mood swung around again a few hours later. He returned to attacking Fritsch and refused to consider Hossbach's suggestion that Rundstedt be called in for consultation. Finally, Hitler consented to see Fritsch in the evening.[611]

Hitler and Göring used the time afforded by the afternoon to make their preparations for confronting Fritsch. Göring even had the witness against Fritsch, a convict who was in the hands of Himmler, brought to the Reichs Chancellery and concealed in a small room adjoining Hitler's library where the interview with Fritsch was to take place. When Fritsch denied the charges before Hitler, the witness was produced and he then claimed to identify Fritsch as the man whom he had seen committing a homosexual act. Fritsch then gave Hitler his word of honour that the accusation was false.[612] Göring was so delighted with the proceedings that he ran from the library to an adjoining room, collapsed onto a sofa with his hands in front of his face howling loudly:

It was he! It was he![613]

Near midnight, Hitler called Beck in for consultation. Beck's reaction was one of puzzlement. He found it difficult to believe that he was witnessing an intrigue of great foulness, but on the other hand, he knew Fritsch too well to believe the accusations against him.[614]

Before Hitler was able to decide how he should deal with the Fritsch affair, he had to take final leave of Blomberg. Blomberg appeared at the Chancellery on 27 January, and was asked by Hitler to nominate a likely successor to himself, excluding Fritsch who was not to be considered because of the charges against him. Blomberg replied that Göring was the senior of those remaining for consideration. Hitler refused to discuss Göring because he felt that Göring was too lazy. Thereupon Blomberg suggested to Hitler that he ought to take over the position of War Minister himself. Hitler made no reply to that idea, but asked who would be suitable to be in charge of the OKW Staff under himself. Blomberg was not able to suggest anybody. Hitler then asked who was in charge of Blomberg's staff. Blomberg replied that it was Keitel, but that there was no question of using him, 'He's nothing but the man who runs my office.' Hitler seized on this at once and said:

That's exactly the man I am looking for![615]

Blomberg then left Germany for a year of exile in Italy.[616]

That afternoon, Hitler met Keitel for the first time.[617] Keitel made no communication with Fritsch, Beck or Hossbach and it was evident that his ambitions had conquered his scruples. He abandoned his loyalty to the Army in favour of the Party and became, from then on, Hitler's devoted and unquestioning servant.

The two pieces of advice given by Blomberg to Hitler had, in all probability, a decisive effect on the future command structure of the Armed Forces. On the evidence given by Hossbach and Blomberg, it seems that Hitler had by no means made up his mind from the very beginning of the period of crisis to become War Minister. Right up until

Blomberg's departure for Italy, Hitler was spending a good deal of time and effort on the problem of selecting a successor. After Blomberg had advised Hitler to become War Minister, Hitler apparently stopped considering other men for the position. No senior officers were called to the Chancellery to advise, and no potential candidate was interviewed (as Brauchitsch was for the post vacated by Fritsch). Therefore, it appears that Blomberg's advice was crucial. Also his description of Keitel as a *Chef de Bureau* was unintentionally instrumental in placing a man who was totally subservient to Hitler in the key position of direction over all Armed Forces planning.

Blomberg, from his long experience of Hitler, must have realized that he was recommending the decapitation of the High Command in this transfer of power from the somewhat conservative hands of the military to those of Hitler which grasped after eastern conquests. The most likely explanation for Blomberg's conduct is his rancour against his colleagues, deliberately excited by Göring in order to create a split within the High Command and to reduce the chances of any general obtaining the Ministry which Göring coveted.

After Blomberg had departed from the scene, the story of the crisis became that of two groups; one which recognized the iniquity of the charges against Fritsch and which sought to rehabilitate him; the other which accepted the *status quo* and regarded the normal functioning of the Army as the most important goal to be achieved.

The first group, composed of the men who were the closest to Fritsch, began to agitate for a full military trial, in order to expose the intriguers publicly and thereby to have Fritsch restored to his position. Hitler's initial aim had been to dismiss Fritsch and set up a special court of inquiry under the control of the Gestapo.[618] Fritsch had refused at first to resign, but when Hitler wrote to him to say that he had granted his request to be retired on grounds of health, Fritsch gave way and wrote out the resignation required of him.[619] Some of Fritsch's supporters including Beck, Hossbach and his adjutant, Both, had counselled him to resist and to attempt a putsch. This Fritsch steadfastly refused to do.[620] Fritsch saw the matter as a personal attack on himself by the Party, and held that the situation did not warrant the bloodshed which such resistance would entail.[621]

Hossbach, assisted by Ministerialdirektor Rosenberg, head of the Armed Forces Legal Office, was able to convince Hitler that he could not get rid of Fritsch by the technique of a Gestapo 'Special Court' without creating a public outcry, and so, with reluctance, Hitler consented to the establishment of a military court to try the case.[622]

In the meantime, the senior officers of the Army had received word of Fritsch's fall, although this was not publicly announced until 4 February. Rundstedt, the next in seniority to Fritsch, protested to Hitler on 29 January that the notion of Fritsch being a homosexual was ridiculous to those who knew him personally. Rundstedt asked Hitler for the sake of the Army to have the matter cleared up at once. Hitler made evasive reply and Rundstedt left without obtaining any definite promise of action.[623]

Hitler then permitted a preliminary examination of the evidence by officials of the Ministry of Justice, but he insisted that all documents used in the examination were to be made available to the Gestapo, so that the latter organization was protected from unpleasant surprises during the course of the examination.[624] The Gestapo intervened frequently and summoned Fritsch three times for interrogation. Fritsch was not legally obliged to tell the Gestapo anything because the case was being tried by military law. However in order to give the opposition as little opportunity as possible to spread the notion that Fritsch had something to hide, he co-operated and submitted to the most detailed questioning which was partly designed to trap him into making hasty admissions.[625]

Fritsch's defence attorney, Graf von der Goltz attempted to attack the credibility of the witness Schmidt, the man who had been used to confront Fritsch in Hitler's library. Goltz discovered that Schmidt had been involved in several other similar accusations, one of which was against the Chief of Police at Potsdam. It was quickly shown that Schmidt's allegations in this case were a pack of lies and the Police Chief agreed to come forward as a witness for the defence. When Heydrich heard of this, he summoned the Police Chief to Gestapo headquarters and had him observed by Schmidt from a concealed position while Heydrich led him through the building. Schmidt was then able to identify the Police Chief as one of the men whom he had seen committing homosexual acts.[626]

Another of those who had been named by Schmidt for committing a homosexual act was an international sportsman. The Gestapo arrested the man at once, proceeded against him on the grounds of Schmidt's allegations and he disappeared into prison leaving Schmidt as Goltz's sole target.[627]

Ever since the commencement of the crisis, Fritsch had remained in isolation in his official residence, becoming increasingly reserved as the inner strains took their toll of his disposition. The preliminary examination continued for most of February, and as time advanced, the risk of Gestapo action to get rid of Fritsch by underhand means mounted. Accordingly a guard of absolutely reliable young officers was formed with orders to shoot any unauthorized person who attempted to force an entry into Fritsch's house. Only eight people, including Beck, Goltz and Hossbach, were permitted access.

Despite the increasingly insistent demands of the Gestapo that Fritsch be made available to them for interrogation, Fritsch's isolation from all possible danger was preserved. Eventually, at Keitel's instigation, a compromise was reached between Fritsch's guardians and the Gestapo and an interrogation was arranged to take place in no-man's-land, in an uninhabited villa in Wannsee. However, the Army did not like to take chances and a unit of picked men was detailed to exercise in the area of the villa from 10 a.m. on the day of the interrogation. Fritsch's escort was provided with a pistol for signalling for assistance.[628] The official who conducted the interrogation went so far as to tell Fritsch that he himself was against the Nazi régime and that Fritsch could therefore speak to him in confidence. Fritsch was not drawn by such crude means.[629]

After the interrogation, Fritsch's escort protested to Keitel about the treatment to which the Gestapo had subjected Fritsch. Keitel replied:

That is all right. You just are not accustomed to the ways of the Gestapo.

The escort was then ordered to be silent about the events he had witnessed.[630]

During the preliminary examination, Goltz had discovered that the Gestapo's case was a clever plot which rested on transferring the details of a real case against a certain retired officer, Rittmeister von Frisch, to the person of Fritsch. Once Goltz had spoken to Frisch, the case was as good as won, provided that the Gestapo did not cause Frisch to disappear. Canaris, the director of counter intelligence, and Gürtner, the Minister of Justice were approached but they were unable to provide adequate safeguard. Canaris then asked Keitel to provide a guard, but Keitel refused.[631] On the following day, Frisch disappeared. He had been arrested by the Gestapo. When the defence asked for him to be made available for interview, the Gestapo refused on the ground that Frisch was in imminent danger of death through illness. This was known to be false and through the efforts of General Heitz, the President of Army Courts Martial, Hitler was persuaded to instruct the Gestapo to hand Frisch over.[632]

Once Heitz had examined Frisch there remained not the least doubt that Fritsch was innocent. Accordingly this was reported to Hitler, who had assigned the post of confirming authority of the court to himself, and who could therefore have stopped the proceedings at any instant. Much to the surprise of the defence, Hitler refused to halt the proceedings as long as Schmidt refused to recant his evidence.[633] Since Schmidt was a prisoner in the hands of the Gestapo, there was little possibility of that.

The trial commenced on Thursday, 10 March 1938. It was broken off on the same day because of the Austrian crisis. It is most significant that the senior officer of the court was Göring. On resumption a week later, the prosecution resorted to claiming that Schmidt had seen both Frisch and Fritsch committing a homosexual act. Goltz was able to show that this also was a fabrication and it was patently clear to the court that there was no real case against Fritsch.[634] Until this point, Göring's behaviour had been consistently biased against the defence in his questions and remarks. Once Schmidt's story had been finally broken down, Göring could not contain his annoyance and frustration. He roared at Schmidt that he was the foulest liar that he had ever seen.[635]

Goltz then pressed for an investigation of the conduct of the prosecution and asked for Himmler and Heydrich to be brought before the court. Göring said that this was out of the question because both were absent on important duty in Austria and because the purpose of the trial had been to investigate the charges against Fritsch, not other matters. The court returned the verdict of

Acquitted on the ground of proven innocence.[636]

This verdict, however, fell unheard on ears which were filled by the celebrations attendant on what the Propaganda Ministry acclaimed as the greatest triumph for German foreign policy since the days of Bismarck—the unification of Austria with the Third Reich.

While the trial had been taking place, the second group within the Army had been concentrating on reorganization and readjustment, so that the passing of Fritsch and the consequent dislocation of the High Command would be as short-lived as possible. Command of the Army passed into the hands of a member of this second group, General der Artillerie Walter von Brauchitsch.

Brauchitsch was a man with an outstanding military record but he was crippled by an infirmity of purpose which made him ineffective when dealing with unfamiliar problems. During the First World War he won the high decoration of the Hohenzollern House Order, as well as the Iron Cross, First Class. He served as a departmental head in the Truppenamt from 1922–25, during which time he distinguished himself by organizing manœuvres to test the possibilities of using motorized troops in conjunction with aircraft, thereby showing himself to be in the forefront of military thought.[637] He became Director of Army Training in January 1930, and Inspector of Artillery in March 1932. He succeeded Blomberg in the important post of Commander of Wehrkreis I, East Prussia, on 1 February 1933, and on 1 April 1937, became the first Commander of the newly formed Fourth Army Group at Leipzig.[638]

Politically he was a keen personal admirer of Hitler, although not a believer in Nazi ideology. His first marriage had broken up, and he wished to obtain a divorce at the time of Fritsch's fall. It is possible that Göring facilitated this divorce. His second wife, whom he married in September 1938, was, in the words of Hassell, '200 per cent rabid' in her support for the Nazis, and she came to exert a dominant influence on Brauchitsch's relations with the Party.[639] Brauchitsch was, therefore, a man most ill-suited to the requirements of standing up to Hitler in cases in which he thought Hitler was wrong. From what we know of the detailed information which the Gestapo possessed concerning senior officers of the Army, it is likely that these were all reasons which assisted Hitler to choose Brauchitsch to replace Fritsch.

Hitler appeared to have decided upon Brauchitsch in the early stages of the crisis. According to Jodl's diary, Hitler's first choice was Reichenau, but Göring persuaded him to choose Brauchitsch.[640] Brauchitsch was summoned by Keitel to Berlin on 28 January 1938, and was asked the following:

Was he prepared to lead the Army closer towards the State and its philosophy?

Was he prepared to choose a more suitable Chief of the General Staff if necessary?

Was he prepared to recognize a new organization of the High Command?

Brauchitsch replied that he was prepared to comply with the first two requirements, but that he would need more time to study the implications of the third point.[641]

However, Hitler was still willing to discuss alternatives to Brauchitsch, for when he spoke to Rundstedt on 31 January, he suggested that Reichenau should become the new commander. Rundstedt rejected this in the name of the Army. They did not want a commander who had been one of Hitler's most enthusiastic supporters if they could help it. Rundstedt suggested Beck. Hitler replied that this was out of the question and then put Brauchitsch's name forward. Rundstedt said that he had no objections to Brauchitsch and presumably, Brauchitsch was confirmed in Hitler's mind as Commander-in-Chief of the Army from then, since no other discussion of the matter has been recorded.[642]

Brauchitsch's conduct during this period is difficult to understand. Beck was very disturbed that Brauchitsch should have dealt with Hitler on the matter, without any prior consultation with him, and without knowledge of what was really happening.[643] By accepting the position of Commander-in-Chief of the Army before Fritsch had even been tried, Brauchitsch was prejudicing the outcome of the issue severely. In these circumstances, Brauchitsch ought never to have thought of accepting the position. It is possible that he regarded Fritsch's case as lost and that he felt he ought to accept the position before it was offered to someone like Reichenau. But he ought never to have committed himself so far without any consultation with other Army leaders to see exactly where the true interests of the Army lay. In acting as he did, Brauchitsch made it impossible for the Army to present a united front to stop Hitler from continuing on his course. His actions implied recognition and approval of Hitler's measures, and must have strengthened the group who regarded the crisis with complacency while spreading confusion in the minds of those who thought that something had gone wrong.

For the next few days until 4 February, little happened of importance for the second group. Apart from Fritsch's close friends, few soldiers knew of the charges which had been made against him, let alone that both Blomberg and Fritsch had been dismissed. On 4 February, Hitler announced to the Army that a complete reorganization of the High Command, and of many other senior positions, had been made. He had summoned a meeting of the senior officers of the Army in the Chancellery. When the various generals arrived in Berlin that morning, they were amazed to make their first acquaintance with the reorganization in the morning papers, or to be congratulated by comparative strangers on receiving some promotion of which they had never been informed officially.[644]

At the meeting, Hitler outlined the details of the new changes, stressing that the centralization of command in his own hands was to be seen as a concentration of authority, and not as an attack on the Armed Forces. He made the details of the charges against Blomberg and Fritsch known, together with the fact that both had departed from active command.[645] He criticized Blomberg for his lack of courage at the re-entry into the Rhineland.[646] The general reaction to this news was one of stunned shock. Few officers could bring themselves to believe that Blomberg and Fritsch were guilty, but Hitler's status was still sufficient to make them think that there must have been some valid reason for his making such grave charges.[647] Hitler also announced that many senior officers were to be shifted to other commands, or were to be retired. It was significant that many of those concerned were officers who had become known to the Party as 'lacking sympathy' for National-Socialism. Amongst these were Leeb, Kleist, Kress von Kressenstein, Lutz, Liese and Manstein.[648]

Brauchitsch's reactions were shown by a letter which he wrote on 11 February to all Army Group and Corps Commanders concerning the interpretation which was to be placed on Hitler's measures. He repeated that the measures were to be regarded only as a concentration of power in the hands of the Head of State.

Any doubt which arises out of this matter concerning the trustworthiness of the Armed Forces with regard to National-Socialism must be decisively refuted. The Armed Forces and the Party each have, in accord with the will of the Führer, their quite separate tasks as parts of the national effort.

There can be no talk of a reinforced influence of the Party in the internal affairs of the Armed Forces.[649]

This instruction was supplemented by another of 28 February 1938. It stated that a number of newspapers had made sharp attacks on the Armed Forces as a result of the measures of 4 February. The retired generals had been described as reactionary, and the entire Wehrmacht was thereby involved. Those officers who were to be retired as a result of the new measures, and who had not yet ceased their duties were to be fare-welled with ceremonies by order. These ceremonies were to be reported in a most friendly manner, so that the impression was given that these officers were being retired with all due form.[650]

By the beginning of March, the Army had begun to readjust to the reorganization and was freer to devote attention to the Fritsch trial. How-ever, no sooner had the trial commenced than the Army became involved in Germany's biggest military operation since 1919. The Anschluss did not only briefly divert Army attention from the Fritsch trial but was suffi-ciently successful to lift the image of Hitler and the Nazi Party to higher levels, creating a new atmosphere of popular enthusiasm which was most inconducive to rational examination of the injustice which had been meted out to Fritsch.

Certainly not all of the Army forgot its old commander. A collection was organized to buy Fritsch a house and many unofficial favours were extended towards him by his old comrades. Pressure was maintained on Hitler for a complete rehabilitation, but Hitler's final concession went only as far as to make Fritsch the Honorary Colonel of his regiment. Fritsch became increasingly depressed at the injustice with which he had been treated and on the outbreak of war accompanied his regiment to Poland probably wishing for the death he found on 22 September 1939 from a sniper's bullet, as a release from the tragedy which had come to dominate his life.

This description of the behaviour of the two groups within the High Command summarizes the major events and reactions of the Army within the period of crisis. How greatly it is to be pitied that there was no third group which saw the crisis in its real shape and significance! Apart from Beck, few realized that Hitler, Göring, Himmler and Heydrich had struck deliberately in order to eliminate any effective independence of the Army of its dictatorial masters. While many officers, such as Weichs and Guderian were shocked and angered by Hitler's treatment of Fritsch, they saw the matter as a case of personal injustice, rather than in terms of the internal struggle for control of the Armed Forces. Trained and educated for the past forty years of their careers to keep themselves apart from politics, most of the senior officers of the Army were not equipped to deal with the complexities of the situation, and so they were easily deceived by Hitler into regarding it as a crisis of secondary, rather than of primary magnitude.

But even if the generals had perceived how these measures endangered the security of Germany, there were many complications to be overcome before the Nazis could have been dislodged from authority by force of arms. In early 1938 Hitler was very popular with the broad mass of the German people, including the men in the ranks of the Army. His rule had brought many benefits to the German nation at large, and Goebbels had not failed to impress this upon the people. Had the generals attempted a revolt against this hero of the masses it is very likely that they would have been leading a force without soldiers. Military obedience is not secured simply by the issuing of an order. Even in battle, the execution of orders depends greatly on the state of mind and enthusiasm of the troops involved. Therefore, how much more unwise it would have been for the leaders of the Army to order their troops into action against the leader of their own nation who was able to make Winston Churchill admit:

I have always said that if Great Britain were defeated in war I hope we should find a Hitler to lead us back to our rightful position among the nations.[651]

It would have been all too easy for the Nazis to have portrayed any attempt at a military putsch as a criminal attempt by a small group of reactionaries to seize power for their own ends. The soldiers lacked a leader of sufficient popularity and status with Germans at large for a revolt to be seen by the people in the vital initial stages as anything other than a military coup for military reasons. Even Fritsch was little known, as was shown by the errors in spelling his name and position made by Germans corresponding with him.[652]

While Fritsch's closer colleagues were convinced of his innocence, this did not mean that the whole Army was smarting under the injustice of Hitler's behaviour towards him. Such a state of affairs would require the non-existence of the vein of cynicism which is apt to run through remarks made about the private lives of the high and mighty by those looking on. It is not at all unlikely, particularly in view of Blomberg's known guilt and of the dry nature of Berlin humour, that many on hearing the accusations against Fritsch said, 'Well, that's what the old devil has been up to!' It must also be remembered that both the proceedings and the verdict of the trial were not given any prominence in the German press, and the press was not even allowed to be present at the sessions of the court.[653]

However even if the leaders of a putsch had waited until the verdict of the trial before striking, another factor had entered to give strength to Hitler's position—the Anschluss. Besides heightening the popularity of Hitler, it took the minds of soldiers away from the Fritsch affair by splitting the activities of the Army, and by giving them a small triumph to discuss in the messes, rather than the gloom of the Fritsch episode.

Unless preconditioned, the natural reaction of an Army in modern Western society to the removal of its commander is not to set about throwing the government out of office, but to examine the reasons given in order to understand the actions of the government as much as possible. In May 1937 Stalin began his great purges against the leadership of the Soviet Army while the mass of the Army watched and waited for him to finish. In November 1937, Hore-Belisha dismissed both the Chief of the Imperial General Staff, Field-Marshal Sir Cyril Deverell and the Adjutant General, General Sir Harry Knox with not the slightest risk of a reaction by force. It may be that the leaders of the German Army took cognizance of both of these cases, and were strengthened thereby in their intention of remaining loyal to the government. At the very least, the German soldiers can hardly be blamed for adhering to normal rules of conduct. They may have been wrong in so doing, but it must be established that they had the means to detect instantaneously the difference between their own situation and that of the other two armies before they can be found guilty of an offence against the code of political-military relations.

It is not considered likely that any one of the above factors would have been decisive in influencing a German general who was considering a putsch at that time, but, taken together and viewed from the standpoint that the course of internal politics was no business of the Army, it is not difficult to understand why the German Army did not react more strongly to the Fritsch crisis.

12

Hitler, the High Command, and the Possibility of War, 1938-1939

THE reorganized High Command had little time for settling smoothly into its functions, for the first of the major crises of the two years which preceded the outbreak of war occurred in March 1938. But this was not a question of mere plans. On this occasion, Hitler wanted action from his Armed Forces.

The Austrian crisis began for the Army in the second week of March 1938. The Austrian Chancellor, Schuschnigg, announced on 9 March, that a plebiscite was to be held on Sunday, 13 March, on terms which were disadvantageous to the Austrian Nazis. Hitler decided at once that Austria had to be occupied and then unified with Germany. On the morning of 10 March, Beck and his Chief of Operations, Manstein, were summoned to the Chancellery, and asked by Hitler what they would recommend for the military occupation of Austria.[654]

Beck told Hitler that relatively few troops were available for use, as no preparations had been made. He suggested the Seventh and the Thirteenth Corps together with the Second Panzer Division. Hitler said that if force was to be used, the troops had to march into Austria on the 12th. The conference finished at one o'clock in the afternoon. Beck calculated that the orders for readiness would have to go out to the formations concerned by six o'clock that same evening. He and Manstein set to work rapidly and the whole operation was improvised within five hours.[655] Although Beck carried out Hitler's orders, he did so with the greatest reluctance. At this stage, Beck and Brauchitsch were not fully aware of the servile attitude which Keitel held towards Hitler, and they concentrated their efforts to have the operation cancelled upon the Chief of Staff of the OKW. Keitel's own record of this period is most interesting:

The next night [10–11 March] was hell for me. There was telephone call after telephone call from the Army General Staff, from Brauchitsch and finally about 4 a.m. from the then Chief of the OKW Operations Staff, General von Viebahn, all imploring me to work on the Führer to give up the move into Austria. I had not the smallest intention even of putting the question to the Führer, I promised to do so and shortly afterwards without having done it rang back to say that he had refused. The Führer never knew anything about all this; if he had, his opinion of the Army Chiefs would have been shattering and I wanted to save both sides that experience.[656]

Even after Seyss-Inquart had taken office as the new Austrian Chancellor on 11 March, Hitler insisted, despite the further protests of Brauchitsch, that the operation planned to take place on the 12th had to go on.[657] The tanks and the infantry rolled across the border at nine o'clock in the morning, depending on encountering no resistance and displaying coloured decoration on the vehicles to accentuate a friendly approach to the Austrians. So improvised was the operation that the tanks relied on refuelling from Austrian motor garages on the way to Vienna, while the commander of the Second Panzer Division had nothing more than a Baedeker's Guide to Austria to assist him to plan the route to Vienna.[658]

Despite the warnings of Beck and Brauchitsch, no Western intervention occurred, and everything went as Hitler had planned. Once again he was able to reinforce his status at the expense of the Army by being proved correct in his judgement by the course of events.

Opposition to the Anschluss on the part of the Army did not extend beyond fear of provoking a wider conflict. The notion of the essential unity of the two countries of Germany and Austria was widely accepted within the Army, and there was much rejoicing by the Army when it was successfully achieved. The German soldiers in Austria were given a wonderful reception and fêted as heroes by the population for several days. This made a great and lasting impression on the minds of the younger men who had not experienced the horrors of the First World War. If Hitler was able to provide easy victories like that, then he was the leader to follow. The detailed records of men such as Weichs and Guderian show that the Anschluss was regarded as the elimination of the restrictive formalities which had kept the two nations apart for so long, to the detriment of both.[659]

Towards the end of April, Hitler began to turn his attention towards Czechoslovakia. On 21 April 1938, he informed Keitel of the political principles which were to govern an attack on Czechoslovakia.[660] Accordingly, *Aufmarsch Grün*, the General Staff plan for a pre-emptive attack on Czechoslovakia before fighting a defensive war against France, had to be re-written. Thus Beck became aware of Hitler's next goal and he set about the preparation of a memorandum which outlined the international situation in Europe as it affected Germany. He placed this memorandum before Brauchitsch on 7 May 1938. The most important parts were as follows:

I

1. Britain and Italy have reached an agreement which frees Britain from the cares both of war with Italy and of a direct threat to the shortest sea route to India and the Far East.

2. The Sino-Japanese war has developed in a direction which gives rise to the supposition that even with a favourable outcome for Japan, the military striking power of this state will be reduced appreciably. . . . Therefore, Britain has gained greater freedom to turn to acute European questions.

3. Britain and France have, once again, taken up closer contact for the purpose of closer political and military co-operation. . . . It is not to be disputed that this military co-operation—aimed primarily at Germany, even though Italy

stands momentarily in the foreground—takes into account, even today, a European or even a World War in the final analysis. In the light of this, the measures of both states to avail themselves even now of deliveries of war material from America are significant, a case which shows a far more advanced situation than in 1914.*

4. Italy has shown a momentary lack of interest in her imperial plans. The background may only be guessed at. Her direct interest in a closer military relationship with Germany may have lost importance.

5. Russia must be regarded as an increasingly more outspoken enemy of Germany. It must be accepted that she will take part at once in any war against Germany with her air force and navy. . . .

6. The conduct of Belgium and Holland depends on that of Britain and France. . . .

7. For the present, no change in the anticipated conduct of Rumania, Yugoslavia and Poland has appeared. Rumania and Poland may, in a war of long duration, be compelled by the pressure of the powers hostile to Germany, to change their attitudes. Similarly, this applies also to the Baltic states.

II

1. Britain, as a world power with many other interests including interests in the powers of the European continent, has tried up till now, with all her means, to prevent a new European war. It may be accepted that she will pursue this policy to the utmost. On the other hand, the possibility of a change in this point of view has shown itself. British rearmament has been thought of from a long way back as the *ultima ratio*, it is progressing and is already striving to exceed the original targets. . . . Britain can appraise the present and future armaments situation of Germany correctly. Germany's economic situation has been known exactly to her for a long time. British opinion against Germany, especially in the circles of the intelligentsia, has hardened appreciably since February and March of this year. . . .

2. France also wants peace, or more correctly, abhors a new war. When faced with a threat, actual or pretended, the French people have always come together as one man. Not least have injury of the French concept of honour and pride and French vanity been contributing factors. While earlier occurrences of this sort have been accepted by the French with resignation the settling of the Austrian question has been widely received in French circles as another Sadowa. . . . France will not succumb to Bolshevism, even though the lowest point in her internal difficulties has not been reached yet. . . . More than ever before, it seems to be out of the question that France and Britain will tread separate paths in matters which touch the power status of the two countries. Therefore, it is to be accepted that if France on her own initiative marches against Germany for the sake of Czechoslovakia, Britain will side with France.

3. The hatred in Britain and in France of a new war with heavy sacrifices in blood as much as the uncertainty which France may experience about being able to hurl the nation into an aggressive war against Germany make it possible that they are seeking new means of waging war. . . . On the grounds of these considerations, one can arrive at the conclusion that France and Britain will place

* This sentence has been difficult to translate because of the expression 'Kriegslieferanten', which appears to have no simple English equivalent. The original German written by Beck was:

Im letzteren Sinne sind auch die Massnahmen beider Staaten bezeichnend, sich schon heute Amerikas als Kriegslieferanten zu bedienen, ein Vorgang, der ein weit fortgeschritteneres Stadium erkennen lässt, als es 1914 der Fall war.

the emphasis of their war effort primarily on the sea and the air and little or none on land attacks. Obviously by such means, the most direct aim of the war, the preservation of Czechoslovakia, will not be achieved. But, one can also impute that they are ready, if need be, to surrender Czechoslovakia and to leave its resurrection, like that of Serbia in its time, to the collective settlement at the end of a long war. The outcome is not a matter of doubt for the two powers, if America supports them, even though this support be confined to deliveries of armaments, raw materials, and food.

III

1. Germany's military situation is, taken as a whole, not to be compared with the weakness of the past years, but it is not as strong as in 1914, because all the powers which might possibly be arrayed against Germany have rearmed to a considerable degree—in some cases to the strongest possible. Besides this, Germany will have for years into the future, Armed Forces which are not ready for use, as is known. The military-political situation of Germany does not provide the prerequisite conditions of space to enable the nation, lying centrally within the continent, to withstand a major war on land, sea and in the air. Hopes based on the neutral nations showed themselves to be insecure in the World War. The very lack of space will make it impossible for Germany to endure a long war successfully.

Germany's defence economy is poor, poorer than in 1917–18. For this reason also Germany is not fit for a long war. . . . However, a European war would be conceived and conducted by our opponents from the outset as a long war.

2. The hope to solve the Czechoslovakian problem by military means during this year without the intervention of Britain and France is groundless. The key to the question: war or peace? lies with either Germany or Britain. Agreement over Czechoslovakia is possible, because Britain wants nothing from this danger spot. The prerequisite is that Germany agree to a solution which is still tolerable for Britain. She will never give us a free hand against Czechoslovakia. If we antagonize Britain over Czechoslovakia, other possible benefits which we might receive from a well disposed Britain, even if only partly so, will disappear. From a Britain which is hostile towards us we will receive nothing. Britain is preparing herself to throw her sword into the balance should Germany seek to force a solution to the Czechoslovakian problem which is not suitable to Britain. It has always been her principle to align herself against the strongest Continental power. Even if the attitude of Britain in relation to Germany is different today from 1914, it is still clear that however strong we may be, we are confronted by a coalition which is more powerful than we are. In this case, France and Russia are already on the side of Britain, America will attach herself to them, perhaps only through supplies of war materials. Britain, with her enormous power, which continues even today, despite the criticisms of personalities who do not know Britain the world power from their own observation, will be able to compel the other small powers who are concerned to go along with her or cut us off economically during the course of a war at the latest.[661]

No significant consequences to this memorandum have been recorded.

Three weeks later, Hitler assembled a group of senior leaders of State and Party and addressed them in the general sense of his speech to the military leaders on 5 November 1937. He stressed the living space problem and stated that this had to be solved by the present generation. Britain and

France would oppose Germany. In the event of a war with the Western Powers, the object of which would be to extend Germany's coast-line by the conquest of Belgium and Holland, Czechoslovakia presented a threat to Germany's rear and stood in the way of a certain German victory. Therefore, Czechoslovakia had to be removed. Britain and France did not want war, Russia would not participate, Poland and Rumania would not be able to oppose Germany out of fear of the Russians, Yugoslavia had disengaged herself, Hungary would join Germany, and Italy was not interested.

Hitler claimed that the situation called for lightning action. British rearmament would not be effective until 1941–42, and that of France would also require many years before completion. There were tensions between Italy on the one side and France and Britain on the other. Italy had to be given clear military support as did Japan also. The right moment had to be grasped. There was no question of Germany's being spared the emergency. Building of the West Wall was to be accelerated, and means for a lightning breakthrough into Czechoslovakia were to be prepared.[662]

Beck was amongst the audience, and on the following day, 29 May 1938, he compiled another memorandum setting out his objection to this policy. He began by stating the points on which he was in agreement with Hitler, viz.: Germany's lack of space, the danger posed by Czechoslovakia to Germany's flank, and the hostility of France. He then proceeded to the main points of the memorandum, his objections to what Hitler had said. These are summarized thus:

1. Germany was not in a stronger position than in 1914. The creation of greater internal unity had to be weighed against the greater unreadiness of the Armed Forces for combat. Furthermore, the danger of air attack on Germany's crowded space was far greater than it was in 1914–18, the financial, food, and raw materials situations were worse than in 1917–18, and the people would be opposed to a war which was not forced upon them.

2. The successes of Hitler's foreign policy in the period 1933–38 were no guarantee that similar decisions would be successful in the future. The opposition to Germany was growing in both military strength and unity. Germany was confronted by a coalition comprising Czechoslovakia, France, Britain and America. These nations would co-operate much more closely than they had done in 1914. Different concepts of religious, racial and national problems had aroused opposition to and even hatred of the Germany of 1938 on the part of the four powers who would oppose her.

3. The appraisals of the military might of France and Britain were unintelligible to a soldier. Both opponents had been underestimated in 1914. Germany, either alone or with the help of Italy, was not in the position to challenge France or Britain militarily.

4. The Czech Army could not be regarded simply as the Army of a nation of seven million people.

5. The cardinal point would always remain whether Germany would become involved in a war merely against Czechoslovakia, or whether she would have to fight against all of Czechoslovakia's supporters. The campaign against Czechoslovakia might well be successful, but in the final analysis, Germany would lose the war.

6. Should France and Britain enter the war, Czechoslovakia would be nothing more than the *casus belli*—the war would be conducted on an entirely different level. It would develop into a European, or a World War. It was a mistake frequently encountered to suppose that such a war would be determined by the initial successes and defeats. Germany's opponents had time and space at their disposal and their resources of men and materials were superior to those of Germany and her allies. If it came to a long major war, the adherence of the other single powers to Germany was not to be expected, either initially, or for the long term.[663]

Beck presented these objections to Brauchitsch on 30 May. Two days previously, Hitler had signed new orders for *Aufmarsch Grün*, beginning:

It is my unalterable decision to smash Czechoslovakia in the near future by military action.[664]

Hitler summoned the Army leaders to a conference at the School of Artillery at Jüterbog on 30 May, at which he communicated his decision to deal with Czechoslovakia by force, by 1 October 1938. The division between the views of Hitler and those of the Army was illustrated by Jodl's diary entry for that day:

The whole contrast becomes acute once more between the Führer's intention that we must do it this year and the opinion of the Army that we cannot do it yet as most certainly the Western Powers will interfere and we are not yet equal to them.[665]

Beck restated his objections to Hitler's policy in a memorandum of 3 June 1938. He took this to Brauchitsch as another step in his campaign to convince the Army commander that war with Czechoslovakia would mean a European war, which Germany would lose. Relations between these two men had become strained as early as their first weeks of co-operation within the High Command.[666] This gradually widened into an unbridgeable gap, which was reinforced by growing divisions between the General Staff and the Army Personnel Office which had been taken over by Keitel's brother, Bodewin, after the Fritsch crisis.[667] Beck offered his resignation to Brauchitsch many times during the summer of 1938 before their final crisis in mutual confidence. Brauchitsch became so exasperated by Beck that he began to by-pass him by dealing directly with the new Chief of the Operations Staff, General Franz Halder.[668] Beck's gloom mounted as he explained to Hossbach one evening that summer that in a Second World War, the war guilt question would play a much greater role than it had in the First World War, and the circumstances of a defeat would be much worse than 1918.[669]

During July, the situation became more critical. All sorts of field exercises were taking place, the civilian population was organized on a war footing, the building of the West Wall was accelerated further, and OKW issued a directive on 4 July that the new *Aufmarsch Grün* was to come into effect on 28 September 1938.[670] Under the pressure of these circumstances, Beck produced his third long memorandum for Brauchitsch.[671] This contained the following points:

1. There was no doubt that an attack on Czechoslovakia would bring France and Britain into the conflict at once, thus causing a European or World War. The outcome of such a war would be a general catastrophe for Germany, not only a military defeat.

2. The German people did not want this war, the purpose of which they did not understand. Similar thoughts were also abroad within the Army. Both the Army and the people feel that such an undertaking would have no prospects of success. The military leaders were responsible for seeing that Germany was not launched into any military campaign which it did not have a good chance of winning. The Czechoslovakian question was creating a crisis of confidence between the people and the military leaders which would influence events for the worse in the event of a war.

3. Military preparations had attracted foreign attention, and had led to increased efforts on the part of the Czechs to improve their defences. Any hope of achieving surprise had thereby been dashed.

4. The possible conduct of Poland and Hungary in the event of a German attack on Czechoslovakia was at best uncertain. They ought not to be relied upon to come to the assistance of Germany. Italy would not be able to prevent France from making an attack to aid Czechoslovakia. There were insufficient forces to cover the German rear on the western front. The removal of troops from East Prussia could excite Polish covetousness.

5. 'From the reasons given above and in my earlier memoranda, I consider myself to be obliged—in consciousness of the significance of such a step, but with reference to responsibility which devolves on me according to my official instructions for the preparation and conducting of a war—to express the urgent request that the Supreme Commander of the Armed Forces halt the preparations for war ordered by him, and defer the intention of solving the Czechoslovakian question by force until the military prerequisites for this have changed fundamentally.'

Beck held that such action as Hitler had planned had no chance of success, and that his views were shared by all department heads within the General Staff. He wanted Brauchitsch to confer with the Wehrkreis Commanders over the attitude of the troops. Closer liaison between the senior officers of the Army was needed. A conference of Army leaders was necessary before Hitler explained his war plans to them, so that Hitler might be presented with a united opinion on the matter. Finally, Brauchitsch was urged to discuss the matter with Raeder and Göring to see whether unity could be reached amongst the commanders of the three services.[672]

Beck laid this memorandum before Brauchitsch on 16 July 1938. At the same time, he urged Brauchitsch to organize a collective measure of resistance of the Army leaders. In his notes for this discussion with Brauchitsch, Beck had written:

History will burden these leaders with blood-guilt if they do not act in accord with their specialized political knowledge and conscience. Their military obedience has a limit where their knowledge, their conscience and their sense of responsibility forbid the execution of a command. If their warnings and counsel receive no hearing in such a situation, then they have the right and the duty to resign from their offices. If they all act with resolution, the execution of a policy of war is impossible. By this they have saved their country from the worst—from ruin. It is a lack of greatness and of recognition of the task if a soldier in the highest position in such times regards his duties and tasks only within the limited framework of his military instructions without being aware of the highest responsibilities towards the nation as a whole. Extraordinary times demand extraordinary measures.[673]

He added that there was a necessity for a showdown with the S.S. and the rising tide of the rule of the bosses (*Bonzokratie*).

On 19 July, Beck repeated to Brauchitsch his ideas for a collective stand against Hitler's plans for aggression. He stressed also that this was perhaps the last opportunity to free Germany and even Hitler himself from the tyranny of a Cheka and oppression by party bosses. They had to demand a return to the rule of law and cessation of the persecution of the churches.[674] Brauchitsch still hesitated, torn between the weight of Beck's arguments, his own admiration for Hitler, and the unrealistic notion that the Army had to be kept out of politics.

On 29 July, Beck went to Brauchitsch again and urged him to tell Hitler that Germany was unprepared for a war, and that the senior generals could not accept responsibility for such adventures. Brauchitsch refused to do this. Beck then demanded that Brauchitsch summon a conference of the senior commanders of the Army so that he could place his views before them. Brauchitsch agreed to this, and the conference was arranged for the end of the first week of August.[675] In the meantime, preparations for war went forward. A new revision of the mobilization plan was issued on 1 August 1938,[676] training was intensified, and troops who were detailed to assist with the harvest had to remain within a short distance of their barracks, ready for movement at short notice.[677]

A useful first-hand report of the conference has been left by Weichs. According to his account,[678] the following took place:

Brauchitsch announced to the generals that he had received the order for the preparation of an attack on Czechoslovakia. He then read a memorandum, which in the opinion of Weichs had been written by Beck, although Brauchitsch was careful to keep the pages covered up while he read them so nobody could see the handwriting. Brauchitsch also claimed that the responsibility for the memorandum was his own. The essence of the document was that general war would result from the Western Powers honouring their obligations to Czechoslovakia. Germany could not stand against them all. The Sudetenland was not worth risking the existence of the nation. Brauchitsch then invited the generals to exert their influence upon Hitler by confronting him with the thoughts expressed in the memorandum as soon as possible.

After a short pause, Brauchitsch asked each of the Wehrkreis Commanders to describe the conditions within their areas of command in the event of a war. This resulted in the general conclusion that the mood of the people and of the soldiers was, in general, against war. The generals were also in agreement that although the standard of training and equipment of the troops was probably sufficient to defeat Czechoslovakia, it was insufficient for a battle with the powers of Europe.

Weichs specifically stated that it was wrong that two of the generals, Reichenau and Busch, dissociated themselves from this opinion (several accounts of this meeting do state this).[679] Weichs wrote that the difference between these two generals and the others was only tactical. Reichenau warned from his personal knowledge of Hitler that it would be far more effective if individual officers were to see Hitler, rather than make a mass confrontation. It is significant that Brauchitsch took this advice. Busch suggested that although the danger of war was imminent, it appeared to be so only from the military point of view, and it was not the place of soldiers to interfere with politicians. Beck spoke out strongly against this notion, stressing that all trained staff officers ought to be capable of making correct judgements in the political-military field.

Brauchitsch then closed the conference with the prophetic observation that a war would be the end of German culture. Weichs then overheard Rundstedt begging Brauchitsch to present these thoughts to Hitler in such a way that he did not damage his own position. Rundstedt was afraid that Brauchitsch would be dismissed and replaced by Reichenau. On looking back, this might not have been a bad thing for the cause of peace. Reichenau's views about Hitler and his policies were undergoing a change at this time,* and he, if any soldier could, was able to stand up to Hitler and to carry some popular support with him. Certainly, Reichenau could hardly have been worse than Brauchitsch as a means of stopping Hitler.

Weichs concluded his account by supposing that Brauchitsch conveyed the thoughts of the conference to Hitler in a milder fashion than the generals thought he would from his tone at the meeting. Weichs did not doubt that Brauchitsch did inform Hitler of the feelings of the generals, because Hitler's response was clear, but certainly Brauchitsch achieved nothing by his protests. Hitler reduced him to a state in which he was prepared to take part in an action which, in his own words, would be the end of German culture. No more damning evidence of the weakness of Brauchitsch could exist than this!

Hitler's first reaction to the views of his senior generals was to attempt to go behind their backs by inviting their Chiefs of Staff to a dinner at the Berghof on 10 August 1938.†[680] At this meeting, he addressed them for three hours on his general political theories. It was apparent to Jodl that Hitler's ideas found opposition in the minds of the audience. He wrote in his diary entry relating to that dinner that attitudes of questioning were widespread throughout the General Staff. The General Staff did not believe in the genius of the Führer. It was in everyone's mouth that the views of the generals were opposed to those of Hitler. This was seeping down throughout the Army, and could eventually affect the morale of the troops. When General von Wietersheim mentioned that it was the opinion of the Commander of the Western Fortifications, General Adam, that these fortifications could not be held for longer than three weeks, Hitler

* See above, Chapter 2, and Warlimont, *Inside Hitler's Headquarters*, p. 59. Reichenau appeared at this time on crutches in Berlin, much to everyone's surprise. WK VII file 611.
† His second reaction was to offer appeasement by formally rehabilitating Fritsch on 11 August 1938. Kielmansegg, *Der Fritsch Prozess, 1938*, p. 130.

exploded with rage. 'That position can be held for not only three weeks, but for three years; the man who does not hold these fortifications is a scoundrel!' [681]

Hitler confronted the senior generals on 15 August, at Jüterbog.* The day began with an exercise, but Weichs said that this was simply a pretext for Hitler to be able to address the generals. [682] Hitler told them that he was firmly resolved to solve the Czechoslovakian question by force that autumn. [683] He stressed that as long as Chamberlain and Daladier were still in power, there would be no European war as a result. He also drew the attention of the generals to his prophetic gifts. [684]

Immediately after Hitler's address, Beck sought an audience with Brauchitsch. Brauchitsch had clearly had enough of Beck by this time. He had Beck informed that he was not available because he was going away on leave, and he would not be able to see Beck until he returned. [685] Brauchitsch may have had other things on his mind in view of his marriage which took place in the following month.

Beck regarded this treatment as the last straw. On Brauchitsch's return on 18 August, Beck had his final stormy talk with the Army commander. Beck realized that it was no use continuing in this way, and that the only course open to him was to resign. Brauchitsch refused to accept Beck's resignation, but Beck simply refused to do any more service. [686] Brauchitsch then discussed the matter with Hitler. Hitler's agreement was communicated to Beck on 21 August, but Brauchitsch also told Beck that Hitler had ordered that 'for reasons of foreign policy' his resignation was not to be communicated to either the Army or to the public. Out of loyalty to Germany in a time of crisis, Beck agreed to this condition. [687]

On 27 August 1938 Beck appeared at his office in the Bendlerstrasse for the last time, to hand over his duties to General Halder, and to give his staff a farewell address. He summoned the departmental heads to his office. He stood by his desk, the famous piece of furniture which had been passed down to successive Chiefs of the General Staff from Moltke. His countenance was strained, and he gazed into the distance without acknowledging the greetings of those who entered. He gave a speech of fifteen minutes' length, beginning with the announcement of his retirement. He spoke of his uncompleted task, exhorted his hearers to independence of views and strength of character, and closed with thanks to those who had worked with him. [688]

Thus Beck's service career closed. He had opposed Hitler's plans for aggression with all his might, and had done his best to precipitate the united resistance of the Army leaders to Hitler. The failure of the latter was due to his being well ahead of his generation in political-military

---

*Buchheit, *Beck*, p. 169, gives the location of this conference as Jüterbog. Weichs' memoirs gives it as the proving ground at Kummersdorf. As the two places are only some twenty miles apart, the difference is not important. Quite likely, the generals met Hitler at Jüterbog, which was the larger centre and journeyed out to Kummersdorf to watch the exercises which both sources mention. The two places had very little apart from forest between them. The Stülper Forst to the north-east of Jüterbog merged with the Forst Kummersdorf to the south-west of Kummersdorf.

Fritsch handing over the Seeckt memorial to members of the Seeckt family at the Invaliden Friedhof on the morning of 2 November 1937.

Oberst Hossbach, who risked his life to warn Fritsch of the intrigues of early 1938, escorting Hitler as Armed Forces Adjutant from the House of the Reichs President.

Heydrich and Himmler,
the directors of the
intrigue against Fritsch.

Himmler and Hitler inspecting a guard of honour of the S.S.
Verfügungstruppe, Himmler's private army.

Brauchitsch before the Führer whom he was unable to resist.

Brauchitsch the soldier—in his element.

Field-Marshal von Brauchitsch, Commander-in-Chief of the German Army, 1938-1941.

Generaloberst Halder—
Chief of the German
General Staff, 1938-1942.

Field Marshal von Manstein—
Director of Operations,
1935-1938, Deputy Chief of
the German General Staff
under Beck, 1936-1938.

Removed from the High
Command when Fritsch was
dismissed.

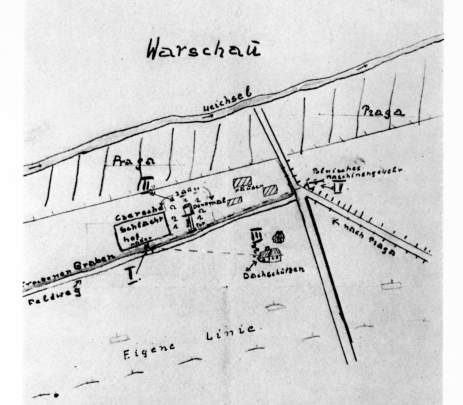

Da der Generaloberd noch zur Armee wollte, ging er aus
den Vorstadthäusern von Praga zurück, bevor das Stosstrupp-
unternehmen beendet war. Er durquerte ein Rübenfeld, Ziff. II.
hier bekam er Feuer aus dem einzelnen Hause Ziff. III
Er suchte Deckung zusammen mit seinem Begleiter in einem
etwa 1 mtr. tiefen Graben Ziff. T. Jetzt schoss noch das polnische
M.G. rechts der Strasse Ziff. IV. Ein Geschoss prallte an de
Mauer von Czersche ab und traf den Generaloberst tödlich X.
Aus dem Rübenfeld hatten deutsche Soldaten 8 Tg. später einen
Ehrenhain gemacht und einen Gedenkstein errichtet.

How Fritsch met his death—a sketch map by an eye witness.
On 22 September 1939 Fritsch accompanied a forward patrol into
no-man's land before the Warsaw district of Praga. While leaving
the patrol to return to Army Headquarters, the conspicuous red
lapels of his general's greatcoat drew the fire of Polish riflemen from
the houses (III in sketch). He and his Adjutant took cover in a ditch
(I) which ran in front of a stone wall. A machine-gun opened up in
enfilade from the house (IV). A shot ricochetted from the wall and
struck Fritsch in the thigh, severing his femoral artery. His Adjutant
attempted to bind Fritsch's leg, but Fritsch removed his monocle,
and brushed the Adjutant away, saying "Oh, just leave be!" One
and a half minutes later, at 9.40 a.m., he was dead. A memorial was
erected in the field which he had just crossed (II). This memorial,
the barracks named after him at Köslin, and his grave, his three sole
monuments, were all destroyed during the war. His horse, Columbus,
he left to General Ulex, a man of Beck's outlook.

A typical scene from the entry of German troops into the Rhineland, Austria, and the Sudetenland. "It was roses, roses, all the way." Browning—*The Patriot*.

Brauchitsch (centre) appointing Fritsch (at left) to be Colonel-in-Chief of Artillery Regiment 12 before a mass parade of troops at Gross Born on 12 August 1938 —the sole gesture of rehabilitation made towards Fritsch after the reasons for his dismissal had been shown false by court-martial in March 1938.

The propaganda battle for the minds of the young soldiers—Hitler addressing 9,000 officer cadets in the Sportpalast, Berlin.

Party propaganda at the exhibition "German Greatness" portraying German soldiers returning from the First World War and finding salvation within the ranks of the Nazi Party.

Epilogue to an Era—the coffin of Generaloberst Freiherr von Fritsch lying in state in the hall of the War Ministry, September 1939.

thought. It was perfectly clear to him that military obedience served no good purpose when it meant obedience to orders which could only ruin the nation. He was also clear in his own mind that an attack on Czechoslovakia would bring this catastrophe about through the intervention of Britain and France. His colleagues seemed to be agreed on the latter but did not regard the former principle as binding upon them.

Whether this principle was really clear in the minds of the other generals at the time is by no means certain. If they were quite certain that they had higher duties than obedience to the Head of State, then collective weakness seems to be the only explanation to their conduct. But these men were capable commanders, used to taking risks and to making decisions affecting many lives, including their own, as their careers in both World Wars have testified.

It seems more likely that the notion of limited obedience was not clearly established in their minds. They had been trained in the simple system of Imperial Germany, by which they were under the personal command of the Kaiser, and that was as far as political connections went. They had fought as small cogs in a great, machine-like war for four years, in which obedience had been of the first importance. In the post-war years, Seeckt reserved the taking of all political decisions to himself. After Seeckt, Schleicher was so active in the political field that a reaction against political soldiers set in. Once Hitler had come to power, the generals' time had been so fully occupied by the demands of the rearmament programme that they had had little scope for broadening their thinking, unless they were of the rare nature of Beck. Therefore, the significance of Beck's thoughts on the limits to obedience to their political masters had small chance of being appreciated.

The strong influence of the oath to Hitler was another obstacle to the full acceptance of Beck's ideas. The observance of this oath was held by many to be sacred. Many of the senior officers had taken the oath solemnly and ceremonially before their own troops and it had taken a hold of their minds which could not be broken by reasons such as Beck advanced.

It is all very well to condemn this failure to perceive wider responsibilities as simply a refusal to recognize an inconvenient state of affairs, for this implies an ability to perceive the essence of the situation. A more accurate description of the conduct of the generals in 1938 would be blindness—they simply lacked the necessary sensory organs to see that the nature of the Third Reich had made the Army the only possible alternative final arbiter to Hitler.

The crux of this failure would seem then to lie in the training of the German officers, but this is hardly a matter for censure, for what nation has ever prepared its soldiers to deal with the civil government whenever it should act in a manner which the soldiers judge to be contrary to the national interest?

After Beck had gone, many generals continued to be worried about what Hitler might do, and about what their duties were, but until they had found a clear answer to these questions, there was work to be got on with. Until they were convinced that it was their duty to oppose Hitler

M

with all their means, it was their duty to obey him. The more they immersed themselves in work, the less acute the other insoluble riddle became as it receded into the background. Once the Munich crisis had turned into Hitler's triumph a wave of relief must have swept over those who had been torturing themselves. The problem was over, the Führer had been right all the time (had he not also been correct at the time of the re-entry of the Rhineland?), Germany was safe in his hands. Even the more cynically minded generals who saw Hitler's success as more due to his luck than to his intuition must have felt that there was no point in worrying until the next time.

In the meantime, they had to take some nasty medicine for their implicit support of Beck, from, of all people, Göring. Göring was ordered by Hitler to put some courage into the generals. According to Weichs, Göring did this in his own brutal and tactless manner. A special course in National-Socialism was run for generals in Berlin. Göring gave the final address. He said:

In this building [i.e. the War Ministry] lives the spirit of faintheartedness. This spirit must go!

He also boasted about the courage and confidence of his Air Force in contrast to that of the other services.[689] The insolence and humiliation of these remarks must have left deep wounds on the pride of many of the audience, while the remorse induced in others would have had a powerful effect in weakening the *esprit de corps* of the Army commanders.

At the conclusion, Hitler spoke on a different theme which also had a most disturbing effect.[690] He said that every nation needed an upper class. The German upper class had failed in the Great War, with the general exception of the officer corps. It was necessary to build a new upper class which could stand the strain of leadership. This could not be achieved without hardship.[691] The implication regarding the conduct of the officer corps in 1938 could hardly have been missed.

While the majority of the German generals regarded obedience to Hitler as their prime duty at the time of the Sudetenland crisis, there was one small group which did not think in this way, and which began to conspire against Hitler. The leader of this group within the High Command was Beck's successor as Chief of the General Staff, General Franz Halder. Halder was of a famous old Bavarian military family which had served Bavaria's rulers for many generations.[692] He had had an outstanding career as an officer of the General Staff, rising to become Beck's deputy and Chief of Operations after Hitler and Keitel had ordered the dismissal of the inconvenient Manstein on 4 February 1938. Halder was a man of conservative leanings and he enjoyed the full confidence of Beck throughout their period of service together.[693] After Beck's resignation, Halder was reluctant to allow Brauchitsch to put forward his name to succeed Beck but after three days, Halder consented. Halder had not been as obstructive as Beck over the Czechoslovakian question and so Brauchitsch probably thought that he would be reducing his own worries by having Halder directly subordinate to him.

Unfortunately for the Army commander's peace of mind, Halder was being drawn into a conspiracy to arrest Hitler and place him on trial as soon as he had given the final order for the execution of *Aufmarsch Grün*. This conspiracy had been set afoot by Admiral Canaris and Oberst Oster of the Abwehr, and had widened to include the commander of Wehr-kreis III, General von Witzleben, the commander of the Potsdam garrison, Graf von Brockdorff-Ahlefeld, the commander of the First Light Division, General Hoepner, Halder's successor as Chief of the Operations Department, General Karl-Heinrich von Stülpnagel, the retired Commander-in-Chief of the Army, von Hammerstein, and Beck.[694]

Once Hitler had been arrested, it was planned that Brauchitsch should issue a decree stating that he was to be the interim supreme authority of government until a civilian caretaker administration had been formed which was then to determine the new form of government for Germany on the basis of popular opinion. But because of Brauchitsch's weakness, it had been decided by the conspirators that he was not to be brought into the plot until the very last moment.[695]

Nevertheless, the conspirators had to have reliable information concerning what was happening at the top so that they could time their blow with precision. Halder therefore was asked to provide advanced notice of Hitler's intention to attack Czechoslovakia, so that Witzleben could arrest Hitler and isolate him. Halder agreed to do this, saying that he could give at least two days' clear notice, and that he would not pass on the order to launch *Aufmarsch Grün* when it came down from Hitler.[696]

After the lack of success of the conspirators' first envoy to London, Herr von Kleist-Schmenzing, in late August 1938, Halder decided to send his own negotiator, Oberstleutnant Böhm-Tettelbach, an industrialist with British connections, to make direct contact with the War Office. Böhm-Tettelbach journeyed to London on 2 September 1938 and repeated the warnings of Kleist that Hitler meant to attack Czechoslovakia at the end of the month. He also hinted at the action proposed by the conspirators,[697] but this mission achieved no result.

Meanwhile, some of the other generals who were not involved in the plot, began to increase their protests against Hitler's plans. Rundstedt and Reichenau urged Brauchitsch to make further representations to Hitler. Brauchitsch conferred with Hitler and Keitel on 3 September at the Berghof, and stressed once again the difficulties of forcing a way into Czechoslovakia and the dangers of Western intervention. His only reward was another tirade of abuse.[698]

On 6 September Halder sounded out the attitude of the Hungarian Chief of the General Staff, General Fischer, and received a briefing from Jodl on Hitler's political attitude. Jodl stressed to Halder that the Führer had ordered that absolutely no hint of the moment of the attack on Czechoslovakia was to be given to anyone involved.[699] Halder's closest contact in the conspiracy, Stülpnagel, approached Jodl two days later and asked for five days' notice of when *Aufmarsch Grün* was to be put into action. Jodl agreed to give this as far as was possible, but he emphasized that the meteorological situation might not permit more than two days' notice. Stülpnagel also inquired whether the basis of the plan, i.e. that the intervention of Britain and France was not to be courted, had not been changed, for Hitler seemed to Stülpnagel to be going ahead at all costs. Even Jodl was becoming worried by this stage. To prevent panic amongst the German public, news circulation was to be restricted, he recorded.[700]

Brauchitsch and Halder again discussed with Hitler the dangers facing Germany, on 9 September 1938, during the Party Rally at Nuremberg. The argument went on till 4 a.m. on the following morning. On his return to Berlin, Keitel complained to Jodl that he was bitterly disappointed in Brauchitsch, in whose appointment he had played so great a part. Keitel then gave a lecture to the staff of the OKW saying that he would not tolerate any doubts or criticism. Jodl added that when Hitler's day of reckoning with Czechoslovakia came, 'many officers would blush with shame at their pusillanimity and smugness'.[701] Jodl summed the situation up in his diary entry for these days thus:

Moreover the Führer is aware that the Commander-in-Chief of the Army asked his commanders to support him in his attempt to make the Führer see sense on the subject of the adventure into which he seems determined to plunge. The Commander-in-Chief himself, so he said, unfortunately had no influence with the Führer. The atmosphere in Nuremberg was consequently cool and frosty. It is tragic that the Führer should have the whole nation behind him with the single exception of the Army generals.

In my opinion it is only by action that they can now atone for their faults of lack of character and discipline. It is the same problem as in 1914. There is only one undisciplined element in the Army—the generals, and in the last analysis this comes from the fact that they are arrogant. They have neither confidence nor discipline because they cannot recognize the Führer's genius. This is no doubt to some extent due to the fact that they still look on him as the Corporal of the World War instead of the greatest statesman since Bismarck.[702]

On another day during the 1938 Party Rally, Göring inspected the camp occupied by the troops who were participating in the Rally, as was the custom for the senior service officer. During the meal which followed his inspection Göring addressed the officers who were at the Rally, saying:

I know that you are afraid of the Czech bunkers, but just throw your heart over and you will come through!

The greater part of the officers present were from Pomerania, and they knew nothing of the situation on the Czechoslovakian border, or of the protests of Beck, so they took Göring's words as a totally unwarranted accusation of cowardice and were very angry. Weichs, as the senior officer present, took the complaints to Brauchitsch, but nothing came of it. One of the unfortunate effects of Göring's taunts was to make the younger officers more intent on proving their bravery by smashing the Czech border defences.[703]

But behind the protests and upheavals which Hitler's policy was causing, preparations and detailed planning for the attack went steadily ahead. Trains carrying material for the western defences were to be kept running on schedule until 20 September. From 21–30 September 1938, the railway time-table for the mobilization period was to be in operation, and all preparations were to be ready for 1 October.[704] OKW was ordered on 15 September to discuss whether forces could be got ready earlier.[705] On 20 September, the Army complained about the arbitrary action of the Sudeten Freikorps on the Czech border, as this was arousing the anxiety of the Czechs and causing troop concentrations at a time when the German Army wished Czech attention to be in any direction but the German border.[706]

The time of striking drew near. On 26 September, Brauchitsch gave orders that the approach march to the Czech border was not to start until the following day, as Hitler did not intend to march in until 30 September. However, although X-day was to be in no circumstances before 30 September, difficulty was encountered in setting the exact time of day at which the attack was to begin. The Army needed the protection of the pre-dawn gloom, while the Air Force could not fly so early because of the early morning fogs.[707] On 27 September, Hitler agreed to the advancing of the first wave of the attack to a line from which they could arrive in the assembly area for the attack of 30 September.[708]

On 28 September, Brauchitsch begged Keitel to remember his responsibilities and to do everything possible to ensure that Hitler did not order the invasion of the Sudetenland.[709] Suddenly, the machine-like process of preparing for war was checked. Chamberlain had announced at 4.15 that afternoon that he was prepared to go to Munich on the following morning to have further discussions with Hitler, Mussolini and Daladier on the Sudetenland crisis.[710]

The German mobilization was not the only plan affected by Chamberlain's statement. During the past weeks, the conspirators, despite the Gestapo and the S.S., had finalized the details of their plans, according to Halder 'to the last gaiter button'.[711] Witzleben told Hossbach in mid-September that all was ready, requiring only the pressing of the button to set the plan in motion.[712] There seems no reason to doubt that this was in fact the case.[713] But once Chamberlain had announced his intention of having further talks with Hitler, it was painfully apparent that the basis for the popular support necessary for such a putsch had been pulled away. Instead of being able to accuse Hitler of casting Germany into the path of the greatest catastrophe of German history, the conspirators were faced with his greatest triumph since coming to power. He had been right, while those who had counselled caution had been proved to be the spreaders of groundless fears.

Even if Chamberlain and Daladier had decided not to come to Munich, such a putsch would have been an extremely risky undertaking.[714] It was to have been led by a group of almost totally unknown civilians and soldiers who were from a group which had been carefully and distinctly labelled by Dr Goebbels as 'reactionary' for years past. The soldiers who were to provide the force necessary had been thoroughly indoctrinated with Hitlerism, if not with Nazism itself, both inside and outside of the Army. The execution of a putsch in the face of enemy confrontation would have reeked of treason to many. However, despite these factors, the conspirators were sufficiently desperate to consider making a putsch under those conditions. But when these difficulties were complicated to the degree that they were after 28 September, they saw that there was nothing to be achieved by betraying their hand, and so they were forced to call off their plans until some new danger arose of sufficient gravity and clarity to be able to shatter the effects of six years of Nazi propaganda on the minds of the German public.

On 1 October 1938, the exhausting atmosphere of tension was relaxed as the Army marched through the open frontiers of the Sudetenland to the accompaniment of triumphal music, applause from the local German population, and the praise of the Party. To most Germans, this was a very sweet victory. The soldiers were only too well aware that it had had nothing to do with them. They knew that it had been a triumph of one man's will. Once more the outcome of events had dragged the balance of political-military relations towards the side of Hitler. Once more the Army had been proved wrong while the Führer's intuition had been shown to be correct. Hitler had one more stick with which to beat his generals on the next occasion they dared to oppose him, while many generals must have become more and more bluffed by the magnitude of Hitler's success in the face of their professional judgement to the contrary.

In the period immediately after the Munich Agreement, Hitler became more distrustful of the Army. He had OKW institute a time-table system, whereby he was continually informed of the whereabouts of each division, and Witzleben was removed from command of Wehrkreis III.[715] Rundstedt, who had requested Hitler's permission to resign after the Fritsch crisis and agreed to serve until autumn, was finally allowed to go.[716] Beck's resignation was announced on 31 October, as was Keitel's promotion to Generaloberst.[717]

Brauchitsch summed up his attitude towards National-Socialism in an order of 18 December 1938.* He emphasized the genius of Hitler in the securing of the new Great-German Reich, and in the creation of a new German being. These great deeds demanded the loyalty of the Army to Hitler, the man who had worked a miracle. Therefore, the officer corps was not to allow anybody to surpass it in the purity and strength of its National-Socialist thought.[718]

During the following three months, a period of training and consolidation took place. New recruits had entered the Army in October, and these had to be given basic training. The operations in Czechoslovakia were fully reported by the participating units, and these reports were analysed on each succeeding level of command. The remainder of Bohemia and Moravia was occupied on 15 and 16 March 1939, and the Memel Land was placed under German rule on 23 March. On the voyage back from Memel after the re-entry ceremonies, Hitler was approached by a number of his military staff in the ward-room of the cruiser on which they were travelling. They were particularly concerned about the growing hostility of Britain towards Nazi-Germany, and asked Hitler if he had given full

* See Chapter 5 above for a fuller quotation of this order.

weight in his deliberations to the power of the Royal Navy, since it could sweep the German Navy from the seas within a few weeks. Hitler replied that he had appreciated Britain's naval power and assured his listeners that:

There is no sacrifice which I will not make to avoid war with Britain.[719]

Towards the end of March, Hitler hinted to Brauchitsch that he had decided to use force against Poland in order to attain his aims of a German strip across the Polish corridor into East Prussia and German control of Danzig.[720] OKW set to work to revise the annually issued *Directive for the Co-ordination of the Preparation of the Armed Forces for War*. During the revision, Warlimont, head of the OKW operations staff, referred the matter to his counterpart in OKH, Stülpnagel, so that the directive would allow the Commander-in-Chief of the Army as much freedom from interference as possible.[721] This document was issued to the three services on 3 April 1939, and planning for an attack on Poland, code-named *Fall Weiss*, was begun.[722]

During the preparation of the plans by the three individual services, OKW was made superfluous by the use of inter-service liaison officers to discuss the inter-service difficulties, and to negotiate matters directly with Hitler.[723] Preparations were also made for emergency assistance for the 1939 harvest to be provided by the Army. Specific distance limits were set on troops working away from their barracks, and they were to be permitted to assist only in such a manner that all mobilization deadlines could be met.[724]

During this time, Hitler allowed members of the OKW staff to confer with members of the Italian General Staff at Innsbruck. The German officers had been forbidden by Hitler to discuss questions of strategy, so the talks were not of great value. However, on 22 May 1939, Hitler announced the signing of the 'Pact of Steel' between Italy and Germany. Although this pact was a military alliance, the military terms were kept secret from the Armed Forces, and no officers participated in drawing them up.[725]

As soon as the pact had been concluded, Hitler summoned the heads of the three services and of the OKW to a meeting in the Chancellery, at which he spoke on the problem of living space and gave his reasons for attacking Poland. He also mentioned the possibility of war in the west, and the need for occupying the Low Countries if this came to pass. At this meeting, Brauchitsch and Halder presented the Army's plans for the attack on Poland to Hitler. Keitel, the sole representative of OKW at the meeting, heard these plans for the first time only then.[726]

Planning and training continued uneventfully until August 1939. The approach of war had become obvious to many members of the High Command. Some considered what might be done to save Germany from a certain catastrophe, while others resigned themselves to their impotence. Amongst the former was General Thomas, head of the Armed Forces Economics Department, who presented a memorandum to Keitel, written with the help of Schacht, stressing that ideas of a lightning war were illusions and that Germany did not have the resources at her disposal necessary to withstand a long war of attrition. Keitel replied that general war would not come to pass because the Western Powers were too decadent and because Hitler's genius would overcome all problems to Germany's advantage.[727]

By late August 1939, Hitler's patience with Poland in the question of the Corridor was running out, while his popularity in the eyes of the Kremlin was growing. On 22 August, he assembled a large gathering of senior officers of the three services and addressed them for several hours on the theme of his future strategy. The main points of his speech were as follows:

He was not able to predict the reactions of Britain and France, but he did not think that they would go to war over Poland, particularly in view of the Nazi-Soviet Pact (which Ribbentrop was on his way to sign). Germany won wars only if she were united. A long period of peace was not good for the nation. The battle would be fought by men, not by machines, and Germany had the better men. The goal of the operation was the elimination of and crushing of the military power of Poland, even though war in the west was a result. It was necessary to crush the enemy's strength wherever it showed itself. The greatest speed in attaining success in the east offered the best prospects for localizing the conflict. The war would be started by propaganda whether this was plausible or not. In starting and waging a war what mattered was not right, but victory. Germans had to steel their hearts and make them hard. Great harshness could mean the greatest mildness in the long run.

He named X-day as 26 August and Y-time 04.30 hours, and abused those of his audience who had doubted his judgement in 1938.[728]

Once the signing of the Nazi-Soviet Pact was announced to a shocked world on the following day, and the British guarantee had been given to Poland on 25 August, the course of Germany was set for war. Disappointed by the reactions of Britain and France, Hitler ordered a postponement of *Fall Weiss*. By 28 August, Hitler had resolved to go to war whatever the cost. He told Brauchitsch that X-day was to be 1 September and that Y-time would be specified later.[729] Late on the evening of 30 August Hitler decided that the attack would begin at 4.45 a.m. on 1 September. This was communicated to the Army High Command on the morning of the 31st, and the final orders were issued to the attacking formations late that evening.[730] Thus was the German Army cast on the road to war and destruction.

Throughout 1939 the senior officers of the Army made but little attempt to oppose Hitler and his policies of aggression which, as many of them realized, risked the whole future of Germany. The protests of 1938 had died out. As events showed, they had been made too soon. Hitler had succeeded in 1938 with a bloodless victory. The generals had struck against empty air and in so doing they had expended their capital of goodwill and respect with the Führer. In 1938 they had a fine and determined leader, Beck. In 1939, apart from the miserable figure of Brauchitsch who had sufficient military insight to see the weaknesses of Germany's position, but not strength enough to force this view on Hitler, there was only Halder. Although approached by the civilian opposition during 1939 to obtain his co-operation for action against Hitler he did not participate in their plans.

Halder may have had very good reasons for not involving the Army at that stage. His readiness to join the plot prepared for November 1939[731] suggests that he was still in favour of the general principle of overthrowing the Nazis. His decision to refrain for the time-being was probably determined by the lack of popular support for a putsch.

The lack of a leader at the centre made these difficulties much harder to solve for any junior leader. Collective professional morale amongst the generals was low in 1939 as a result of their defeat by Hitler's intuition, so they did not feel like taking more revolutionary steps until the chances of success had improved significantly. Moreover, nagging at the minds of some and dominating the minds of others was the old notion that politics was no business of the Army. The government had ordered the Army to war, therefore it had to go and uphold the national interest. Even though the prospects looked black to many, this was a ground only for protest. After the protest had been made (or after everyone had supposed that it had been made by the Commander-in-Chief) the government had the power of command, and the Army had to cope as well as it was able.

Even though the situation in September looked gloomy and the future appeared even darker, those generals who were opposed to Hitler still had to search for a means of breaking the vicious cycle in which they were trapped before they were able to think further about displaying their opposition. The course of the following six years showed that there was no means ready to hand. The greater bulk of the Army remained loyal to Hitler until the bitter end. In 1944 when the myth of Hitler's invincibility had been broken, wide support within the Army for a putsch was lacking. Any such attempt made in 1939 would have been hopeless. What else remained for the Army but to trust to its success in battle to minimize the effect of the coming catastrophe?

Conclusion

THE remarkable chain of events which formed the story of the German
Army in its relations with the Nazi Government of Germany in the pre-
war years is particularly rich in examples of the gradual growth of power
of a political movement at the expense of an army. The balance of political-
military relations as described in the introduction may be summarized
thus:

(a) The desires of politicians to attain their own political goals.

(b) Their recognition of the need for compromises for the sake of
national security.

(c) The desires of soldiers for progress towards their military goals.

(d) The awareness of the soldiers for their part that they must compromise with the politicians in order to achieve them.

If (a) and (d) pull in the one direction, (b) and (c) tend, of course, to
pull in the other.

Force (a) was of great strength in the Third Reich. The Nazi Party,
under the leadership of Hitler, began its period of office with a widely
based and far reaching programme of policy, which the Party showed it
would pursue with fanaticism. The Party regarded itself as the sole bearer
of the *Weltanschauung*, and buttressed itself in a dictatorial position in
order to realize its policy. In particular, the Party would not tolerate being
pulled off its path by the Army, unless the Army had extremely pressing
reasons. Throughout the 'twenties, Hitler had impinged upon barriers
held by the Army across his course towards the Chancellorship, and he
had come to dislike generals. He was prepared to use guile and deception
in order to achieve his ends. Because the Army did not operate so willingly
by such methods, Hitler's ability to go his own way was further enhanced.

The frequent occurrence of surprise tasks, such as the re-entry of the
Rhineland, the Anschluss and the Czechoslovakian operations kept the
Army off-balance and intensified greatly the atmosphere of rush and
improvisation which accompanied the process of rapid, large-scale rearmament. This caused Army policy to degenerate into a series of dis-
jointed improvisations and gave little time for the organization of united
resistance by the High Command to each of Hitler's aggressive projects.
The nature of the Third Reich gave an extraordinary amount of initiative
to Hitler in political-military relations and he exploited it.

Hitler was further strengthened by the lack of an organized political opposition capable of exerting sanctions on his general policy, while the infirmity of purpose and disunity amongst the military leaders greatly reduced the need for him to heed criticism, either civil or military. During the years after 1933, his respect for the generals as experts within their own field was seriously eroded by their mistaken assessments of the reactions of the Western Powers.

Nonetheless, Hitler had to come to terms with force (b) and face up to some military limitations upon his ambitions. Militarily, Germany was, until 1938, a very weak nation. As a result, Hitler was compelled to proceed slowly for the first few years of his rule. He had to arouse the enthusiasm of some generals at least, in order to have the immense work of the rearmament carried out effectively. Until 1938, he maintained a front of respect for the generals, and appeared to treat their views seriously. This may even have been more than a front. During his first year of power, the challenge of the S.A. presented itself. Hitler could not afford to become completely isolated from a source of physical strength, and so he encouraged the natural tendencies of the Army to resist Röhm's attempts to dominate the military establishment. During the life of Hindenburg, Hitler had to contend with a Head of State who was the personification of German military tradition, and who resented the efforts of his Chancellor to interfere in internal Army affairs. However, after 1934, the force of many of these factors was spent, and the degree of compromise which Hitler had to make with the Army to maintain his position against internal and external threats declined severely.

Force (c) had strong roots in the traditions of the German Army. It was accustomed to choosing its own military policies, and to a great amount of freedom in their pursuit. The Army knew how to formulate policy and was used to accepting responsibility for its execution. It was not a vacuum waiting for Hitler to fill. This suited Hitler very well because it made for military efficiency. While the strength of the Army was low it was no serious threat to his position and he allowed it considerable control over its own internal affairs until 1938.

The Army was assisted further in adhering to its own policy by the presence of Hindenburg as Head of State for the transitional period. Despite his age, the old Field-Marshal remained intolerant of interference in military matters and he maintained direct relations with Hammerstein and Fritsch in matters of Army administration. The senior officers within the High Command were for the most part, true to the old conservatism which had dominated their earlier careers. In particular, Fritsch and Beck had clear ideas of the measures required to restore German military strength and they made the most of the new atmosphere offered by the Nazi government to put these measures into operation. They were also repelled by the intrusions of Nazism in the form of political indoctrination of the soldiers and made determined efforts to keep the Army free of such contamination.

However, these influences were heavily outweighed by the components of force (d). At the top of the political structure was a man who gave a high priority to military considerations, who openly supported the Army as an essential instrument of national policy and who attracted the sympathies of all ranks. Immediately beneath Hitler in the military hierarchy was the extraordinary Blomberg, who dedicated himself to bringing the Army and the Party into intimate union, in such a way that the Army was required to make most of the adjustment. His naïve but sincere attempts to ensure German security through faith in the Führer made heavy contribution to the catastrophes of 1939–45. Nazism was disseminated throughout the Armed Forces by Blomberg's special political instructions and since these came from the seat of highest military authority, it was extremely difficult for the subordinate officers who opposed these views to prevent their spread. Once these instructions had been promulgated to the troops, the opposing officers could but issue warnings which resulted in many cases in loss of authority because the troops then associated these officers with the reactionaries and ultra-conservatives ridiculed by Nazi propaganda.

The Army was further confused by the part played by Brauchitsch. He accepted office under Hitler at a time when the Army High Command might have been able to expose the corruptness of the Party in the Fritsch affair. Brauchitsch then proceeded to allow Hitler to drag the Army further into his militarily unsound plans for aggression. In some ways, Brauchitsch continued the role of Blomberg by maintaining the stream of pro-Nazi decrees and instructions which reached all ranks. His political influence on the Army was scarcely less profound than that of the War Minister.

Amongst those beneath these leaders were men of driving personal ambition of types as widely differing as Keitel and Reichenau who did not hesitate to seek the favour of the Party at the expense of Army solidarity. These men existed at all levels and provided a permanent threat to the holders of high positions who were not openly enthusiastic about Hitler and Nazism. Apart from anything else which they did for Hitler, the mere presence of these men was a powerful coercive force on the others who attempted to keep the Army apart from politics. Hitler showed that he was prepared to use his supporters to replace the 'obstructionists' when it came to the time for action, and so the threat was shown to be no bluff.

The majority of officers averse to Nazism were like rudderless ships amidst swift currents. Their education and traditions had kept them apart from politics and so their realization of the significance of events taking place around them was at best, slow. The criminal character of Hitler's rule was not appreciated by many until the last years of the war. The purge of 30 June 1934 was regarded as a private affair between Hitler and the S.A. The growth of Party influence was not regarded with abhorrence by many until it was too late to be able to resist it effectively. Some of these men have since maintained that, even had the evil nature of the Nazi régime been perceived, it was no business of the Army to make itself the *ultima ratio* in internal politics. These circumstances made it impossible for the few perceptive members of the High Command to gather enough support to be able to confront Hitler with unified resistance. Once Hitler had seized the initiative in January 1933, the background of the greater part of the officer corps permitted him to maintain it with relative ease, even in cases in which their military judgement warned of impending disaster.

This lack of political consciousness made the literal significance of the Oath to the Führer far greater than the duties of the defence of Germany required. The question of loyalty to Hitler was seen by some in terms of a man's absolute honour in fidelity to his pledged word rather than in terms of Hitler's opportunist exploitation of a remarkable combination of circumstances which combined to give Hitler claim on the Army's loyalty in circumstances which the Army had never foreseen. When this outlook was combined with the strict code of military obedience which inhibits protest against orders, the Nazi Party was given a degree of control over the German Army quite unknown to the armies of western democracies.

The expansion of the Army by the induction of thousands of youths who had been indoctrinated for some years into the spirit of Nazism placed further limits on the Army's political freedom. Not only did it make support for a putsch extremely difficult to obtain but it provided a built-in surveillance system by which the Party might observe the conduct and attitudes of individual soldiers of all ranks. The young conscripts were keen and enthusiastic about the achievements of the Third Reich and the officers who were in close contact with their men could not have expected to obtain the full co-operation and arouse the enthusiasm of their troops without making at least an outward concession to the political feelings of the soldiers. Junior officers affected senior officers in a similar if less marked fashion. These circumstances made it professionally advantageous for officers to acknowledge the apparently good points of the National-Socialist régime and to ignore the bad. Mass conscription of German youths in the years after 1935 made it possible and indeed inevitable for Nazism to spread upwards throughout the Army like a cancerous growth.

By 1939, what had been conscious submission to Nazism on the part of some officers had grown into inability to oppose it. In 1933, only a small number of officers, mostly of junior rank, were convinced supporters of Nazism and attempted to spread Party ideology amongst their troops. By 1939, there were few senior officers who were able to inhibit Nazi indoctrination of their soldiers. A gradual change had occurred. What had been the exception in 1932 had become the rule in 1939, and vice versa.

Broad forces were exerted by the course of events in pre-war Germany which helped to restrict the political initiative and self-confidence of the High Command. The presence of the S.A. under the leadership of Röhm, covetous of the position of the Army, made the Army more dependent upon the favour of the Chancellor than would otherwise have been the case. When this Chancellor, who was also the head of the Nazi Party, struck down the leaders of the old guard of the Party, and assigned the Party's troops who had borne the brunt of the physical struggle for power to a minor role within the new state for which they had fought, he earned the gratitude of the Army. The different natures of the personalities of Hitler and Röhm made what was a struggle for personal power portrayable as a contest between the forces of white and the forces of black. Part of

Hitler's reward for defeating the purported evil designs of Röhm was the Oath. The caution displayed by senior officers over the questions of rearmament, the Rhineland and Czechoslovakia, was shown by events to have been unnecessary. Hitler's apparent temerity was justified and he used these successes as a foundation for the myth of his military invincibility and political infallibility. Those officers who had dared to doubt the wisdom of the Führer were humiliated by the success of an amateur in their professional field. Hitler's status in the eyes of some soldiers mounted while his contempt of the competence of the High Command increased in more than equal proportion.

Apart from the strictures imposed by discipline, the German Army faced another difficulty in dealing with political matters which was not shared by many of the other professions. As in most armies, an officer could not resign as of right. He could merely request permission to do so. In view of the shortage of trained officers in the German Army resignations were not permitted easily, particularly on the higher levels at which the personal approval of Hitler was necessary for a resignation. Submission of a resignation in such circumstances did little more than to brand the officer concerned as an opponent of the régime and thus expose him to the terrors of the Nazi system of coercion. This required the issue at question to have been one of unmistakable clarity for a man of principle to request permission to resign. Most of the points of dispute between the Party and the Army during this period were too vague to allow of this measure of clarity and furnished all too little direction to men unattuned to the political significance of events. Against any urge to resign in protest was opposed the military duty of obedience, reinforced by tradition. There was also the repercussion on the officer's own family.

The possibilities open to an officer who was opposed to an order which had been given to him were full obedience, open insubordination, or apparent obedience with concealed insubordination. Thus there were considerable forces, conscious and subconscious, tending to make an officer give the benefit of any doubt of interpretation to an order.

The military efficiency of the Nazi dictatorship was another factor which tended to influence soldiers in Hitler's favour. The greater availability, compared with the days of the Weimar Republic, of materials, men, and finance, the improved conditions of service, the modernization of the Army, the fascination of new work and the emphasis on professional proficiency were associated in the minds of many soldiers, and with considerable justification, with the National-Socialist government. Apart from local friction with minor Party officials which was often rationalized in terms of the Führer's ignorance of the misconduct of his juniors, there was much about the Third Reich in its pre-war years which seemed to the German Army at large to be wholly right and proper. The overall system had provided the good things—it only remained for Hitler to clean up the defects on the lower levels, when he had time, for Germany to be put back on her feet again as a healthy and vigorous nation which had cast off the gloom and shame of the 'twenties. It was only too easy for the Party propaganda machine to impress this sort of thinking upon the receptive minds of many soldiers and to make others, who were less credulous, more hesitant in criticizing the Party.

Thus the German Army came to be dominated by Hitler. The forces acting on the Nazi Party enabled it to pursue its own policy with little need for compromise with the Army, while the Army was subject to an overwhelming number of influences which combined on many levels to make it subservient to its political master.

Appendix A

Some Additional Cases in Army-Party Relations

One of the most frequent means of contact between the Army and the Party in matters of an ideological nature was in the public ceremonies, which were attended by both in official capacities. Initially, the Army had not attempted to make any recognition of Party formations which happened to be at the same place in uniform. This situation did not last for more than several months. On 19 September 1933, Blomberg ordered that soldiers should salute members of the S.A., S.S. and other Party formations, when both met in uniform, out of doors.[732] The Nazi salute had to be used on all occasions when a soldier was not wearing headgear, even when he was saluting another soldier.[733] On 29 August 1934, Fritsch signed an order for the introduction of the Nazi salute into further ceremonies for the Army.[734]

The military salute was in danger of vanishing completely in March 1935, when the Luftwaffe was unveiled. Göring, and possibly Blomberg, wanted a unified salute for the entire Wehrmacht. Until then, the Luftwaffe had used the Nazi salute. Hitler and Göring together decided that the Army would have to change to the Nazi salute also. Hossbach then went to Hitler, and explained how unpopular this would have been with the Army, and Hitler agreed to let the Army retain its traditional salute.[735] The final alteration to be made in the salute, as far as records show, was the introduction of the response 'Heil Hitler!' after the 1936 Nuremberg Rally to be used by soldiers who were greeted by civilians with the Party salute.[736]

The various insignia of the Party did not immediately spread to the uniform of the Army, but by February 1934, Blomberg had decided that the Party emblem was to be worn on Wehrmacht uniforms, to advertise that the Armed Forces were as loyal to Hitler as his other forces.[737] The number of Party badges permitted to be worn was increased by Blomberg's order of 31 August 1935, which detailed six more, related to the Party's history.[738] On 26 March 1936, Wehrmacht members were permitted to wear the Golden Decoration of the Hitler Youth.[739]

One vexed question at combined parades of the Army and the Party was the order of march. On 24 March 1934, Fritsch asked Reichenau to obtain a ruling on the matter, so that the disputes which had been taking place might be avoided.[740] The answer to this request is not known, but on 22 April 1936, Keitel issued an order cancelling an arrangement whereby the S.A. had been permitted to march in front of the Army. The new regulation gave the Army priority over the Party organizations when the soldiers were armed, but when unarmed they were to march behind all of the detachments of the Party and its organizations.[741]

In addition to these, there were many similar small points, too numerous to be described here, but exemplified by Hitler's order that 'Sieg Heil!' was to be used for all loyal toasts,[742] and by the participation of the Army in the Party Rallies.[743] The general impression one gets from all these small incidents is of a reluctance on the part of some officers to accept the Party's presence at one function or another, or of a disinclination to have to march behind Party contingents. These feelings would then provoke small incidents, which came before Reichenau or Keitel for settlement. The final ruling seldom, if ever, put the interests of the Army above those of the Party.

One particular Party organization which came to play a sizeable role in Army-Party relations in the years after the Röhm crisis was the Hitler Youth. According to the Nazi system, boys belonged to the Hitler Youth between the ages of 10 and 18, approximately, i.e. until shortly before their entry into the Army. The Army had always taken an interest in the development of German youth, and there was ample reciprocal interest to ensure frequent contacts.

Formal co-operation between the Army and the Hitler Youth for the purposes of military training began in late 1936. Initially, it was done on a local basis, under the co-ordination of the Wehrkreise, since it was not possible to make a national ruling until the passage of a special law overcoming the difficulties of the Army's giving help to a political body.[744] This law, the *Reichs Jugend Gesetz*, was passed on 1 December 1936. It entrusted the physical and spiritual training of the youth of Germany to the Hitler Youth.[745] On the following day, Reichenau issued a directive on Army-Hitler Youth co-operation to Wehrkreis VII. Whether this was a purely local measure is not known, but because its wording closely follows that of the *Jugend Gesetz*, it is likely that the law was quickly promulgated to each of the Wehrkreis Headquarters, with instructions that they were to draft interim regulations at once.

This directive illustrated the extent of Army-Hitler Youth co-operation. It covered shooting, instruction of leaders, small manœuvres, visits to Army barracks, sport, films, talks and social gatherings.[746] This co-operation was supervised by a specially appointed Hitler Youth Liaison Officer, who was a member of the Wehrkreis staff. Reichenau's directive was supplemented by an order from Fritsch of 26 April 1937,[747] covering similar points with the addition of the appointment of Oberstleutnant Rommel as Liaison Officer of the Wehrmacht and of the Army with the Hitler Youth.

In order to make the political aspects perfectly clear, Keitel issued an order on 29 April 1937, which stated:

> According to § 26 of the Defence Law, soldiers are not permitted to engage in political activities, their membership to the N.S.D.A.P. and its organizations is to be in abeyance.
>
> Amongst the organizations of the N.S.D.A.P. is the Hitler Youth. However, since the leadership of the national youth has been entrusted with the education of the entire German youth, it has been raised to the status of a government body.[748]

An indication of the manner in which the co-operation was progressing was given by a report from the Commandant of Munich, of 9 December 1937. He described the co-operation as

> mainly good—the Hitler Youth is well disposed towards co-operation with the Army. In difficult cases, trouble has been due more to unfamiliarity than to malevolence.[749]

This was confirmed for the Army as a whole by a directive signed by Beck, in the absence of Fritsch, on 19 January 1938. This directive then went into further detail concerning the responsibilities and tasks of the Wehrkreise, stating that all Hitler Youth leaders were to receive military training in week-end or other short courses.[750] Many other directives and orders in connection with the Hitler Youth were issued by OKW and OKH during 1938 and 1939, but they were all of an administrative nature, detailing funds, transport, accommodation and other facilities to be used by the Army expressly for giving assistance to the Hitler Youth.

In view of the strong appeal which military training on a game basis has for boys, and the usual affection of armies for organizations like the Boy Scouts and the Cadet Corps, it is not surprising that work with the Hitler Youth was welcomed within the German Army. What is significant, however, is that the Hitler Youth was not only a youth organization, but also a Nazi one. In this way, it is likely that some of the enthusiasm for youth work on the part of the soldiers concerned was transferred to the National-Socialist movement as a whole. But even more insidious were some of the possible effects of placing soldiers in a position of pre-eminence in front of boys. In such an environment, a politically uncommitted soldier, asked a question the answer to which would reveal his own attitude towards the National-Socialist state, would have been under strong pressure to allow his beliefs to crystallize into Nazism. The enthusiasm of the moment, coupled with the tendency of youth to view life in black and white terms, would have been continually pulling the mind of a man towards clear commitment.

During the pre-war years, the relationships between the Army and many of the Party organizations were defined in Army orders. In an order governing relations with the National-Socialist Industrial Organization (N.S. Betriebstellen Organisation), of 31 October 1933, Blomberg said:

No doubt may be permitted to exist over the fact that establishments of the N.S.D.A.P., therefore also the N.S.B.O., are not to be regarded as party establishments in the sense of the old party-state, with respect to which the Wehrmacht remained detached.

The N.S.B.O. has the task of broadening and deepening the National-Socialist philosophy amongst industry. In this activity, it is to be supported by the Wehrmacht.

But this task of the N.S.B.O. does not relieve the directors of Wehrmacht industrial establishments from the duty of educating their subordinates in the spirit of the National-Socialist philosophy.[751]

Blomberg's attitude towards the National-Socialist Motor Corps (N.S. Kraftfahr Korps) was shown in an order of 17 April 1934. He stated:

The order of 1 March 1934 may give the false impression that officers are to hold themselves apart from the N.S.K.K. I desire close co-operation between the local branches of the N.S.K.K. and the Wehrmacht, especially in matters such as sporting competitions.[752]

The National-Socialist welfare organization, *Kraft durch Freude* was another important link between the Army and the Party. On 29 June 1934, an 'Important Political Instruction' was issued by the Reichswehr Minister, entitled 'National Work and the Allocation of Free Time in the Wehrmacht—Participation in the N.S. Fellowship *Kraft durch Freude*'. In this, Blomberg stressed that part of the philosophical training of the Wehrmacht lay in the appreciation of culture of all kinds. Therefore, Blomberg had arranged for all units to receive, gratis, copies of the Nazi magazine, *Volkstum und Heimat*. He went on to emphasize the importance of the *Kraft durch Freude* organization for developing a corporate spirit between the German people and their Armed Forces. He wanted civilians to be invited to a massive scale to take part in the off-duty life of the Army. They were to be able to watch ceremonial parades and to take part in festivities and remembrances. All possible varieties of entertainment were to be thought of by units, for contributing to the welfare of the people. Conducted tours through barracks and other establishments were to be arranged. Groups of workers were to be invited to watch field exercises. Shooting competitions were to be made open, and sporting competitions were to be arranged. Groups of workers were to be accommodated in barracks and in the ski and mountain huts of the Army, for recreational purposes.

> He who recognizes the necessity of this work of fellowship will discover even more ways in which the Wehrmacht can participate in the work of the N.S. fellowship, *Kraft durch Freude*.[753]

On 10 December 1935, Blomberg announced that it was most desirable that officers should give talks at various National-Socialist schools for adults, and at functions of *Kraft durch Freude*.[754] This relationship continued to be a close and popular one throughout the pre-war period.

The establishment of Party courts as separate entities from the State courts created difficulties. Blomberg outlined some of the ensuing complications in a letter to the Minister for the Interior of 25 May 1934. As a result of the Law for the Maintenance of the Unity of Party and State, a Party court proceeding had the full force of law, he wrote. It was then possible that a person might have been tried twice, and given two different punishments for the same offence. He appealed for Party courts to let matters rest, in the case of military offences, until the military authorities had completed their proceedings. In the case of a soldier who had committed an offence against the Party regulations only, the Party courts were requested to inform the Commanding Officer of the man concerned about what actions were being taken against the man, so that the Army could take appropriate action, such as arresting or dismissing him.[755] On 7 February 1936, Blomberg ordered the Wehrmacht to give closer co-operation to the Party courts, by furnishing all documents which the courts might require for the investigation of an offence, and by providing witnesses when they were called for by the courts.[756]

The extensive powers of scrutiny which these rulings gave to the Party were further enhanced by an order from Blomberg, immediately before his resignation, on 25 January 1938. This required that specially recalcitrant men be handed over to the Gestapo for the remainder of their service time. After the Gestapo had taken appropriate proceedings against these men, they were to be put into a concentration camp.[757]

Despite all of these formal rulings on matters affecting Nazi ideology, friction continually erupted in the form of clashes, insults and arbitrary acts. There were so many incidents recorded in the files of the War Ministry, the Army High Command, and the Wehrkreise that a full account is impossible, but a few are described below for the sake of example.

In May 1934, Julius Streicher, Gauleiter of Franconia and self-appointed 'Frankenführer', made a speech in which he severely criticized the political outlook of the officers of the Army.[758] On 26 August 1934, the Gestapo suddenly arrested Leutnant von Loessel, and removed him to Berlin for interrogation, without any explanation.[759] On 29 August 1935, a Party member named Osmers, called on Hauptmann Konitzky at his home, and asked him what his attitude to the Party was, and many other personal questions. Konitzky reminded Osmers that the only people who were entitled to ask him questions on his doorstep were the police. Thereupon Osmers tapped his chest and said, 'Who are the police today?'[760]

An Unteroffizier named Eggers entered a bar on the evening of 10 September 1935, to find four S.A. leaders at the counter. When he moved up to the counter, they threw beer mats at him, then called him 'Scheiss Reichswehr!' Eggers asked the bar tender to restrain them. They then threatened Eggers with being sent to a concentration camp, and added further obscene insults.[761]

On 9 November 1935, Reichsamtleiter Geiger, of the German Workers Front, the Nazi substitute for the trade unions, said to a large audience at Münster, 'The sooner that professors, officers, and other senior men regard themselves as workers, the happier Münster will be!'[762]

In late 1935, evidence reached the Headquarters of Wehrkreis VIII, Silesia, that the Gestapo had been conducting systematic and extensive inquiries into the political views of Army officers within the Wehrkreis. The Gestapo had even addressed letters to some commanders, asking for whatever information they were able to provide. The matter was reported to Blomberg, who asked the Gestapo for an explanation. The Gestapo attempted to tell Blomberg that the inquiries had been made at the request of Wehrkreis VIII, itself. This was denied by Wehrkreis VIII. The Gestapo then stated that Wehrkreis VIII had objected to a report made by the Gestapo in October 1935, which alleged that there were many reactionaries in the officer corps. Because the Army had contested this, the matter had to be cleared up. Furthermore, as the incident had been expanded so greatly, it had become urgently necessary for even fuller investigations of the officers to be made. The Breslau Gestapo then named twelve 'reactionary officers' in a letter to the Commander of Wehrkreis VIII. The Commander replied that only the Army was responsible for investigating the personal lives of its members, and that the twelve officers named were all serving members, who had taken the Oath to Hitler, and who would keep it. Fighting rumours was not a new matter for the Army, he added, and it would be appreciated if the Gestapo were to stamp them out as well. This appears to have ended the matter as far as Blomberg was concerned.[763]

However, despite constant threats against individuals of being taken before a 'People's Court', or a Party court, or threats to confiscate property and supplies as a means of disciplining Wehrkreis Commanders, the Army continued to show a lack of respect for the Party in some matters. On 22 September 1935, a group of soldiers lined up in the restaurant Sonneneck in Stahnsdorf, each with a lighted match which they proceeded to apply to the tail feathers of the Party eagle on their uniforms, reciting, 'Now let us incinerate the *Pleitergeier* [or 'bankrupt vulture']* of Germany'. They made further facetious remarks about the Party and its organizations, and said that they were off to join the League of German Maidens when they had finished with the Army.[764]

At a dance in Neustadt, Upper Silesia, five young subalterns rose and gave the

---

* The term 'Pleitergeier' was originally a nickname given by the Reichswehr to the eagle on the cockade which was worn on military headgear of the Weimar Republic. The name was suggested by the condition of the Weimar Republic's finances. Frequent use of this nickname before 1933 gave rise to its occasional incorrect application to the eagle of the Nazi Party badge by soldiers during the life of the Third Reich.

toast, 'Heil Moscow!' in a spirit of devilment. Fifteen S.A. men then armed themselves with chairs, and set about belabouring the officers. When the matter came before Blomberg, he approved of the assignment of guilt to the officers by the Minister of Justice. The S.A. men were not brought to trial, because of the publicity which it would involve, and because 'all they had done was to be over-zealous in their fight for National-Socialism'.[765]

In October 1935, the wife of Major von Broich was reported to the Party for giving only RM 0.40 to a *Winterhilfe* collection, when, in the opinion of the man making the collection, a Major's wife could have afforded to give more. In conse-quence, Frau von Broich was approached soon after, by the same collector who was collecting for a different cause. Again she did not contribute satisfactorily, stating that she had to pay so much to the Party and to the S.S. that there was nothing left for other collections. When called to account for the behaviour of his wife, Major von Broich said that they gave RM 9 automatically each month for the *Winterhilfe*. Furthermore, he had given money to the S.S. since 1933, and his wife had Party dues to pay.[766]

In November 1935, an S.A. man who was on an eight weeks' course with the Army applied to be released, in order to see Lutze, the Chief of Staff of the S.A. The Commanding Officer of the man refused permission, because this was a Party matter, and therefore could wait.[767]

On 12 December 1935, an S.A. man struck one soldier and stabbed two others at Braunsberg, East Prussia. The mayor of Braunsberg complained that the soldiers had been creating tension by shouting remarks around the town, such as:

> Erst kommt das Heer, dann eine ganze Weile gar nichts, dann ein grosser Haufen Scheisse, dann vielleicht die N.S.D.A.P.

> [First comes the Army, then for a long while nothing, then a great heap of shit, then perhaps the N.S.D.A.P.]

and by referring to the locals as 'schnoddrige Ochspreussen'.[768]

In 1936, a Gefreiter Mandelke was tried for making the following remarks to some of his squad:

> Dr. Goebbels is the greatest blackguard of the Twentieth Century.
> If a putsch were to be made by the Wehrmacht, Generaloberst von Blom-berg would scarcely subordinate himself to the Führer as a former corporal.
> > *Lieber ein Kaiser von Gottes Gnaden,*
> > *Als einen Hitler aus Berchtesgaden.*
> The Nazis will not last long—the day is coming when they will be over-thrown by the Wehrmacht.
> In the next general election, the N.S.D.A.P. will not have a majority.

Mandelke's defence was that he had only been illustrating the manner in which a drunk man might talk. This was unanimously denied by Mandelke's squad.[769]

These incidents continued to occur throughout the years preceding the war, showing both that there was much discontent with Hitler and the Nazi move-ment, on the part of a few individuals, and that there were many others, even comrades of the former, who were prepared to report these deviant views, and to play a part in the prosecution of the men who had been rash enough to express their views openly. Thus was National-Socialism able to make an even greater show of strength and deterrent ability than its other ideological tools and supports allowed.

By these formal, outward means, the Nazi Party was able to give the whole of German life a consistent appearance for the soldier. Whenever he saw the Party on parade with the Army, it was there in a place of importance, often having priority over the Army. Relationships with the organizations of the Party with which he was likely to come into contact were defined and regulated, so that every incentive was given to the development of an almost automatic acceptance of the Party's dominance in all aspects of German life and of the Party's infallibility in executing this role. In an organization such as an army, this emphasis on outward form was likely to have had a great effect.

Thus, the Party bound the Army to its service by a very clever and effective means. By penetrating the minds of the men in the ranks, it was made less necessary for the consent of the more conservative of the senior officers to be obtained. This process short-circuited the opposition to Nazism in the higher ranks, robbing the High Command of independence of movement and thought, while simultaneously helping to provide the National-Socialist movement with armed forces which would obey its orders with the minimum of questioning.

Biographical Details of some Senior German Officers

This appendix outlines the service careers of, and other points of interest relating to the more prominent of the senior officers mentioned above in this study. Apart from the officers at the very top of the Army, I have added some whose writings have provided me with important evidence, such as Weichs and Dollmann, and others who occupied lower positions, but whose careers illustrate the background of an officer of the rank of Oberst during the mid-'thirties, such as Manstein and Heinrici.

This appendix is intended to show not only the individual background of each of the officers dealt with, but also to give a picture of the career patterns of the senior officers of the German Army collectively. It should be noted that while the military training of all of these officers, in their various ranks, was excellent, they were given little opportunity for any wider development.

The officers included in this appendix are (omitting ranks):

Adam	Dollmann	Heinrici	Reichenau
Beck	Fritsch	Hossbach	Rundstedt
Blomberg	Halder	Keitel	Viebahn
Brauchitsch	Hammerstein	Manstein	Weichs
			Witzleben

This information has been compiled from the Record Cards of the Heeres Personalamt, from rank lists and organization directories published by the German Army, from Allied Intelligence material gathered before and during the Second World War, and supplemented by conversations with survivors amongst the officers listed, and with friends and relatives of some of the deceased.

Adam Wilhelm

15. 9. 1877	Born at Ansbach (Mittelfranken)
19. 7. 1897	Entered the Bavarian Railway Battalion as *Fahnenjunker*
10. 3. 1899	*Leutnant*
21. 9. 1902	Posted to the Bavarian Telegraph Company
28. 10. 1905	*Oberleutnant*
22. 3. 1906	Posted to the Bavarian Railway Battalion
1. 10. 1907	Seconded to the Bavarian Kriegsakademie
1. 10. 1911	*Hauptmann*
1. 10. 1912	Company Commander in the Bavarian Pioneer Battalion
8. 8. 1914	Company Commander in the Second Bavarian Field Pioneer Battalion
7. 9. 1914	General Staff Officer on the staff of General von Falkenhayn
14. 12. 1917	*Major* (temporary)

24. 6. 1918	Commander of the Seventeenth Bavarian Pioneer Battalion
11. 6. 1919	Liaison Officer with the Bavarian government
26. 9. 1919	*Major* (substantive, with seniority 18.8.1918)
1. 10. 1920	General Staff Officer in the Headquarters of Wehrkreis VII
1. 2. 1923	*Oberstleutnant*
1. 4. 1923	Commander of the Third Battalion of the Twentieth Infantry Regiment
1. 10. 1925	Chief of Staff to the Seventh Division
1. 2. 1927	*Oberst*
1. 4. 1928	Commander of the Nineteenth Infantry Regiment
1. 2. 1930	Chief of Staff to Gruppenkommando I (possibly slightly earlier), promoted *Generalmajor*
1. 10. 1930	Reichswehr Ministry—Chief of the General Staff (Chef des Truppenamts)
1931	*Generalleutnant* (the first figures of this date are obscured on the HPA Card)
1. 10. 1933	Commander in Wehrkreis VII (and of the Seventh Division)
1. 10. 1934	Commander of Wehrkreis VII
1. 4. 1935	*General der Infanterie*
1. 10. 1935	Commandant of the Wehrmacht Akademie
15. 11. 1938	Placed at the disposal of the Commander-in-Chief of the Army
31. 12. 1938	Was retired

General Adam was a Protestant, spoke English, and was married on 29.9.1906.

Beck Ludwig

29. 6. 1880	Born at Biebrich, near Wiesbaden
1886–1898	Educated in Biebrich and at the Humanistisches Gymnasium, where he completed his Abitur
12. 3. 1898	Entered the Fifteenth Prussian Field Artillery Regiment
1898–1899	Attended the Kriegsschule Neisse
18. 8. 1899	*Leutnant*
1. 10. 1902	School of Artillery and Engineering, Charlottenburg
18. 9. 1903	Battalion Adjutant, Fifteenth Field Artillery Regiment
1. 10. 1908	Kriegsakademie
17. 9. 1909	*Oberleutnant*
1. 7. 1911	Fifteenth Field Artillery Regiment
1. 3. 1912	Grosser Generalstab, Berlin
1. 10. 1913	*Hauptmann*
2. 8. 1914	2. General Staff Officer to the Sixth Reserve Corps
1915–1916	1. General Staff Officer to the 117th and 13th Reserve Divisions
1916–1918	General Staff Officer to the Army Group *Deutscher Kronprinz*
18. 4. 1918	*Major*
1918–1919	Grosser Generalstab, Berlin
1919–1922	Special duties assigned by General von Seeckt
1. 10. 1922	Battalion Commander, Sixth Artillery Regiment, Münster
15. 4. 1923	*Oberstleutnant*
1. 10. 1923	Director of Staff Officer Training, Wehrkreis VI
1. 10. 1925	Chief of Staff, Wehrkreis IV
1. 10. 1929	Commander of the Fifth Artillery Regiment, Fulda
1. 11. 1929	*Oberst*
1. 2. 1931	*Generalmajor*

1931–1932	Preparation of manual *Die Truppenführung*
1. 2. 1932	*Artillerieführer* IV, Dresden
1. 10. 1932	Commander of the First Cavalry Division, Frankfurt a.d. Oder
1. 12. 1932	*Generalleutnant*
1. 10. 1933	*Chef des Truppenamts*
1. 7. 1935	*Chef des Generalstabs des Heeres*
1. 10. 1935	*General der Artillerie*
16–20. 6. 1937	Visit to Paris, talks with Marshal Pétain, General Gamelin, and War Minister Daladier
27. 8. 1938	Hands over his office to *General der Artillerie* Halder
1–30. 9. 1938	In temporary command of the First Army (Westwall)
31. 10. 1938	Official retirement, promoted *Generaloberst*
20. 7. 1944	Death

Beck was a Protestant, and he spoke French and English. He married Amalie Pagenstecher on 12.5.1916. His wife died on 16.11.1917. His decorations included the Iron Cross, First Class, and the Hohenzollern House Order.

Blomberg Werner Eduard Fritz von

2. 9. 1878	Born at Stargard in Pomerania
1894–1897	Attended the Hauptkadettenanstalt, Gross-Lichterfelde
13. 3. 1897	*Leutnant* in the Seventy-Third Fusilier Regiment
1904–1907	Seconded to the Kriegsakademie
18. 5. 1907	*Oberleutnant*
1908–1911	General Staff Officer, Grosser Generalstab
20. 3. 1911	*Hauptmann*
1911–1913	Generalstab der Armee
August 1914	General Staff Officer in the Nineteenth Reserve Division
1916	General Staff Officer in the Eighteenth Reserve Corps
22. 3. 1916	*Major*
1917	General Staff Officer in the Headquarters of the Seventh Army
1920	Chief of Staff to the Döberitz Brigade
1. 10. 1920	*Oberstleutnant*
1. 5. 1921	Chief of Staff to the Fifth Division
1. 4. 1925	*Oberst* and *Abteilungsleiter* in the Reichswehr Ministry (Operations)
1. 4. 1927	Chief of the General Staff (*Chef des Truppenamts*)
1. 4. 1928	*Generalmajor* (substantive—presumably he was given temporary promotion a year earlier because the position of CGS required the rank of Generalmajor)
1928–1929	Visits to Russia, Austria and Hungary
1. 10. 1929	*Generalleutnant*
1930–1933	Commander of Wehrkreis I, East Prussia
1930	Visit to U.S.A.
1932	Leader of the German Military Delegation to the Disarmament Conference at Geneva
30. 1. 1933	Minister for Defence and promoted to *General der Infanterie*
30. 8. 1933	*Generaloberst*
July 1934	Visit to Denmark, Sweden, Lithuania and Finland
20. 4. 1936	*Generalfeldmarschall*
1937	Leader of the German Delegation to the Coronation of King George VI
4. 2. 1938	Retired on grounds of health

Blomberg's decorations included the Iron Cross, First Class, the Wound Decoration, and the *Pour le Mérite*. He was married to Charlotte Hellmich, 20.4.1904, and had two sons and three daughters. His first wife died in 1932. He was remarried on 12.1.1938 to Erica Gruhn.

Brauchitsch Walther von

4. 10. 1881	Born at Berlin
22. 3. 1900	*Leutnant*, Dritte Garderegiment zu Fuss
1901	Third Guards Field Artillery Regiment
15. 2. 1906	Battalion Adjutant
13. 4. 1909	Regimental Adjutant
18. 10. 1909	*Oberleutnant*
1910–1912	Kriegsakademie
1912	Grosser Generalstab, Berlin
18. 12. 1913	*Hauptmann*
22. 3. 1914	Generalstab der Armee
1. 8. 1914	General Staff Officer, Sixteenth Corps
17. 10. 1915	General Staff Officer, Thirty Fourth Division
19. 2. 1918	General Staff Officer, First Guards Reserve Division
15. 7. 1918	*Major*
6. 8. 1918	First General Staff Officer, Guards Reserve Corps
26. 1. 1919	Staff Officer to Wehrkreis II
1. 10. 1920	*Major im Generalstab* and attached to the staff of *Artillerieführer* II
1. 10. 1921	Commander of the Second Battery of the Second Field Artillery Regiment
1. 11. 1922	Staff Officer in the Truppenamt
1. 4. 1925	*Oberstleutnant* with seniority from 1.6.1923
1. 10. 1925	Commander of the Second Battalion of the Sixth Artillery Regiment
1. 11. 1927	Chief of Staff to Wehrkreis VI
1. 4. 1928	*Oberst*
15. 1. 1930	Director of Army Training, Truppenamt
1. 2. 1930	Departmental Head in the Truppenamt
1. 10. 1930	*Generalmajor*
1. 3. 1932	Inspector of Artillery
1. 2. 1933	Commander of Wehrkreis I and the First Division
1. 10. 1933	*Generalleutnant*
21. 6. 1935	Commander of the First Army Corps
1. 4. 1936	*General der Artillerie*
1. 4. 1937	Commander of Heeresgruppe 4, Leipzig
4. 2. 1938	*Generaloberst* and Commander-in-Chief of the Army
19. 7. 1940	*Generalfeldmarschall*
19. 12. 1941	Retired

Brauchitsch's decorations included the Hohenzollern House Order and Iron Cross, First Class (W.W.I.) and the *Ritterkreuz* (30.9.1939). He was awarded the Party Gold Badge on 21.3.1939. He was married to Elizabeth von Karstedt on 29.12.1910 and divorced in February 1938. In September 1938 he married Charlotte Schmidt (*née* Rüpper).

Dollmann Friedrich

2. 2. 1882	Born at Würzburg
15. 7. 1899	*Fahnenjunker*
4. 3. 1901	*Leutnant*
1. 10. 1903	School of Artillery and Engineering, Charlottenburg
1. 10. 1909	Kriegsakademie
23. 10. 1910	*Oberleutnant*
1. 10. 1913	*Hauptmann*
1914–1918	War Service as an Adjutant and as a General Staff Officer
16. 3. 1919	Appointed to the administration of the Peace Commission
1. 10. 1921	*Major*
1. 4. 1923	General Staff Officer, Wehrkreis VII
1. 4. 1927	*Oberstleutnant*
1. 12. 1927	Staff of the First Battalion of the Seventh Artillery Regiment
1. 2. 1928	Commander of the First Battalion of the Seventh Artillery Regiment
1. 10. 1929	Chief of Staff, Wehrkreis VII
1. 2. 1930	*Oberst*
1. 2. 1931	Commander of the Sixth Artillery Regiment
1. 10. 1932	*Artillerieführer* VII
1. 2. 1933	Inspector of Artillery
1. 10. 1933	*Generalmajor*
1. 10. 1934	Area Headquarters, Kassel
1. 5. 1935	Commander of Wehrkreis IX, Kassel
1. 10. 1935	Commander of the Ninth Army Corps
1. 4. 1936	*General der Artillerie*
1. 3. 1939	Commander of the Seventh Army
19. 7. 1940	*Generaloberst*

Dollmann was a Catholic, and married on 15.3.1919.

Fritsch Freiherr Werner Thomas Ludwig von

4. 8. 1880	Born at Benrath, near Düsseldorf
1886–1898	Educated at Düsseldorf, Posen and Hanau
21. 9. 1898	*Fahnenjunker* in the Twenty-Fifth Hessian Artillery Regiment
27. 1. 1900	*Leutnant*
1. 10. 1907	Kriegsakademie, Berlin
18. 10. 1909	*Oberleutnant*
1. 4. 1911	Grosser Generalstab, Berlin
1913	Anti-aircraft observer training
22. 3. 1913	*Hauptmann im Grossen Generalstab*
1914–1918	General Staff Officer to the Fourth Army, the Forty-Seventh Reserve Division, the First Guards Division, the Tenth Army, the Air Force, the Sixth Reserve Corps and Grenzschutz Nord
16. 9. 1917	*Major*
1919	1. General Staff Officer to General von der Goltz, Baltic Area, Grenzschutz Nord, and other General Staff appointments
1920	Reichswehr Ministry
1922	Commander of the Second Battalion of the Fifth Artillery Regiment
1. 2. 1923	*Oberstleutnant*
1924–1926	Chief of Staff to the First Division, Königsberg

January 1926 Director of Operations, Truppenamt
1. 3. 1927 *Oberst*
1928 Commander of the Second Artillery Regiment
1930 *Artillerieführer* II
1. 11. 1930 *Generalmajor*, Commander of the First Cavalry Division, Frankfurt a.d. Oder
1. 10. 1932 *Generalleutnant*, Commander of Wehrkreis III
1. 2. 1934 *General der Artillerie* and Commander-in-Chief of the Army
20. 4. 1936 *Generaloberst*
4. 2. 1938 Retired
12. 8. 1938 Honorary Colonel of the Twelfth Artillery Regiment
22. 9. 1939 Shot, before Warsaw
Fritsch was a Protestant, and his decorations included the Iron Cross, First Class and the Hohenzollern House Order.

Halder Franz

30. 6. 1884 Born at Würzburg
14. 7. 1902 Entered the Third Bavarian Field Artillery Regiment as *Fahnenjunker*
9. 3. 1904 *Leutnant*
7. 3. 1912 *Oberleutnant*, passed the Interpreter Examination in French
16. 5. 1914 Kriegsakademie, Munich
2. 8. 1914 Ordnance Officer, Headquarters of the Third Army Corps
6. 1. 1915 2. General Staff Officer to the Sixth Infantry Division
9. 8. 1915 *Hauptmann*
26. 3. 1917 Headquarters of the Second Army
14. 6. 1917 General Staff Officer to the Fourth Army
12. 7. 1917 General Staff Officer to the Supreme Commander, East
30. 10. 1917 Headquarters of the Fifteenth Reserve Corps
20. 12. 1918 Adjutant, Bavarian General Staff
1. 10. 1919 Reichswehr Ministry
17. 8. 1920 Kommandatur, Munich
1. 10. 1921 Instructor in Tactics, Wehrkreis VII
1. 10. 1923 Commander of the Fourth Battery of the Seventh Artillery Regiment
1. 3. 1924 *Major* (seniority from 1.4.1923)
1. 12. 1925 General Staff Officer to the Seventh Division
3. 7. 1928 Seventh Mechanized Battalion
1. 2. 1929 *Oberstleutnant*
1. 4. 1929 Second in Command of the Directorate of Training, Truppenamt
1. 10. 1931 Chief of Staff of the Sixth Division
1. 12. 1931 *Oberst*
1. 10. 1934 *Generalmajor*, *Artillerieführer* VII
15. 10. 1935 Commander of the Seventh Division
1. 8. 1936 *Generalleutnant*. Also in charge of the Manœuvres Staff during Army general manœuvres 1936
12. 11. 1936 Department head, General Staff of the Army, Berlin
12. 10. 1937 Director of Training, General Staff of the Army
1. 2. 1938 *General der Artillerie*
10. 2. 1938 Director of Operations, General Staff of the Army
1. 9. 1938 Chief of the Army General Staff

1. 7. 1939	Head of the German Military Mission to the Italian manœuvres
19. 7. 1940	*Generaloberst*
24. 9. 1942	Removed from office and transferred to the reserve
21. 7. 1944	Arrested by the Gestapo
31. 1. 1945	Dismissed from the Army
7. 2. 1945	Imprisoned in Flossenburg Concentration Camp
7. 4. 1945	Imprisoned in Dachau Concentration Camp

Halder is a Protestant, he married Gertrud Erl on 25.9.1907, and his decorations included the Iron Cross, First Class and the Hohenzollern House Order from World War I and the *Ritterkreuz*, awarded on 29.10.1939.

Hammerstein-Equord Freiherr Kurt von

16. 9. 1878	Born at Hinrichshagen, Mecklenburg-Strelitz
1884–1898	Educated at Plön and Gross Lichterfelde
1898	*Leutnant*, Dritte Garderegiment zu Fuss
1907–1910	Kriegsakademie, Berlin
1909	*Oberleutnant*
1911–1913	Grosser Generalstab, Berlin
22. 3. 1913	*Hauptmann*
1. 5. 1914	Adjutant to Oberquartiermeister III, War Ministry
1914–1918	General Staff Officer, serving on the General Headquarters of the Field Army, and with the Sixty-Fifth Corps
1917	*Major*
1920	*Oberstleutnant*
1921	Chief of Staff to the Second Army Group, Kassel
1. 5. 1925	*Oberst*
1925–1929	Chief of Staff, Wehrkreis III
1. 2. 1929	*Generalmajor*
1929	Chief of Staff to the First Army Group, Berlin
Late 1929	*Chef des Truppenamts*
	Generalleutnant
18. 10. 1930	*Chef der Heeresleitung* (Commander-in-Chief of the Army), and *General der Infanterie*, with seniority from 1.3.1929
1. 2. 1934	Resignation and promotion to *Generaloberst*
1. 10. 1938	Mentioned as likely Commander-in-Chief of either the Western or Eastern Fronts if war resulted from the Czechoslovakian crisis, during which he actually commanded an Army Group in a static role
September 1939	Commander-in-Chief, Armee Abteilung A, charged with the defence of the Low Countries

Hammerstein's decorations included the Iron Cross, First Class and the Hohenzollern House Order from the First World War.

Heinrici Gotthard

25. 12. 1886	Born at Gumbinnen, East Prussia
8. 3. 1905	*Fahnenjunker*, 95 Infantry Regiment
18. 8. 1906	*Leutnant*
17. 2. 1914	*Oberleutnant*
18. 6. 1915	*Hauptmann*

27. 8. 1916	Brigade Adjutant
7. 12. 1916	General Staff Officer, 115 Infantry Division
13. 3. 1917	Generalstab der Armee
9. 10. 1917	Headquarters, Seventh Army Corps
28. 2. 1918	General Staff Officer, 203 Infantry Division
18. 2. 1919	General Staff Officer, First Army Corps
23. 8. 1924	Commander of the Fourteenth Company of the Thirteenth Infantry Regiment (Württ.)
1. 2. 1926	*Major*
1. 10. 1927	Organizations Department, Truppenamt
1. 8. 1930	*Oberstleutnant*
1. 11. 1930	Commander of the Third Battalion of the Third Infantry Regiment, Osterode, East Prussia
1. 10. 1932	Headquarters of First Army Group
1. 2. 1933	Reichswehr Ministry, later head of the Central Department of the Allgemeines Heeresamt (General Army Office)
1. 3. 1933	*Oberst*
1. 1. 1936	*Generalmajor*
25. 5. 1937	*Chef Amtsgruppe Ersatz und Heereswesen* (Group for Replacement and Army Affairs)
12. 10. 1937	Commander of the Sixteenth Division
1. 3. 1938	*Generalleutnant*
1. 2. 1940	Commander of the Seventh Army Corps
9. 4. 1940	Commander of the Twelfth Army Corps
1. 6. 1940	*General der Infanterie*
17. 6. 1940	Commander of the Forty-Third Army Corps
20. 1. 1942 4. 6. 1944	} Commander of the Fourth Army
1. 1. 1943	*Generaloberst*
19. 8. 1944	Commander of the First Panzer Army
20. 3. 1945 29. 4. 1945	} Commander of Army Group Vistula

Heinrici was married to Gertrud Strupp on 16.10.1920. He speaks French and English .His decorations included the Iron Cross, First Class and the Hohenzollern House Order (W.W.I.) and the *Ritterkreuz* (18.9.1941) with Oakleaves (24.11.1943) and Swords (3.3.1945).

Hossbach Friedrich

21. 11. 1894	Born at Unna (Westphalia)
29. 10. 1913	*Fähnrich*, 82 Infantry Regiment
19. 6. 1914	*Leutnant*
1. 11. 1914	Battalion Adjutant
15. 9. 1916	Regimental Adjutant
2. 3. 1918	Ordnance Officer, Eighteenth Army Corps
20. 9. 1918	*Oberleutnant*
14. 11. 1918	Battalion Second in Command
22. 11. 1918	Company Commander
23. 11. 1919	Commander of a Signal Platoon
17. 12. 1919	Battalion Adjutant
22. 3. 1923	Wehrkreis Examination (for General Staff Selection)

I. 10. 1923	Commander of the Eighth (Machine Gun) Company of the Seventeenth Infantry Regiment
I. 10. 1924	Fifteenth Cavalry Regiment
I. 10. 1925	Seventeenth Infantry Regiment
I. 3. 1927	*Hauptmann*
I. 10. 1927	Reichswehr Ministry
I. 10. 1931	Seventeenth Infantry Regiment
I. 7. 1933	Reichswehr Ministry (HPA)
I. 3. 1934	*Major*
2. 8. 1934	Armed Forces Adjutant to the Führer and Reichs Chancellor
I. 7. 1935	Head of the Central Department, General Staff of the Army (in addition to being Hitler's Armed Forces Adjutant)
I. 9. 1935	*Oberstleutnant*
I. 3. 1937	*Oberst* (with seniority from 1.10.1938)
28. 1. 1938	Dismissed from the post of Adjutant to Hitler
15. 9. 1938	Commander of 82 Infantry Regiment
I. 9. 1939	Chief of Staff to the Thirtieth Army Corps
25. 10. 1939	Commander of 82 Infantry Regiment
21. 1. 1942 28. 2. 1942	Temporary Commander of 31 Infantry Division
I. 3. 1942	*Generalmajor*
I. 4. 1942	Commander of 82 Infantry Division
I. 8. 1942	*Generalleutnant*
16. 5. 1943	Commander 31 Infantry Division
2. 8. 1943 10. 8. 1943	Deputy Commander of LVI Panzer Corps
12. 8. 1943	Commander, LVI Panzer Corps
I. 11. 1943	*General der Infanterie*
19. 7. 1944 28. 1. 1945	Commander of the Fourth Army

Hossbach married Margarethe Jahns on 24.5.1921. He speaks English and French. His decorations included the Iron Cross, First Class (W.W.I.), and the *Ritterkreuz* (7.10.1940) with Oakleaves (11.9.1943).

Keitel Wilhelm

22. 9. 1882	Born at Helmscherode, near Brunswick
9. 3. 1901	*Fahnenjunker*
18. 8. 1902	*Leutnant*
23. 11. 1908	Regimental Adjutant
18. 8. 1910	*Oberleutnant*
8. 10. 1914	*Hauptmann*
11. 11. 1914	Battery Commander
9. 3. 1915	General Staff Officer to the Fifteenth Reserve Corps
20. 7. 1916	General Staff Officer to the Nineteenth Reserve Division
3. 5. 1917	General Staff Officer to 199 Infantry Division
19. 8. 1917	Army Special Employment List
21. 12. 1917	Generalstab der Armee
7. 5. 1920	Instructor at the School of Cavalry
I. 5. 1923	*Major*
15. 9. 1923	Sixth Artillery Regiment

1. 2. 1925	Reichswehr Ministry
1. 11. 1927	Commander of the Second Battalion of the Sixth Artillery Regiment
1. 2. 1929	*Oberstleutnant*
1. 10. 1929	Head of the Organizations Department, Truppenamt
1. 10. 1931	*Oberst*
1. 10. 1933	*Infanterieführer* III, Potsdam
1. 4. 1934	*Generalmajor*
1. 10. 1934	*Infanterieführer* VI
9. 9. 1935	Wehrmachtsamt
1. 10. 1935	Head of the Wehrmachtsamt
1. 1. 1936	*Generalleutnant*
1. 8. 1937	*General der Artillerie*
4. 2. 1938	Head of OKW
1. 11. 1938	*Generaloberst*
19. 7. 1940	*Generalfeldmarschall*

Keitel was married on 18.4.1909. His decorations included the Iron Cross, First Class and the Hohenzollern House Order (W.W.I.) and the *Ritterkreuz* (29.10.1939).

His brother, Bodewin, was Head of the Army Personnel Office from 1938–1942.

Manstein Fritz Erich von Lewinski genannt von

24. 11. 1887	Born at Berlin
6. 3. 1906	*Fähnrich*, Dritte Garderegiment zu Fuss
27. 1. 1907	*Leutnant*
1. 7. 1911	Battalion Adjutant
19. 6. 1914	*Oberleutnant*
2. 8. 1914	Regimental Adjutant
1. 10. 1914	Kriegsakademie
17. 6. 1915	Staff Officer to Army Group von Gallwitz
24. 7. 1915	*Hauptmann*
19. 8. 1915	Adjutant, Headquarters of the Twelfth Army
22. 1. 1916	General Staff Officer, Headquarters of the Eleventh Army
July 1916	General Staff Officer, Headquarters of the First Army
late 1917	1. General Staff Officer to the Fourth Cavalry Division, Estonia
May 1918	1. General Staff Officer to 213 Assault Infantry Division
early 1919	Area Headquarters Magdeburg
1919	General Staff Officer, Grenzschutz Ost, Southern Headquarters, Breslau
late 1919	Staff Officer to General von Lossberg in Berlin and then in Kassel, Headquarters of Army Group II
1. 10. 1921	Commander of the Sixth Company of the Fifth Infantry Regiment
1. 10. 1923	General Staff Officer to Wehrkreis II
1. 10. 1924	General Staff Officer to Wehrkreis IV
1. 2. 1927	*Major*
1. 10. 1927	General Staff Officer to Infanterieführer IV
1. 9. 1929	Operations Department of the Truppenamt
1. 4. 1931	*Oberstleutnant*
1. 10. 1932	Commander of the Second Battalion of the Fourth Infantry Regiment
1. 12. 1933	*Oberst*

1. 2. 1934	Chief of Staff to Wehrkreis III
1. 7. 1935	Head of the Operations Department, General Staff of the Army
1. 10. 1936	*Generalmajor*
6. 10. 1936	Deputy Chief of the General Staff (*Oberquartiermeister I*)
4. 2. 1938	Commander of the Eighteenth Division
1. 4. 1939	*Generalleutnant*
18. 8. 1939	Chief of Staff to the Commander-in-Chief, East
23. 10. 1939	Chief of Staff, Army Group A
15. 2. 1940	Commander of 38 Army Corps
1. 6. 1940	*General der Infanterie*
May 1941	Commander of 56 Motorized Corps
13. 9. 1941	Commander of the Eleventh Army
1. 1. 1942	*Generaloberst*
1. 7. 1942	*Generalfeldmarschall*
November 1942	Commander of Army Group South
31. 4. 1944	Transferred to the Reserve

Manstein speaks English and French. He married Jutta Sibylle von Loesch on 10.6.1920. His decorations included the Iron Cross, First Class and the Hohenzollern House Order (W.W.I.) and the *Ritterkreuz* (19.7.1940) with Oakleaves (March 1943) and Swords (March 1944).

Reichenau Walther von

8. 10. 1884	Born at Karlsruhe
1903	*Fahnenjunker*, First Guards Field Artillery Regiment
1904	*Leutnant*
8. 8. 1912	*Oberleutnant*
1. 5. 1914	Kriegsakademie, Berlin
1914–1918	Adjutant, First Guards Reserve Artillery Regiment, General Staff Officer 47 Reserve Division and Sixth Army Corps
28. 11. 1914	*Hauptmann*
1919	General Staff Officer, Headquarters Kolberg
1920	General Staff Officer, Wehrkreis VI
1922–1923	Commander of the Eighth (Machine Gun) Company of the Eighteenth Infantry Regiment
1. 7. 1923	*Major*, General Staff Officer Wehrkreis III
1. 6. 1926	Visit to England
1927	General Staff Officer, First Army Group Headquarters
1. 11. 1927	Commander of the Fifth Signal Battalion
1. 4. 1929	*Oberstleutnant*
4. 9. 1929	Language study in England
1. 10. 1929	Chief of Staff to the Inspector of Signals, Reichswehr Ministry
1. 2. 1931	Chief of Staff to Wehrkreis I
1. 2. 1932	*Oberst*
1. 2. 1933	Head of the Ministerial Office, Reichswehr Ministry
1. 1. 1934	*Generalmajor*
1. 2. 1934	Head of the Armed Forces Office (Ministerial Office enlarged)
1. 8. 1935	*Generalleutnant* and Commander of Wehrkreis VII
12. 5. 1936	Attached to General Chiang Kai-shek, China
1. 10. 1936	*General der Infanterie*
4. 2. 1938	Commander-in-Chief, Fourth Army Group

8.	6. 1939	Reported to have requested permission to retire
1.	9. 1939	Commander of the Tenth Army, in Poland
1.	10. 1939	*Generaloberst*
2.	5. 1940	Commander of the Sixth Army, Western Front
9.	7. 1940	*Generalfeldmarschall*
12.	6. 1941	Commander of the Sixth Army, in Russia
3.	12. 1941	Commander-in-Chief, Army Group South
7.	1. 1942	Death

Reichenau was a Protestant, he spoke English, and his decorations included the Iron Cross, First Class and Hohenzollern House Order (W.W.I.) and the *Ritterkreuz* (W.W.II.). He was married.

Rundstedt Gerd von

12.	12. 1875	Born at Aschersleben, near Halle
22.	3. 1892	*Fahnenjunker*
17.	6. 1893	*Leutnant*
1.	10. 1896	Battalion Adjutant
22.	3. 1900	Regimental Adjutant
12.	9. 1902	*Oberleutnant*
1.	10. 1902	Kriegskademie, Berlin
1.	4. 1907	Grosser Generalstab, Berlin
24.	3. 1909	*Hauptmann*
1.	10. 1910	General Staff Officer, Eleventh Army Corps
13.	9. 1912	Company Commander, 171 Infantry Regiment
1.	8. 1914	General Staff Officer, 22 Reserve Division
6.	11. 1914	Special Duties List
28.	11. 1914	*Major*
1.	10. 1920	*Oberstleutnant* and Chief of Staff, Third Cavalry Division
1.	2. 1923	*Oberst*
1.	10. 1923	Chief of Staff, Wehrkreis II
1.	3. 1925	Commander of the Eighteenth Infantry Regiment
1.	10. 1926	Chief of Staff, Headquarters of the Second Army Group
1.	11. 1927	*Generalmajor*
1.	11. 1928	Commander of the Second Cavalry Division
1.	3. 1929	*Generalleutnant*
1.	1. 1932	Commander of Wehrkreis III
1.	10. 1932	*General der Infanterie* and Commander-in-Chief of the First Army Group
1.	3. 1938	*Generaloberst*
1.	11. 1938	Retired from active service, and Honorary Colonel of the Eighteenth Infantry Regiment
1.	6. 1939	Recalled to duty
20.	10. 1939	Commander-in-Chief Army Group A
19.	7. 1940	*Generalfeldmarschall*
3.	12. 1941	Transferred to the Reserve
8.	3. 1942	Acting Commander-in-Chief West, and Commander-in-Chief of Army Group D
1.	5. 1942	Commander-in-Chief West, and Commander-in-Chief of Army Group D
2.	7. 1944	Transferred to the Reserve

4. 9. 1944   Commander-in-Chief West, and Commander-in-Chief of Army Group D

10. 3. 1945   Transferred to the Reserve

Rundstedt was married on 22.1.1902. He was a qualified interpreter in French. His decorations included the Iron Cross, First Class and Hohenzollern House Order (W.W.I.) and the *Ritterkreuz* (30.9.1939) with Oakleaves (30.6.1944) and Swords (18.2.1945).

Viebahn Max von

27. 3. 1888   Born at Detmold

1894–1906   Educated at Sondershausen, Oppeln, Meiningen and Mainz (Abitur 1906)

1906–1915   *Kaiser Alexander* Garde-Grenadier-Regiment Nr. 1

1906   *Leutnant*

1915   *Hauptmann*

1915–1916   General Staff Officer, Headquarters of the Guards Corps

1916–1917   General Staff Officer to the Twenty First Reserve Division

1917–1918   General Staff Officer to the Army Group *Deutscher Kronprinz*

1919–1920   General Staff Officer to General von Lüttwitz, Berlin

1920–1923   Third Battalion of the Ninth Infantry Regiment, Spandau

1923–1924   Instructor in General Staff Training, Wehrkreis II

1924   *Major*

1924–1929   Training Department, Truppenamt

1929   *Oberstleutnant*

1929–1932   Head of the First Department of the Army Personnel Office (Heeres Personalamt), Officer Records, Transfers and Promotions

1932   *Oberst*

1932–1934   Commander of the Fifth Infantry Regiment, Stettin

1934–1937   Chief of Staff to the Headquarters of the Second Army Group Kassel

1. 12. 1935   *Generalmajor*

1937–1938   Commander of 34 Division, Koblenz

1. 1. 1938   *Generalleutnant*

4. 2. 1938   Director of Operations, OKW

April 1938   Placed at the disposal of the Chief of the General Staff of the Army

1939–1941   Commander of 257 Division, Poland, France and Russia

1941   Commander, Area Headquarters, St. Lô

1942   Retired

Viebahn speaks French and English. His decorations included the Iron Cross, First Class and the Hohenzollern House Order (W.W.I.). He is married.

Weichs Freiherr Maximilian von

12. 11. 1881   Born at Dessau, Anhalt

15. 7. 1900   *Fahnenjunker*, Second Bavarian Heavy Cavalry Regiment

9. 3. 1902   *Leutnant*

23. 2. 1906   Regimental Adjutant

1. 10. 1908   School of Cavalry

1. 10. 1910   Kriegsakademie

3. 3. 1911   *Oberleutnant*

22. 2. 1914	*Rittmeister*
2. 8. 1914	Bavarian Cavalry Division
14. 10. 1914	Brigade Adjutant
27. 5. 1915	2. General Staff Officer, Fifth Infantry Division
24. 6. 1917	General Staff Officer, Headquarters of the Second Army Corps
9. 4. 1920	General Staff Officer to the Third Cavalry Division
1. 4. 1922	Eighteenth Cavalry Regiment
1. 2. 1923	*Major* with seniority, 1.7.1921
1. 2. 1925	School of Infantry
October 1927	Second in Command of the Eighteenth Cavalry Regiment
1. 2. 1928	*Oberstleutnant* and Commander of the Eighteenth Cavalry Regiment
1. 3. 1930	General Staff Officer to the First Cavalry Division
1. 11. 1930	*Oberst*
1. 12. 1932	General Staff Officer to the Headquarters of the Second Army Group
1. 2. 1933	*Infanterieführer* III
1. 4. 1933	*Generalmajor*
1. 12. 1933	Commander of the Third Cavalry Division
1. 4. 1935	*Generalleutnant*
15. 10. 1935	Commander of the First Panzer Division
12. 5. 1936 ⎫ 1. 10. 1936 ⎭	Also temporary Commander of Wehrkreis III, during the absence in China of Reichenau
1. 10. 1936	*General der Kavallerie*
12. 10. 1937	Commander of the Thirteenth Army Corps
23. 9. 1939	Commander of the Second Army
9. 7. 1940	*Generaloberst*
13. 7. 1942	Commander-in-Chief, Army Group B
1. 2. 1943	*Generalfeldmarschall*
10. 7. 1943	Transferred to the Reserve
25. 8. 1943	Commander-in-Chief, Army Group F, Commander-in-Chief, South East
22. 3. 1945	Transferred to the Reserve

Weichs was married on 28.7.1928. His decorations included the Iron Cross, First Class (W.W.I.) and the *Ritterkreuz* (26.6.1940) with Oakleaves (5.2.1945).

Witzleben Erwin von

4. 12. 1881	Born at Breslau
22. 3. 1901	*Leutnant*, Seventh Grenadier Regiment, Liegnitz
1. 10. 1908	Adjutant, Area Command, Hirschberg
16. 6. 1910	*Oberleutnant*
2. 8. 1914	Adjutant to the Nineteenth Reserve Infantry Brigade
8. 10. 1914	*Hauptmann*
15. 2. 1915	Company Commander in the Sixth Infantry Regiment
6. 9. 1916	General Staff Officer
15. 4. 1917	Battalion Commander
2. 8. 1918	General Staff Officer, 108 Infantry Division
16. 1. 1919	Company Commander in the Seventh Grenadier Regiment
11. 3. 1919	General Staff Officer
1. 1. 1921	Commander of the Eighth (Machine Gun) Company of the Eighth Infantry Regiment

3. 8. 1922   General Staff Officer, Wehrkreis IV
1. 4. 1923   *Major*
1. 10. 1925   Twelfth Cavalry Regiment
1. 2. 1926   General Staff Officer to Infanterieführer III
1. 2. 1928   Commander of the Third Battalion of the Sixth Infantry Regiment
1. 1. 1929   *Oberstleutnant* and Chief of Staff to Wehrkreis VI
1. 1. 1930   Sixth Cavalry Regiment
1. 2. 1930   Chief of Staff to Wehrkreis VI
1. 4. 1931   *Oberst*
1. 10. 1931   Commander of the Eighth Infantry Regiment
1. 10. 1933   Area Command, Hanover
1. 2. 1934   *Generalmajor* and Commander of Wehrkreis III
1. 12. 1934   *Generalleutnant*
1. 10. 1936   *General der Infanterie*
10. 11. 1938   Commander of the Second Army Group, Frankfurt am Main
26. 6. 1939   Commander of the Fifth and Twelfth Army Corps in the Siegfried Line
1. 11. 1939   *Generaloberst*
19. 7. 1940   *Generalfeldmarschall*
4. 12. 1941   Commander-in-Chief, Army Group D
21. 3. 1942   Retired

Witzleben married on 21.5.1907. He spoke English and French. His decorations included the Iron Cross, First Class (W.W.I.) and the *Ritterkreuz* (28.6.1940).

Appendix C

The Organization of the German Army 1934-1939

This appendix shows the organization of the German Army during the process of expansion. Formations are shown down to approximately divisional level and the movements of most general officers throughout the period are given. There are a few exceptions because of the creation of special temporary staff appointments and because some general officers were placed at the disposal of the War Minister, or of the Commander-in-Chief of the Army, or of the Chief of the Army General Staff and full records of these special postings have not been systematically kept. The information used in this appendix is derived from the official *Stellungbesetzungen* or lists of appointments of officers issued by the German Army correct to the following dates:

> April 1934
> October 1935
> October 1936
> October 1937
> January 1939

Photocopies of these *Stellungbesetzungen* are held by the Bundesarchiv, Koblenz.
The following abbreviations have been used in this appendix:

Ranks:

GFM	Generalfeldmarschall
Genob	Generaloberst
GdI	General der Infanterie
GdA	General der Artillerie
GdK	General der Kavallerie
GdPi	General der Pioniere
GdPzTruppen	General der Panzer Truppen
GL	Generalleutnant
GM	Generalmajor
Ob	Oberst
Obstlt	Oberstleutnant

Appointments:

Ob d W	Oberbefehlshaber der Wehrmacht (Commander-in-Chief of the Armed Forces)
RWMinister	Reichswehr Minister (Minister for Defence)
RKM	Reichskriegsminister (Minister for War)
Chef HL	Chef der Heeresleitung (Commander-in-Chief of the Army)
Ob d H	Oberbefehlshaber des Heeres (Commander-in-Chief of the Army)

Offices:

HPA	Heeres Personalamt (Personnel Branch)
TA	Truppenamt (General Staff of the Army)
Gen St d H	Generalstab des Heeres (General Staff of the Army)
VA	Heeres Verwaltungsamt (Army Administration Branch)
Wa A	Heeres Waffenamt (Army Ordnance Branch)
AHA	Allgemeines Heeresamt (General Army Office)

Formations:

GKdo	Gruppenkommando (Headquarters of an Army Group)
AK	Armeekorps (Corps)
Div	Division (All divisions are infantry unless otherwise stated)
HDSt	Heeres Dienststelle (Frontier Zone Command)

Figure 1

The German Army in April 1934

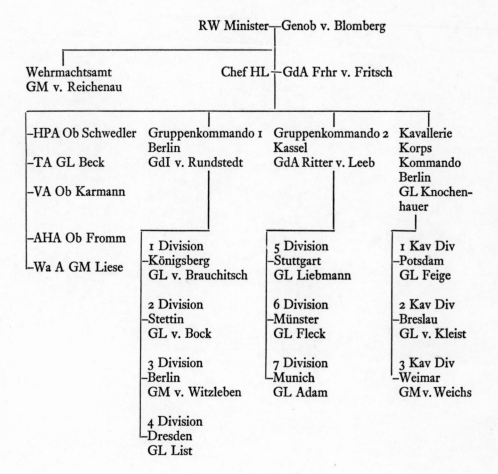

RW Minister—Genob v. Blomberg

Wehrmachtsamt
GM v. Reichenau

Chef HL—GdA Frhr v. Fritsch

–HPA Ob Schwedler

–TA GL Beck

–VA Ob Karmann

–AHA Ob Fromm

└Wa A GM Liese

Gruppenkommando 1
Berlin
GdI v. Rundstedt

Gruppenkommando 2
Kassel
GdA Ritter v. Leeb

Kavallerie
Korps
Kommando
Berlin
GL Knochen-
hauer

1 Division
–Königsberg
GL v. Brauchitsch

2 Division
–Stettin
GL v. Bock

3 Division
–Berlin
GM v. Witzleben

4 Division
└Dresden
GL List

5 Division
–Stuttgart
GL Liebmann

6 Division
–Münster
GL Fleck

7 Division
└Munich
GL Adam

1 Kav Div
–Potsdam
GL Feige

2 Kav Div
–Breslau
GL v. Kleist

3 Kav Div
–Weimar
GM v. Weichs

Figure 2

The German Army in October 1935

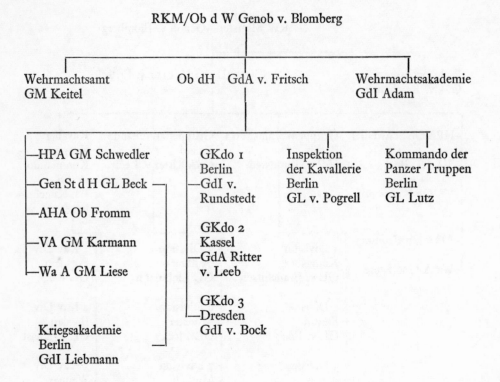

RKM/Ob d W Genob v. Blomberg

Wehrmachtsamt
GM Keitel

Ob dH GdA v. Fritsch

Wehrmachtsakademie
GdI Adam

—HPA GM Schwedler

—Gen St d H GL Beck —

—AHA Ob Fromm

—VA GM Karmann

—Wa A GM Liese

Kriegsakademie
Berlin
GdI Liebmann

GKdo 1
Berlin
—GdI v.
Rundstedt

GKdo 2
Kassel
—GdA Ritter
v. Leeb

GKdo 3
—Dresden
GdI v. Bock

Inspektion
der Kavallerie
Berlin
GL v. Pogrell

Kommando der
Panzer Truppen
Berlin
GL Lutz

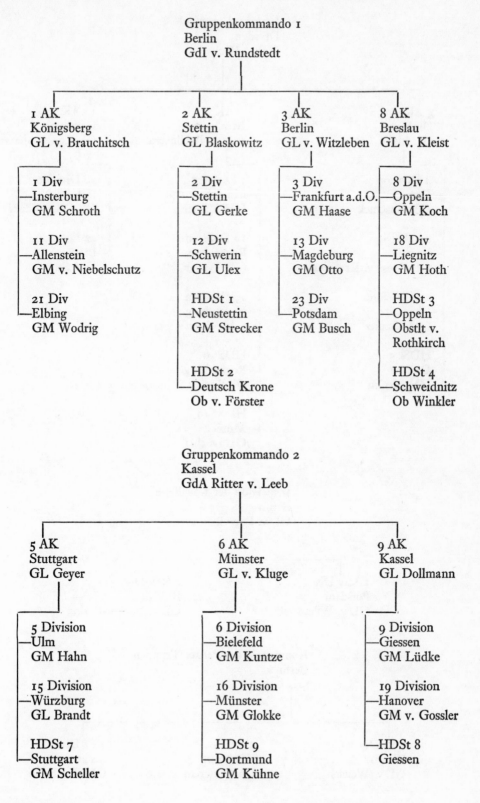

Gruppenkommando 1
Berlin
GdI v. Rundstedt

1 AK	2 AK	3 AK	8 AK
Königsberg	Stettin	Berlin	Breslau
GL v. Brauchitsch	GL Blaskowitz	GL v. Witzleben	GL v. Kleist

1 Div	2 Div	3 Div	8 Div
—Insterburg	—Stettin	—Frankfurt a.d.O.	—Oppeln
GM Schroth	GL Gerke	GM Haase	GM Koch

11 Div	12 Div	13 Div	18 Div
—Allenstein	—Schwerin	—Magdeburg	—Liegnitz
GM v. Niebelschutz	GL Ulex	GM Otto	GM Hoth

21 Div	HDSt 1	23 Div	HDSt 3
—Elbing	—Neustettin	—Potsdam	—Oppeln
GM Wodrig	GM Strecker	GM Busch	Obstlt v. Rothkirch

	HDSt 2		HDSt 4
	—Deutsch Krone		—Schweidnitz
	Ob v. Förster		Ob Winkler

Gruppenkommando 2
Kassel
GdA Ritter v. Leeb

5 AK	6 AK	9 AK
Stuttgart	Münster	Kassel
GL Geyer	GL v. Kluge	GL Dollmann

5 Division	6 Division	9 Division
—Ulm	—Bielefeld	—Giessen
GM Hahn	GM Kuntze	GM Lüdke

15 Division	16 Division	19 Division
—Würzburg	—Münster	—Hanover
GL Brandt	GM Glokke	GM v. Gossler

HDSt 7	HDSt 9	HDSt 8
—Stuttgart	—Dortmund	—Giessen
GM Scheller	GM Kühne	

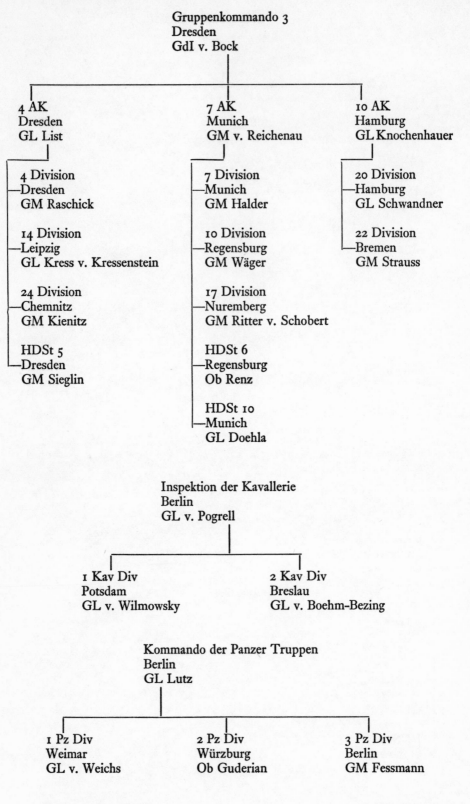

Gruppenkommando 3
Dresden
GdI v. Bock

4 AK
Dresden
GL List

7 AK
Munich
GM v. Reichenau

10 AK
Hamburg
GL Knochenhauer

4 Division
—Dresden
GM Raschick

14 Division
—Leipzig
GL Kress v. Kressenstein

24 Division
—Chemnitz
GM Kienitz

HDSt 5
—Dresden
GM Sieglin

7 Division
—Munich
GM Halder

10 Division
—Regensburg
GM Wäger

17 Division
—Nuremberg
GM Ritter v. Schobert

HDSt 6
—Regensburg
Ob Renz

HDSt 10
—Munich
GL Doehla

20 Division
—Hamburg
GL Schwandner

22 Division
—Bremen
GM Strauss

Inspektion der Kavallerie
Berlin
GL v. Pogrell

1 Kav Div
Potsdam
GL v. Wilmowsky

2 Kav Div
Breslau
GL v. Boehm-Bezing

Kommando der Panzer Truppen
Berlin
GL Lutz

1 Pz Div
Weimar
GL v. Weichs

2 Pz Div
Würzburg
Ob Guderian

3 Pz Div
Berlin
GM Fessmann

Figure 3

The German Army in October 1936

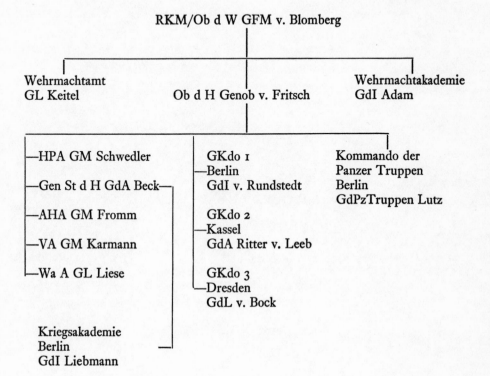

RKM/Ob d W GFM v. Blomberg

Wehrmachtamt
GL Keitel

Ob d H Genob v. Fritsch

Wehrmachtakademie
GdI Adam

—HPA GM Schwedler

—Gen St d H GdA Beck—

—AHA GM Fromm

—VA GM Karmann

—Wa A GL Liese

GKdo 1
—Berlin
GdI v. Rundstedt

GKdo 2
—Kassel
GdA Ritter v. Leeb

GKdo 3
—Dresden
GdL v. Bock

Kommando der
Panzer Truppen
Berlin
GdPzTruppen Lutz

Kriegsakademie
Berlin
GdI Liebmann

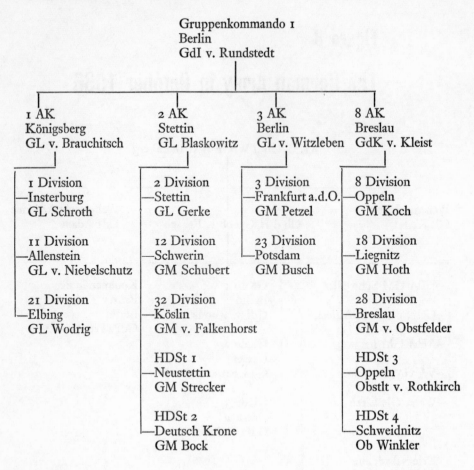

Gruppenkommando 1
Berlin
GdI v. Rundstedt

1 AK
Königsberg
GL v. Brauchitsch

2 AK
Stettin
GL Blaskowitz

3 AK
Berlin
GL v. Witzleben

8 AK
Breslau
GdK v. Kleist

1 Division
—Insterburg
GL Schroth

2 Division
—Stettin
GL Gerke

3 Division
—Frankfurt a.d.O.
GM Petzel

8 Division
—Oppeln
GM Koch

11 Division
—Allenstein
GL v. Niebelschutz

12 Division
—Schwerin
GM Schubert

23 Division
—Potsdam
GM Busch

18 Division
—Liegnitz
GM Hoth

21 Division
—Elbing
GL Wodrig

32 Division
—Köslin
GM v. Falkenhorst

28 Division
—Breslau
GM v. Obstfelder

HDSt 1
—Neustettin
GM Strecker

HDSt 3
—Oppeln
Obstlt v. Rothkirch

HDSt 2
—Deutsch Krone
GM Bock

HDSt 4
—Schweidnitz
Ob Winkler

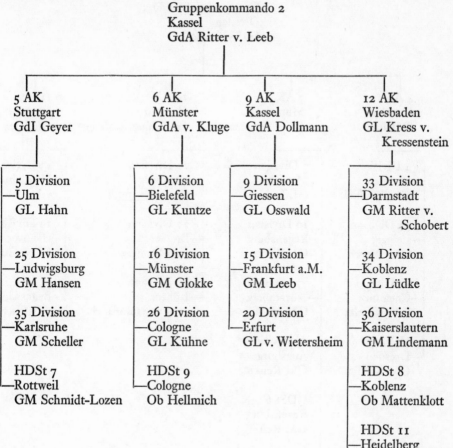

Gruppenkommando 2
Kassel
GdA Ritter v. Leeb

5 AK	6 AK	9 AK	12 AK
Stuttgart	Münster	Kassel	Wiesbaden
GdI Geyer	GdA v. Kluge	GdA Dollmann	GL Kress v. Kressenstein

5 Division
—Ulm
GL Hahn

6 Division
—Bielefeld
GL Kuntze

9 Division
—Giessen
GL Osswald

33 Division
—Darmstadt
GM Ritter v. Schobert

25 Division
—Ludwigsburg
GM Hansen

16 Division
—Münster
GM Glokke

15 Division
—Frankfurt a.M.
GM Leeb

34 Division
—Koblenz
GL Lüdke

35 Division
—Karlsruhe
GM Scheller

26 Division
—Cologne
GL Kühne

29 Division
—Erfurt
GL v. Wietersheim

36 Division
—Kaiserslautern
GM Lindemann

HDSt 7
—Rottweil
GM Schmidt-Lozen

HDSt 9
—Cologne
Ob Hellmich

HDSt 8
—Koblenz
Ob Mattenklott

HDSt 11
—Heidelberg
Ob Gallenkamp

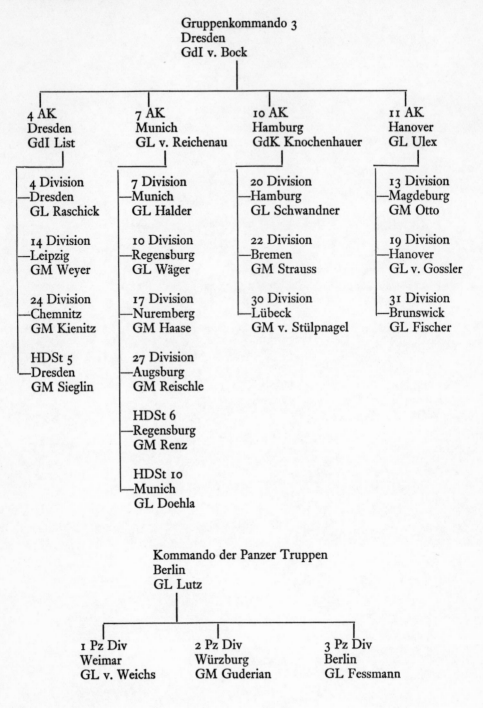

Gruppenkommando 3
Dresden
GdI v. Bock

4 AK	7 AK	10 AK	11 AK
Dresden	Munich	Hamburg	Hanover
GdI List	GL v. Reichenau	GdK Knochenhauer	GL Ulex

4 Division	7 Division	20 Division	13 Division
Dresden	Munich	Hamburg	Magdeburg
GL Raschick	GL Halder	GL Schwandner	GM Otto
14 Division	10 Division	22 Division	19 Division
Leipzig	Regensburg	Bremen	Hanover
GM Weyer	GL Wäger	GM Strauss	GL v. Gossler
24 Division	17 Division	30 Division	31 Division
Chemnitz	Nuremberg	Lübeck	Brunswick
GM Kienitz	GM Haase	GM v. Stülpnagel	GL Fischer
HDSt 5	27 Division		
Dresden	Augsburg		
GM Sieglin	GM Reischle		
	HDSt 6		
	Regensburg		
	GM Renz		
	HDSt 10		
	Munich		
	GL Doehla		

Kommando der Panzer Truppen
Berlin
GL Lutz

1 Pz Div	2 Pz Div	3 Pz Div
Weimar	Würzburg	Berlin
GL v. Weichs	GM Guderian	GL Fessmann

Figure 4

The German Army in October 1937

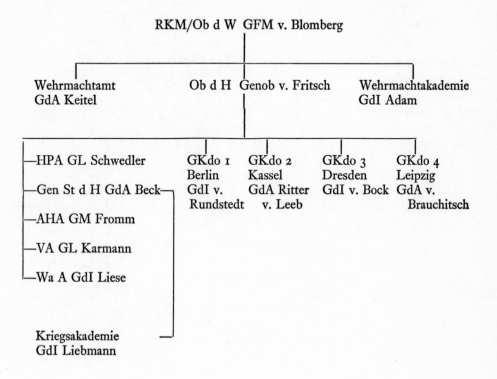

RKM/Ob d W GFM v. Blomberg

Wehrmachtamt
GdA Keitel

Ob d H Genob v. Fritsch

Wehrmachtakademie
GdI Adam

—HPA GL Schwedler

—Gen St d H GdA Beck—

—AHA GM Fromm

—VA GL Karmann

—Wa A GdI Liese

Kriegsakademie
GdI Liebmann

GKdo 1
Berlin
GdI v.
Rundstedt

GKdo 2
Kassel
GdA Ritter
v. Leeb

GKdo 3
Dresden
GdI v. Bock

GKdo 4
Leipzig
GdA v.
Brauchitsch

P

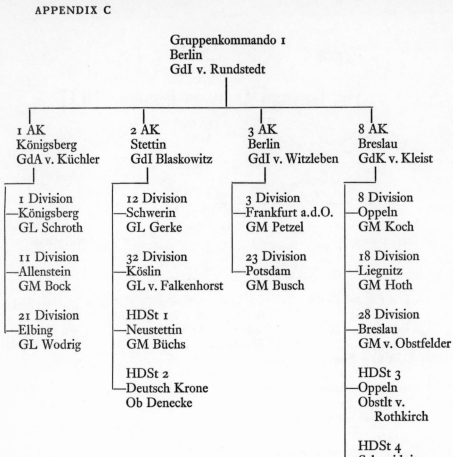

Gruppenkommando 1
Berlin
GdI v. Rundstedt

1 AK	2 AK	3 AK	8 AK
Königsberg	Stettin	Berlin	Breslau
GdA v. Küchler	GdI Blaskowitz	GdI v. Witzleben	GdK v. Kleist

1 Division
—Königsberg
GL Schroth

12 Division
—Schwerin
GL Gerke

3 Division
—Frankfurt a.d.O.
GM Petzel

8 Division
—Oppeln
GM Koch

11 Division
—Allenstein
GM Bock

32 Division
—Köslin
GL v. Falkenhorst

23 Division
—Potsdam
GM Busch

18 Division
—Liegnitz
GM Hoth

21 Division
—Elbing
GL Wodrig

HDSt 1
—Neustettin
GM Büchs

28 Division
—Breslau
GM v. Obstfelder

HDSt 2
—Deutsch Krone
Ob Denecke

HDSt 3
—Oppeln
Obstlt v.
Rothkirch

HDSt 4
—Schweidnitz
Ob Winkler

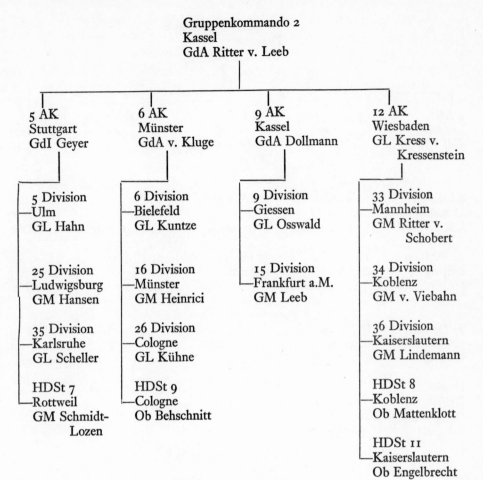

Gruppenkommando 2
Kassel
GdA Ritter v. Leeb

5 AK
Stuttgart
GdI Geyer

6 AK
Münster
GdA v. Kluge

9 AK
Kassel
GdA Dollmann

12 AK
Wiesbaden
GL Kress v.
Kressenstein

5 Division
—Ulm
GL Hahn

6 Division
—Bielefeld
GL Kuntze

9 Division
—Giessen
GL Osswald

33 Division
—Mannheim
GM Ritter v.
Schobert

25 Division
—Ludwigsburg
GM Hansen

16 Division
—Münster
GM Heinrici

15 Division
—Frankfurt a.M.
GM Leeb

34 Division
—Koblenz
GM v. Viebahn

35 Division
—Karlsruhe
GL Scheller

26 Division
—Cologne
GL Kühne

36 Division
—Kaiserslautern
GM Lindemann

HDSt 7
—Rottweil
GM Schmidt-
Lozen

HDSt 9
—Cologne
Ob Behschnitt

HDSt 8
—Koblenz
Ob Mattenklott

HDSt 11
—Kaiserslautern
Ob Engelbrecht

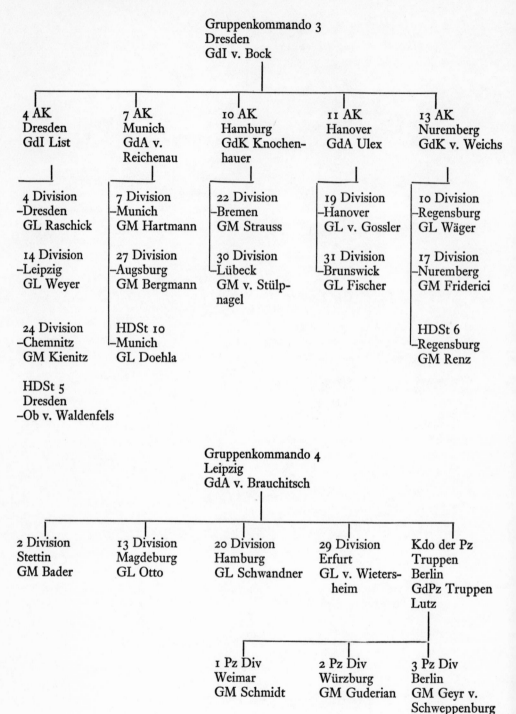

Gruppenkommando 3
Dresden
GdI v. Bock

4 AK
Dresden
GdI List

7 AK
Munich
GdA v.
Reichenau

10 AK
Hamburg
GdK Knochen-
hauer

11 AK
Hanover
GdA Ulex

13 AK
Nuremberg
GdK v. Weichs

4 Division
–Dresden
GL Raschick

7 Division
–Munich
GM Hartmann

22 Division
–Bremen
GM Strauss

19 Division
–Hanover
GL v. Gossler

10 Division
–Regensburg
GL Wäger

14 Division
–Leipzig
GL Weyer

27 Division
–Augsburg
GM Bergmann

30 Division
–Lübeck
GM v. Stülp-
nagel

31 Division
–Brunswick
GL Fischer

17 Division
–Nuremberg
GM Friderici

24 Division
–Chemnitz
GM Kienitz

HDSt 10
–Munich
GL Doehla

HDSt 6
–Regensburg
GM Renz

HDSt 5
Dresden
–Ob v. Waldenfels

Gruppenkommando 4
Leipzig
GdA v. Brauchitsch

2 Division
Stettin
GM Bader

13 Division
Magdeburg
GL Otto

20 Division
Hamburg
GL Schwandner

29 Division
Erfurt
GL v. Wieters-
heim

Kdo der Pz
Truppen
Berlin
GdPz Truppen
Lutz

1 Pz Div
Weimar
GM Schmidt

2 Pz Div
Würzburg
GM Guderian

3 Pz Div
Berlin
GM Geyr v.
Schweppenburg

Figure 5

The German Army in January 1939

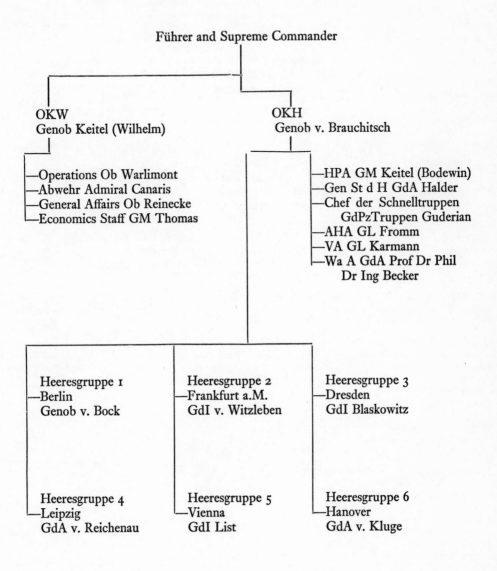

Führer and Supreme Commander

OKW
Genob Keitel (Wilhelm)

OKH
Genob v. Brauchitsch

—Operations Ob Warlimont
—Abwehr Admiral Canaris
—General Affairs Ob Reinecke
—Economics Staff GM Thomas

—HPA GM Keitel (Bodewin)
—Gen St d H GdA Halder
—Chef der Schnelltruppen
    GdPzTruppen Guderian
—AHA GL Fromm
—VA GL Karmann
—Wa A GdA Prof Dr Phil
    Dr Ing Becker

Heeresgruppe 1
—Berlin
Genob v. Bock

Heeresgruppe 2
—Frankfurt a.M.
GdI v. Witzleben

Heeresgruppe 3
—Dresden
GdI Blaskowitz

Heeresgruppe 4
—Leipzig
GdA v. Reichenau

Heeresgruppe 5
—Vienna
GdI List

Heeresgruppe 6
—Hanover
GdA v. Kluge

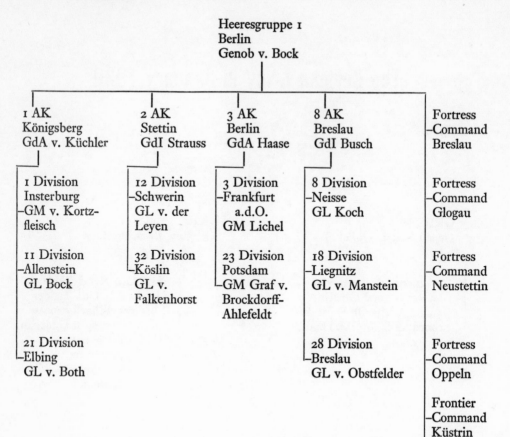

Heeresgruppe 1
Berlin
Genob v. Bock

1 AK Königsberg GdA v. Küchler	2 AK Stettin GdI Strauss	3 AK Berlin GdA Haase	8 AK Breslau GdI Busch	Fortress –Command Breslau
1 Division Insterburg –GM v. Kortz-fleisch	12 Division –Schwerin GL v. der Leyen	3 Division –Frankfurt a.d.O. GM Lichel	8 Division –Neisse GL Koch	Fortress –Command Glogau
11 Division –Allenstein GL Bock	32 Division –Köslin GL v. Falkenhorst	23 Division Potsdam –GM Graf v. Brockdorff-Ahlefeldt	18 Division –Liegnitz GL v. Manstein	Fortress –Command Neustettin
21 Division –Elbing GL v. Both			28 Division –Breslau GL v. Obstfelder	Fortress –Command Oppeln
				Frontier –Command Küstrin
				Inspectorate of –the Eastern Fortifications

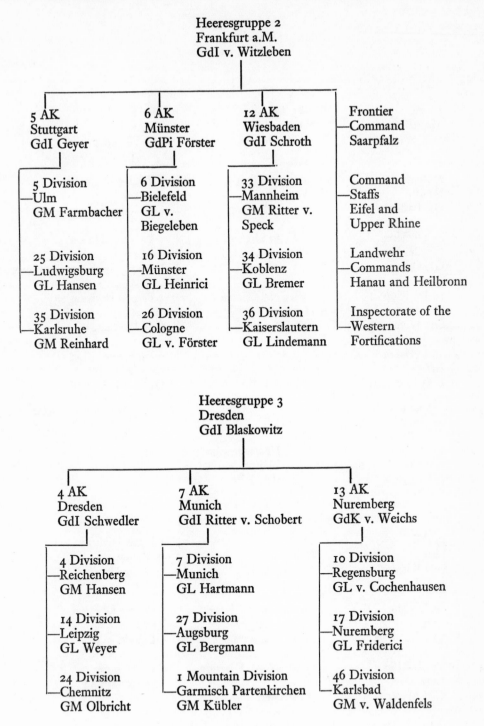

Heeresgruppe 2
Frankfurt a.M.
GdI v. Witzleben

5 AK
Stuttgart
GdI Geyer

6 AK
Münster
GdPi Förster

12 AK
Wiesbaden
GdI Schroth

Frontier
—Command
Saarpfalz

5 Division
—Ulm
GM Farmbacher

6 Division
—Bielefeld
GL v.
Biegeleben

33 Division
—Mannheim
GM Ritter v.
Speck

Command
—Staffs
Eifel and
Upper Rhine

25 Division
—Ludwigsburg
GL Hansen

16 Division
—Münster
GL Heinrici

34 Division
—Koblenz
GL Bremer

Landwehr
—Commands
Hanau and Heilbronn

35 Division
—Karlsruhe
GM Reinhard

26 Division
—Cologne
GL v. Förster

36 Division
—Kaiserslautern
GL Lindemann

Inspectorate of the
—Western
Fortifications

Heeresgruppe 3
Dresden
GdI Blaskowitz

4 AK
Dresden
GdI Schwedler

7 AK
Munich
GdI Ritter v. Schobert

13 AK
Nuremberg
GdK v. Weichs

4 Division
—Reichenberg
GM Hansen

7 Division
—Munich
GL Hartmann

10 Division
—Regensburg
GL v. Cochenhausen

14 Division
—Leipzig
GL Weyer

27 Division
—Augsburg
GL Bergmann

17 Division
—Nuremberg
GL Friderici

24 Division
—Chemnitz
GM Olbricht

1 Mountain Division
—Garmisch Partenkirchen
GM Kübler

46 Division
—Karlsbad
GM v. Waldenfels

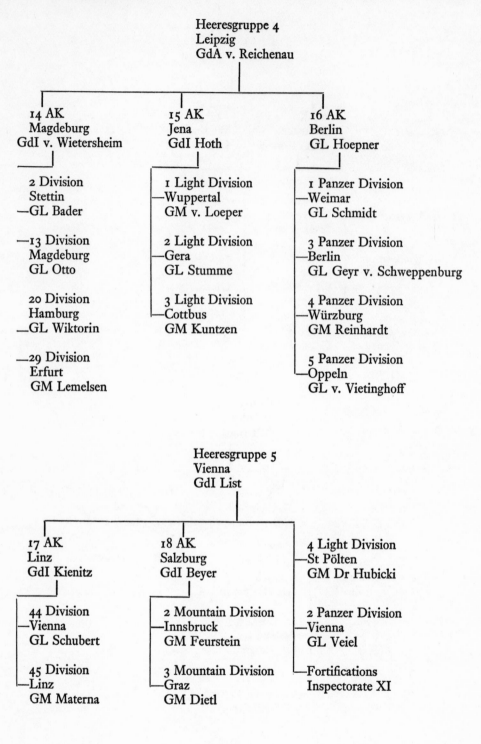

Heeresgruppe 4
Leipzig
GdA v. Reichenau

14 AK
Magdeburg
GdI v. Wietersheim

2 Division
Stettin
—GL Bader

—13 Division
Magdeburg
GL Otto

20 Division
Hamburg
—GL Wiktorin

—29 Division
Erfurt
GM Lemelsen

15 AK
Jena
GdI Hoth

1 Light Division
—Wuppertal
GM v. Loeper

2 Light Division
—Gera
GL Stumme

3 Light Division
—Cottbus
GM Kuntzen

16 AK
Berlin
GL Hoepner

1 Panzer Division
—Weimar
GL Schmidt

3 Panzer Division
—Berlin
GL Geyr v. Schweppenburg

4 Panzer Division
—Würzburg
GM Reinhardt

5 Panzer Division
—Oppeln
GL v. Vietinghoff

Heeresgruppe 5
Vienna
GdI List

17 AK
Linz
GdI Kienitz

44 Division
—Vienna
GL Schubert

45 Division
—Linz
GM Materna

18 AK
Salzburg
GdI Beyer

2 Mountain Division
—Innsbruck
GM Feurstein

3 Mountain Division
—Graz
GM Dietl

4 Light Division
—St Pölten
GM Dr Hubicki

2 Panzer Division
—Vienna
GL Veiel

—Fortifications
Inspectorate XI

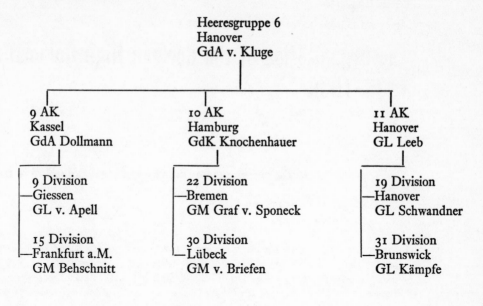

Heeresgruppe 6
Hanover
GdA v. Kluge

9 AK
Kassel
GdA Dollmann

9 Division
—Giessen
GL v. Apell

15 Division
—Frankfurt a.M.
GM Behschnitt

10 AK
Hamburg
GdK Knochenhauer

22 Division
—Bremen
GM Graf v. Sponeck

30 Division
—Lübeck
GM v. Briefen

11 AK
Hanover
GL Leeb

19 Division
—Hanover
GL Schwandner

31 Division
—Brunswick
GL Kämpfe

The Organization of the German High Command 1933-1939

This appendix shows the organization of the German High Command in two stages

        (a) 1933–1937, and
        (b) 1938–1939

Figures 1, 2, and 4 show the organization of the High Command as a whole as at January 1933, December 1937, and September 1939, respectively. Figure 3 shows the organization of the Army General Staff in greater detail for the period between the establishment of the OKW (February 1938) and mobilization of the German Forces (August 1939). The commentary which follows the figures describes the major changes within the High Command which occurred during the two intervals between the figures showing the High Command organization, i.e. 1933–1937, and 1938–1939.

Figure 1

The German High Command in January, 1933

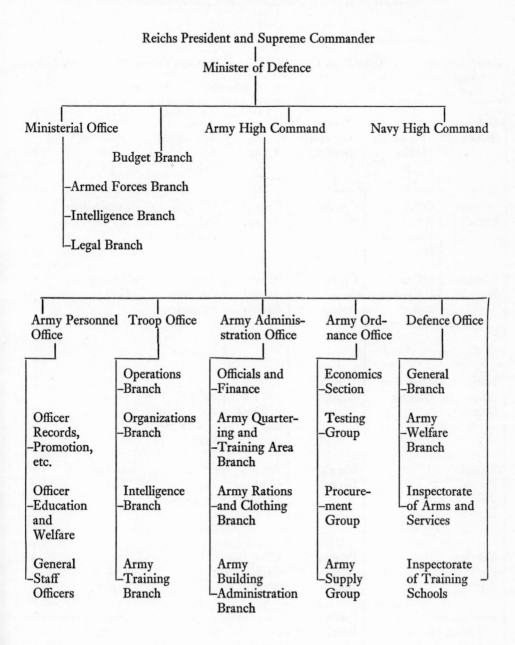

Reichs President and Supreme Commander

Minister of Defence

Ministerial Office   Army High Command   Navy High Command

Budget Branch

–Armed Forces Branch

–Intelligence Branch

–Legal Branch

Army Personnel Office	Troop Office	Army Administration Office	Army Ordnance Office	Defence Office
	Operations –Branch	Officials and –Finance	Economics –Section	General –Branch
Officer Records, –Promotion, etc.	Organizations –Branch	Army Quartering and –Training Area Branch	Testing –Group	Army –Welfare Branch
Officer –Education and Welfare	Intelligence –Branch	Army Rations –and Clothing Branch	Procure- –ment Group	Inspectorate –of Arms and Services
General –Staff Officers	Army –Training Branch	Army Building –Administration Branch	Army –Supply Group	Inspectorate of Training Schools

Figure 2
The German High Command in December 1937

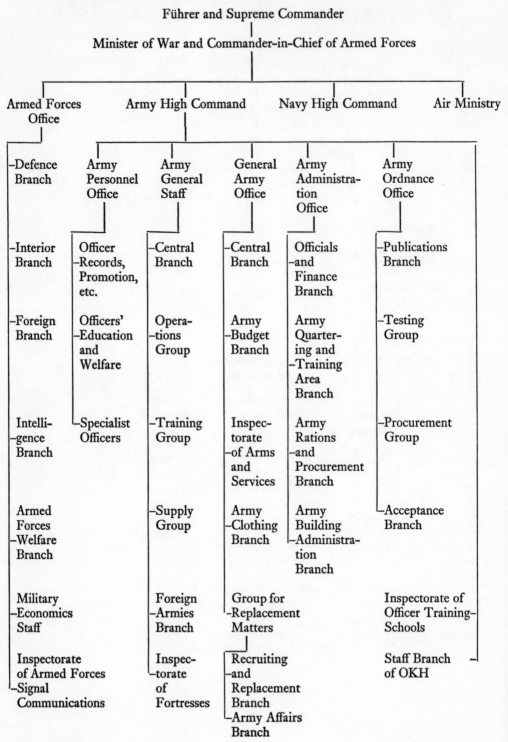

Führer and Supreme Commander

Minister of War and Commander-in-Chief of Armed Forces

| Armed Forces Office | Army High Command | | Navy High Command | | Air Ministry |

Armed Forces Office	Army Personnel Office	Army General Staff	General Army Office	Army Administration Office	Army Ordnance Office
–Defence Branch					
–Interior Branch	Officer –Records, Promotion, etc.	–Central Branch	–Central Branch	Officials –and Finance Branch	–Publications Branch
–Foreign Branch	Officers' –Education and Welfare	Opera- –tions Group	Army –Budget Branch	Army Quarter- ing and –Training Area Branch	–Testing Group
Intelli- –gence Branch	–Specialist Officers	–Training Group	Inspec- torate –of Arms and Services	Army Rations –and Procurement Branch	–Procurement Group
Armed Forces –Welfare Branch		–Supply Group	Army –Clothing Branch	Army Building –Administra- tion Branch	–Acceptance Branch
Military –Economics Staff		Foreign –Armies Branch	Group for –Replacement Matters		Inspectorate of Officer Training– Schools
Inspectorate of Armed Forces –Signal Communications		Inspec- –torate of Fortresses	Recruiting –and Replacement Branch –Army Affairs Branch		Staff Branch of OKH –

Figure 3

Organization of the Army General Staff 1938

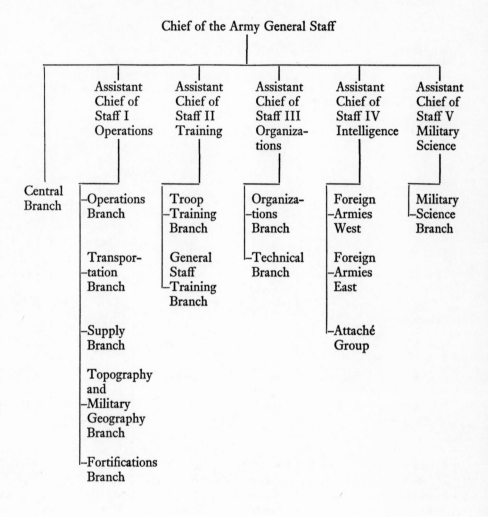

Chief of the Army General Staff

Assistant Chief of Staff I Operations	Assistant Chief of Staff II Training	Assistant Chief of Staff III Organizations	Assistant Chief of Staff IV Intelligence	Assistant Chief of Staff V Military Science

Central Branch

—Operations Branch

Transpor-—tation Branch

—Supply Branch

Topography and —Military Geography Branch

—Fortifications Branch

Troop —Training Branch

General Staff —Training Branch

Organiza--tions Branch

—Technical Branch

Foreign —Armies West

Foreign —Armies East

—Attaché Group

Military —Science Branch

Figure 4

The German High Command in September 1939

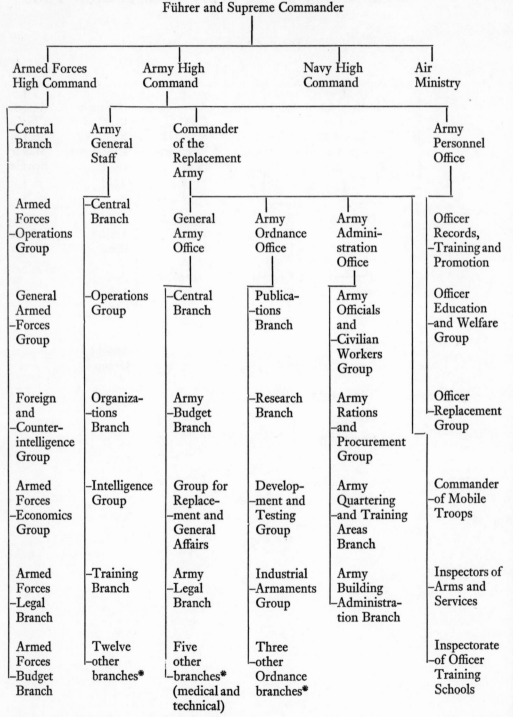

Führer and Supreme Commander

| Armed Forces High Command | Army High Command | Navy High Command | Air Ministry |

–Central Branch

Army General Staff

Commander of the Replacement Army

Army Personnel Office

| Armed Forces –Operations Group | –Central Branch | General Army Office | Army Ordnance Office | Army Administration Office | Officer Records, –Training and Promotion |

| General Armed –Forces Group | –Operations Group | –Central Branch | Publica- –tions Branch | Army Officials and –Civilian Workers Group | Officer Education –and Welfare Group |

| Foreign and –Counter- intelligence Group | Organiza- –tions Branch | Army –Budget Branch | –Research Branch | Army Rations –and Procurement Group | Officer –Replacement Group |

| Armed Forces –Economics Group | –Intelligence Group | Group for Replace- –ment and General Affairs | Develop- –ment and Testing Group | Army Quartering –and Training Areas Branch | Commander –of Mobile Troops |

| Armed Forces –Legal Branch | –Training Branch | Army –Legal Branch | Industrial –Armaments Group | Army Building –Administra- tion Branch | Inspectors of –Arms and Services |

| Armed Forces –Budget Branch | Twelve –other branches* | Five other ᴸbranches* (medical and technical) | Three –other Ordnance branches* | | Inspectorate ᴸof Officer Training Schools |

* For details see the full summary given in this Appendix.

Section 1

THE ORGANIZATION OF THE GERMAN HIGH COMMAND 1933-1937

Review of Period from Figure 1 (1933) to Figure 2 (1937)

I. FÜHRER AND SUPREME COMMANDER (*Führer und Oberster Befehlshaber*)

30 Jan. 1933 Hitler appointed Chancellor of Reich.

1 Aug. 1934 By the Law regarding the Head of the State (*Gesetz über das Staatsoberhaupt des Deutschen Reiches*) the office of Reichs President was combined with the office of Chancellor of the Reich. As a result, Hitler assumed the former authority of the Reich President.

21 May 1935 In accordance with Article 3 of the Military Defence Law (*Wehrgesetz*) the Supreme Commander of the Armed Forces was the Führer and Reich Chancellor (*Oberster Befehlshaber der Wehrmacht ist der Führer und Reichskanzler*). Subordinate to him was the Reich War Minister as the C-in-C of the Armed Forces (*Unter ihm übt der Reichskriegsminister als Oberbefehlshaber der Wehrmacht Befehlsgewalt über die Wehrmacht aus*).

II. MINISTER OF WAR AND C-IN-C ARMED FORCES (*Reichskriegsminister und Oberbefehlshaber der Wehrmacht*)

21 May 1935 By the Military Defence Law (*Wehrgesetz*) the title of Reich Defence Minister (*Reichswehrminister*) was changed to Reich War Minister (*Reichskriegsminister*). The Reich War Minister exercised the powers of C-in-C Armed Forces under the authority of the Supreme Commander. (*Unter ihm—dem Obersten Befehlshaber der Wehrmacht—übt der Reichskriegsminister als Oberbefehlshaber der Wehrmacht Befehlsgewalt über die Wehrmacht aus.*)

III. ARMED FORCES OFFICE (*Wehrmachtamt*)

Late 1933 Title of Ministerial Office changed to Armed Forces Office (*Wehrmachtsamt*) and included:

A. National Defence Branch (*Landesverteidigungsabteilung*) under the previous Chief of the Armed Forces Branch (*Wehrmachtsabteilung*) which was disbanded.

B. Interior Branch (*Inlandsabteilung*) (formed out of Armed Forces Branch).

C. Foreign Intelligence Branch (*Auslandsabteilung*) (Ausl.) (formed out of Armed Forces Branch).

D. Counter Intelligence Branch (*Abwehrabteilung*).

E. Legal Branch (*Rechtsabteilung*).

F. Armed Forces Budget Branch (*Wehrmachthaushaltsabteilung*) (WH) (not to be confused with Budget Branch (H), see Section 4.

Nov. 1934 Military Economics and Ordnance Group (*Wehrwirtschafts- und Waffenwesen*) (W) created.

July 1935 Armed Forces Welfare Branch (*Wehrmachtversorgungsabteilung*) first appears.

Nov. 1935 Military Economics and Ordnance Group (*Wehrwirtschafts- und Waffen-wesen*) (W) renamed the Military Economics Staff (*Wehrwirtschaftsstab*).

Oct. 1936 Now called *Wehrmachtamt* instead of *Wehrmachtsamt*.

June 1937 *Wehrmachthaushaltsabteilung* became *Wehrmachthaushalts-und Verwalt-ungsabteilung* (WH).

Oct. 1937 Inspector of Armed Forces Signal Communications (*Inspekteur der Wehrmachtnachrichtenverbindungen*) (Insp.NV) added. Also Armed Forces Signal Communications Branch (*Abteilung für Wehrmachtnachrichtenverbind-ungen*) (WNV).

Agencies in Armed Forces Office in October 1937:

A. NATIONAL DEFENCE BRANCH (*Landesverteidigungsabteilung*)

B. INTERIOR BRANCH (*Inlandsabteilung*)

C. FOREIGN INTELLIGENCE BRANCH (*Auslandsabteilung*)

D. COUNTER-INTELLIGENCE BRANCH (*Abwehrabteilung*)

E. LEGAL BRANCH (*Rechtsabteilung*)

F. ARMED FORCES BUDGET AND ADMINISTRATION BRANCH (*Wehrmachthaushalts- und Verwaltungsabteilung*) (WH)

G. MILITARY ECONOMICS STAFF (*Wehrwirtschaftsstab*) (W.Stb.)
Formed Nov. 1934 as the Military Economics and Ordnance Group (*Wehrwirt-schafts- und Waffenwesen*) (W) with the following organization:
Military Economics Branch (*Wehrwirtschaftliche Abteilung*) WWi). Con-tracts and Price Control (*Vertrags- und Preispr fwesen*) (WPreispr).
Contracts and Price Control, Administration Office (*Vertrags- und Preis-prüfwesen Verwaltungsamt*) (WPreisprVA).
Contracts and Price Control, Army Ordnance Office (*Vertrags- und Preis-prüfwesen Heereswaffenamt*) (WPreisprWaA).
Contracts and Price Control, Navy Directorate (*Vertrags- und Preisprüf-wesen Marineleitung*) (WPreisprML).
In November 1935 the Military Economics and Ordnance Group (*Wehrwirt-schafts- und Waffenwesen*) (W) was renamed the Military Economics Staff (*Wehrwirtschaftsstab*) without any apparent change in the organization.
By December 1936 the Military Economics Branch (*Wehrwirtschaftliche Abteilung*) of the Military Economics Staff had been renamed the Operations Staff (*Führungsstab des Chef des Wehrwirtschaftsstabes*). An Armaments Industry Branch (*Rüstungswirtschaftliche Abteilung*) (WRü) and a Raw Materials Branch (*Rohstoffabteilung*) (W.Ro) had been added to the Military Economics Staff.
By October 1937 the Operations Staff (*Führungsstab des Chef des Wehrwirt-schaftsstabes*) had been expanded and renamed Military Economics Branch (*Wehrwirtschaftliche Abteilung*) (WWi).
Organization of Military Economics Staff in October 1937:
Military Economics Branch (*Wehrwirtschaftliche Abteilung*) (WWi).
Armaments Industry Branch (*Rüstungswirtschaftliche Abteilung*) (WRü).
Raw Materials Branch (*Rohstoffabteilung*) (W.Ro).
Contracts and Price Control (*Vertrags- und Preisprüfwesen*) (WPreispr).

H. ARMED FORCES WELFARE BRANCH (*Wehrmachtversorgungs-abteilung*).

I. INSPECTOR OF ARMED FORCES SIGNAL COM-
MUNICATIONS (*Inspekteur der Wehrmachtnachrichtenverbindungen*)
(Insp. WNV).

J. ARMED FORCES SIGNAL COMMUNICATIONS BRANCH,
(*Abteilung für Wehrmachtnachrichtenverbindungen*) (WNV).

IV. BUDGET BRANCH (*Haushaltsabteilung*)

This remained directly subordinate to the Reichs Defence Minister until 1935
organized as follows:

Army Section (*Gruppe Heer*) (H.Heer)
Navy Section (*Gruppe Marine*) (H.Mar. bei MLE).

Although the Budget Branch was directly subordinate to the Reichs Defence
Minister, the Army Section was available to the Chief of the General Army
Office for work on budget matters, and the Navy Section was subordinate to the
Chief of the Navy Directorate.

In 1935 the Budget Branch (*Haushaltsabteilung*) (H) was dissolved, the Army
Section going to the General Army Office to become Army Budget Branch
(*Heeres-Haushaltsabteilung*) (H.Haush) and the Navy Section going to the
Navy High Command.

V. ARMY HIGH COMMAND (*Oberkommando des Heeres*)

By April 1934 the Defence Office (*Wehramt*) had become General Army Office
(*Allgemeines Heeresamt*).

On 21 May 1935 the Army Directorate (*Heeresleitung*) became the Army High Command (*Oberkommando des Heeres*).

On 21 May 1935 the title of Chief of the Army Directorate (*Chef der Heeresleitung*)
was changed to Commander-in-Chief of Army (*Oberbefehlshaber des Heeres*).

On 1 June 1935 the title of Troop Office (*Truppenamt*) was changed to Army
General Staff (*Generalstab des Heeres*).

Agencies in Army High Command in October 1937:

A. ARMY GENERAL STAFF (*Generalstab des Heeres*)

1933 Army Transport Section (*Heeres-Transportgruppe*) (T.1.IV) appeared under
under Operations Branch T.1 of Troop Office.

1934 League of Nations Branch, Army Section (*Völkerbundstabteilung Gruppe Heer*)
was disbanded.

1934–35 Central Section (*Zentralgruppe*) (TZ) was added. Transportation Branch
(T.5) was added. Military Science Branch (TK) was added. Contracts Section
(TV) was added.

1 June 1935 The Troop Office (*Truppenamt*) became the Army General Staff
(*Generalstab des Heeres*), and the Chief of the Troop Office changed his title
to Chief of Army General Staff, with the following changes in designation of
agencies within the Troop Office:

Central Section (*Zentralgruppe*) (TZ) became Central Branch (*Zentralabteilung*)
(GZ) of Army General Staff.

Army Branch (*Heeresabteilung*) (T.1) became the 1st (Operations) Branch
(*1. Abteilung—Operationsabteilung*).

Army Organization Branch (*Heeres-Organisationsabteilung*) (T.2) became the
2nd (Organization) Branch (*2. Abteilung—Organisationsabteilung*).

Foreign Armies Branch (*Abteilung Fremde Heere*) (T.3) became the 3rd (Foreign Armies) Branch (*3. Abteilung—Abteilung Fremde Heere*).

Army Training Branch (*Heeres-Ausbildungsabteilung*) (T.4) became the 4th (Army Training) Branch (*4. Abteilung—Heeres-Ausbildungsabteilung*).

Transportation Branch (*Transportabteilung*) (T.5) became the 5th (Transportation) Branch (*5. Abteilung—Transportabteilung*).

Section V of the Army Branch (*Gruppe V der Heeresabteilung*) (T.1.V) became the 6th (Supply) Branch (*6. Abteilung—Quartiermeisterabteilung*).

Military Science Branch (*Kriegswissenschaftliche Abteilung*) (TK) became the 7th (Military Science) Branch (*7. Abteilung—Kriegswissenschaftliche Abteilung*).

Contracts Section (*Vertragsgruppe*) (TV) became Contracts Section (*Vertragsgruppe*) (GV).

In addition, an Assistant Chief of Staff I (*Oberquartiermeister* I) was appointed to take control of the 1st (Operations) Branch and the 2nd (Organization) Branch.

Between July 1935 and October 1935 an 8th (Technical) Branch was added to the General Staff, and placed under the control of the Assistant Chief of Staff I.

An Assistant Chief of Staff II was appointed to take control of the 5th, 6th and 7th Branches.

The Attaché Section first appeared subordinate to *3. Abteilung*.

The Inspector of Fortifications (*Inspekteur der Festungen*) with subordinate Inspectorate of Fortifications was transferred from the General Army Office (In.5) to the General Staff. The Inspector of Fortifications continued to hold the dual appointment of Inspector of Engineers in the General Army Office (In.5).

An appointment list (*Stellenbesetzungsliste*) issued during this period in 1935 showed the following organization:

Central Branch.
Assistant Chief of Staff I
  1st (Operations) Branch
  2nd (Organization) Branch
  8th (Technical) Branch
  3rd (Foreign Armies) Branch
  Attaché Section
  4th (Army Training) Branch
Assistant Chief of Staff II
  5th (Transport) Branch
  6th (Supply) Branch
  7th (Military Science) Branch
Inspector of Fortifications
Inspectorate of Fortifications

15 Oct. 1935 A correction was issued to the above Appointment List (*Stellenbesetzungsliste*) of 1935, deleting Assistant Chief of Staff II, and inserting in his place an Assistant Chief of Staff III, at the same time removing the 7th Branch from the control of A.C. of S III and apparently making it independent.

1 Apr. 1936 The following agencies were added to the Army General Staff:

Army Film Centre (*Heeresfilmstelle*) became a subordinate (*Nachgeordnete*) agency of General Staff and subordinate to the 4th (Training) Branch.

Commander of Railway Units (*Befehlshaber der Eisenbahneinheiten*) became subordinate to Transport Branch.

Chief of Military Survey (*Kriegsvermessungschef*).

14 Aug. 1936 9th (Topographical) Branch (*9. Abteilung—Heeres-Vermessungswesen und Militärgeographie*) was formed and placed under control of Assistant Chief of Staff I.

6 Oct. 1936 An appointment list showed the following organization:
Central Branch
Assistant Chief of Staff I
  1st (Operations) Branch
  2nd (Organization) Branch
  8th (Technical) Branch
  9th (Topographical) Branch
Assistant Chief of Staff III
  5th (Transport) Branch
  6th (Supply) Branch
  3rd (Foreign Armies) Branch
    The Attaché Section was no longer shown, but its personnel formed part of the 3rd Branch.
  7th (Military Science) Branch
Inspectorate of Fortifications (In. Fest) headed by the Inspector of Fortifications who was also the Inspector of Engineers in General Army Office (In.5).

1 Apr. 1937 Army Archive (*Heeresarchiv*) formed, its Chief subordinate to the Chief of the Army General Staff.

1 Apr. 1937 Research Institute for Army and War History (*Forschungsanstalt für Kriegs- und Heeresgeschichte*) transferred to Army General Staff, and renamed Army Historical Research Institute (*Kriegsgeschichtliche Forschungsanstalt des Heeres*).

12 Oct. 1937 The Assistant Chief of Staff II was re-established and given control of:
  4th (Troop Training) Branch
  7th (Military Science) Branch
  11th (Officer Training) Branch—newly formed.
  In addition a 10th (Fortifications) Branch (*10. Abteilung—Landesbefestigungstabteilung*) was formed and placed under the Assistant Chief of Staff I.

The Organization of the Army General Staff in October 1937:

  1. Central Branch (*Zentralabteilung*)
  2. Assistant Chief of Staff for Operations (*Oberquartiermeister I*) (OQuI)
     1st (Operations) Branch (*1. Abteilung—Operationsabteilung*)
     2nd (Organization) Branch (*2. Abteilung—Organisationsabteilung*)
     8th (Technical) Branch (*8. Abteilung—Technische Abteilung*)
     9th (Army Topographical) Branch (*9. Abteilung—Heeresvermessungswesen und Militärgeographie*)
     10th (Land Fortifications) Branch (*10. Abteilung—Landesbefestigungsabteilung*)
  3. Assistant Chief of Staff for Training (*Oberquartiermeister II*) (OQuII)
     4th (Troop Training) Branch (*4. Abteilung—Truppenausbildungsabteilung*)
     7th (Military Science) Branch (*7. Abteilung—Kriegswissenschaftliche Abteilung*)
     11th (Officer Training) Branch (*11. Abteilung—Offizierausbildungsabteilung*)
  4. Assistant Chief of Staff for Supply (*Oberquartiermeister III*) (OQuIII)
     5th (Transport) Branch (*5. Abteilung—Transportabteilung*) Commander of Railway Units
     6th (Supply) Branch (*6. Abteilung—Quartiermeisterabteilung*)
  5. 3rd (Foreign Armies) Branch (*3. Abteilung—Abteilung Fremde Heere*)

6. Inspectorate of Fortifications (*Inspektion der Festungen*) (In.Fest) headed by the Inspector of Fortifications, who was also the Inspector of Engineers in General Army Office (In.5)

Shown as agencies under the control of (*nachgeordnet dem*) General Staff:

Army Historical Research Institute (*Kriegsgeschichtliche Forschungsanstalt des Heeres*)

Chief of Army Archives (*Chef der Heeresarchiv*), controlling Army Archives (*Heeresarchiv*)

Army Film Centre (*Heeresfilmstelle*)

B. ARMY PERSONNEL OFFICE (*Heeres-Personalamt*)

1933 Army Personnel Branch 4 (*Heeres-Personalabteilung 4*) (P.4) E-Officers formed (E-Officers=former regular officers recalled to active service).

1935 Personnel Section P.3 (General Staff Officers) disappears, its functions being taken over by the Central Branch of Army General Staff.

The Organization of the Army Personnel Office in October 1937:

1. Army Personnel Branch 1 (*Heeres-Personalabteilung 1*) (P.1) Officer Records, Transfers and Promotions.
2. Army Personnel Branch 2 (*Heeres-Personalabteilung 2*) (P.2) Officer Education and Welfare.

Transfers and Promotions.
3. Army Personnel Branch 4 (*Heeres-Personalabteilung 4*) (P.4) E-Officers.

C. GENERAL ARMY OFFICE (*Allgemeines Heeresamt*)

By April 1934 the Defence Office (*Wehramt*) had become the General Army Office.

Also the Ordnance Inspectorate (*Feldzeuginspektion beim Allgemeinen Heeresamt*) (Fz.In.) was added.

1935 The Central Branch (*Zentralabteilung*) (Z) was added.

The Army Budget Branch (*Heeres-Haushaltsabteilung*) (H.Haush.) was added, formerly part of the Budget Branch under Reichs Defence Minister.

The Inspectorate of Cavalry (*Inspektion der Kavallerie*) (In.3) changed its title to Cavalry Branch (*Kavallerieabteilung*) (In.3).

The Inspectorate of Engineers and Fortifications (*Inspektion der Pioniere und Festungen*) (In.5) became the Inspectorate of Engineers (*Inspektion der Pioniere*) (In.5), and the Inspectorate of Fortifications (*Inspektion der Festungen*) was transferred to the Army General Staff. The former Inspector of Engineers and Fortifications in the General Army Office now held the dual appointment of Inspector of Fortifications (General Staff) and Inspector of Engineers (General Army Office).

The Inspectorate of Motor Transport Troops (*Inspektion der Kraftfahrtruppen* (In.6) was now called Inspectorate of Motor Transport Troops and Army Motorization (*Inspektion der Kraftfahrkampftruppe und für Heeresmotorisierung*).

The Supply Branch (*Nachschubabteilung*) (In.8) was added.

The Ordnance Stores Inspectorate (*Feldzeuginspektion beim Allgemeinen Heeresamt*) (Fz.In) became the Army Ordnance Stores Branch (*Heeres-Feldzeugabteilung*) (Fz).

1 May 1936 The Inspectorate of Chemical Warfare Troops and Anti-Gas Defence (*Inspektion der Nebeltruppe und für Gasabwehr*) (In.9) was formed; Section IV of the Inspectorate of Artillery was transferred to it.

1 June 1937 The General Branch (*Allgemeine Abteilung*) was reorganized and renamed Group for Replacement and Army Affairs. (*Amtsgruppe für Ersatz- und Heerwesen*) (Ag.EH). Organization of Ag.EH as follows:

Replacement Branch (*Abteilung für Ersatzwesen*) (Abt.E)
Army Affairs Branch (*Abteilung für Heerwesen*) (Abt.H)
Punishments Section (*Gruppe Strafgefangenenwesen*) (Gruppe Str.).

1937 The Inspectorate of Motor Transport Troops and Army Motorization (*Inspektion der Kraftfahrkampftruppen und für Heeresmotorisierung*) (In.6) was called the Inspectorate of Panzer Troops and Army Motorization (*Inspektion der Panzertruppen und für Heeresmotorisierung*) (In.6).
The Supply Branch (*Nachschubabteilung*) (In.8) became the Supply Troops Branch (*Fahrtruppenabteilung*) (In.8).

1 Sep. 1937 The Army Clothing Branch (*Heeresbekleidungsabteilung*) (V.5) and the *Referat* of V.3 dealing with Army Clothing Offices, were transferred from the Army Administration Office to the General Office to form the Army Clothing Branch (*Heeresbekleidungsabteilung*) (Bk1) as part of the Group for Replacement and Army Affairs.

The Organization of the General Army Office in October 1937:

1. Central Branch (*Zentralabteilung*) (Z)
   Army Publications Administration (*Heeres-Druckvorschriftenverwaltung*) (H.Dv.).
2. Army Budget Branch (*Heeres-Haushaltsabteilung*) (H. Haush).
3. Group for Replacement and Army Affairs (*Amtsgruppe für Ersatz- und Heerwesen*) (Ag.EH).
   a. Replacement Branch (*Abteilung für Ersatzwesen*) (Abt.E)
   b. Army Branch (*Abteilung für Heerwesen*) (Abt.H)
   c. Army Clothing Branch (*Heeresbekleidungsabteilung*) (Bk1)
   d. Punishment Section (*Gruppe Strafgefangenenwesen*) (*Gruppe Str*).
4. Army Ordnance Stores Branch (*Heeres-Feldzeugabteilung*) (Fz).
5. Inspectorates of Arms and Services (*Waffeninspektionen*)
   a. Inspectorate of Infantry (*Inspektion der Infanterie*) (In.2)*
   b. Cavalry Branch (*Kavallerieabteilung*) (In.3)†
   c. Inspectorate of Artillery (*Inspektion der Artillerie*) (In.4)*
   d. Inspectorate of Engineers (*Inspektion der Pioniere*) (In.5)*
   e. Inspectorate of Panzer Troops and Army Motorization (*Inspektion der Panzertruppen und für Heeresmotorisierung*) (In.6)*
   f. Inspectorate of Signal Troops (*Inspektion der Nachrichtentruppen*) (In.7)*
   g. Supply Troops Branch (*Fahrtruppenabteilung*) (In.8)†
   h. Inspectorate of Chemical Warfare Troops and Anti-Gas Defence (*Inspektion der Nebeltruppe und für Gasabwehr*) (In.9).*
6. Army Medical Inspectorate (*Heeres-Sanitätsinspektion*) (S.In).*
7. Veterinary Inspectorate (*Veterinärinspektion*) (V.In).*

D. ARMY ORDNANCE OFFICE (*Heeres-Waffenamt*)

1933 The Economics Section (*Wirtschaftsgruppe*) (Wa.Wi) became the Economics Branch (*Wirtschaftsabteilung*) (Wa.Wi).
The Statistical Section (*Statistische Gruppe*) (Wa.Prw.8) of the Testing Group was disbanded.

---

* Headed by an Inspector (*Inspekteur*)
† Headed by a Departmental Chief (*Abteilungschef*) possibly the former Inspector of In.3.

The Army Supply Branch (*Heeres-Nachschubabteilung*) (Wa.N) became the Supply System (*Nachschubwesen*) (Wa.N) controlling an Army Supply Branch (*Heeres-Nachschubabteilung*) (Wa.N.1).

1934 The Branch for Optics and Survey (*Abteilung für Optik und Messwesen*) (Wa.Prw.8) was formed.

The Army Equipment Branch (*Heeres-Geräteabteilung*) (Wa.B.1) became the Army Equipment Procurement Branch (*Heeres-Gerätebeschaffungsabteilung*) (Wa.B.1).

The Army Weapons and Ammunition Branch (*Heeres-Waffen und Munitions-abteilung*) (Wa.B.2) split into the Army Weapons Procurement Branch (*Heeres-Waffenbeschaffungsabteilung*) (Wa.B.2), and

The Army Ammunition Procurement Branch (*Heeres-Munitionsbeschaffungs-abteilung*) (Wa.B.3).

The Supply System (*Nachschubwesen*) (Wa.N) and the Army Supply Branch (*Heeres-Nachschubabteilung*) (Wa.N.1) were disbanded; personnel were transferred to the Ordnance Inspectorate (Fz.In) in the General Army Office.

The Army Acceptance Branch (*Heeres-Abnahmeabteilung*) (Wa.Abn) was added, apparently as part of the Procurement Group (Wa.B).

1935 The Economics Branch (*Wirtschaftsabteilung*) (Wa.Wi) was transferred to Military Economics Staff in OKW.

The Anti-Gas Defence (*Gasschutzabteilung*) (Wa.Prw.9) was added.

The Branch for Ordnance Proving Grounds (*Abteilung für Versuchsschiess-plätze*) (Wa.Prw.12) was added.

The Section for Procurement of Motor Transport Vehicles (*Beschaffungs-gruppe für Kraftfahrwesen*) (Wa.B.6) was added.

By Apr. 1935 the following agencies had been formed:

Technical Press-Reading Centre (*Zeitschriftenstelle*) (Ztschr).

Publications Centre (*Vorschriftenstelle*) (Wa.Vs).

Central Agency for Army Physics and Chemistry (*Zentralstelle für Heeresphysik und Chemie*) (W.Prw.Z), forming part of the Testing Group.

Production Branch (*Fabrikationsabteilung*) (Wa.B.4) forming part of the Procurement Group.

1936 The Branch for Optics and Survey (*Abteilung für Optik und Messwesen*) (Wa.Prw.8) became Branch for Survey, Optics and Meteorology (*Abteilung für Messwesen, Optik und Wetterkunde*) (Wa.Prw.8).

The Organization Section for Procurement (*Organisationsgruppe des Beschaffungs-wesens*) (Wa.B.5) first appeared.

The Section for Procurement of Motor Transport Vehicles (*Beschaffungs-gruppe für Kraftfahrwesen*) (Wa.B.6) changed title to Procurement Branch for Motor Transport Equipment (*Beschaffungsabteilung für Kraftfahrgerät*) (Wa.B.6).

1937 By 1937 the following changes and additions had been made:

The Chief Designer (*Chefkonstrukteur*) (Wa.Prw.3) first appeared.

The Air Defence Branch (*Flugabwehrabteilung*) (Wa.Prw.10) was added.

The Research Branch (*Forschungsabteilung*) (Wa.Prw.11) was added.

The Branch for Special Equipment (*Abteilung für Sondergerät*) (Wa.Prw.13) was added.

The Organization Section for Procurement (*Organisationsgruppe des Beschaff-ungswesens*) (Wa.B.5) became the Organization Branch for Procurement (*Organisationsabteilung des Beschaffungswesens*) (Wa.B.5).

The Procurement Branch for Signals Equipment (*Beschaffungsabteilung für Nachrichtengerät*) (Wa.B.7) was added.

The Army Acceptance Branch (*Heeres-Abnahmeabteilung*) (Wa.Abn) which apparently had been part of the Procurement Group, appeared to become an independent branch in the Ordnance Office.

The Technical Press-Reading Centre (Ztschr) and the Publications Centre (Wa.Vs) had expanded to Branches.

The Central Agency for Army Physics and Chemistry (Wa.Prw.Z) no longer appeared.

The Organization of the Army Ordnance Office in October 1937:

1. Technical Press-Reading Branch (*Zeitschriftenabteilung*) (Ztschr)
2. Publications Branch (*Vorschriftenabteilung*) (Wa.Vs)
3. Testing Group (*Prüfwesen*) (Wa.Prw)
   Ballistics and Ammunition Branch (*Ballistische und Munitionsabteilung*) (Wa.Prw.1)
   Infantry Branch (*Infanterieabteilung*) (Wa.Prw.2)
   Chief Designer (*Chefkonstrukteur*) (Wa.Prw.3)
   Artillery Branch (*Artillerieabteilung*) (Wa.Prw.4)
   Engineers and Fortifications Branch (*Pionier u. Festungsabteilung*) (Wa.Prw.5)
   Motor Transportation and Motorization Branch (*Kraftfahr- und Motorisierungsabteilung*) (Wa.Prw.6)
   Signals Branch (*Nachrichtenabteilung*) (Wa.Prw.7)
   Branch for Survey, Optics, and Meteorology (*Abteilung für Messwesen, Optik und Wetterkunde*) (Wa.Prw. 8)
   Anti-Gas Defence Branch (*Gasschutzabteilung*) (Wa.Prw.9)
   Air Defence Branch (*Flugabwehrabteilung*) (Wa.Prw.10)
   Ordnance Research Branch (*Forschungsabteilung*) (Wa.Prw.11)
   Branch for Ordnance Proving Grounds (*Abteilung für Versuchsschiessplätze*) (Wa.Prw.12)
   Branch for Special Equipment (*Abteilung für Sondergerät*) (Wa.Prw.13)
4. Procurement Group (*Beschaffungswesen*) (Wa.B)
   Army Equipment Procurement Branch (*Heeres-Gerätebeschaffungsabteilung*) (Wa.B.1)
   Army Weapons Procurement Branch (*Heeres-Waffenbeschaffungsabteilung*) (Wa.B.2)
   Army Munition Procurement Branch (*Heeres-Munitionsbeschaffungsabteilung*) (Wa.B.3)
   Production Branch (*Fabrikationsabteilung*) (Wa.B.4)
   Organization Branch for Procurement (*Organisationsabteilung des Beschaffungswesens*) (Wa.B.5)
   Procurement Branch for Motor Transport Equipment (*Beschaffungsabteilung für Kraftfahrgerät*) (Wa.B.6)
   Procurement Branch for Signals Equipment (*Beschaffungsabteilung für Nachrichtengerät*) (Wa.B.7)
5. Army Acceptance Branch (*Heeres-Abnahmeabteilung*) (Wa.Abn).

E. ARMY ADMINISTRATION OFFICE (*Heeres-Verwaltungsamt*)

1935 The Army Clothing Branch (*Heeres-Bekleidungsabteilung*) (V.5) appeared for the first time.

Army Rations and Clothing Branch (V.3) became Army Rations and Procurement Branch (*Heeres-Verpflegungs- und Beschaffungsabteilung*) (V.3).

1 Sep. 1937 The Army Clothing Branch (V.5) was transferred to the General Army Office, together with the *Referat* of V.3 dealing with Army Clothing Offices.

The Organization of the Army Administration Office in October 1937:

1. Army Officials and Finance Branch (*Heeres-Beamten- und Kassenabteilung*) (V.1). Cashier's Office of the Army High Command (*Amtskasse des Ober-kommando des Heeres*) (AK.OKH)
   Pay Offices of the Army High Command I–IV (*Gebührnisstellen des OKH I–IV*) (GSt. I–IV)
2. Army Quartering and Training Area Branch (*Heeres-Unterkunfts- und Übungsplatzabteilung*) (V.2)
   Office Administration, Army High Command (*Hausverwaltung, OKH*) (Hv.Heer)
3. Army Rations and Procurement Branch (*Heeres-Verpflegungs- und Beschaffungsabteilung*) (V.3)
4. Army Building Administration Branch (*Heeres-Bauverwaltungsabteilung* (V.4)

F. INSPECTORATE OF OFFICER TRAINING SCHOOLS
(*Inspektion der Kriegsschulen*) (In.1)

1935 The Inspectorate of Arms and Service Schools (*Inspektion der Waffenschulen*) (In.1) became the Inspectorate of Officer Training Schools (*Inspektion der Kriegsschulen*) (In.1), headed by an Inspector (*Inspekteur*).

Section 2

THE ORGANIZATION OF THE GERMAN HIGH COMMAND 1937-1939

Review of Period from Figure 2 (1937) to Figure 4 (1939)

I. FÜHRER AND SUPREME COMMANDER (*Führer und Oberster Befehlshaber*)

4 Feb. 1938 With the dismissal of v. Blomberg and the elimination of the post of Minister of War and C-in-C Armed Forces, the Führer and Supreme Commander assumed personal command of the Armed Forces. (*Führer und Reichskanzler übt die Befehlsgewalt über die gesamte Wehrmacht persönlich aus—Erlass über die Führung der Wehrmacht.*)

II. ARMED FORCES HIGH COMMAND (*Oberkommando der Wehrmacht*) (OKW)

4 Feb. 1938 The Armed Forces Office (*Wehrmachtamt*) became the Armed Forces High Command (*Oberkommando der Wehrmacht*) with the functions of a military staff under the command of the Führer and Supreme Commander. The Chief of the Armed Forces High Command (*Chef OKW*) was equivalent in status to other *Reich* Ministers. The Armed Forces High Command also assumed the duties of the former Ministry of War (*Reichskriegsministerium*). The *Chef OKW* exercised the authority of the former Minister of War. (*Wehrmachtamt steht als OKW und als militärischer Stab unter dem Befehl des Führers und Reichskanzlers. Chef OKW ist den Reichsministern gleichgestellt. Das OKW nimmt zugleich die Geschäfte des Reichskriegsministers wahr. Chef OKW übt bisher dem Reichskriegsminister zustehenden Befugnisse aus.*)

1 June 1938 The following organization of the Armed Forces High Command came into effect: Four groups were formed:

A. OPERATIONS STAFF GROUP (*Amtsgruppe Führungsstab*) (WFA)
   1. National Defence Branch (*Landesverteidigungsabteilung*) (L)
   2. The Inspector of Armed Forces Signal Communications (*Inspekteur der Wehrmachtnachrichtenverbindungen*) was directly subordinate to the *Chef OKW*
   The position of Chief of the Operations Staff Group (*Chef der Amtsgruppe Führungsstab*) was to be held until further notice by the Chief of the National Defence Branch
   3. Armed Forces Signal Communications Branch (*Abteilung Wehrmachtnachrichtenverbindungen*) (Abt WNV)

B. GENERAL ARMED FORCES GROUP (*Amtsgruppe Allgemeine Wehrmachtangelegenheiten*) (AWA)
   1. Interior Branch (*Inlandsabteilung*) (J)
   2. Armed Forces Welfare Branch (*Wehrmachtversorgungsabteilung*)

C. FOREIGN AND COUNTER INTELLIGENCE GROUP (*Amtsgruppe Auslandnachrichten und Abwehr*) (A.Ausl)
   1. Foreign Intelligence Branch (*Auslandsabteilung*)
   2. Counter Intelligence Branch (*Abwehrabteilung*)

D. MILITARY ECONOMICS GROUP (*Amtsgruppe Wehrwirtschaftsstab*) (WStb)

No change in internal organization was made.

In addition to the Armed Forces Signals Inspector, the following agencies were directly subordinate to the *Chef OKW*:

E. CENTRAL SECTION (*Zentralgruppe*) (WZ)

F. ARMED FORCES LEGAL BRANCH (*Wehrmachtrechtsabteilung*) (WR)

G. ARMED FORCES BUDGET AND ADMINISTRATION BRANCH (*Wehrmachthaushalt- und Verwaltungsabteilung*) (WH)

H. SPECIAL ECONOMICS STAFF (*Sonderstab W*)

Aug. 1939 The war-time Organization (*Kriegsspitzengliederung*) of the Armed Forces High Command became effective, involving the following changes:

A. The Operations Staff Group (*Amtsgruppe Führungsstab*) (WFA) became the Armed Forces Operations Office (*Wehrmacht-Führungsamt*) (WFA)

B. The General Armed Forces Group (*Amtsgruppe Allgemeine Wehrmachtangelegenheiten*) (AWA) became the General Armed Forces Office (*Allgemeines Wehrmachtsamt*) (AWA)

C. The Foreign and Counter Intelligence Group (*Amtsgruppe Auslandsnachrichten und Abwehr*) (A.Ausl/Abw) became the Foreign and Counter Intelligence Office (*Amt Ausland/Abwehr*) (A.Ausl/Abw)

D. The Military Economics Group (*Amtsgruppe Wehrwirtschaftsstab*) (W.Stb) became the Military Economics Office (*Wehrwirtschaftsamt*) (W.Stb).

Agencies in the Armed Forces High Command in September 1939:

A. ARMED FORCES OPERATIONS OFFICE (*Wehrmacht-Führungsamt*) (WFA)

The following were added:

The Armed Forces Propaganda Branch (*Abteilung für Wehrmachtpropaganda*) (W.Pr).

The Chief of Armed Forces Transportation (*Chef des Transportwesens der Wehrmacht*), the appointment being held by the same man as Chief of Army Transportation (*Chef des Transportwesens im OKH*).

The Organization of the Armed Forces Operations Office in September 1939:

1. National Defence Branch (*Abteilung Landesverteidigung*) (L).
2. Inspector of Armed Forces Signal Communications (*Inspekteur der Wehrmachtnachrichtenverbindungen*) (Although subordinate to the Chief of the Armed Forces Operations Office, he had the right of direct consultation with the Chief of the Armed Forces High Command, and, if senior to the *Chef WFA*, had a direct personal subordination to the *Chef OKW*. He was authorized to issue directives to the Armed Forces Signal Communications Branch in consultation with the *Chef WFA*)
3. Armed Forces Signal Communications Branch (*Abteilung Wehrmachtnachrichtenverbindungen*) (Abt.WNV)
4. Armed Forces Propaganda Branch (*Abteilung für Wehrmachtpropaganda*) (W.Pr)
5. Chief of Armed Forces Transportation (*Chef des Transportwesens der Wehrmacht*) (The same man as the Chief of Army Transportation).

B. GENERAL ARMED FORCES OFFICE (*Allegemeines Wehrmacht-amt*) (AWA)

The Armed Forces Welfare Branch (*Wehrmachtversorgungsabteiling*) became the Armed Forces Welfare and Pensions Branch (*Wehrmachtfürsorge u. Versorgungsabteilung*) (W.Vers).

The Armed Forces Vocational Training Schools Branch (*Abteilung Wehrmachtfachschulunterricht*) (WU) was added.

The Science Branch (*Abteilung Wissenschaft*) (W.Wiss.) was added.

The Armed Forces Administration Branch (*Wehrmachtverwaltungsabteilung*) (WV) was added. This was formerly part of the Armed Forces Budget and Administration Branch (*Wehrmachthaushalt- und Versorgungsabteilung*) (WH) which split into the Armed Forces Administration Branch to form part of the General Armed Forces Office, and the Armed Forces Budget Branch (*Wehrmachthaushaltsabteilung*) (WH) which became directly subordinate to the Chief of OKW.

A General for Special Employment on Prisoner-of-War Affairs (*General z.b.V. für das Kriegsgefangenenwesen*) was added.

The Branch for Armed Forces Casualties and Prisoner-of-War Affairs (*Abteilung Wehrmachtverluste und Kriegsgefangenenwesen*) was added.

The Organization of the General Armed Forces Office in September 1939:

1. General Branch (*Allgemeine Abteilung*) (Allg)
2. Interior Branch (*Abteilung Inland*) (J)
3. Armed Forces Welfare and Pensions Branch (*Wehrmachtfürsorge- und Versorgungsabteilung*) (W.Vers)
4. Armed Forces Vocational Training Schools Branch (*Abteilung Wehrmachtfachschulunterricht*) (WU)
5. Science Branch (*Abteilung Wissenschaft*) (W.Wiss.).
6. Armed Forces Administration Branch (*Wehrmachtverwaltungsabteilung*) (WV)
7. General for Special Employment on Prisoner-of-War Affairs (*Gen. z.b.V. für das Kriegsgefangenenwesen*). (He was directly subordinate to Chief of General Armed Forces Office He worked in close collaboration with the Branch for Armed Forces Casualties and Prisoner-of-War Affairs, but had no authority over it. His main function was to visit prisoner-of-war and internment camps and make recommendations to the Branch for Armed Forces Casualties and Prisoner-of-War Affairs.)
8. Branch for Armed Forces Casualties and Prisoner-of-War Affairs (*Abteilung Wehrmachtverluste und Kriegsgefangenenwesen*).

C. FOREIGN AND COUNTER INTELLIGENCE OFFICE (*Amt Ausland/Abwehr*) (A.Ausl/Abw)

The Central Branch (*Zentralabteilung*) was added.

Counter Intelligence Branch (*Abwehrabteilung*) became the Counter Intelligence Branches I, II and III.

The Organization of the Foreign and Counter Intelligence Office in September 1939:

1. Central Branch (*Zentralabteilung*)
2. Foreign Intelligence Branch (*Abteilung Ausland*) (Ausl)
3. Counter Intelligence Branch I—Procurement of Intelligence (*Abteilung Abwehr I—Nachrichtenbeschaffung*) (Abw.I)
4. Counter Intelligence Branch II—Special Service (*Abteilung Abwehr II—Sonderdienst*) (Abw. II)

5. Counter Intelligence Branch III—Counter-intelligence (*Abteilung Abwehr III—Abwehr*) (Abw. III).

D. MILITARY ECONOMICS OFFICE (*Wehrwirtschaftsamt*) (W.Stb)
No changes during the period 1937–1939.

Organization of Military Economics Office in September 1939:

1. Military Economics Branch (*Wehrwirtschaftliche Abteilung*) (W.Wi)
2. Armament Industry Branch (*Rüstungswirtschaftliche Abteilung*) (W.Rü)
3. Raw Materials Branch (*Rohstoffabteilung*) (W.Ro)
4. Contracts and Price Control Branch (*Abteilung Vertrag u. Preisprüfwesen*) (*W.Preispr*).

E. ARMED FORCES CENTRAL BRANCH (*Wehrmacht Zentralabteilung*) (WZ) Mobilization, Personnel, Administration.

F. ARMED FORCES LEGAL BRANCH (*Wehrmachtrechtsabteilung*) (WR) (The Chief of the Armed Forces Legal Branch was also Chief of Judicial Agencies in the OKW) (*Chef der Justizdienststelle beim Chef OKW*).

G. ARMED FORCES BUDGET BRANCH (*Wehrmachthaushaltsabteilung*) (WH) Formerly part of Armed Forces Budget and Administration Branch (*Wehrmachthaushalt– und Verwaltungsabteilung*) (WH) which split into the Armed Forces Administration Branch (*Wehrmachtverwaltungsabteilung*) (WV), which became part of the General Armed Forces Office, and the Armed Forces Budget Branch, which remained directly subordinate to the Chief of OKW.

III. ARMY HIGH COMMAND (*Oberkommando des Heeres*)

Upon mobilization in August 1939, the Army High Command divided into a Field Headquarters and a Home Command. A Commander of the Replacement Army (*Befehlshaber des Ersatzheeres*) was appointed to take control of the Home Command.

Agencies in the High Command in September 1939:

A. ARMY GENERAL STAFF (*Generalstab des Heeres*)
On 1 Nov. 1938 the following reorganization came into effect:
A.C. of S–I (*Oberquartiermeister I*) now controlled:
Operations Branch (*Operationsabteilung*) (1. Abt)
Transport Branch (*Transportabteilung*) (5. Abt)
Supply and Administration Branch (*Quartiermeisterabteilung*) (6. Abt)
Army Topographical Branch (*Heeres-Vermessungswesen und Militärgeographie*) (9. Abt)
Land Fortifications Branch (*Landesbefestigungsabteilung*) (10. Abt)
A.C. of S–II (*Oberquartiermeister II*) now controlled:
Troop Training Branch (*Truppenausbildungsabteilung*) (4. Abt)
General Staff Training and Manuals Branch (*Abteilung für Generalstabsausbildung und Vorschriften*) (11. Abt) which was formerly called the 11th (Officer Training) Branch (*11. Abteilung—Offizierausbildungsabteilung*)
A.C. of S–III (*Oberquartiermeister III*) now controlled:
Organization Branch (*Organisationsabteilung*) (2. Abt)
Technical Branch (*Technische Abteilung*) (8. Abt)
A.C. of S–IV (*Oberquartiermeister IV*) was appointed to control Foreign Armies West Branch (*Fremde Heere West*) (3. Abt)
Foreign Armies East Branch (*Fremde Heere Ost*) (12. Abt)

These two branches were formed out of the former 3rd (Foreign Armies) Branch (*3. Abteilung—Abteilung Fremde Heere*)

In addition an Attaché Section (*Attachegruppe*) was formed and became directly subordinate to A.C. of S–IV.

A.C. of S–V (*Oberquartiermeister V*) was appointed to control Military Science Branch (*Kriegswissenschaftliche Abteilung*) (7. Abt)

In August 1939 the war-time organization (*Kriegsspitzengliederung*) of the Army General Staff came into effect, involving the following changes:

The A.C. of S–I (*Oberquartiermeister I*) no longer had any branches of the General Staff shown directly subordinated to him, but it was indicated that he was Deputy to Chief of Army General Staff and would represent him in his absence; also that the duties of the A.C. of S–I would be indicated to him from time to time by the Chief of General Staff, and might include the direct control of such branches of the General Staff as the occasion demanded.

The Operations Branch became an independent agency in the General Staff.

The Transport Branch was placed under a Chief of Army Transportation (*Chef des Transportwesens*).

The Supply and Administration Branch (6. Abt) was placed under a Chief of Field Supply and Administration (*Generalquartiermeister*).

The Army Topographical Branch (9. Abt) became the Mapping and Survey Branch (*Abteilung für Kriegskarten und Vermessungswesen*).

The A.C. of S–II was removed from the establishment.

The Troop Training Branch (4. Abt) and General Staff Training and Manuals Branch (11. Abt) were merged to form a new Training Branch (*Ausbildungsabteilung*) as an independent agency in the General Staff, controlling the Army Film Centre (*Heeresfilmstelle*).

The A.C. of S–III was removed from the establishment.

The Organization Branch (*Organisationsabteilung*) now became an independent agency in the General Staff.

The Technical Branch (*Technische Abteilung*) (8. Abt) became the Army Technical Section (*Gruppe Heerestechnik*).

In addition the following new agencies were created:

Chief of Meteorology (Army) (*Chef des Wetterdienstes—Heer*)

Chief of Army Signals (*Chef des Heeres-Nachrichtenwesens*) (Chef HNW)

Air Force General with C-in-C Army (*General der Luftwaffe b.Ob.d.H.*)

Chiefs of Arms and Services attached to C-in-C Army (*Waffengenerale beim Oberbefehlshaber des Heeres*)

Upon mobilization, the Army General Staff also split into a Field Headquarters (*1. Staffel*) and a Rear Echelon (*2. Staffel*) with the following allocation of agencies to each echelon:

Field Headquarters (*1. Staffel*):

Chief of the Army General Staff (*Chef des Generalstabs des Heeres*)
1. Central Branch (*Zentralabteilung*) (GZ)
2. A.C. of S–I (*Oberquartiermeister I*) (O.Qu.I)
3. Operations Branch (*Operationsabteilung*)
4. Organization Branch (*Organisationsabteilung*)
5. Land Fortifications Branch (*Landesbefestigungsabteilung*)
6. Chief of Field Army Supply and Administration (*Generalquartiermeister*)
   Section Qu. *1* (*Gruppe Qu. 1*)
   Ref. Ia
   Ref. Ib

Section Qu. 2 (*Gruppe Qu. 2*)
Section Qu. 3 (*Gruppe Qu. 3*)
Army Supply Section (*Gruppe Heeresnachschubführer*)
Chief Army Administration Officer (*Gruppe IVa, Heeresintendant*)
Chief Army Medical Officer (*Gruppe IVb, Heeresarzt*)
Chief Army Veterinarian (*Gruppe IVc, Heeresveterinär*)
Chief of Army Postal Services (*Gruppe F.P. Heeresfeldpostmeister*)
Civil Commissioner for Operational Areas (*Gruppe Z, Zivilbeauftragter*)
Army Field Judical Section (*Gruppe III, Feldjustizverwaltung*)
Adjutant Section (*Gruppe IIa, Adjutantur*)
Headquarters Commander (*Kommandant des Stabsquartiers*) Registry (*Registratur*)

7. Chief of Army Transportation (*Chef des Transportwesens*)
   Commander of Railway Units (*Befehlshaber der Eisenbahneinheiten*)
8. Training Branch (*Ausbildungsabteilung*)
   Army Film Centre (*Heeresfilmstelle*)
9. A.C. of S–IV—Foreign Armies (*Oberquartiermeister IV—Fremde Heere*) (O.Qu IV)
   Eastern Branch (*Abteilung Ost*)
   Western Branch (*Abteilung West*)
10. Chief of Meteorology (Army) (*Chef des Wetterdienstes—Heer*)
11. Chief of Army Signals (*Chef des Heeres—Nachrichtenwesens*) (Chef HNW)
12. Air Force General with C-in-C Army (*General der Luftwaffe b.Ob.d.H.*)
13. Chiefs of Combat Arms attached to C-in-C Army (*Waffengenerale beim Oberbefehlshaber des Heeres*)
    Director of Infantry (*General der Infanterie*)
    Director of Artillery (*General der Artillerie*)
    Director of Engineers and Fortifications (*General der Pioniere und Festungen*)

Rear Echelon (*2. Staffel*):

14. A.C. of S–V (*Oberquartiermeister V*), who controlled the rear echelons of the Army General Staff, as follows:
15. Military Science Branch (*Kriegswissenschaftliche Abteilung*)
16. Mapping and Survey Branch (*Abteilung für Kriegskarten und Vermessungswesen*)
17. Attaché Section (*Attachegruppe*) (Subordinate to O.Qu. IV)
18. Army Technical Section (*Gruppe Heerestechnik*)
19. Radio Interception Centre (*Horchleitstelle*)
20. Central Branch, Rear Echelon (*Organisationsabteilung 2. Staffel*)
    Foreign Armies Branch, Rear Echelon (*Abt. Fremde Heere 2. Staffel*)
    Organization Branch, Rear Echelon (*Organisationsabteilung 2. Staffel*)
    Training Branch, Rear Echelon (*Ausbildungsabteilung 2. Staffel*)

In September 1939 the organization of the Army General Staff remained unchanged.

B. ARMY PERSONNEL OFFICE (*Heeres-Personalamt*)
In August 1939 the War-time Organization (*Kriegsspitzengliederung*) of the Army Personnel Office became effective, involving the following changes:

A Field Headquarters (*1. Staffel*) was established, including the Chief of the Army Personnel Office (*Chef des Heerespersonalamts*)

1. Forward Echelon of the Army Personnel Office

The Home Command (2. *Staffel*) comprised:
2. Army Personnel Branch 1 (*Heeres-Personalabteilung* 1) (P.*1*)
   Officer Records, Transfers and Promotions.
3. Army Personnel Branch 2 (*Heeres-Personalabteilung* 2) (P.2)
   Officer Education and Welfare.
4. Army Personnel Branch 3 (*Heeres-Personalabteilung* 3) (P.*3*)
   E-Officers. (Formerly designated as P.*4*).

In September 1939 the organization of the Army Personnel Office remained unchanged.

IV. COMMANDER OF THE REPLACEMENT ARMY (*Befehlshaber des Ersatzheeres*) (BdE), controlling the General Army Office and Army Administration Office. The appointment of the Commander of the Replacement Army was held provisionally by the Chief of the General Army Office.

C. GENERAL ARMY OFFICE (*Allgemeines Heeresamt*) (AHA)

1938 Inspectorate of Artillery (*Inspektion der Artillerie*) (In.4) now controlled:
The Senior Artillery Officer for Land Fortifications (*Höherer Artillerieoffizier für die Landesbefestigung*), and the Senior Officer for Artillery Observation Troops (*Höherer Offizier der Artilleriebeobachtungstruppen*).

1938 The Inspectorate of Fortifications (*Inspektion der Festungen*) (In.Fest) was transferred from Army General Staff back to General Army Office.

1938 The Inspector of Engineers and Fortifications (*Inspekteur der Pioniere und Festungen* was re-established, controlling the Inspectorate of Engineers (*Inspektion der Pioniere*) (In.5) and the Inspectorate of Fortifications (*Inspektion der Festungen*) (In.Fest).

24 Nov. 1938 The Army Ordnance Stores Branch (*Heeres-Feldzeugabteilung*) (Fz) became the Ordnance Stores Inspectorate (*Feldzeuginspektion*) (Fz.In).

24 Nov. 1938 The Cavalry Branch (*Kavallerieabteilung*) (In. 3), and the Inspectorate of Panzer Troops and Army Motorization (*Inspektion der Panzertruppen und für Heeresmotorisierung*) (In.6) were both reorganized into the Branch for Panzer Troops, Cavalry and Army Motorization (*Abteilung Panzertruppen, Kavallerie und Heeresmotorisierung*) (In.6).

24 Nov. 1938 The Inspectorate of Riding and Driving (*Inspektion des Reit- und Fahrwesens*) was formed, and was designated (In.3) formerly applicable to the Cavalry Branch—see above.

24 Nov. 1938 The Supply Troops Branch (*Fahrtruppenabteilung*) (In.8) became the Inspectorate of Supply Troops (*Inspektion der Fahrtruppe*) (In.8).

24 Nov. 1938 The Inspectorate of Railway Engineers (*Inspektion der Eisenbahnpioniere*) (In.10) was formed.

By 1939 the Army Legal Branch (*Heeres-Rechtsabteilung*) (HR) had been formed.

By 1939 In.2 had become *Infanterie Abteilung*
   In.4 had become *Artillerie Abteilung*
   In.5 had become *Pionier Abteilung*
   In.7 had become *Nachrichtentruppen Abteilung*
   In.9 had become *Abteilung Nebeltruppe und Gasabwehr*.

By 1939 *Heeresbekleidungsabteilung* (Bk.1) had become *Bekleidungsabteilung* (Bk.1).

The Organization of the General Army Office in September 1939:

1. Central Branch (*Zentralabteilung*) (Z)
   Army Publications Administration (*Heeres-Druckvorschriftenverwaltung*) (H.Dv)
   Office Administrator (*Bürodirektor beim BdE*) (Bd.BdE)
   Message Centre (*Kurierstelle*) (Kurierst)
   Accounts Offices I and II OKH (*Wirtschaftsstelle I and II OKH*) (WiSt. I and II OKH).
2. Army Budget Branch (*Heeres-Haushaltsabteilung*) (H.Haush)
3. Group for Replacement and Army Affairs (*Amtsgruppe Ersatz- und Heerwesen*) (Ag.EH)
   a. Recruiting and Conscription Branch (*Abteilung Ersatzwesen*) (Abt.E)
   b. Army Branch (*Abteilung Heerwesen*) (Abt.H)
   c. Clothing Branch (*Bekleidungs-Abteilung*) (Bk.1)
   d. Penal Section (*Gruppe Strafgefangenenwesen*) (Str)
   e. Chaplain's Section (*Gruppe Seelsorge*) (S)
   f. Commander of the Bendler Block (*Kommandant des Bendlerblocks*)
4. Army Legal Branch (*Heeres-Rechtsabteilung*) (HR)
5. Army Ordnance Stores Inspectorate (*Heeres-Feldzeuginspektion*) (Fz.In) headed by a Feldzeugmeister
6. Arms and Services Branches (*Waffen Abteilung*)
   a. Infantry Branch (*Infanterieabteilung*) (In.2)*
   b. Inspectorate of Riding and Driving (*Inspektion des Reit- und Fahrwesens*) (In.3)*
   c. Artillery Branch (*Artillerieabteilung*) (In.4)*
      Senior Artillery Officer for Land Fortifications (*Höherer Artillerieoffizier für die Landesbefestigung*)
      Senior Officer for Artillery Observation Troops (*Höherer Offizier der Artilleriebeobachtungstruppen*)
   d. Engineer's Branch (*Pionier Abteilung*) (In.5)*
   e. Panzer Troops, Cavalry and Army Motorization Branch (*Abteilung Panzertruppen, Kavallerie u. Heeresmotorisierung*) (In.6)*
   f. Signals Troops Branch (*Nachrichtentruppenabteilung*) (In.7)*
   g. Supply Troops Inspectorate (*Inspektion der Fahrtruppe*) (In.8)*
   h. Chemical Warfare Troops and Anti-Gas Defence Branch (*Abteilung Nebeltruppe und Gasabwehr*) (In.9)*
   i. Inspectorate of Railway Engineers (*Inspektion der Eisenbahnpionere*) (In.10)*
7. Inspectorate of Fortifications (*Inspektion der Festungen*) headed by an Inspector (*Inspekteur der Festungen*)
8. Army Medical Inspectorate (*Heeres-Sanitätsinspektion*) (S.In) headed by an Inspector (*Heeres-Sanitätsinspekteur*) who was directly responsible to C-in-C Army
9. Veterinary Inspectorate (*Veterinärinspektion*) (V.In) headed by an Inspector (*Veterinärinspekteur*) who was directly responsible to C-in-C Army
10. Inspectorate of the General Technical Troop Service (*Inspektion des Allgemeinen Technischen Truppendienstes*) (In.T).

* Headed by Branch Chief (*Abteilungschef*).
The Arms and Services Inspectors (*Waffeninspekteure*) formerly at the head of the Inspectorates became independent of General Army Office and directly subordinate to Chef H.Rü u.BdE.

D. ARMY ORDNANCE OFFICE (*Heeres-Waffenamt*) (Wa.A)

Aug. 1939 The war-time Organization (*Kriegsspitzengliederung*) of the Army Ordnance Office came into effect, involving the following changes:

Prüfwesen (Wa.Prw) became the Development and Testing Group (*Amtsgruppe für Entwicklung und Prüfung*) (Wa. Prüf).

The Chief Designer (*Chefkonstrukteur*) (Wa.Prw.3) was no longer shown as independent agency in the Army Ordnance Office, but became a subordinate to the Chief Ordnance Engineer.

The Branch of Survey, Optics and Meteorology (Wa.Prw.8) became the Branch for Optics, Survey and Meteorology (*Abteilung für Optik, Messwesen und Heeres-Wetterdienst*) (Wa.Prüf.8).

The Air Defence Branch (*Flugabwehrabteilung*)(Wa.Prw.10) no longer appeared. (Wa.Prüf.10 reappeared towards the end of the war as the agency which had been secretly engaged on rocket development; it is not known whether it retained the title of Air Defence Branch.)

The Ordnance Research Branch (*Forschungsabteilung*) (Wa.Prw.11) became an independent agency in the Army Ordnance Office and changed its abbreviation to Wa.F.

Wa.Prüf.12 changed its title to *Abteilung für Versuchsplätze*.

The Branch for Special Equipment (*Abteilung für Sondergerät*) (Wa.Prw.13) changed its abbreviation to Wa.Prüf. 11.

The Procurement Group (*Beschaffungswesen*) (Wa.B) was disbanded.

The Group for the Armaments Industry (*Amtsgruppe für Industrielle Rüstung*) (Wa.J.Rü) was added.

The Army Acceptance Branch (Wa.Abn) became the Acceptance Group (*Amtsgruppe für Abnahme*) (Wa.Abn).

The Chief Ordnance Engineer (*Chefingenieur*) first appeared.

The Organization of the Army Ordnance Office in September 1939:

1. Armed Forces Technical Press Reading Branch (*Wehrmachtzeitschriftenabteilung*) (*Ztschr*)
2. Publications Branch (*Vorschriftenabteilung*) (Wa.Vs)
3. Development and Testing Group (*Amtsgruppe für Entwicklung und Prüfung*) (Wa.Prüf.)
    a. Ballistics and Ammunition Branch (*Ballistische- und Munitionsabteilung*) (Wa.Prüf.1)
    b. Infantry Branch (*Infanterieabteilung*) (Wa.Prüf.2)
    c. Artillery Branch (*Artillerieabteilung*) (Wa.Prüf.4)
    d. Engineers and Fortification Engineers Branch (*Pionier- und Festungspionierabteilung*) (Wa.Prüf.5)
    e. Motor Transportation and Motorization Branch (*Kraftfahr- und Motorisierungsabteilung*) (Wa.Prüf.6)
    f. Signals Branch (*Nachrichtenabteilung*) (Wa.Prüf.7)
    g. Branch for Optics, Survey and Meteorology (*Abteilung für Optik, Messwesen und Heeres-Wetterdienst*) (Wa.Prüf.8)
    h. Gas Defence Branch (*Gasschutzabteilung*) (Wa.Prüf.9)
    i. Special Equipment Branch (*Abteilung für Sondergerät*) (Wa.Prüf.11)
    j. Branch for Ordnance Proving Grounds (*Abteilung für Versuchsplätze*) (Wa.Prüf.12)
4. Group for the Armaments Industry (*Amtsgruppe für Industrielle Rüstung*) (Wa.J.Rü).

a. Battle Equipment Branch (*Kampfgerätabteilung*) (Wa.J.Rü.1)
b. Weapons Branch (*Waffenabteilung*) (Wa.J.Rü.2)
c. Ammunition Branch (*Munitionsabteilung*) (Wa.J.Rü.3)
d. Engineers and Fortifications Engineers Equipment Branch (*Pionier- und Festungspioniergerätabteilung*) (Wa.J.Rü.5)
e. Motor Vehicle Equipment Branch (*Kraftfahrgerätabteilung*) (Wa.J.Rü.6)
f. Signals Equipment Branch (*Nachrichtengerätabteilung*) (Wa.J.Rü.7)
g. Organization Branch (*Organisationsabteilung*) (Wa.J.Rü.8)
h. Powder and Explosives Manufacture Branch (*Pulver und Sprengstofffabrikationsabteilung*) (Wa.J.Rü.9)
i. Economic Administration Branch (*Betriebswirtschaftliche Abteilung*) (Wa.J.Rü10).
5. Acceptance Group (*Amtsgruppe für Abhahme*) (Wa.Abn)
6. Chief Ordnance Engineer (*Chefingenieur*)
7. Ordnance Research Branch (*Forschungsabteilung*) (Wa.F).

E. ARMY ADMINISTRATION OFFICE (*Heeresverwaltungsamt*) (VA)

1 Feb. 1939 Reorganization of the Army Administration Office took place, involving the following changes:
1. The Civilian Personnel and Finance Group (*Amtsgruppe Allgemeine Heeresbeamten- Angesteleten- Arbliter- und Kassenangelegenheiten*) (Ag.V.I) was formed, controlling:
   a. The Army Administration Officials and Finance Branch (*Heeresverwaltungsbeamten und Kassenabteilung*) (V.1); formerly called the Army Officials and Finance Branch
   b. The Technical Army Officials Branch (*Technische Heeresbeamtenabteilung*) (V.6) newly formed
   c. The Civilian Employees Section (*Gruppe Angestellten und Arbeiter*) (Anga) newly formed
   d. The Section for Training of Army Administrative Officials (*Gruppe Ausbildung der Heeresverwaltungsbeamten*) (Ausb) newly formed
2. The Army Rations and Procurement Group (*Amtsgruppe Heeres-Verpflegungs- und Beschaffungswesen*) (Ag.V.III) was formed, controlling:
   a. The Army Rations Branch (*Heeres-Verpflegungsabteilung*) (V.3)
   b. The Army Procurement Branch (*Heeres-Beschaffungsabteilung*) (V.5)
   These two branches had been formed from the former Army Rations and Procurement Branch (V.3)
3. The Army Quartering and Training Area Branch (*Heeres-Unterkunfts- und Übungsplatzabteilung*) (V.2) remained unchanged
4. The Army Building Administration Branch (*Heeres-Bauverwaltungsabteilung*) (V.4) remained unchanged.
Sep. 1939 The war-time Organization (*Kriegsspitzengliederung*) of the Army Administration Office came into effect, without any change to the organization as of 1 Feb. 1939.

F. INSPECTORS OF ARMS AND SERVICES (*Waffen-Inspekteure*)

Upon mobilization, the Inspectors of Arms and Services became independent of the General Army Office and instead became directly subordinate to the Commander of the Replacement Army.

Organization of Inspectors of Arms and Services in September 1939:
1. Inspector of Infantry (*Inspekteur der Infanterie*).
2. Inspector of Riding and Driving (*Inspekteur des Reit- und Fahrwesens*).

3. Inspector of Artillery (*Inspekteur der Artillerie*).
4. Inspector of Engineers and Railway Engineers (*Inspekteur der Pioniere und Eisenbahnpioniere*)
5. Inspector of Mobile Troops (*Inspekteur der Schnellen Truppen*)
6. Inspector of Signal Troops (*Inspekteur der Nachrichtentruppen*)
7. Inspector of Supply Troops (*Inspekteur der Fahrtruppen*)
8. Inspector of Chemical Warfare Troops (*Inspekteur der Nebeltruppen*).

G. INSPECTOR OF OFFICER CADET COURSES (*Inspekteur der Offizieranwärten-Lehrgänge*) (In.OAL). Replaces Inspectorate of Officer Training Schools (*Inspektion der Kriegsschulen*) (In.1).

H. CHIEF OF ARMY JUDICATURE (*Chef des Heeres-Justizwesens*) (Appointment held by same man as Chief of Army Legal Branch).

I. CHIEF OF MOBILE TROOPS (*Chef der Schnellen Truppen*) (Formed in November 1938, but disbanded on mobilization).

Appendix E

Table of Comparative Ranks

German (pre-1939)	British (1960's)
Generalfeldmarschall	Field-Marshal
Generaloberst	
	General
General der Infanterie, etc.	
	Lieutenant-General
Generalleutnant	
	Major-General
Generalmajor	
	Brigadier
Oberst	
	Colonel
Oberstleutnant	
	Lieutenant-Colonel
Major	
	Major
Hauptmann, Rittmeister	
	Captain
Oberleutnant	
	Lieutenant
Leutnant	
	Second Lieutenant

Unteroffizier: corresponds approximately with Sergeant
Gefreiter: corresponds approximately with Corporal

Fähnrich ⎫	Officer Cadet
Fahnenjunker ⎭	or Ensign

Appendix F

A Note on the 'Pact of the Deutschland'

Wheeler-Bennett in *The Nemesis of Power* (p. 312) has described an agreement which was supposed to have been made between Hitler and Blomberg on board the cruiser *Deutschland* while voyaging between Kiel and Königsberg on 11 and 12 April 1934. This agreement provided for the support of the Armed Forces for Hitler's candidacy as Hindenburg's successor in return for Hitler's promise to eliminate the threat of the S.A. to the position of the Wehrmacht. Fritsch and Raeder were supposed to have taken part in preliminary discussions regarding the succession to Hindenburg on the night of 11 April.

The evidence cited by Wheeler-Bennett for this 'Pact' is the *Weissbuch über die Erschiessungen des 30. Juni*, Paris 1935, pp. 52–53. This book was published by a group of left-wing political refugees who had escaped to France. Examination shows this book to be more of the nature of a political pamphlet than an objective historical study. Its authorship was anonymous and it does not quote any sources for its information, hence it is unverifiable. While this is no sufficient reason for believing this account to be false, there are certain other circumstances of relevance:

(a) In view of the pact signed on 28 February 1934 between Blomberg and Röhm, the Wehrmacht stood to gain nothing more from the Pact of the *Deutschland* than it had already been promised.

(b) Hitler already had the unquestioning support of Blomberg, while the attitudes of Fritsch and Raeder do not appear to have altered as a result of any agreement reached about this time.

(c) Wheeler-Bennett states that the 'Pact' went into 'almost immediate effect'. He supports this statement with two pieces of evidence, viz. that Hitler made an offer on 16 April 1934 to Britain to reduce the S.A. to 800,000 men, and that Blomberg ordered that the Party emblem was to be worn on Wehrmacht uniforms as a result of the 'Pact'. As Wheeler-Bennett himself states, the offer to reduce the S.A. was merely a repetition of another made in February to the same effect, and therefore the second offer shows no change in Hitler's policy as a result of any new 'Pact' reached with the Wehrmacht. Rather, it was a continuation of Hitler's policy which he had determined many months previously. The second piece of evidence, regarding the wearing of the Party emblem, has been shown to be incapable of supporting any supposition of a pact reached in April, because Blomberg had ordered the adoption of the Party emblem for Wehrmacht uniforms in the *Militärwochenblatt* of 25 February 1934.

(d) The nature of this 'Pact', a highly important and secret agreement, reached between two men, with the possible knowledge of two others, raises the question of how a group of political refugees came by such information. As far as present knowledge indicates, no details of the 'Pact' were committed to writing.

The negotiations were supposed to have been carried out by conversations and from what is known of Hitler's methods of working, it is extremely improbable that there were any witnesses who would have been disposed to breaking the secrecy of these conversations.

In view of the above, it would seem that further evidence is required before the 'Pact of the *Deutschland*' can be reasonably regarded as a historical fact.

Bibliography

(Items marked * are particularly important)

A. PRIMARY SOURCES

1. UNPUBLISHED DOCUMENTS AND PAPERS

(a) German Sources

(i) *Bundesarchiv, Koblenz*

Nachlass GROENER	H 08 – 46/152
Nachlass SCHLEICHER	H 08 – 42/88
	H 08 – 42/92
*Nachlass BECK	H 08 – 28/2
	H 08 – 28/6
Nachlass FRITSCH	H 08 – 33/1
*Nachlass WEICHS	H 08 – 19/1
	H 08 – 19/14

Akten HEERESDIENSTSTELLE 6, REGENSBURG, *Zusammenarbeit mit Parteigliederungen in Fragen des Grenzschutzes*, 7.7.34–20.9.38   H 64 – 6/1

Reden anlässlich der 125 Jahrfeier der Kriegsakademie   H 81 – 1/2

(ii) *Militärgeschichtliches Forschungsamt* (MGFA), *Freiburg im Breisgau*

Files quoted in the text:

Haushalt der S.A. (1933–1334)

File no.	H 7/30	(MGFA no.)
,, ,,	H 24/88A	,, ,,
,, ,, II	H 252	,, ,,
,, ,, II	L 51/7	,, ,,
,, ,, II	W 22	,, ,,
,, ,, III	H 287	,, ,,

The following files were referred to by the MGFA by their Wehrmacht classification numbers:

*OKW / 848	WK VII / 754
OKW / 867	WK VII / 759
*OKW / 888	WK VII / 760
OKW / 1551	WK VII / 897
	WK VII / 1299
*OKH / H – 24/6	*WK VII / 1320
*OKH / H – 24/35	*WK VII / 1652
*OKH / H – 24/37	WK VII / 2196
OKH / H – 24/38	*WK VII / 2210
OKH / H – 24/39	*WK VII / 2306
OKH / H – 24/40	WK VII / 2310
OKH / H – 24/74	WK IX / 9
	WK IX / 134
WK VII / 335	WK IX / 137
WK VII / 611	
WK VII / 741	WK XII / 15C

WK XIII / 16	WK XIII / 268
WK XIII / 184	WK XIII / 294
WK XIII / 188	WK XIII / 337
WK XIII / 189	WK XIII / 423
WK XIII / 190	*WK XIII / 823
WK XIII / 192	WK XIII / 924
WK XIII / 264	

Other files containing relevant information and used as background material:

OKW / 847	WK XIII / 240
OKW / 891	WK XIII / 241
	WK XIII / 335
WK VII / 213	WK XIII / 345
WK VII / 240	WK XIII / 483
WK VII / 347	WK XIII / 571
WK VII / 405	WK XIII / 656
WK VII / 406–1	WK XIII / 660
WK VII / 450	WK XIII / 661
WK VII / 1342	WK XIII / 662
WK VII / 1343	WK XIII / 663
WK VII / 1451	WK XIII / 664
WK VII / 1631	WK XIII / 665
WK VII / 1873	WK XIII / 703
WK VII / 2136	WK XIII / 721
WK VII / 3058	WK XIII / 863
	WK XIII / 872
WK XII / 15B	WK XIII / 888
WK XII / 15D	WK XIII / 893
WK XII / 15E	WK XIII / 987
WK XII / 15G	WK XIII / 1021
WK XII / 15H	WK XIII / 1027
WK XII / 203	WK XIII / 1029
WK XII / 333	WK XIII / 1033
	WK XIII / 1034
WK XIII / 65	WK XIII / 1035
WK XIII / 180	WK XIII / 1036
WK XIII / 181	WK XIII / 1037
WK XIII / 182	WK XIII / 1142
WK XIII / 183	WK XIII / 1294
WK XIII / 185	WK XIII / 1306
WK XIII / 186	WK XIII / 1420
WK XIII / 187	WK XIII / 1490

(iii) INSTITUT FÜR ZEITGESCHICHTE, MUNICH

Zeugenschrifttum Nr. 44 – GAERTNER
     „   „   66 – HEINRICI
     „   „   105 – MELLENTHIN
     „   „   152 – STAPF
     „   „   217 – BUSSCHE
     „   „   279 – OTT

LIEBMANN, *Notizen.*

D. MENDE, *Die Geburt des Dritten Reiches*, (Manuscript).

Völkischer Beobachter.

(iv) A private memorandum by Dr Max Rehm of Nürtingen, *Generaloberst Ludwig Beck*.

(b) British Sources

THE PAPERS OF CAPTAIN SIR BASIL LIDDELL HART, Medmenham, Bucks.
Letter from Generalfeldmarschall a.D. von RUNDSTEDT to Captain Liddell Hart, 9 November 1945.
Letter from Generalleutnant a.D. RÖHRRICHT to Captain Liddell Hart, November 1945.
Letter from General DITTMAR to Captain Liddell Hart, undated.
Memorandum written by General der Infanterie a.D. BLUMENTRITT in 1946.
Official Interrogation Record of Oberst von LINDEINER, Grizedale Hall, 1945.
Record of a private interview with Generalfeldmarschall a.D. von RUNDSTEDT by Captain Liddell Hart, 6 January 1946, Grizedale Hall.

2. PUBLISHED DOCUMENTS

Documents on German Foreign Policy, published by Her Majesty's Stationery Office, abbr. DGFP. Series C vols. I–IV and Series D, vols. I–VII.
Documents on British Foreign Policy (second series) (DBFP), Vol. II.
Nuremberg Documents
(a) *The Trials of the Major War Criminals*, produced for the International Military Tribunal and published at Nuremberg 1947–49, abbr. IMT. Cases and documents have been referred to in the text by their serial numbers.
(b) *Nazi Conspiracy and Aggression*, published by the United States Government Printing Office 1946, abbr. NCA.
(c) *Nuremberg Military Tribunals*, USGPO, Washington, 1951.
Stellenbesetzungen of the German Army, 1932–38, published by the Army High Command at approximately yearly intervals. A complete set is held by the *Bundesarchiv*, Koblenz. H 10–4/8 to H 10–4/17.
VOGELSANG, Thilo (editor), Neue Dokumente zur Geschichte der Reichswehr 1930–33, in *Vierteljahrshefte für Zeitgeschichte*, April 1954.
Text of a letter from Hitler to Reichenau of 2 December 1932, in *Vierteljahrshefte für Zeitgeschichte*, October 1959.
Offiziere im Bild von Dokumenten aus drei Jahrhunderten, issued by Hans Meier-Welcker, Schriften des Militärgeschichtlichen Forschungsamt, Band 6, Stuttgart, 1964.

3. DIARIES, PRIVATE PAPERS AND OTHER PRIMARY SOURCES WHICH HAVE BEEN PUBLISHED

BECK, Generaloberst Ludwig, in:
FÖRSTER, Wolfgang, *Ein General Kämpft gegen den Krieg*, Munich, 1949.
Ludwig Beck—Sein Kampf gegen den Krieg, Munich, 1953.
LUDWIG BECK, *Studien*, ed. by Hans Speidel, Stuttgart, 1955.
BLOMBERG, Generalfeldmarschall Werner von, 'Aufbau und Aufgaben der deutschen Wehrmacht' in, *Deutsche Gedenkhalle—das neue Deutschland*, Berlin, 1939.
'Wehrhaftigkeit oder Pazifismus', in *Almanach der nationalsozialistischen Revolution*, issued by Wilhelm Kube, Berlin, 1934.
CHURCHILL, Sir Winston, Letter published in *The Times* of 7 November 1938.
HALDER, Generaloberst Franz, *Kriegstagebuch*, Stuttgart, 1962.

HASSELL, Ulrich von, *Vom Anderen Deutschland*, Zürich, 1946.

HITLER, Adolf, *Mein Kampf*, Munich, 1933.

JODL, Generaloberst Alfred, in *Nuremberg Documents*, 1780 PS, for fragments of his diary, January 1937—August 1939.

RÖHM, Ernst, 'S.A. und deutsche Revolution', in *Nationalsozialistische Monatshefte*, No. 31, 1933.

B. SECONDARY SOURCES

4. MEMOIRS AND OTHER RETROSPECTIVE FIRST HAND ACCOUNTS

*BENNECKE, Heinrich, *Die Reichswehr und der Röhm-Putsch*, Munich, 1964.
Hitler und die S.A., Munich, 1962.
   Both of these are valuable accounts of Reichswehr-S.A. relations, by a former senior officer of the S.A. Bennecke describes how institutional factors were exploited by a few individuals to disrupt the normally good relations which existed between the Reichswehr and the S.A. on the local level.

BOEHM, General Admiral, in: *Frankfurter Allgemeine Zeitung*, 25 October 1961 (letter concerning Fritsch as a guest on the *Gneisenau*, 12–17 June 1939).

BONHOEFFER, Dietrich, *Offiziere gegen Hitler*, Munich, 1951.

CHURCHILL, Sir Winston, *The Second World War*, Vol. I—'The Gathering Storm', London, 1948.

DÖNITZ, Karl, *Zehn Jahre und Zwanzig Tage*, Bonn, 1958.

DUESTERBERG, Theodor, *Der Stahlhelm und Hitler*, Hanover, 1949.

FABER du FAUR, Moriz von, *Macht und Ohnmacht—Erinnerungen eines alten Offizers*, Stuttgart, 1953.

FECHTER, Paul, *Menschen und Zeiten—Begegnungen aus fünf Jahrhunderten*, Gütersloh, 1949. A good account of the personality of Beck.

GESSLER, Otto, *Reichswehrpolitik in der Weimarer Zeit*, ed. Kurt Sendtner, Stuttgart, 1958.

GAMELIN, Maurice Gustave, *Servir*, 3 vols., Paris, 1946–47.

GEYR von SCHWEPPENBURG, Leo Freiherr, *Erinnerungen eines Militärattaches London 1933–1937*, Stuttgart, 1949.
Gebrochenes Schwert, Berlin, 1952.

GISEVIUS, Hans Bernd, *Bis zum bittern Ende*, Hamburg, 1960.

*GUDERIAN, Heinz, *Panzer Leader*, London, 1952.
   An excellent account of events through the eyes of an officer for whom patriotism was of supreme importance.

HALDER, Franz, *Hitler als Feldherr*, Munich, 1949.

HAUSSER, Paul, *Waffen SS im Einsatz*, Göttingen, 1953.
   This contains a brief but worthwhile account of the development of the Waffen SS 1933–39.

HEUSINGER, Adolf, *Befehl im Widerstreit*, Stuttgart, 1950.
   A record of dialogues illustrating some key problems for German officers, 1924–45.

*HOSSBACH, Friedrich, *Zwischen Wehrmacht und Hitler*, Hanover, 1949.
   An excellent, objective account of the Army's relations with Hitler and Blomberg 1934–38—one of the most valuable sources for this subject.

LIDDELL HART, Sir Basil, *Memoirs*, London, 1965.
   These memoirs contain an excellent description of the personality of Blomberg.

*MANSTEIN, Erich von, *Aus einem Soldatenleben*, Bonn, 1958.

A most valuable and full autobiography, covering the pre-war years. There are a few slips of the author's memory.

*PAPEN, Franz von, *Memoirs*, London, 1952.

An interesting and detailed account, but must be treated with caution.

RAEDER, Erich, *Mein Leben*, Bd. I., Tübingen, 1956.

RÖHM, Ernst, *Die Geschichte eines Hochverräters*, Munich, 1933.

SCHACHT, Hjalmar, *Account Settled*, London, 1949.

SCHELLENBERG, Walter, *The Schellenberg Memoirs*, London, 1956.

Valuable description of Heydrich's role, 1936–38, by one of his assistants.

SPRANGER, Eduard, 'Generaloberst Beck in der Mittwochgesellschaft', in *Universitas*, 1956, Heft 2.

WARLIMONT, Walter, *Inside Hitler's Headquarters*, London, 1964.

This contains a brief but good summary of the pre-war problems of the German High Command.

WEIZSÄCKER, E. von, *Erinnerungen*, Munich, 1950.

WESTPHAL, Siegfried, *Heer in Fesseln*, Bonn, 1950.

5. OTHER SECONDARY SOURCES

ABSOLON, Rudolf, *Wehrgesetz und Wehrdienst 1935–1945—das Personalwesen in der Wehrmacht*, Schriften des Bundesarchivs Band 5, Boppard/Rhein, 1960.

ARETIN, Karl Otmar Freiherr von, 'Die deutschen Generale und Hitlers Kriegspolitik', in *Politische Studien* 10, 1959.

BARTHEL, Konrad, 'Zur Problematik zeitgeschichtlichen Verstehens—Bemerkungen zu Wheeler-Bennetts *Nemesis der Macht*', in *Geschichte in Wissenschaft und Unterricht*, October, 1955.

BENOIST-MECHIN, Jacques, *Histoire de l'Armée Allemande*, Vol. III, 1925–37, Vol. IV, 1937–38 and Vol. V, 1938–39, Paris, 1964.

BERGMANN, Robert, 'Die Reichswehr', in *Das Buch der Hitler Jugend—Die Jugend im Dritten Reich*, ed. by Ulf Uweson and Walther Ziersch, Munich, 1934.

BERNDORFF, Hans, *General zwischen Ost und West*, Hamburg, 1951.

A superficial biography of Schleicher, but containing a good account of his death.

BLUMENTRITT, Günther, *von Rundstedt—the Soldier and the Man*, London, 1952.

BOENINGER, Hildegard, 'Hitler and the German Generals 1934–1938', in *Journal of Central European Affairs*, Vol. 14, No. 1, 1954.

BOR, Peter, *Gespräche mit Halder*, Wiesbaden, 1950.

This contains some very interesting anecdotes and opinions by Halder.

*BRACHER, K. D., SAUER, W., and SCHULZ, G., *Die Nationalsozialistische Machtergreifung*, Cologne and Opladen, 1962.

This extremely full work is of the greatest importance as a history of the years 1932–34 in Germany. It is accurate, objective and thoroughly documented, based on the widest selection of primary material yet used for a study of the early years of the Third Reich.

BRACHER, K. D., *Die Auflösung der Weimarer Republik*, Stuttgart, 1960.

This is also a work of prime importance, covering the collapse of the Weimar Republic, and of the same quality as *Die Nationalsozialistische Machtergreifung*.

BREYER, Richard, *Das deutsche Reich und Polen, 1932–1937*, Würzburg, 1955.

BUBER, Fritz, ed., *Europäische Politik im Spiegel der Prager Akten*, Essen, 1942.

*BUCHHEIT, Gert, *Soldatentum und Rebellion*, Rastatt/Baden, 1961.

Ludwig Beck, Munich, 1964.

Both works are thorough, accurate and objective collations of mostly well-known material, but assembled in new convenient forms. One book repeats the other to a moderate extent. Footnotes are plentiful, but are extremely brief.

BULLOCK, Alan, *Hitler, a Study in Tyranny*, London, 1952.

*CARSTEN, F. L., *Reichswehr und Politik 1918–1933*, Cologne, 1964.

A very thorough and detailed examination of political military relations in the Weimar Republic, providing an important extension of the work of Harold Gordon to cover the interval 1926–33. This work is particularly useful for understanding the formation of political opinion in the Reichswehr in the years before 1933.

'From Scharnhorst to Schleicher—the Prussian Officer Corps in Politics 1806–1933', in *Soldiers and Governments*, ed. Michael Howard, London, 1957.

CRAIG, G. A., *The Politics of the Prussian Army, 1940–1945*, Oxford, 1955.

Daily Mail of 29 December 1933.

*DEMETER, Karl, *Das deutsche Offizierkorps in Gesellschaft und Staat 1650–1945*, Frankfurt, 1964.

This has been for thirty years the basic text on the social position of the German Officer. The recent edition includes treatment of the Nazi era.

DONNEVERT, Richard, *Wehrmacht und Partei*, Leipzig, 1938.

ENGELBRECHTEN, Julius Karl von, *Eine braune Armee entsteht. Die Geschichte der Berlin-Brandenburger S.A.*, Berlin, 1937.

*ERFURTH, Waldemar, *Die Geschichte des deutschen Generalstabes 1918–1945*, Göttingen, 1957.

A valuable account, by the former head of the Military History Section, OKH. It thus has the benefit (and defects) of 'inside information', although it is inclined to be too brief.

*ERICKSON, John, *The Soviet High Command 1918–1941*, London, 1962.

This contains the most detailed account of the dealings of the Reichswehr with the Red Army and of the part of Heydrich in the great purges of the Red Army, 1937–39. But since the theme of the book is the Red Army, some distillation is necessary to extract the details relating to the German Army. It is a work of the greatest importance.

EYCK, Erich, *Geschichte der Weimarer Republik*, Stuttgart, 1954.

FLECHTHEIM, Ossip K., *Die Kommunistische Partei Deutschlands in der Weimarer Republik*, Offenbach, 1948.

A useful account of the internal troubles of Germany before Hitler's rise to power.

FOERTSCH, Hermann, *Unsere deutsche Wehrmacht*, Berlin, 1935.

Die Wehrmacht im nationalsozialistischen Staat, Hamburg, 1935.

Schuld und Verhängnis, Stuttgart, 1951.

A most interesting and well written account of events leading up to the Fritsch crisis, which the author, an officer on the staff of OKH, treats as a fundamental turning point in the Nazi era.

FOLTMANN, J., and MOLLER, H., *Opfergang der Generale*, Berlin, 1952.

An interesting collection of biographical details relating to German generals and their fates during and after the Second World War.

FÖRSTER, Wolfgang, 'Generaloberst Freiherr von Fritsch', in *Deutscher Soldaten-kalendar*, 1960.

Frankfurter Zeitung of 26 September 1933.

FRANZ, Georg, 'Die Haltung des Offizierkorps 1919–1937', in *Wehrwissenschaftliche Rundschau*, July 1957.

FREDE, G., and SCHÜDDEKOPF, O., *Wehrmacht und Politik 1933–1945*, Hanover, 1951.

GELLERMANN, J. E., *Generals as Statesmen*, New York, 1959.
Very superficial, but with some interesting details concerning Schleicher.

GORDON, Harold, *The Reichswehr and the German Republic 1919–1926*, Princeton, 1957.
This is the most thorough and balanced account of its subject, and is of great importance for an understanding of the problems which faced the Reichswehr under the Weimar governments.

GÖRLITZ, Walter, 'Die deutsche Militäropposition 1939–1945', in *Frankfurter Hefte*, Vol. IV, No. 3, 1949.
Hindenburg—ein Lebensbild, Bonn, 1953.
The German General Staff 1657–1945, New York, 1953.
Keitel—Verbrecher oder Offizier, Göttingen, 1961.
All of these works lack depth, rather than interest.

GROENER-GEYER, Dorothea, *General Groener—Soldat und Staatsmann*, Frankfurt, 1955.

GUMBRUCH, Wierner, 'Zur Gleichschaltung der bewaffneten Macht unter der Herrschaft des Nat onalsozialismus', in: *Wehrwissenschaftliche Rundschau*, 1958, pp. 81–92.

HALLGARTEN, George, *Hitler, Reichswehr und Industrie*, Frankfurt, 1955.

HAMMERSTEIN, Kunrat Freiherr von, 'Schleicher, Hammerstein und die Machtübernahme 1933', in *Frankfurter Hefte* 11, 1956.
This is a most interesting account, based on the writings of Generaloberst von Hammerstein after his retirement from command of the Army, and presented by his son.

HARSCH, Joseph C., *Pattern of Conquest*, New York, 1941.
This book, written in the opening stage of the war, is remarkable for its description of the strong points of Nazism, as well as of its weaknesses. The section on the Wehrmacht describes how the major problems in the minds of German officers were tactical, rather than political. It was written to shake the United States out of isolationism, and it presents its case convincingly without recourse to distortion.

HERZFELD, Hans, 'Zur neureren Literatur über das Heeresproblem in der deutschen Geschichte', in *Vierteljahrshefte für Zeitgeschichte*, 4, 1956.

HOSSBACH, Friedrich, *Die Entwicklung des Oberbefehls über das Heer in Brandenburg Preussen und im Deutschen Reich von 1655–1945*, Würzburg, 1957.

HUBER, E., *Heer und Staat in der deutschen Geschichte*, Hamburg, 1938.

HUNTINGTON, Samuel P., *The Soldier and the State*, Harvard, 1957.
An interesting theoretical analysis of political-military relations, based partly on Nazi Germany and Japan. Huntington draws the conclusion that the pursuit of professionalism will save an army from interference in politics. This seems inconsistent with the fate of the highly professional (as he admits) German Army.

Jahrbuch des deutschen Heeres, 1936, 1937, 1938, 1939, 1940, published at Leipzig in each following year on the authority of OKH.

JAKOB, Berthold, *Das neue deutsche Heer und seine Führer*, Paris, 1936.

JOST, Walter, *Die wehrpolitische Revolution des Nationalsozialismus, mit einem Geleitwort von Generaloberst von Blomberg*, Hamburg, 1936.

KANIS, I., *Waffen SS im Bild*, Göttingen, 1957.

KAYSER, Walther, *Die nationalpolitische Bedeutung der Wehrmacht*, Hamburg, 1937.

*KEILIG, Wolf, ed., *Das deutsche Heer 1939–1945—Gliederung, Einsatz, Stellenbesetzungen*, Bad Nauheim, 1957.
This work aims to gather together all available information on the composition and employment of, and the command and staff appointments in, the German Army during World War II. It is a single, comprehensive work, and likely to be surpassed only perhaps by the forthcoming work edited by Georg

Tessin—*Formationsgeschichte der deutschen Wehrmacht, 1939–1945*, which is due to appear in approximately twelve volumes in the next few years.

Das deutsche Heer is not yet complete, but many instalments have been issued, and the work forms an indispensable research tool particularly for investigating the organization of the Army and the careers of senior officers.

*KIELMANSEGG, Adolf Graf von, *Der Fritsch Prozess 1938*, Hamburg 1949.

The only full account of the Fritsch trial and its background. All other accounts appear to be derived from it. Unfortunately it is very deficient in foot-notes and has no index. The introductory chapter on Fritsch's life is the fullest and most penetrating biographical record which is available. It is a great pity that this has not been expanded since 1949.

KILIANI, Emanuel von, '1914 und 1939—die Einstellung der Obersten Führungs-schicht des deutschen Heeres zum Ausbruch beider Weltkriege', in *die Wehrkunde*, November and December 1964.

KOHN, Hans, *The Mind of Germany*, London, 1962.

KRAUSNICK, Helmut, 'Die Wehrmacht im Dritten Reich', in *Schicksalfragen der Gegenwart*, Tübingen, 1957.

KUHN, Otto, *Vom 100,000 Mann Heer zum Volksheer*, Cologne, 1937.

LEBER, Annedore, *Das Gewissen steht auf*, Berlin, 1954.

LIDDELL HART, Basil Sir, *The Other Side of the Hill*, London, 1948.

This work deals mainly with the Second World War, but there are interesting early chapters on the influence of Seeckt and containing brief biographies of the senior generals. The book was the first to take into account the views of the German officers as expressed by them.

LOHMANN, Heinz, *S.A. räumt auf! Aus der Kampfzeit der Bewegung. Aufzeichnungen*, Hamburg, 1933.

LOWIE, R. H., *Toward understanding Germany*, Chicago, 1954.

LUTZE, Viktor, *Wehrmacht und politisches Soldatentum*, Munich, 1937.

MANVELL, Roger, and FRAENKEL, Heinrich, *Hermann Göring*, London, 1962.

MARCKS, Erich, 'Das Reichsheer von 1919 bis 1935', in *Deutsche Heeresgeschichte*, issued by Karl Linnebach, Hamburg, 1935.

MAU, H., and KRAUSNICK, H., *Deutsche Geschichte der jüngsten Vergangenheit 1933–1945*, Stuttgart, 1961.

*MEINCK, Gerhard, *Hitler und die deutsche Aufrüstung 1933–1939*, Wiesbaden, 1959.

A most important work describing German rearmament and the relative roles of Hitler and the Army in determining the speed of the process. It also provides a valuable insight into the continuity of Hitler's plans for war.

'Der Reichsverteidigungsrat', in *Wehrwissenschaftliche Rundschau*, No. 6, 1956.

MEINECKE, Friedrich, *Die deutsche Katastrophe*, Zürich, 1946.

MENDELSSOHN, Peter de, *Die Nürnberger Dokumente*, Hamburg, 1947.

An interesting selection of IMT documents, linked by a commentary designed to show how Hitler planned aggression from 1937.

*MUELLER-HILLEBRAND, Burkhart, *Das Heer 1933–1945*, Darmstadt, 1954.

A statistical account of the growth of the German Army and of its changes in organization.

NAMIER, Sir Lewis, *In the Nazi Era*, London, 1952.

Die Nationalversammlung von Potsdam. Deutschlands grosse Tage 21–23 März, 1933, with supplements by Hans Wendt, Berlin, 1933.

OBERMANN, Emil, *Soldaten, Bürger, Militaristen. Militär und Demokratie in Deutsch-land*, Stuttgart, 1958.

PFIZER, Theodor, 'Die Brüder Stauffenberg', in Robert Böhringer, *Eine Freundesgabe*, Tübingen, 1957.

PINSON, Koppel S., *Modern Germany*, New York, 1954.

POLIAKOV, L., and WULF, J., *Das Dritte Reich und seine Diener*, Berlin, 1956.

POLLMÜLLER, I., 'Die Rolle der Reichswehr von 1918 bis 1933', in *Frankfurter Heeft*, December 1946.

RABENAU, Friedrich von, *Hans von Seeckt—Aus seinem Leben 1918–1936*, Leipzig, 1940.

REICHE, Helmut, *Wehrmacht und Bewegung*, Düsseldorf, 1937.

RITTER, Gerhard, *Carl Goerdeler und die deutsche Widerstandsbewegung*, Stuttgart, 1955. 'The Military and Politics in Germany', in *Journal of Central European Affairs*, No. XVII, October 1957.

*ROBERTSON, E. M., *Hitler's Pre-War Policy and Military Plans 1933–1939*, London, 1963.
    This is a useful description of some of Hitler's pre-war preparations and military policy. It is particularly good for events relating to the S.A., 1933–34, but scant use has been made of the masses of documents held by the U.S.A. and now returned to Germany and the book falls a little short of the claims of its title.

ROOS, H., 'Die Präventivkriegspläne Pilsudskis von 1933', in *Vierteljahrshefte für Zeitgeschichte*, No. 3, 1955.

ROSENBERGER, H., 'Die Entlassung des Generalobersten Freiherr von Fritsch', in *Deutsche Rundschau*, November 1946.

ROSINSKI, Herbert, *The German Army*, London, 1939.
    This book is very superficial, containing a high proportion of myths.

ROTHFELS, Hans, *Die deutsche Opposition gegen Hitler*, Frankfurt, 1960.

ROYCE, Hans, JACOBSEN, Hans-Adolf, and ZIMMERMANN, Erich, *20 Juli 1944*, Bonn, 1960.

S.A. Geist im Betrieb, issued by Oberste S.A. Führung, Munich, 1938.

*SAUER, Wolfgang, 'Die Mobilmachung der Gewalt', in K. D. Bracher et al., *Die Nationalsozialistische Machtergreifung*, Cologne and Opladen, 1962.
    This is the fullest account of the impact of the first two years of the Nazi régime upon the Army. It is accurate and extremely thorough. The sections on the development of Hitler's ideas on war and on Army-S.A. relations are excellent.

'Die Reichswehr', in K. D. Bracher, *Die Auflösung der Weimarer Republik*, Stuttgart, 1960.

'Armee und Politik in Deutschland', in *Neue Politische Literatur*, 4, 1959.

SCHLIEFFEN, Graf Alfred von, *Cannae*, Berlin, 1925.

SCHRAMM, Percy Ernst, *Hitler als militärischer Führer*, Bonn, 1962.

SCHRAMM, Wilhelm Ritter von, 'Das Politisch-militärische Testament des General-obersten Beck', *die Wehrkunde*, No. 7, 1959.

SCHÜDDEKOPF, Otto Ernst, *Das Heer und die Republik*, Frankfurt, 1955.

Schultheiss' Europäischer Geschichtskalendar 1934, Munich, 1935.

SCHWEITZER, Arthur, *Big Business in the Third Reich*, London, 1964.
    This book is better on the general economic topics than on military economic matters.

SEABURY, Paul, *The Wilhelmstrasse*, Berkeley, 1954.

SHIRER, William, *The Rise and Fall of the Third Reich*, London, 1962.

SNELL, John L., ed., *The Outbreak of the Second World War—Design or Blunder?* Boston, 1962.
    The Nazi Revolution—Germany's Guilt or Germany's Fate? Boston, 1959.

SNYDER, L. L., German Nationalism, Penn., 1952.

SPEIDEL, Hans, 'Ludwig Beck', in *Die Grossen Deutschen*, Berlin, 1957.

SPEIDEL, Helm, 'Reichswehr und Rote Armee', in *Vierteljahrshefte für Zeitgeschichte*, No. 1, 1953.

STADELMANN, Rudolf, *Scharnhorst—Schicksal und geistige Welt*, Wiesbaden, 1952.

TAYLOR, A. J. P., *The Course of German History*, London, 1945.
  The Origins of the Second World War, London, 1961.

TAYLOR, Telford, *Sword and Swastika—Generals and Nazis in the Third Reich*, New York, 1952.

*TESSIN, Georg, *Formationsgeschichte der Wehrmacht 1933–1939*, Schriften des Bundesarchivs, Band 7, Boppard/Rhein, 1959.
  An excellent, detailed account of the growth of the Wehrmacht.

THOMAS, Georg, 'Wehrwirtschaft' in *Die deutsche Wehrmacht 1914–1939, Rückblick und Ausblick*, ed. Georg Wetzell, Berlin, 1939.

THOMÉE, Gerhard, *Der Wiederaufstieg des deutschen Heeres 1918–1938*, Berlin, 1939.
  'Die Wehrmacht des Dritten Reiches', in *Die deutsche Soldatenkunde*, Leipzig, 1937.

The Times, 10 October 1934 and 28 August 1937.

VAGTS, Alfred, *A History of Militarism*, New York, 1937.
  Defence and Diplomacy. The Soldier and the Conduct of Foreign Relations, New York, 1957.

VIERECK, Peter, *Metapolitics—The Roots of the Nazi Mind*, New York, 1941.

VOGELSANG, Thilo, *Reichswehr, Staat und NSDAP*, Stuttgart, 1962.
  A most detailed account of the role of the Reichswehr in politics in the years immediately before Hitler's accession to power. It is an accurate and very well documented work.
  'Zur Politik Schleichers gegenüber der NSDAP 1932', in *Vierteljahrshefte für Zeitgeschichte*, No. 6, 1958.

VOLZ, Hans, *Die Geschichte der S.A. von den Anfängen bis zur Gegenwart*, Berlin, 1934.

WACKER, Wolfgang, *Der Bau des Panzerschiffs 'A' und der Reichstag*, Tübinger Studien zur Geschichte und Politik, Tübingen, 1959.
  Wehrgeist und Schule im Ausland, Hamburg, 1935.

Weissbuch über die Erschiessungen des 30. Juni 1934, Paris, 1935.
  This anonymous chronicle published by a group of leftist German political refugees in Paris in 1935 makes wild claims without any substantiating evidence and contains many errors of fact. It should be treated with the greatest reserve.

WHEELER-BENNETT, Sir John W., *The Nemesis of Power*, London, 1953.
  This is a valuable work covering the period 1918–45, and most facts of importance in German political-military relations in the period are to be found in it, particularly with reference to the bomb plot of 20 July 1944. It is consistently critical of the actions of the German officers, and at times is over-critical. The mid-'thirties receive brief treatment.
  Hindenburg—Wooden Titan, New York, 1936.
  Munich—Prologue to Tragedy, New York, 1964.

ZELLER, Eberhard, *Geist der Freiheit—der Zwanzigste Juli 1944*, Munich, 1954.

LIST OF PERSONS INTERVIEWED

The following persons have assisted the writer by granting interviews which have provided additional material for this book:

(a) *In Germany*

Dr Heinrich Bennecke
Grossadmiral a.D. Karl Dönitz
Generalleutnant a.D. Hermann Flörke
Vizeadmiral a.D. W. Fröhlich
Generaloberst a.D. Franz Halder
General der Artillerie a.D. Friedrich Hauck
Generaloberst a.D. Paul Hausser
Generaloberst a.D. Gotthard Heinrici
Generalmajor a.D. von Hellermann
Oberst i.G. Hans-Joachim Kraaz
Generalfeldmarschall a.D. Erich von Manstein
Frau Gertrud Neubaur-Beck
Konteradmiral a.D. J. von Puttkamer
Oberst a.D. Hans Refior
Generalmajor a.D. Frhr Ludwig Rudt von Collenberg
General a.D. Dr Hans Speidel
General der Infanterie a.D. Max von Viebahn

(b) *In England*

Captain Sir Basil Liddell Hart
General Sir Andrew Thorne
Sir John Wheeler-Bennett

Source Notes

1 For an excellent exposition of the military ethic, see Samuel P. Huntington, *The Soldier and the State*, Belknap, Harvard, 1957, Ch. 3.

2 J. W. Wheeler-Bennett, *The Nemesis of Power*, Macmillan, London, 1953, pp. 213–222; Thilo Vogelsang, *Reichswehr, Staat und NSDAP*, Deutsche Verlagsanstalt, Stuttgart, 1962, pp. 82–83; F. L. Carsten. *Reichswehr und Politik 1918–1933*, Cologne, 1964, pp. 341–347.

3 Wheeler-Bennett, *Nemesis*, p. 216.

4 G. A. Craig, *The Politics of the Prussian Army, 1640–1949*, Oxford, 1955, p. 441.

5 Wolfgang Sauer, 'Die Mobilmachung der Gewalt', p. 703, in K. D. Bracher, W. Sauer, G. Schulz, *Die Nationalsozialistische Machtergreifung*, Westdeutscher Verlag, Cologne and Opladen, 1962.

6 Wheeler-Bennett, *Nemesis*, p. 218, and *Frankfurter Zeitung*, 26 September 1930,

7 Hjalmar Schacht, *Account Settled*, London, 1949, pp. 209–210.

8 Erich von Manstein, *Aus einem Soldatenleben*, Athenäum Verlag, Bonn, 1958, p. 175, and conversations with Generalleutnant a.D. Hermann Flörke, February 1964.

9 Manstein, *op. cit.*, pp. 168–169.

10 Karl Demeter, *Das deutsche Offizierkorps in Gesellschaft und Staat, 1650–1945*, Bernard und Graefe, Frankfurt am Main, 1964, p. 56.

11 Manstein, *op. cit.*, p. 170.

12 Friedrich Meinecke, *Die deutsche Katastrophe*, Zürich, 1946, p. 69.

13 This view is based on conversations with General Dr. Hans Speidel, Generaloberst a.D. Gotthard Heinrici, Generaloberst a.D. Franz Halder, Generalfeldmarschall a.D. Erich von Manstein, Grossadmiral a.D. Karl Dönitz, February–April 1964.

14 OKH File H 24/6.

15 *Ibid.*

16 Vogelsang, *op. cit.*, p. 316.

17 *Ibid.*

18 For details of Pilsudski's plans, see Alfred Vagts, *Defence and Diplomacy—the Soldier and the Conduct of Foreign Relations*, Kings Crown Press, New York, 1957, p. 310. H. Roos, 'Die Präventivkriegspläne Pilsudskis von 1933', in *Vierteljahrshefte für Zeitgeschichte*, 3 (1955), pp. 344–363. Czech report from Warsaw of 10 March 1933, in *Europäische Politik im Spiegel der Prager Akten*, edited by Fritz Buber, Deutsches Institut für aussenpolitische Forschungen, Essen, 1942, p. 24. A most interesting resumé of Germany's strategic problems in the East is given in a letter written by Hitler on 2 December 1932, to Reichenau. See E. M. Robertson, *Hitler's Pre-War Plans and Military Policy*, Longmans, 1963, pp. 4–5. The full text of the letter has been published by Thilo Vogelsang in *Vierteljahrshefte für Zeitgeschichte*, October 1959.

19 *Vortragsnotiz des Oberstleutnant Ott für den Reichswehrminister von Schleicher*, Institut für Zeitgeschichte, Munich, F41, Band 4, fol. 142. Details of this conference and of its conclusions are also given in a letter by Generalleutnant a.D. Röhrricht to Captain B. H. Liddell Hart, of November 1945. This letter is in the possession of Sir Basil Liddell Hart. Röhrricht was a Hauptmann in the Ministeramt, directly under Schleicher, and was later in charge of the Reichswehr Presseabteilung, where he prepared speeches for Schleicher, Hindenburg and Blomberg. However, in this letter, Röhrricht gives the wrong date for this conference, viz. 20 November 1932. The actual orders for the calling of the conference, contained in OKH File H 24/6, show that the dates of the conference were 25 and 26 November. Institut für Zeitgeschichte *Zeugenschrifttum Nr.* 279 contains Ott's account of the conclusions reached at the Planspiel itself. From henceforward, these documents will be referred to by the '*Zeugenschrifttum Nr.* . . . .'.

20 OKH File H 24/74.

21 *Ibid.*

22 OKH File H 24/6.

23 Few men knew Hammerstein better than Field-Marshal von Manstein, who described Hammerstein as one of the cleverest men whom he had ever met. Manstein had served in the same Regiment as Hammerstein, the Dritte Garderegiment zu Fuss. This was also the Regiment of Hindenburg and Schleicher, and was one of the most celebrated of the Prussian Guards Regiments. From 1929 to 1931, Manstein had worked under Hammerstein as Head of the Employment of Units Section of the Operations Branch (Abteilung T1) of the General Staff. Manstein, *op. cit.*, p. 108. One of Hammerstein's favourite sayings was 'Vorschriften sind für die Dummen', or, 'Rules are for the stupid'. Manstein, *op. cit.*, p. 109.

24 Generaloberst a.D. Gotthard Heinrici relates a typical incident from the year 1929, when he was a Major in the Mobilization Office of the High Command, under Oberstleutnant Wilhelm Keitel. It was urgently necessary at one stage for Hammerstein to give a decision on the composition of the Army after mobilization. It was several weeks before Hammerstein was able to spare the time from his hunting to deal with the matter. In the meantime, the planners had to make their own decision. Conversation with Generaloberst a.D. Heinrici, 12 March 1964.

25 Wheeler-Bennett, *Nemesis*, pp. 224–225.

26 *Ibid.*

27 Wheeler-Bennett, *Nemesis*, p. 279.

28 Vogelsang, *op. cit.*, p. 378.

29 Vogelsang, *op. cit.*, p. 375.

30 Vogelsang, *op. cit.*, p. 387.

31 Vogelsang, *op. cit.*, p. 375.

32 *Ibid.*

33 Vogelsang, *op. cit.*, p. 387.

34 Franz von Papen, *Memoirs*, André Deutsch, London, 1952, p. 240.

35 *Ibid.*

36 Vogelsang, *op. cit.*, p. 387.

37 Vogelsang, *op. cit.*, pp. 388–389.

38 *Ibid.*, and *Zeugenschrifttum Nr.* 217, for the personal account of General Bussche, written after the war.

39 Vogelsang, *op. cit.*, p. 396.

40 Wheeler-Bennett, *Nemesis*, p. 282.

41 Vogelsang, *op. cit.*, p. 393. The details regarding the following events of 29 January 1933 are set out in detail in Vogelsang, *op. cit.*, pp. 393–396.

42 Wheeler-Bennett, *Nemesis*, p. 282.

43 Wheeler-Bennett, *Nemesis*, p. 283.

44 Vogelsang, *op. cit.*, pp. 394–395.

45 Vogelsang, *op. cit.*, pp. 378–379, and D. Mende, *Die Geburt des Dritten Reiches*, Institut für Zeitgeschichte manuscript, p. 2.

46 Wheeler-Bennett, *Nemesis*, p. 285.

47 Craig, *op. cit.*, pp. 466–467.

48 Gerhard Ritter, 'The Military and Politics in Germany', *Journal of Central European Affairs*, XVII (October 1957), pp. 259–270.

49 Wheeler-Bennett, *Nemesis*, p. 285.

50 See Alan Bullock, *Hitler—a Study in Tyranny*, Penguin, 1962, Ch. 7, pp. 372–410, 568–569, 668, 670–673, 676–677, 705–707, and Friedrich Hossbach, *Zwischen Wehrmacht und Hitler*, Wolfenbüttler Verlag, Hanover, 1949, pp. 19–36, 44–50.

51 Hossbach, *op. cit.*, pp. 34–35, 134–135.

52 Hossbach, *op. cit.*, p. 19.

53 Hossbach, *op. cit.*, p. 20.

54 Hossbach, *op. cit.*, p. 24.

55 Hossbach, *op. cit.*, p. 46.

56 Hossbach, *op. cit.*, p. 45.

57 *Ibid.*

58 *Ibid.*
59 *Ibid.*
60 Hossbach, *op. cit.*, p. 50.
61 Hossbach, *op. cit.*, p. 47.
62 Vogelsang, *op. cit.*, p. 387, and Manstein, *op. cit.*, p. 172.
63 Wheeler-Bennett, *Nemesis*, p. 297.
64 Manstein, *op. cit.*, pp. 172–173. Wheeler Bennett, *Nemesis*, p. 298, and a memorandum written by General der Infanterie Günther Blumentritt, for Allied Interrogation Officers, during his captivity, 1946. Blumentritt was a G.S.O.1 to Reichenau in Wehrkreis VII, Munich, in 1936. A copy of this memorandum is in the possession of Sir Basil Liddell Hart.
65 See above, Chapter 1, p. 9.
66 Vogelsang, *op. cit.*, p. 387.
67 John Erickson, *The Soviet High Command, 1918–1941*, Macmillan, London, 1962, p. 258.
68 Wheeler-Bennett, *Nemesis*, p. 296.
69 Craig, *op. cit.*, p. 441.
70 Hossbach, *op. cit.*, p. 109.
71 Conversations with: Field-Marshal von Manstein, March 1964, General Sir Andrew Thorne, former British Military Attaché, Berlin, 1932–35, January 1965, Captain Sir Basil Liddell Hart, September 1964. Although Hossbach, *op. cit.*, p. 131, mentions that Blomberg was peculiarly calm at his final interview with Hitler on 27 January 1938.
72 Memoirs of Field-Marshal Maximilian Freiherr von Weichs, Bundesarchiv, Koblenz, File H 08–19/5.
73 Hossbach, *op. cit.*, p. 22.
74 Generaloberst Werner Freiherr von Fritsch in a memorandum written on 1 February 1938. Beck Papers, Bundesarchiv, File H 08–28/3.
75 Hossbach, *op. cit.*, p. 77.
76 Burkhart Mueller-Hillebrand, *Das Heer, 1933–1945*, E. S. Mittler und Sohn, Darmstadt, 1954, p. 77.
77 Manstein, *op. cit.*, pp. 172–173. Wheeler-Bennett, *Nemesis*, p. 298.
78 Robertson, *op. cit.*, pp. 4–5.
79 Wheeler-Bennett, *Nemesis*, p. 298.
80 Heinz Guderian, *Panzer Leader*, Michael Joseph, London, 1952, p. 29.
81 Blumentritt, *op. cit.*
82 Conversations with Generaloberst Heinrici, March 1964, and Generalleutnant Flörke, February 1964.
83 William Shirer, *The Rise and Fall of the Third Reich*, Reprint Society Limited, London, 1962, p. 335.
84 Blumentritt, *op. cit.* See Hermann Foertsch, *Schuld und Verhängnis*, Deutsche Verlags Anstalt, Stuttgart, 1951, p. 33, and Walter Warlimont, *Inside Hitler's Headquarters*, Weidenfeld and Nicolson, London, 1964, p. 59.
85 Blumentritt, *op. cit.*, and Interrogation Record, Oberst von Lindeiner, Grizedale Camp, 1945. A copy of this record is in the possession of Sir Basil Liddell Hart. Lindeiner had been one of Reichenau's Staff Officers from 1937–1939.
86 See note 84 above.
87 Robertson, *op. cit.*, pp. 4–5.
88 *Ibid.*
89 The full text of this letter is published by Thilo Vogelsang in *Vierteljahrshefte für Zeitgeschichte*, October 1959.
90 Fritsch, *op. cit.*
91 Wheeler-Bennett, *Nemesis*, p. 300.
92 *Ibid.*
93 Gerhard Meinck, 'Der Reichsverteidigungsrat', in *Wehrwissenschaftliche Rundschau*, 6 (1956), p. 411 *et seq.*
94 Wheeler-Bennett, *Nemesis*, pp. 753–754.
95 The details of these moves are given by Weichs, *op. cit.*

96 Ludwig Beck, *Studien*, ed. by General Dr Hans Speidel, K. F. Koehler Verlag, Stuttgart, 1955, p. 18.

97 The information on Generaloberst Ludwig Beck stems chiefly from documents and photographs belonging to his daughter, Frau Gertrud Neubaur, and from conversations with Frau Neubaur in March 1964. Other supplementary information was provided by conversations with General der Infanterie Max von Viebahn, February and March 1964, who had known Beck from his youth, served with him during the First World War, and remained a close friend until Beck's death in 1944. I am also grateful to Dr Max Rehm of Nürtingen, for a private memorandum on Beck, and to General Sir Andrew Thorne, Military Attaché, Berlin, 1932–35, for his recollections of Beck's personality.

The best description of Beck's characters are presented in two studies by General Dr Hans Speidel. One of these is the foreword to his collection of the strategic writings of Beck—Ludwig Beck, *Studien*. The other is in *Die Grossen Deutschen*, Propyläen Verlag, Berlin, 1957, Vol. 4, p. 564.

The following also contain useful information:

Wheeler-Bennett, *Nemesis*, pp. 391–394.

Eberhard Zeller, *Geist der Freiheit—der Zwanzigste Juli*, Verlag Hermann Rinn, Munich, 1954.

Hans Royce, Erich Zimmermann, Hans-Adolf Jacobsen, *20 Juli 1944*, Bundes Zentral für Heimatdienst, Berto Verlag, Bonn, 1960.

Annedore Leber, *Das Gewissen Steht Auf*, Mosaik Verlag, Berlin, 1954, pp. 152 fol.

Hans Rothfels, *Die Deutsche Opposition gegen Hitler*, Fischer Bücherei, Frankfurt am Main, 1960.

Wolfgang Förster, *Generaloberst Ludwig Beck—Sein Kampf gegen den Krieg*, Isar Verlag, Munich, 1953.

Manstein, *op. cit.*

Gerhard Ritter, *Carl Goerdeler und die deutsche Widerstandsbewegung*, Deutsche Verlags Anstalt, Stuttgart, 1955.

Eduard Spranger, 'Generaloberst Beck in der Mittwochgesellschaft', *Universitas*, 1956, Heft 2, pp. 183 fol.

Paul Fechter, *Menschen und Zeiten—Begegnungen aus fünf Jahrzehnten*, Bertelsmann Verlag, Gütersloh, 1949, pp. 395 fol.

Rudolf Stadelmann, *Scharnhorst—Schicksal und geistige Welt*, Limes Verlag, Wiesbaden, 1952.

Walter Görlitz, 'Die deutsche Militäropposition 1939–1945', *Frankfurter Hefte*, Vol. IV, 3, 1949.

Theodor Pfizer, 'Die Brüder Stauffenberg', in Robert Böhringer, *Eine Freundesgabe*, J. C. B. Mohr, Tübingen, 1957, pp. 487 fol.

98 The *Mittwochgesellschaft* was a circle of intellectuals, founded in 1863, which met every Wednesday in Berlin to discuss cultural, political and scientific problems.

The other members in Beck's time were:

Albrecht Penck, Geographer
Hans Lietzmann, Theologian
Ferdinand Sauerbruch, Surgeon
Hermann Oncken, Historian
Wilhelm Pinder, Art Historian
Ludwig Diels, Botanist
Eugen Fischer, Biologist
Eduard Spranger, Philosopher
Ulrich Wilcken, Classical Historian
Julius Petersen, Professor of German
Ulrich von Hassell, Diplomat
Jens Jessen, Economic Historian
Werner Heisenberg, Physicist
Johannes Popitz, Economist

Paul Fechter, Writer
Hans Heinrich Schaeder
Wolfgang Schadewalt
Johannes Stroux.
The circle developed into an opposition group to the Nazis, and was active in preparing plans for the restoration of a democratic government in Germany. See Gert Buchheit, *Ludwig Beck*, List Verlag, Munich, 1964, pp. 238-248.

99 Guderian, *op. cit.*, p. 32.

100 Manstein, *op. cit.*, p. 241.

101 Conversation with General der Infanterie von Viebahn, February 1964.

102 Wheeler-Bennett, *Nemesis*, p. 300.

103 *Ibid.*

104 The details of the reactions of Hindenburg are from Papen, *op. cit.*, p. 288.

105 *Ibid.*

106 Harold Gordon, *The Reichswehr and the German Republic 1919-1926*, Princeton, 1957, pp. 164-165.

107 *Wehrgesetz* of June 1923. Friedrich von Rabenau, *Hans von Seeckt, Aus seinem Leben 1918-1936*, Verlag von Hase und Koehler, Leipzig, 1940, pp. 472-473.

108 Papen, *op. cit.*, p. 288.

109 *Daily Mail* of 29 December 1933.

110 Hossbach, *op. cit.*, p. 73.

111 Adolf Graf von Kielmansegg, *Der Fritsch Prozess 1938*, Hoffmann und Campe Verlag, Hamburg, 1949, p. 26.

112 Kielmansegg, *op. cit.*, pp. 24-26.

113 *Ibid.*

114 Fritsch, *op. cit.*

115 *Ibid.*

116 *Ibid.*

117 For various estimates of Fritsch see: Wheeler-Bennett, *Nemesis*, pp. 301-304, 358-359. Hossbach, *op. cit.*, pp. 73, 103-109, 140-141. Wolfgang Sauer in *Die Nationalsozialistische Machtergreifung*, by Karl Dietrich Bracher, Wolfgang Sauer, Gerhard Schulz, West Deutscher Verlag, Cologne, 1962, pp. 735-737, 920. Papen, *op. cit.*, pp. 240, 288. Guderian, *op. cit.*, pp. 31-32. Waldemar Erfurth, *Die Geschichte des deutschen Generalstabes 1918-1945*, Musterschmidt Verlag, Göttingen, 1957, pp. 151-152. Shirer, *op. cit.*, pp. 215, 315. Gert Buchheit, *Ludwig Beck*, p. 40, and *Soldatentum und Rebellion*, Grote Verlag, Rastatt/Baden, 1961, pp. 6, 7, 16-18. Walter Görlitz, *The German General Staff 1657-1945*, Praeger, New York, 1953, pp. 282-283. Craig, *op. cit.*, pp. 473-474, 484-487. Liddell Hart, *The Other Side of the Hill*, Cassell, London, 1948, pp. 27-30 (Panther Edition). These references all give brief pictures of a few pages in length, although their content varies considerably. There is only one reasonably full attempt to treat the character of Fritsch, viz. Kielmansegg, *op. cit.* My treatment of Fritsch has drawn heavily on this account. I have attempted to supply some new information based on conversations with men who knew Fritsch personally, while treating material which has been published as briefly as possible. One of the greatest handicaps is Fritsch's aversion to writing anything about himself. What few papers he did leave behind fell mostly into the hands of the Gestapo, or were destroyed. Before his death, he left a considerable amount of his papers with a friend, but they were discovered by the Gestapo in 1945, and so they were lost to the future. After his death, his house at Achterburg was ransacked by the Gestapo, who confiscated whatever they found. The most significant remnants are those of his letters in the possession of the Bundesarchiv, Koblenz, and the copies of his letters to Baroness von Schutzbar-Milchling held by St. Antony's College, Oxford.

118 Kielmansegg, *op. cit.*, p. 19.

119 *Ibid.*

120 Kielmansegg, *op. cit.*, p. 20.

121 Wheeler-Bennett, *Nemesis*, pp. 301-302.

122 Letter written by Fritsch to Major Hagemann, 31 August 1919, part of which is quoted in Kielmansegg, *op. cit.*, pp. 21–22.
123 Memorandum written by Fritsch, 28 March 1920, part of which is reproduced in Kielmansegg, *op. cit.*, p. 22.
124 Hossbach, *op. cit.*, p. 53.
125 Kielmansegg, *op. cit.*, p. 23.
126 Kielmansegg, *op. cit.*, p. 24.
127 *Ibid.*
128 Guderian, *op. cit.*, pp. 31–32.
129 Kielmansegg, *op. cit.*, pp. 16–17.
130 Kielmansegg, *op. cit.*, p. 17.
131 Conversations with: Field Marshal von Manstein, March 1964; Generaloberst Halder, March 1964; Frau Gertrud Neubaur, March 1964; General Sir Andrew Thorne, January 1965.
132 Kielmansegg, *op. cit.*, p. 18.
133 Weichs, *op. cit.*
134 *Ibid.*
135 Kielmansegg, *op. cit.*, pp. 22 and 119.
136 Kielmansegg, *op. cit.*, p. 27. Fritsch wrote this on 17 May 1937.
137 Conversation with Generaloberst Heinrici, February 1964.
138 Shirer, *op. cit.*, p. 315. Shirer was standing next to Fritsch at this parade.
139 Kielmansegg, *op. cit.*, pp. 12, 34.
140 Hossbach, *op. cit.*, pp. 107–108.
141 *Ibid.*
142 *Ibid.*
143 *Ibid.*
144 *Ibid.*
145 *Ibid.*
146 Wolfgang Förster, *Ein General kämpft gegen den Krieg*, Münchener Dom Ver,lag Munich, 1949, p. 21.
147 Hossbach, *op. cit.*, p. 144.
148 Hossbach, *op. cit.*, pp. 107–108.
149 Fritsch letter, 1 February 1938.
150 *Ibid.*
151 Weichs, *op. cit.*
152 Conversations with General der Infanterie Max von Viebahn, February 1964.
153 OKW file H 24/6. Other committee members were: Generalleutnant Ritter von Leeb, Generalleutnant von Bock, Oberstleutnant Busch.
154 Förster, *op. cit.*, p. 20.
155 Conversation with Frau Gertrud Neubaur, March 1964.
156 Hossbach, *op. cit.*, pp. 99–107.
157 *Ibid.*
158 Fritsch letter of 1 February 1938.
159 Conversation with Frau Neubaur, March 1964.
160 The S.A. had 300,000 troops. Heinrich Bennecke, *Hitler und die S.A.*, Günter Olzog Verlag, Munich, 1962, p. 213.
161 Craig, *op. cit.*, p. 441. Bennecke, *Hitler und die S.A.*, p. 158.
162 Photographs of this type of support are in the possession of Generalleutnant Hermann Flörke, and were examined by the writer in Jan.–Feb. 1964, and Dec. 1964–Jan. 1965.
163 Robertson, *op. cit.*, p. 29.
164 *Ibid.*
165 *Ibid.*
166 *Ibid.*
167 *Ibid.*
168 *Ibid.*
169 OKH file H 24/6.
170 Shirer, *op. cit.*, p. 252.

171 Sauer, *op. cit.*, p. 887. Hitler was also present on 1 July.
172 *Wichtige Politische Verfügungen des Reichswehrministers*, WK VII file 2306.
173 Sauer, *op. cit.*, p. 886.
174 Sauer, *op. cit.*, p. 889. The speeches in which Hitler made direct reference to the superiority of the Army in defence matters included: at Kiel, to S.A. leaders, 7 May 1933, in the Reichstag, 17 May 1933, at Bad Reichenhall, to the S.A., 1 July 1933, at Bad Godesburg, to the S.A., 19 August 1933, and on the radio, 14 October 1933, on the withdrawal of Germany from the League of Nations.
175 Heinrich Bennecke, *Die Reichswehr und der Röhm-Putsch*, Beiheft 2 der *Zweimonatsschrift Politische Studien*, Günter Olzog Verlag, Munich, 1964, p. 27. Dr Bennecke, former Obergruppenführer of the S.A., was at that time directly under Krüger, as chief of the Reichs S.A. Hochschulamt. Much of the information given concerning the youth movements and the S.A.-Army co-operation was confirmed by Dr Bennecke in conversation with the writer, February 1964.
176 Bennecke, *Die Reichswehr und der Röhm-Putsch*, p. 27.
177 *Ibid.*
178 Supplement to *Verordnung über die Ergänzung des Heeres*, issued in August 1933. Sauer, *op. cit.*, p. 918.
179 Hermann Foertsch, *Schuld und Verhängnis*, Deutsche Verlags Anstalt, Stuttgart, 1951, p. 46.
180 *Ibid.*
181 *Ibid.*
182 Wheeler-Bennett, *Nemesis*, pp. 307–308.
183 For Krüger's position in these affairs, see Bennecke, *Die Reichswehr und der Röhm-Putsch*, pp. 26–29, Robertson, *op. cit.*, p. 29.
184 Wheeler-Bennett, *Nemesis*, p. 308.
185 WK VII file 759.
186 OKH file H 24/6.
187 *Militär-Wochenblatt* of 4 October 1933, para. 426, and Sauer, *op. cit.*, p. 917.
188 OKH file H 24/6.
189 *Zeugenschrifttum Gaertner Nr.* 44, p. 5, and Sauer, *op. cit.*, p. 890.
190 Wheeler-Bennett, *Nemesis*, pp. 308–309.
191 I.M.T., Vol. XLII, p. 214, and Sauer, *op. cit.*, p. 892.
192 Robertson, *op. cit.*, p. 29.
193 WK VII file 2306.
194 *Zeugenschrifttum Gaertner Nr.* 44, p. 4, and Sauer, *op. cit.*, p. 885.
195 Liebmann *Notizen*, Institut für Zeitgeschichte, Munich, p. 59. These notes were written for a Wehrkreis conference of 15–18 January 1934.
196 *Ibid.*, and Sauer, *op. cit.*, p. 941.
197 These negotiations were carried out by Oberstleutnant (later General) Stapf, Deputy Chief of the *Organisations-Abteilung*. *Zeugenschrifttum Stapf, Nr.* 152, p. 1.
198 Sauer, *op. cit.*, p. 941.
199 Wheeler-Bennett, *Nemesis*, p. 761.
200 Liebmann, *op. cit.*, p. 67.
201 *Ibid.*
202 *Ibid.*
203 Liebmann, *op. cit.*, p. 68.
204 Weichs, *op. cit.*
205 WK VII file 2306.
206 Manstein, *op. cit.*, pp. 209–210.
207 *Ibid.*
208 Wheeler-Bennett, *Nemesis*, p. 309.
209 Wheeler-Bennett, *Nemesis*, p. 311, and Robertson, *op. cit.*, p. 30.
210 WK VII file 2306.
211 Graf von Schlieffen, *Cannae*, Berlin, 1925, p. XIII.
212 Weichs, *op. cit.*

213 As confirmed by Weichs, *op. cit.*, and by conversations with Field-Marshal von Manstein and Generaloberst Heinrici, February and March 1964.
214 Sauer, *op. cit.*, p. 949.
215 Robertson, *op. cit.*, p. 31.
216 WK VII file 760.
217 Robertson, *op. cit.*, p. 31.
218 Liebmann, *op. cit.*, p. 79.
219 *Haushalt der S.A.*, held by the Militärgeschichtliches Forschungsamt, Freiburg im Br.
220 Weichs, *op. cit.*
221 OKH file H 24/6.
222 I have found this order only in the files of units within WK VII. Presumably it was a local order, the product of the tenseness in Munich. There is no mention in the heading of the order that it came from a higher authority. WK VII file 741.
223 Sauer, *op. cit.*, p. 951. This conference was also described to the writer by Generaloberst Heinrici, February 1964, and Konteradmiral von Puttkamer, March 1964, who were two of the participants.
224 WK VII file 2306.
225 Sauer, *op. cit.*, p. 952.
226 Sauer, *op. cit.*, p. 951.
227 Evidence of S.S. Obergruppenführer Wolff, Adjutant to Himmler, Sauer, *op. cit.*, p. 951.
228 Foertsch, *op. cit.*, p. 53.
229 *Ibid.*
230 OKH file H 24/6.
231 Guderian, *op. cit.*, p. 33.
232 Wheeler-Bennett, *Nemesis*, p. 319.
233 Sauer, *op. cit.*, p. 955.
234 *Ibid.*
235 Sauer, *op. cit.*, p. 956.
236 *Ibid.*
237 *Ibid.*
238 WK VII file 1652.
239 Heinrici, *op. cit.*, p. 166. Minutes of a conference held by Fromm, Head of the General Army Office, undated, but deducible to 24–25 June 1934.
240 Sauer, *op. cit.*, p. 958.
241 *Ibid.*
242 *Ibid.*
243 Sauer, *op. cit.*, pp. 956–957.
244 Instruction of the Commandant of the Bendler Block, Dr Grobbels. OKH file H 24/6.
245 WK VII file 1652.
246 *Zeugenschrifttum Mellenthin, Nr.* 105, p. 36.
247 *Ibid.*
248 *Völkischer Beobachter*, 29 June 1934, and Foertsch, *op. cit.*, p. 54.
249 WK VII file 1652.
250 Report of S.A. man Gerheuser, member of an S.A. machine-gun company. WK VII file 1652.
251 Affidavit of Ewald von Kleist, given at Nuremberg, and reproduced by Bennecke in *Die Reichswehr und der Röhm-Putsch*, Appendix Four.
252 Sauer, *op. cit.*, pp. 955–958.
253 Written statement of Arno Moysischewitz, written in Berlin, 1935, and now with the Schleicher papers, Bundesarchiv, file H 08-42/92.
254 Statement of Marie Guntel, quoted by Hans Berndorff, in *General zwischen Ost und West*, Hamburg, 1951, pp. 306–309, 314–315. A different time for Schleicher's death was given to Sir John Wheeler-Bennett by Major von Goldammer, who stated that he telephoned Schleicher between 9 and 10 a.m. While they were conversing, Schleicher was interrupted. Goldammer then

heard sounds like shots and then the line went silent. See Wheeler-Bennett, *Nemesis*, p. 323.

255 WK VII file 1652.
256 *Ibid.*
257 *Ibid.*
258 *Ibid.*
259 *Ibid.*
260 *Ibid.*
261 Report of a participant to the writer. The participant prefers to remain anonymous.
262 Hossbach, *op. cit.*, p. 70.
263 WK VII file 1652.
264 *Ibid.*
265 *Ibid.*
266 Conversations with many witnesses in the larger cities, January–May 1964.
267 Heinrici, *op. cit.*, p. 168.
268 Bennecke, *Die Reichswehr und der Röhm-Putsch*, pp. 87–88.
269 Conversation with Frau Gertrud Neubaur, March, 1964.
270 Wheeler-Bennett, *Nemesis*, pp. 328–331.
271 Correspondence contained in OKW file 867.
272 WK VII file 1652.
273 *Ibid.*
274 WK VII file 2306 and OKH file 867.
275 *Das Archiv*, 10 July 1934, p. 516.
276 *Völkischer Beobachter*, 14 July 1934, and Foertsch, *op. cit.*, p. 61.
277 Bennecke, *Die Reichswehr und der Röhm-Putsch*, p. 77.
278 Manstein, *op. cit.*, p. 194.
279 Berndorff, *op. cit.*, p. 310.
280 Conversations with Generalleutnant Flörke, February 1964, and General Dr Speidel, January 1964.
281 The documents associated with this case are to be found in OKH file H 24/6.
282 Wheeler-Bennett, *Nemesis*, p. 329.
283 Wheeler-Bennett, *Nemesis*, pp. 335–337.
284 Wheeler-Bennett, *Nemesis*, pp. 337. This account was given by an officer who was present at the conference. No official record was made.
285 The documents relating to this case are to be found in OKH file H 24/6.
286 The Schleicher Papers, Bundesarchiv file Ho 8–42/88.
287 Conversation with Generaloberst Franz Halder, March 1964.
288 Robertson, *op. cit.*, pp. 53–56.
289 Buchheit, *Soldatentum und Rebellion*, p. 41.
290 *Ibid.*
291 Buchheit, *Beck*, p. 46.
292 Buchheit, *Soldatentum und Rebellion*, p. 42.
293 Wheeler-Bennett, *Nemesis*, p. 332.
294 Hossbach, *op. cit.*, p. 12.
295 Hossbach, *op. cit.*, p. 13.
296 *Ibid.*
297 *Befehlsverhältnisse, Vorgesetzten und Rangverhältnisse, Reichswehr Ministerium—Infanterie Abteilung, 1925–1935*, p. 55. Militärgeschichtliches Forschungsamt, Freiburg im Br. File No. II H 252.
298 Wheeler-Bennett, *Wooden Titan*, Morrow, New York, 1936, p. 472.
299 Wheeler-Bennett, *Wooden Titan*, p. 475.
300 Generaloberst Walter Warlimont, *Der Deutsche Generalstab*, memorandum written by Warlimont while he was in American hands after the War.
301 Foertsch, *op. cit.*, p. 67.
302 These details were taken from the Weichs Memoirs. Weichs was the senior Army officer in Nuremberg from 1937 to 1939, and has recorded a great deal about the Party Rallies in his memoirs. He relates that his position was far from that of a

Commanding General—it was 'a cross between a film producer and a drill sergeant'. Fortunately the files of Wehrkreis XIII (Nuremberg-Fürth) dealing with the Party Rallies have survived. Full details are given in the following:

WK XIII file '*Reichparteitag* 1935',
" " " 1936,
" " " 1937,
" " " 1938.

Militärgeschichtliches Forschungsamt, Freiburg im Br.

303 Weichs, *op. cit.*
304 Bullock, *op. cit.*, pp. 50–56.
305 Adolf Hitler, *Mein Kampf*, Munich, 1933, p. 476.
306 *Militär Wochenblatt* of 18 April 1934, p. 1299. Sauer, *op. cit.*, p. 915.
307 Weichs, *op. cit.*
308 For an interesting account of this side of Blomberg's personality, see Sir Basil Liddell Hart, *Memoirs*, Cassell, London, 1965, Vol. I, pp. 200–203.
309 WK VII file 2306.
310 *Militärgeschichtliches Forschungsamt* (hereafter MGFA), file II L 51/7, pp. 128–131.
311 For examples of Fritsch's directives, see his order of 21 December 1934, OKH file H 24/6, and his order of 13 April, MGFA III H 287, pp. 4–5.
312 Fritsch memorandum of 1 February 1938.
313 MGFA file H 7/30.
314 See WK VII file 335 for Brauchitsch's speech to the Party leaders at the Ordensburg Sonthofen on 26 March 1939, and also MGFA file H 7/30 for several other examples.
315 OKH file H. 24/6.
316 WK VII file 2306.
317 *Ibid.*
318 *Ibid.*
319 *Ibid.*
320 Instruction of Generalkommando 3, Dresden, to 10 Division, Regensburg, and passed on by 10 Division to units under command on 19 December 1936. WK XIII file 16.
321 Order signed by Keitel, 15 December 1937, WK XIII file 289.
322 WK XII file 15C.
323 WK VII file 2306.
324 *Ibid.*
325 *Ibid.*
326 *Ibid.*
327 Speech by Blomberg before officials of the N.S.D.A.P at the Ordensburg Vogelsang, 27 April 1937. MGFA file II W 22.
328 *Ibid.*
329 WK XIII file 289—order of General Reichenau, Commander of Wehrkreis VII, 30 June 1937. (When Wehrkreis XIII was formed at Nuremberg, on 1 October 1937, all earlier documents were kept in files labelled WK XIII, whether they had been issued by WK XIII, or by the former administrating headquarters, WK VII.)
330 *Ibid.*
331 WK XIII file 184—Order of the Day of 17 Division, 10 March 1939.
332 WK VII file 2306.
333 OKH file H 24/6.
334 *Ibid.*
335 *Ibid.*
336 Reichswehr Ministry directive on Army Public Relations, 8 June 1935, in WK VII file 2306.
337 WK IX file 137.
338 *Wichtige Politische Verfügung* (hereafter WPV) of 16 December 1933, WK VII file 2306.

339 Minutes of a conference in the Headquarters of Artillerie Führer VII, Munich, 19 November 1934, conducted by Oberstleutnant Körbitz. WK VII file 2306.
340 WPV of 29 April 1936, WK VII file 2306.
341 OKW Memorandum of 13 October 1938, OKH file H 24/40.
342 WK VII file 2306.
343 Demeter, *op. cit.*, p. 199.
344 *Ibid.*
345 WK VII file 2306.
346 *Ibid.*
347 *Ibid.*
348 *Ibid.*
349 *Ibid.*
350 See WK IX file 9 (Dollmann was Commander of WK IX).
351 Letter of Keitel to Dollmann, 19 February 1936. WK IX file 9.
352 These notes occur in WK IX file 9, between the documents dated 25 January 1938 and 12 November 1936.
353 Demeter, *op. cit.*, p. 200.
354 These were circulated by the Commander of 10 Division to units under his command on 19 December 1936. They are to be found in WK XIII file 16.
355 WK IX file 9.
356 See, for example, the contents of OKW file 848 and OKH file H 24/6. This latter file also contains the records of Beck's efforts to find positions for Jewish soldiers with the mission in China.
357 MGFA file H 24/88A.
358 WK IX file 134.
359 WK VII file 2306.
360 Order No. 364 in *Heeres Verordnungsblatt, Nr.* 13 of 1936, p. 121, in OKH file H 24/35.
361 WK XIII file 924.
362 WK VII file 2196.
363 *Ibid.*
364 WK VII file 2306.
365 *Ibid.*
366 WK XIII file 16.
367 *Ibid.*
368 WK VII file 2196.
369 Order of Fritsch of 18 June 1936, WK IX file 134.
370 WPV of 26 May 1936, WK VII file 2306.
371 Order of Blomberg of 28 September 1936, WK XIII file 289.
372 WK IX file 137.
373 Order of the Commander, 7 Division, Munich, of 5 July 1937, WK VII file 1652.
374 WK VII file 1652.
375 WK VII file 2306.
376 Correspondence of WK II to Blomberg of 7 October 1935, OKW file 848.
377 Letter from Blomberg to Hess, 12 October 1935, OKW file 848.
378 Foertsch, *op. cit.*, p. 71. Hossbach, *op. cit.*, p. 53.
379 WK XII file 15/C.
380 Kielmansegg, *op. cit.*, p. 34.
381 WK XIII file 184.
382 Erickson, *op. cit.*, pp. 26–27.
383 F. P. Walters, *A History of the League of Nations*, Oxford University Press, 1960, p. 515.
384 G. Meinck, *Hitler und die deutsche Aufrüstung, 1933–1939*, Wiesbaden, 1959, pp. 86–88.
385 *Ibid.*
386 *Ibid.*
387 *Ibid.*
388 *Ibid.*

389 Weichs, *op. cit.*
390 Meinck, *Hitler, etc.*, p. 87.
391 See above, p. 41. Robertson, *op. cit.*, p. 30, and DBFP (second series), Vol. II, doc. No. 206.
392 Liebmann, *op. cit.*, p. 61.
393 WK VII file 1320. 7 Division was asked to provide 726 N.C.O.s and men.
394 Conversation with Generaloberst Halder, March 1964.
395 Meinck, *Hitler, etc.*, p. 88.
396 *Ibid.*
397 G. Tessin, *Formationsgeschichte der Wehrmacht 1933–1939*, Boppard am Rhein 1959, pp. 19–21.
398 Meinck, *Hitler, etc.*, p. 89.
399 *Das Archiv*, April 1934, p. 49.
400 Förster, *Ein General*, pp. 22–23.
401 OKH file H 24/6.
402 WK XIII file 337. This report was reproduced in a special *Gestapo* handbook. It was taken from the *Prager Tagesblatt* of 22 November 1934, and appeared also in the *Prager Presse* of 25 November. In the same collection of press reports, similar extracts based on the Czech reports were taken from *Le Temps* and *Le Journal* of 26 November 1934.
403 The writer is grateful to Generaloberst a.D. Heinrici for this account of the struggle between the Army and the Reichs Arbeits Dienst, which was given during conversations in March 1964. This clash, like so many others which occurred during the Third Reich, is not documented. General Heinrici was at that time a departmental head in the Allgemeines Heeresamt, and was himself involved in the negotiations. Reichenau described himself to Heinrici as 'the R.A.D.'s most deadly enemy'.
404 WK VII file 2310.
405 Robertson, *op. cit.*, pp. 53–56.
406 Meinck, *Hitler, etc.*, p. 96.
407 Meinck, *Hitler, etc.*, p. 97.
408 This account is taken from Hossbach, *op. cit.*, pp. 95–96.
409 *Ibid.*
410 *Ibid.*
411 *Ibid.*
412 Foertsch, *op. cit.*, pp. 69–70.
413 Manstein, *op. cit.*, p. 216.
414 Weichs, *op. cit.*
415 Foertsch, *op. cit.*, pp. 69–70.
416 Tessin, *op. cit.*, pp. 248–252.
417 WK XIII file 342.
418 Mueller Hillebrand, *op. cit.*, p. 27.
419 Wheeler-Bennett, *Nemesis*, p. 340.
420 Erfurth, *op. cit.*, p. 165. Mueller Hillebrand, *op. cit.*, p. 180.
421 Mueller Hillebrand, *op. cit.*, pp. 27–28.
422 Hossbach, *op. cit.*, p. 66.
423 Hossbach, *op. cit.*, p. 47.
424 Erfurth, *op. cit.*, pp. 124–127.
425 Speech of Beck, 15 October 1935, Bundesarchiv file H 81/1/2.
426 Bundesarchiv file H 81/1/2.
427 Blomberg's speech, Bundesarchiv file H 81/1/2.
428 Liebmann's speech, Bundesarchiv file H 81/1/2.
429 Bundesarchiv file H 81/1/2.
430 Order of the Reichskriegs Minister of 31 August 1935. WK VII file 2306.
431 Speeches of Fritsch and Seeckt contained in Bundesarchiv file H 81/1/2.
432 Tessin, *op. cit.*, p. 14.
433 Mueller Hillebrand, *op. cit.*, p. 66.
434 Meinck, *Hitler, etc.*, p. 89.

435 In accordance with official practice, the author is not permitted to cite the reference particulars of this document.
436 Hossbach, *op. cit.*, pp. 181–182. Förster, *Ein General*, pp. 23–24.
437 Hossbach, *loc. cit.*
438 Guderian, *op. cit.*, pp. 29–30.
439 Weichs, *op. cit.*
440 Meinck, *Hitler, etc.*, p. 238.
441 In particular, Hossbach and Manstein.
442 Sauer, *op. cit.*, p. 886, and WK VII file 759.
443 Bennecke, *Die Reichswehr und der Röhm-Putsch*, p. 26.
444 Report of II Battalion, Infanterie Regiment 19, of 1 August 1934, WK VII file 1652.
445 Bundesarchiv, file H 64 6/1.
446 *Ibid.*
447 This whole incident is described in Fritsch's own words in his memorandum of 1 February 1938, *op. cit.*
448 From the diary of General Admiral Boehm. This extract was published in the *Frankfurter Allgemeine Zeitung* on 25 October 1961. The introductory remark in Admiral Boehm's diary to this incident was:
'When one goes into an S.S. building now, one does not know whether one will come out or not.'
449 Fritsch, *op. cit.*
450 This report is to be found in WK XIII file 337.
451 Fritsch, *op. cit.*
452 *Ibid.*
453 OKH file H 24/6.
454 See correspondence on this subject between Infanterie Regiment 40, Augsburg, and General Halder, April 1935, WK VII file 1299.
455 Wheeler-Bennett, *Nemesis*, pp. 341–342.
456 *Ibid.*
457 OKW file 848.
458 *Ibid.*
459 *Ibid.*
460 *Ibid.*
461 *Ibid.*
462 WK VII file 1652.
463 *Ibid.*
464 *Ibid.*
465 See correspondence between Himmler's adjutant Wolff, and General Dollmann, in WK IX file 9.
466 For many of the details concerning the growth and development of the S.S. Verfügungstruppe, the writer is grateful to Generaloberst der Waffen S.S. Paul Hausser, for conversations in February 1964. General Hausser retired from the Reichswehr in 1932 as a Generalleutnant. He became Inspekteur der S.S. Verfügungstruppe in 1936, and eventually became the senior field commander of the Waffen S.S. He has written a history of the Waffen S.S., *Meine Ehre heisst Treu*, but this has met with certain publication difficulties. General Hausser gave the writer a condensed account of the development of the S.S. Verfügungstruppe, based on his researches for this book.
467 Hossbach, *op. cit.*, p. 32.
468 *Ibid.*
469 *Ibid.*
470 WK VII file 1320.
471 *Ibid.*
472 Bundesarchiv file H 64 6/1.
473 Conversation with General Hausser, February 1964.
474 I. Kanis, *Waffen S.S. im Bild*, Göttingen, 1957, pp. 13–14.
475 Hossbach, *op. cit.*, p. 32.

476 Fritsch, *op. cit.*
477 WK VII file 2210.
478 OKW file 1551.
479 WK VII file 1652.
480 *Ibid.*
481 This account of the organizational disputes which occurred between 1933 and 1934 is based on a collection of extracts from German documents entitled *Extracts from German High Command Memoranda, 1933–1934,* (GHCM). These memoranda were taken from the files of Section III (High Command Structure) of the Organizations Branch of the General Staff. The lecture by von Belli is extract 1 in the series (GHCM 1). In accordance with official practice, the author is not permitted to cite further reference particulars of these documents.
482 GHCM, *op. cit.*, 2.
483 GHCM, *op. cit.*, 10.
484 GHCM, *op. cit.*, 12.
485 GHCM, *op. cit.*, 4.
486 GHCM, *op. cit.*, 6.
487 GHCM, *op. cit.*, 5.
488 GHCM, *op. cit.*, 6.
489 GHCM, *op. cit.*, 7.
490 GHCM, *op. cit.*, 9.
491 GHCM, *op. cit.*, 10.
492 GHCM, *op. cit.*, 20.
493 GHCM, *op. cit.*, 21–24, 26.
494 Erfurth, *op. cit.*, p. 177.
495 Erfurth, *op. cit.*, pp. 177–178.
496 GHCM, *op. cit.*, 26.
497 GHCM, *op. cit.*, 27.
498 GHCM, *op. cit.*, 31.
499 GHCM, *op. cit.*, 34.
500 GHCM, *op. cit.*, 35.
501 GHCM, *op. cit.*, 45, 46.
502 Erfurth, *op. cit.*, p. 179.
503 In accordance with official practice, the author is not permitted to cite the reference particulars of this document.
504 See above.
505 See above.
506 Warlimont, *Inside Hitler's Headquarters*, p. 12.
507 Hossbach, *op. cit.*, pp. 45 and 77.
508 Gordon, *op. cit.*, pp. 273–274.
509 Manstein, *op. cit.*, pp. 111, 117–118, 120–123.
510 Meinck, *Hitler, etc.*, p. 19.
511 Vagts, *op. cit.*, p. 310.
512 Text of a Czechoslovakian report from Warsaw of 10 March 1933, contained in Buber, *op. cit.*
513 Roos, *op. cit.*, pp. 344–363.
514 Craig, *op. cit.*, p. 472.
515 Craig, *op. cit.*, p. 471.
516 Wheeler-Bennett, *Nemesis*, pp. 304–306.
517 Hossbach, *op. cit.*, p. 117.
518 Bucheit, *Beck*, pp. 40–41. Conversations with Frau Gertrud Neubaur, March 1964, and with Field-Marshal von Manstein, March 1964.
519 Liebmann, *op. cit.*, p. 109, and Meinck, *Hitler, etc.*, p. 126.
520 Robertson, *op. cit.*, p. 89.
521 *Ibid.*
522 This may be deduced from Beck's reply of 3 May 1935, in which he actually mentions Czechoslovakia by name. Beck Papers, Bundesarchiv file Ho 8/28/2.
523 Beck Papers, *loc. cit.*

524 *Ibid.*
525 *Ibid.*
526 Robertson, *op. cit.*, p. 90.
527 Peter Bor, *Gespräche mit Halder*, Wiesbaden, 1950, p. 117.
528 Hossbach, *op. cit.*, p. 153.
529 Bor, *op. cit.*, p. 117.
530 Meinck, *Hitler, etc.*, p. 127.
531 Manstein, *op. cit.*, pp. 111–115, 119–126, 226.
532 Manstein, *op. cit.*, p. 227.
533 Manstein, *op. cit.*, pp. 227–228.
534 Manstein, *op. cit.*, p. 228.
535 Letter of Beck to Brauchitsch, 5 May 1938, quoted in Förster, *Ein General*, pp. 82 *et seq.*
536 Manstein, *op. cit.*, pp. 228–229.
537 Peter de Mendelssohn, *Die Nürnberger Dokumente*, Hamburg, 1947, p. 19. This document replaced one dated 26 June 1936, of which no copies have survived. Most of the text of this directive is given by Mendelssohn, pp. 19–29.
538 Hossbach, *op. cit.*, p. 77.
539 Robertson, *op. cit.*, p. 92.
540 Meinck, *Hitler, etc.*, pp. 136–138.
541 Manstein, *op. cit.*, p. 231.
542 Manstein, *op. cit.*, p. 232.
543 Manstein, *op. cit.*, p. 233.
544 Letter of General Dittmar to Sir Basil Liddell Hart (undated), and Manstein, *op. cit.*, p. 234.
545 Manstein, *loc. cit.*
546 Hitler, *op. cit.*, pp. 144–153, 440, 492, 738–754 *et passim.*
547 Sauer, *op. cit.*, p. 747.
548 Sauer, *op. cit.*, pp. 719–720, and conversations with General Sir Andrew Thorne, British Military Attaché, Berlin, 1932–1935, who knew many of the officers at this dinner personally.
549 Field-Marshal Gerd von Rundstedt in the record of an interview with Captain B. H. Liddell Hart at Grizedale Hall, 6 January 1946. A copy of this record is in the possession of Sir Basil Liddell Hart.
550 *Zeugenschrifttum Ott*, Nr. 279, I, p. 19, Institut für Zeitgeschichte, Munich.
551 Sauer, *op. cit.*, p. 735.
552 *Ibid.*
553 *Ibid.*
554 *Documents on German Foreign Policy*, H.M.S.O., Series C, Vol. III, pp. 698–699 —details of a conversation which took place between State Secretary von Bülow and General Beck on 1 December 1934, outlining the military reasons for stationing German troops in the Rhineland.
555 Hossbach, *op. cit.*, p. 97.
556 OKH file H 24/38.
557 Hossbach, *op. cit.*, p. 97.
558 *Ibid.*
559 These moves are described in detail by Robertson, *op. cit.*, pp. 71–80.
560 OKH file H 24/35.
561 Robertson, *op. cit.*, p. 77, and Meinck, *Hitler, etc.*, pp. 151–152.
562 Robertson, *op. cit.*, p. 78.
563 Hossbach, *op. cit.*, p. 98.
564 Shirer, *op. cit.*, p. 291 footnote.
565 Tessin, *op. cit.*, p. 256. The Landespolizei formed the 25th, 26th, 33rd and 34th Divisions.
566 Tessin, *op. cit.*, p. 255.
567 Maurice G. Gamelin, *Servir, Vol. II, Le Prologue du Drame*, Paris, 1946, p. 201, and A. J. P. Taylor, *The Origins of the Second World War*, Hamish Hamilton, London, 1961, p. 98.

568 Weichs, *op. cit.*
569 The details of this incident are taken from Hossbach, *op. cit.*, p. 98.
570 Manstein, *op. cit.*, p. 237, IMT, Vol. XX, p. 657, and Foertsch, *op. cit.*, p. 74.
571 Meinck, *Hitler, etc.*, p. 164.
572 Meinck, *Hitler, etc.*, p. 234.
573 Meinck, *Hitler, etc.*, pp. 164–166.
574 Förster, *Ein General*, p. 31.
575 Förster, *Ein General*, pp. 43–52.
576 Beck's report on his journey, Beck, *Studien*, p. 295.
577 Hossbach, *op. cit.*, pp. 137–138.
578 *Ibid.*
579 Hossbach, *op. cit.*, pp. 219–220.
580 Hossbach, *op. cit.*, pp. 216–217.
581 Wheeler-Bennett, *Nemesis*, p. 361.
582 IMT, Vol. XIV, pp. 34–37. Affidavit of Field-Marshal von Blomberg sworn at Nuremberg, 26 February 1946, and evidence of Grand Admiral Raeder at Nuremberg, 16 May 1946.
583 Wheeler-Bennett, *Nemesis*, p. 362.
584 *Ibid.*, and Buchheit, *Beck*, p. 100.
585 Wheeler-Bennett, *loc. cit.*
586 Kielmansegg, *op. cit.*, p. 34.
587 *Ibid.*
588 *Ibid.*
589 Kielmansegg, *op. cit.*, p. 36.
590 Buchheit, *Beck*, p. 102.
591 Buchheit, *Beck*, p. 101.
592 Hossbach, *op. cit.*, p. 218.
593 Förster, *Ein General*, pp. 61–65.
594 The text of this address was published to the Army in orders. WK XIII file 823. Jodl mentioned the address in his diary entry for 21 January 1938. Robertson, *op. cit.*, p. 110. From the official nature of the published account, which gave the date of the address as 22 January 1938, it seems more likely that the date given by Jodl was in error.
595 Wheeler-Bennett, *Nemesis*, p. 357.
596 Papen, *op. cit.*, p. 365.
597 Kielmansegg, *op. cit.*, p. 53.
598 Buchheit, *Beck*, p. 108.
599 Erickson, *op. cit.*, pp. 433–436.
600 Wheeler-Bennett, *Nemesis*, p. 364.
601 Hossbach, *op. cit.*, p. 122.
602 Buchheit, *Beck*, p. 107.
603 *Ibid.*
604 Kielmansegg, *op. cit.*, p. 37.
605 Förster, *Generaloberst Ludwig Beck*, p. 86.
606 Kielmansegg, *op. cit.*, pp. 36–37.
607 Blomberg's own statement to Graf von der Goltz at Nuremberg, June 1945, Kielmansegg, *op. cit.*, p. 39, and Hossbach, *op. cit.*, p. 133.
608 Hossbach, *op. cit.*, p. 125.
609 Hossbach, *op. cit.*, p. 126.
610 Hossbach, *op. cit.*, p. 127.
611 Hossbach, *op. cit.*, p. 129.
612 Hossbach, *op. cit.*, p. 130.
613 Hossbach, *op. cit.*, p. 129.
614 Hossbach, *op. cit.*, p. 130.
615 Warlimont, *Inside Hitler's Headquarters*, p. 13.
616 Wheeler-Bennett, *Nemesis*, p. 368.
617 Hossbach, *op. cit.*, p. 133.

618 Kielmansegg, *op. cit.*, pp. 43–44.
619 Kielmansegg, *op. cit.*, p. 42.
620 Kielmansegg, *op. cit.*, p. 120.
621 *Ibid.* and Hossbach, *op. cit.*, p. 141.
622 Kielmansegg, *op. cit.*, p. 46.
623 Kielmansegg, *op. cit.*, pp. 47–48.
624 Kielmansegg, *op. cit.*, p. 50.
625 Kielmansegg, *op. cit.*, pp. 57–58.
626 Kielmansegg, *op. cit.*, pp. 69–70.
627 Kielmansegg, *op. cit.*, p. 70.
628 Kielmansegg, *op. cit.*, pp. 71–72.
629 Kielmansegg, *op. cit.*, pp. 72–74.
630 Kielmansegg, *op. cit.*, p. 74.
631 Kielmansegg, *op. cit.*, pp. 80–83.
632 Kielmansegg, *op. cit.*, pp. 83–84.
633 Kielmansegg, *op. cit.*, pp. 84–85.
634 Kielmansegg, *op. cit.*, p. 93.
635 Kielmansegg, *op. cit.*, p. 94.
636 Kielmansegg, *op. cit.*, pp. 94–96.
637 Guderian, *op. cit.*, p. 21.
638 Except where otherwise stated these details are taken from the personal records cards of Brauchitsch which were kept by the Heerespersonalamt.
639 Ulrich von Hassell, *Vom anderen Deutschland*, Zürich, 1946, p. 80.
640 Buchheit, *Soldatentum und Rebellion*, pp. 110–111.
641 Hossbach, *op. cit.*, p. 155.
642 Buchheit, *Soldatentum und Rebellion*, p. 111.
643 Hossbach, *op. cit.*, p. 156.
644 Weichs, *op. cit.*
645 *Ibid.*
646 *Ibid.*
647 *Ibid.* and Guderian, *op. cit.*, p. 47.
648 *Decree Concerning the Leadership of the Wehrmacht of 4* February 1938, *Reichsgesetzblatt, 1938.*
649 OKH file H 24/40.
650 *Ibid.*
651 Open letter to Hitler by Winston Churchill, *The Times*, 7 November 1938.
652 OKH file H 24/37.
653 Kielmansegg, *op. cit.*, pp. 88, 110.
654 Buchheit, *Beck*, p. 127.
655 Buchheit, *Beck*, p. 128, and Hossbach, *op. cit.*, p. 148.
656 W. Görlitz, *Keitel—Verbrecher oder Offizier*, Göttingen, 1961, p. 179, and Warlimont, *Inside Hitler's Headquarters*, p. 15.
657 E. von Weizsäcker, *Erinnerungen*, Munich, 1950, p. 148. Notes made by Staatssekretär von Weizsäcker on 26 March 1938.
658 Guderian, *op. cit.*, pp. 50–51.
659 *Ibid.* and Weichs, *op. cit.*
660 Wheeler-Bennett, *Nemesis*, pp. 396–397, and IMT document PS–388, Item 2.
661 Förster, *Ein General*, pp. 82 *et seq.*
662 Buchheit, *Soldatentum und Rebellion*, pp. 152–153.
663 Förster, *Ein General*, pp. 90 *et seq.*, and Buchheit, *Soldatentum*, pp. 154–155.
664 IMT document PS–388, Item 11.
665 Jodl's diary for 30 May 1938.
666 Hossbach, *op. cit.*, p. 146.
667 *Ibid.*
668 Hossbach, *op. cit.*, p. 148.
669 Hossbach, *op. cit.*, p. 156.
670 Buchheit, *Beck*, p. 147.
671 *Ibid.*

672 Förster, *Ein General*, pp. 98 *et seq.*
673 Förster, *Ein General*, pp. 102 *et seq.*
674 Förster, *Ein General*, pp. 105–106.
675 Wheeler-Bennett, *Nemesis*, p. 402.
676 WK VII file 897.
677 WK VII file 2210.
678 Weichs, *op. cit.*
679 Wheeler-Bennett, *Nemesis*, p. 403, and Buchheit, *Beck*, p. 162.
680 Jodl's Diary for 10 August 1938, Buchheit, *Beck*, p. 168, and Manstein, *op. cit.*, pp. 336–337.
681 Jodl, *loc. cit.*, and Wheeler-Bennett, *Nemesis*, pp. 403–404.
682 Weichs, *op. cit.*
683 Buchheit, *Beck*, p. 169.
684 Weichs, *op. cit.*
685 Buchheit, *Beck*, p. 170.
686 Wheeler-Bennett, *Nemesis*, p. 405.
687 Buchheit, *Beck*, p. 170.
688 Hossbach, *op. cit.*, p. 149.
689 Weichs, *op. cit.*
690 *Ibid.*
691 *Ibid.*
692 Conversation with Generaloberst Halder, March 1964.
693 Wheeler-Bennett, *Nemesis*, pp. 408–409.
694 Wheeler-Bennett, *Nemesis*, pp. 407–408.
695 *Ibid.*
696 Wheeler-Bennett, *Nemesis*, pp. 408–409.
697 Wheeler-Bennett, *Nemesis*, pp. 413–414, and Bor, *op. cit.*, p. 122.
698 Wheeler-Bennett, *Nemesis*, p. 419.
699 Jodl's diary for 6 September 1938.
700 Jodl's diary for 8 September 1938.
701 Warlimont, *Inside Hitler's Headquarters*, p. 116.
702 *Ibid.* and Jodl's diary for 10, 12, and 13 September 1938.
703 Weichs, *op. cit.*
704 Robertson, *op. cit.*, p. 136.
705 Robertson, *op. cit.*, p. 138.
706 Jodl's diary for 20 September 1938.
707 Jodl's diary for 26 September 1938.
708 Jodl's diary for 27 September 1938.
709 Jodl's diary for 28 September 1938.
710 J. W. Wheeler-Bennett, *Munich—Prologue to Tragedy*, Viking, New York, 1964, pp. 169–170.
711 Wheeler-Bennett, *Nemesis*, p. 420.
712 Hossbach, *op. cit.*, p. 157.
713 Wheeler-Bennett, *Nemesis*, p. 420.
714 This view is based on conversations with many Germans of widely differing political views and social positions, who were either soldiers or adult civilians at the time of the Munich Agreement.
715 Bor, *op. cit.*, p. 124.
716 Letter of Rundstedt to Captain Liddell Hart of 9 November 1945, which is in Sir Basil Liddell Hart's possession.
717 Wheeler-Bennett, *Nemesis*, p. 427.
718 MGFA file H 7/30.
719 Conversation with Admiral Rothe-Roth and Admiral von Puttkamer, Naval Adjutant to the Führer, March 1964. The admirals also said that the fleet war games took into account only the French and Polish navies.
720 Warlimont, *Inside Hitler's Headquarters*, p. 19.
721 Warlimont, *Inside Hitler's Headquarters*, p. 20.
722 *Ibid.*, and IMT document C-120.

723 *Ibid.*
724 WK VII file 2210—order of 12 May 1939.
725 Warlimont, *Inside Hitler's Headquarters*, p. 23.
726 Warlimont, *Inside Hitler's Headquarters*, pp. 22–23, Wheeler-Bennett, *Nemesis*, p. 483, *Documents on German Foreign Policy, Series D*, HMSO, Vol. VI, pp. 578–580, and IMT documents L–79 and C–126.
727 Wheeler-Bennett, *Nemesis*, p. 445.
728 Several accounts of this conference exist, viz.: IMT documents PS–1014 and PS–798 (both anonymous), Raeder–27 (by Admiral Böhm) and L–3 (also anonymous). Document L–3 differs from the others in that its content is highly coloured, mentioning that Hitler had ordered his *Totenkopf* Units to Poland 'with the order to kill without pity or mercy all men women and children of Polish race or language', and that at the conclusion of the first part of the meeting, Göring leapt onto the table and after offering 'bloodthirsty thanks and bloody promises', danced around 'like a savage'. (Wheeler-Bennett, *Nemesis*, pp. 447–448.) There are many other points of difference which suggest that L–3 is of doubtful authenticity in comparison with the other accounts. L–3 was not used as evidence by the prosecution at Nuremberg (IMT, Vol. 14, p. 64). L–3 was given by an unidentified informant to Louis Lochner one week before Hitler's attack on Poland.
729 Halder's diary for 28 August 1939.
730 Halder's diary for 31 August 1939, and Wheeler-Bennett, *Nemesis*, p. 454.
731 Wheeler-Bennett, *Nemesis*, p. 470.
732 OKH file H 24/6.
733 Sauer, *op. cit.*, p. 917.
734 OKH file H 24/6.
735 Hossbach, *op. cit.*, p. 28.
736 WK XIII file 188.
737 Liebmann, *op. cit.*, pp. 76, 79.
738 WK VII file 1652.
739 *Ibid.*
740 OKH file 24/6.
741 WK VII file 1652.
742 WPV of 31 August 1935, WK VII file 2306.
743 WK XIII files 188, 189.
744 Correspondence of 14 August 1936, and of Blomberg to WK IX, 3 September 1936, in OKW file 888.
745 Memorandum signed by Fritsch of 26 April 1937, WK XIII file 246.
746 WK XIII file 246.
747 *Ibid.*
748 *Ibid.*
749 WK VII file 2210.
750 WK XIII 246.
751 WK VII file 2306.
752 *Ibid.*
753 *Ibid.*
754 *Ibid.*
755 OKH file H 24/6.
756 WK VII file 2306.
757 WK VII file 2196.
758 OKH file H 24/6.
759 *Ibid.*
760 OKW file 848.
761 *Ibid.*
762 *Ibid.*
763 *Ibid.*
764 *Ibid.*
765 *Ibid.*
766 *Ibid.*
767 *Ibid.*
768 *Ibid.*
769 *Ibid.*

Index